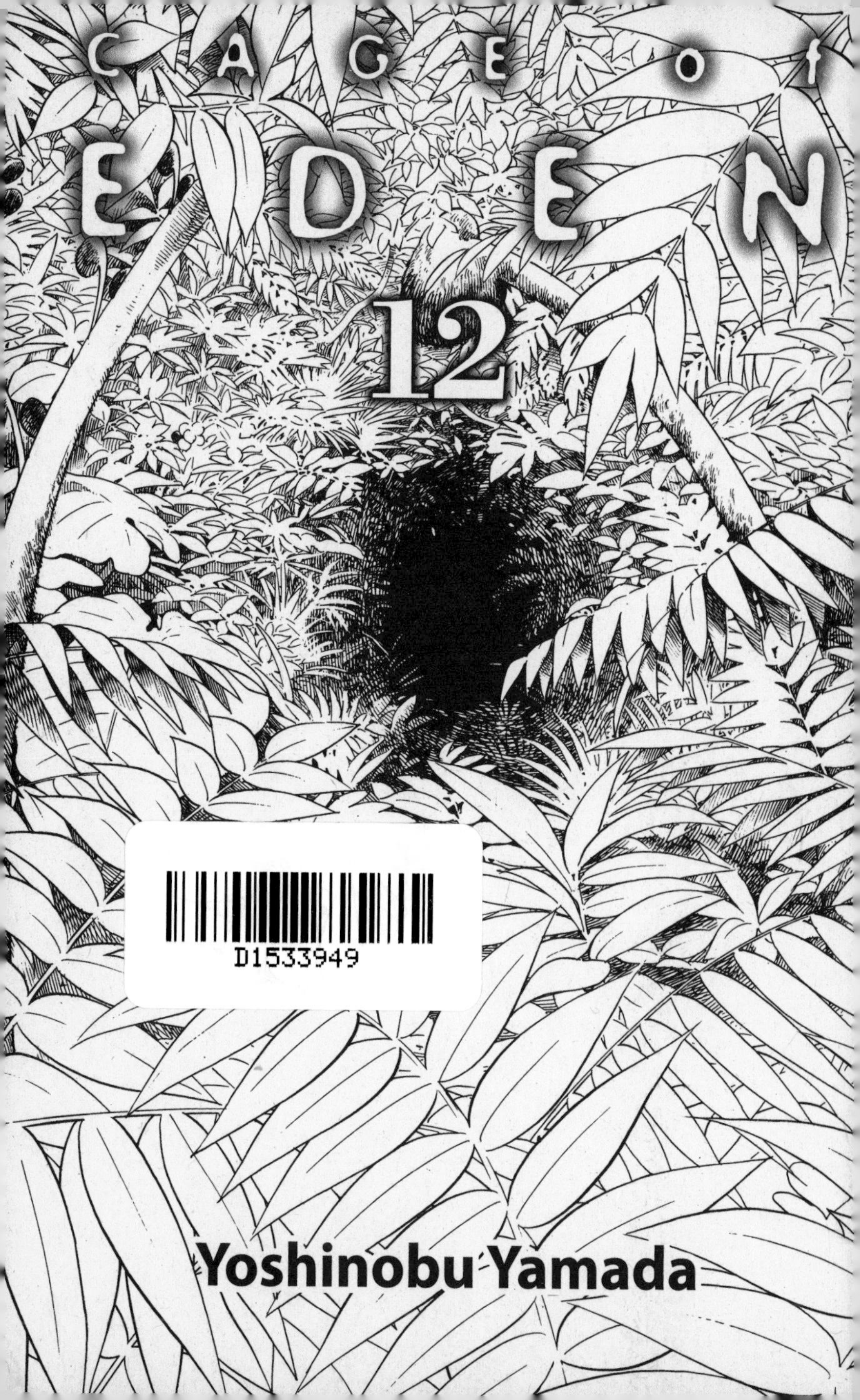
CAGE of
EDEN
12
Yoshinobu Yamada

CAGE of EDEN

CONTENTS

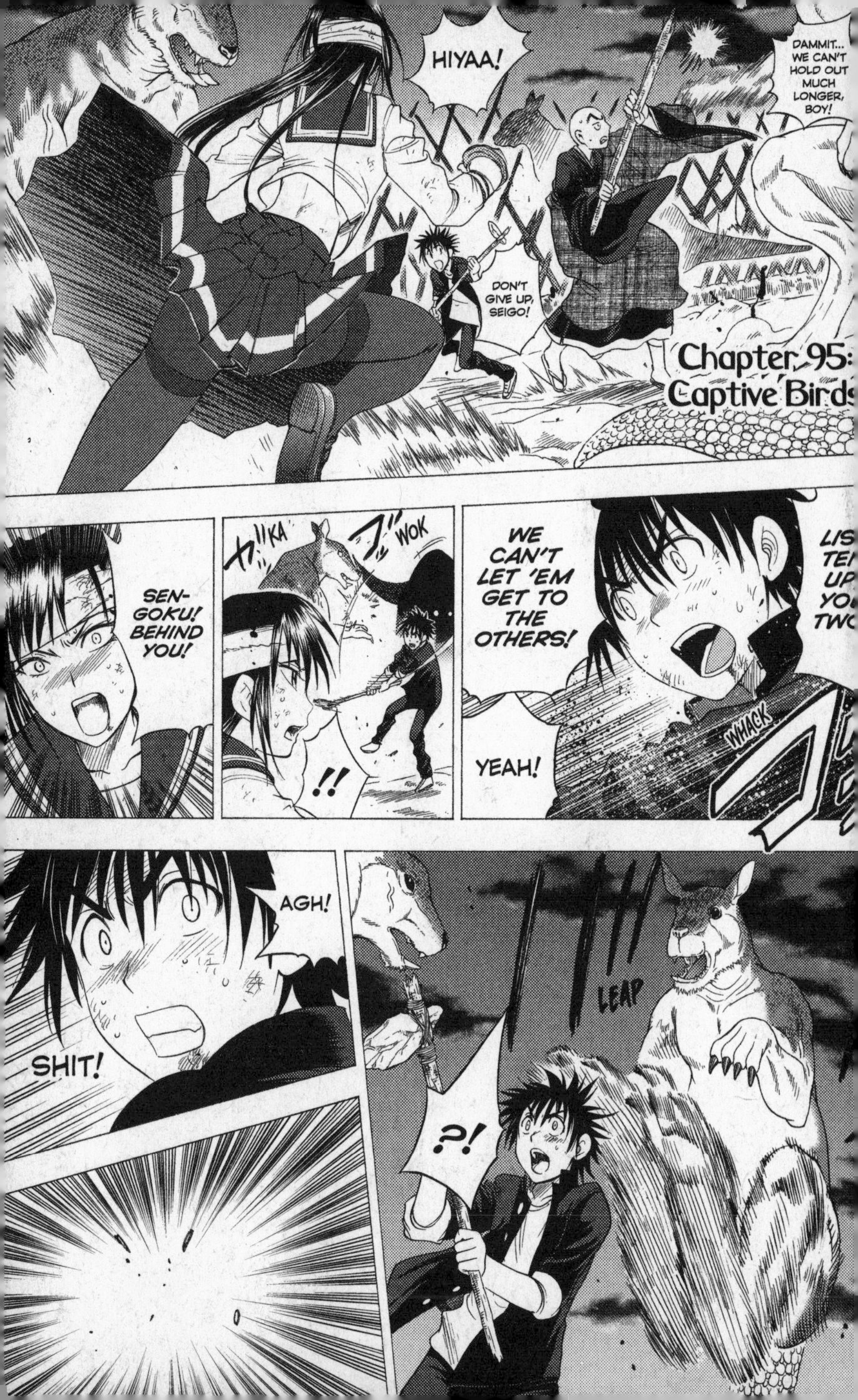
DAMMIT... WE CAN'T HOLD OUT MUCH LONGER, BOY!
HIYAA!
DON'T GIVE UP, SEIGO!
Chapter 95: Captive Birds
WE CAN'T LET 'EM GET TO THE OTHERS!
WHACK
YEAH!
KA
WOK
!!
SEN-GOKU! BEHIND YOU!
LEAP
?!
AGH!
SHIT!

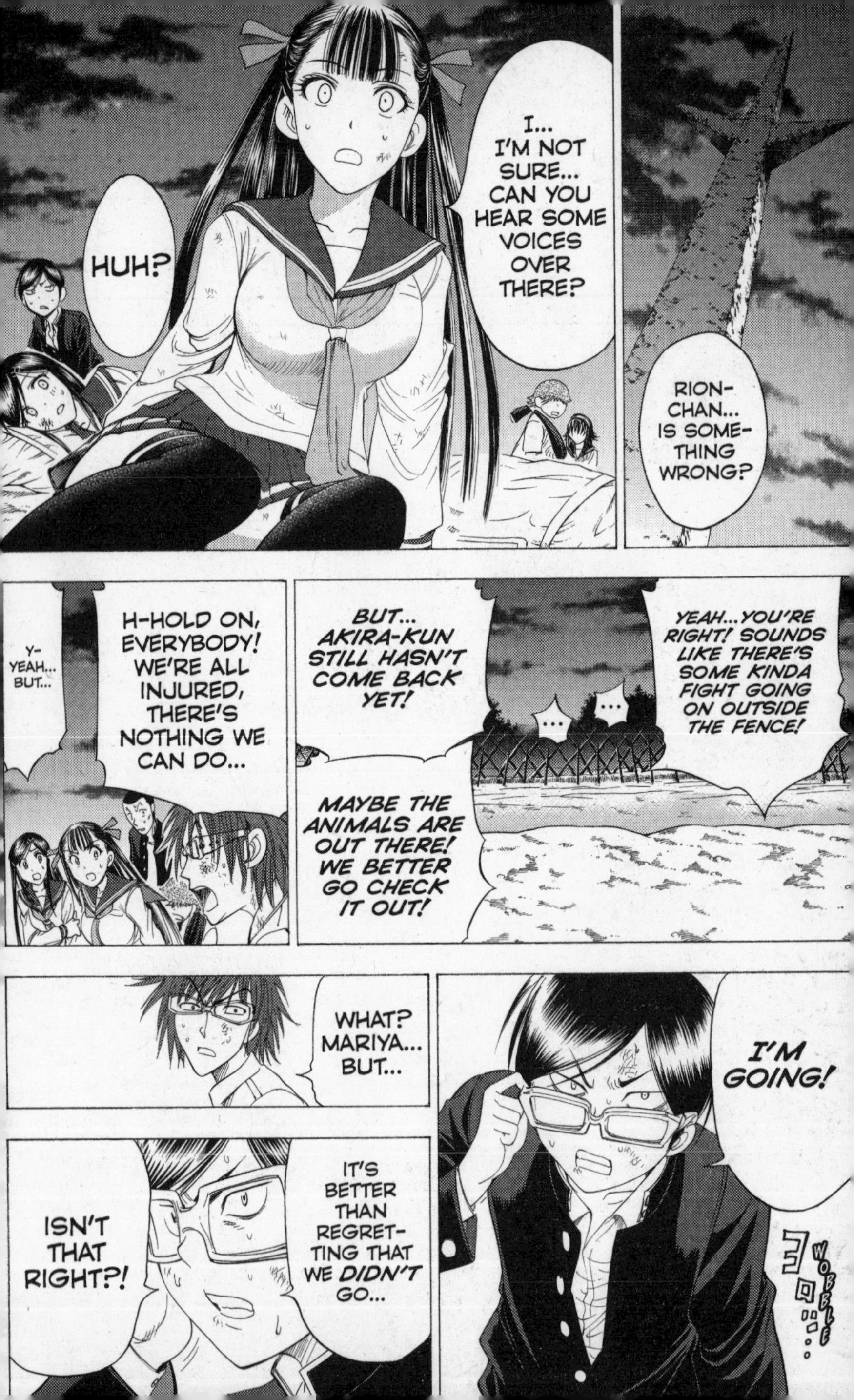
RION-CHAN... IS SOMETHING WRONG?
I... I'M NOT SURE... CAN YOU HEAR SOME VOICES OVER THERE?
HUH?
YEAH...YOU'RE RIGHT! SOUNDS LIKE THERE'S SOME KINDA FIGHT GOING ON OUTSIDE THE FENCE!
...
...
BUT... AKIRA-KUN STILL HASN'T COME BACK YET!
MAYBE THE ANIMALS ARE OUT THERE! WE BETTER GO CHECK IT OUT!
H-HOLD ON, EVERYBODY! WE'RE ALL INJURED, THERE'S NOTHING WE CAN DO...
Y-YEAH... BUT...
I'M GOING!
WOBBLE
WHAT? MARIYA... BUT...
IT'S BETTER THAN REGRETTING THAT WE DIDN'T GO...
ISN'T THAT RIGHT?!

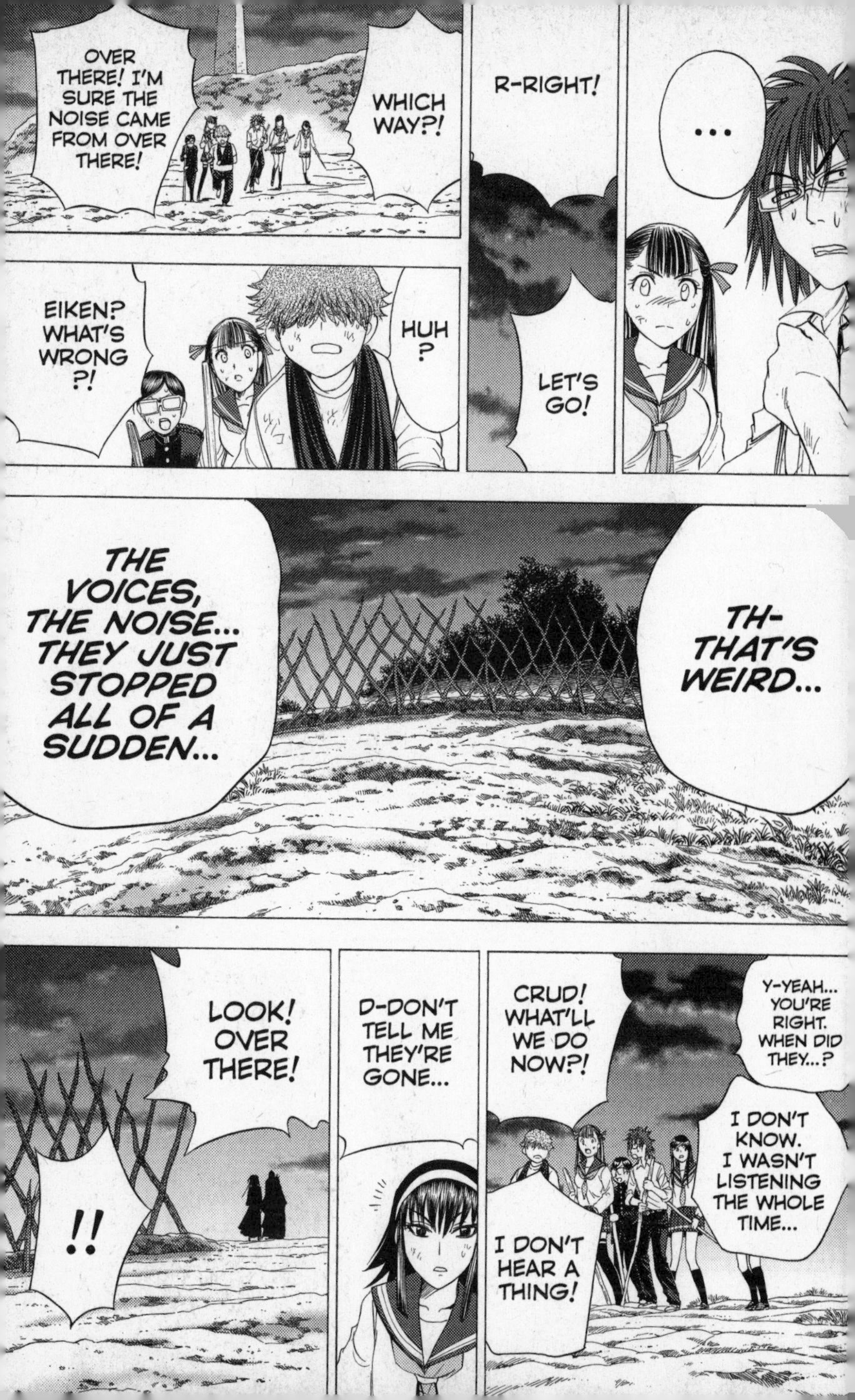
...
R-RIGHT!
LET'S GO!
WHICH WAY?!
OVER THERE! I'M SURE THE NOISE CAME FROM OVER THERE!
HUH?
EIKEN? WHAT'S WRONG?!
TH-THAT'S WEIRD...
THE VOICES, THE NOISE... THEY JUST STOPPED ALL OF A SUDDEN...
Y-YEAH... YOU'RE RIGHT. WHEN DID THEY...?
CRUD! WHAT'LL WE DO NOW?!
I DON'T KNOW. I WASN'T LISTENING THE WHOLE TIME...
I DON'T HEAR A THING!
D-DON'T TELL ME THEY'RE GONE...
LOOK! OVER THERE!
!!

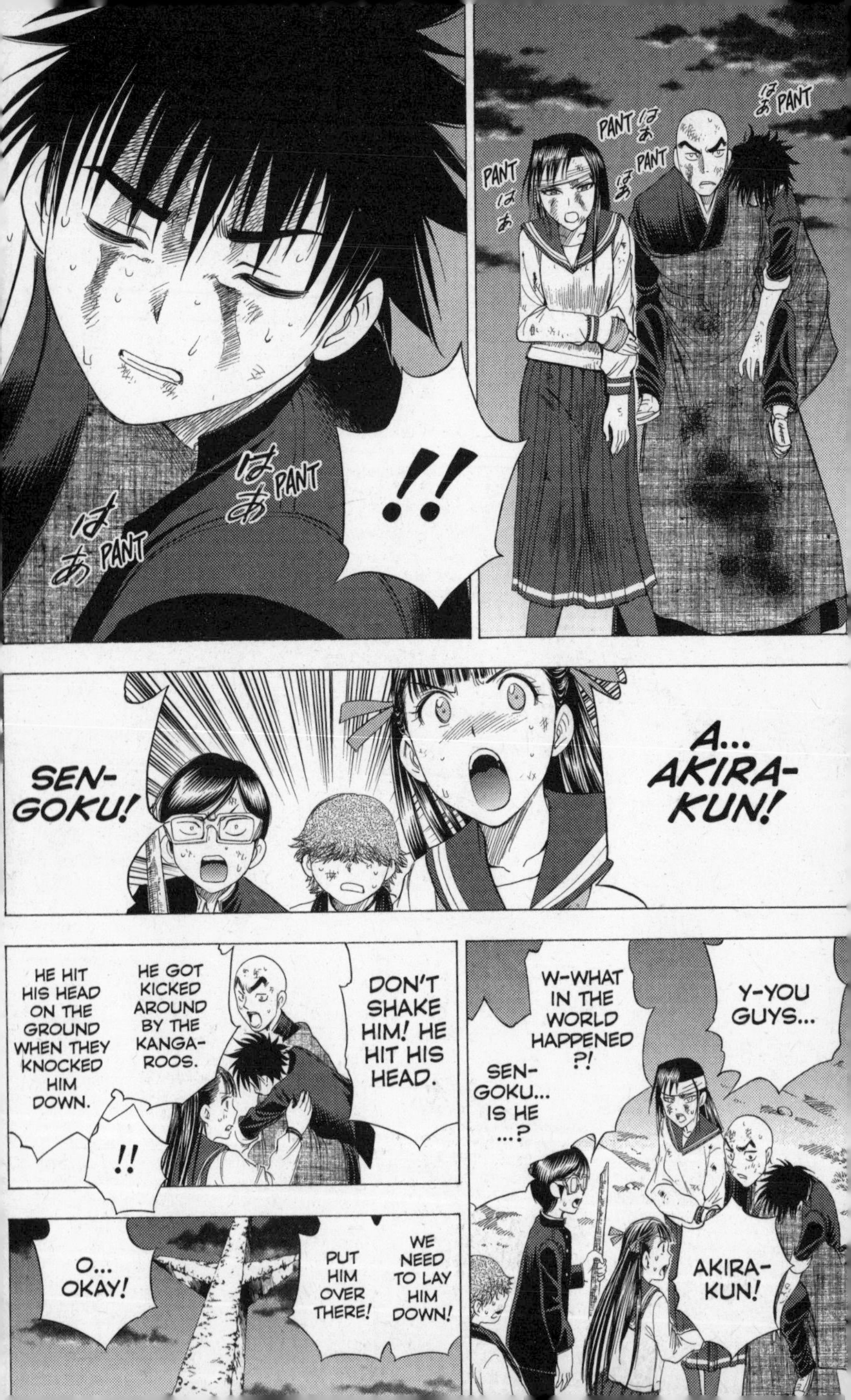

はあ PANT
PANT はあ
PANT はあ
PANT はあ
はあ PANT
はあ PANT
!!
A... AKIRA-KUN!
SEN-GOKU!
Y-YOU GUYS...
W-WHAT IN THE WORLD HAPPENED?!
SEN-GOKU... IS HE ...?
AKIRA-KUN!
DON'T SHAKE HIM! HE HIT HIS HEAD.
HE GOT KICKED AROUND BY THE KANGA-ROOS.
HE HIT HIS HEAD ON THE GROUND WHEN THEY KNOCKED HIM DOWN.
!!
WE NEED TO LAY HIM DOWN!
PUT HIM OVER THERE!
O... OKAY!

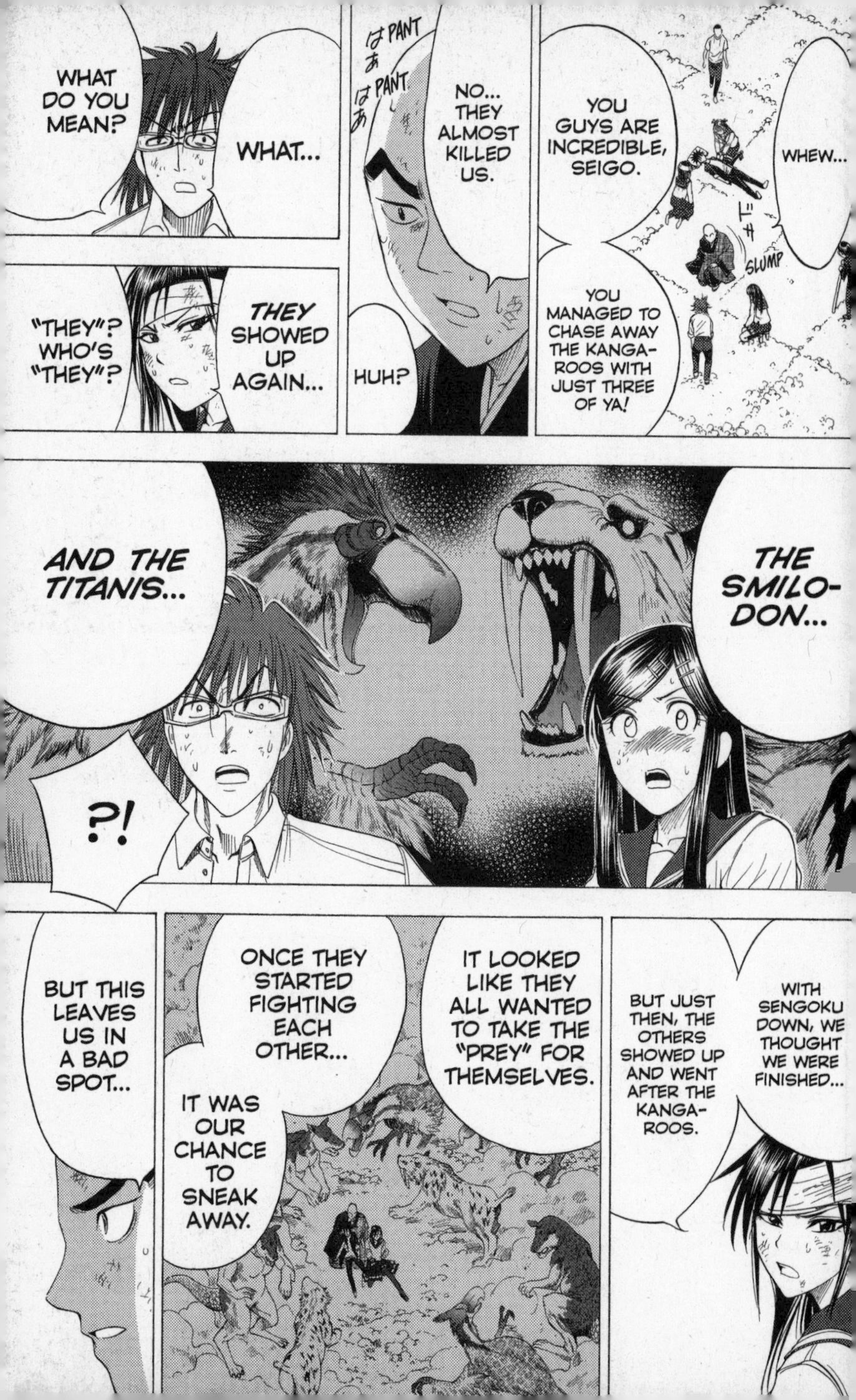
WHEW...
YOU GUYS ARE INCREDIBLE, SEIGO.
ドサ SLUMP
YOU MANAGED TO CHASE AWAY THE KANGA-ROOS WITH JUST THREE OF YA!
はぁ PANT はぁ PANT
NO... THEY ALMOST KILLED US.
HUH?
WHAT...
WHAT DO YOU MEAN?
THEY SHOWED UP AGAIN...
"THEY"? WHO'S "THEY"?
THE SMILO-DON...
AND THE TITANIS...
?!
WITH SENGOKU DOWN, WE THOUGHT WE WERE FINISHED...
BUT JUST THEN, THE OTHERS SHOWED UP AND WENT AFTER THE KANGA-ROOS.
IT LOOKED LIKE THEY ALL WANTED TO TAKE THE "PREY" FOR THEMSELVES.
ONCE THEY STARTED FIGHTING EACH OTHER...
IT WAS OUR CHANCE TO SNEAK AWAY.
BUT THIS LEAVES US IN A BAD SPOT...

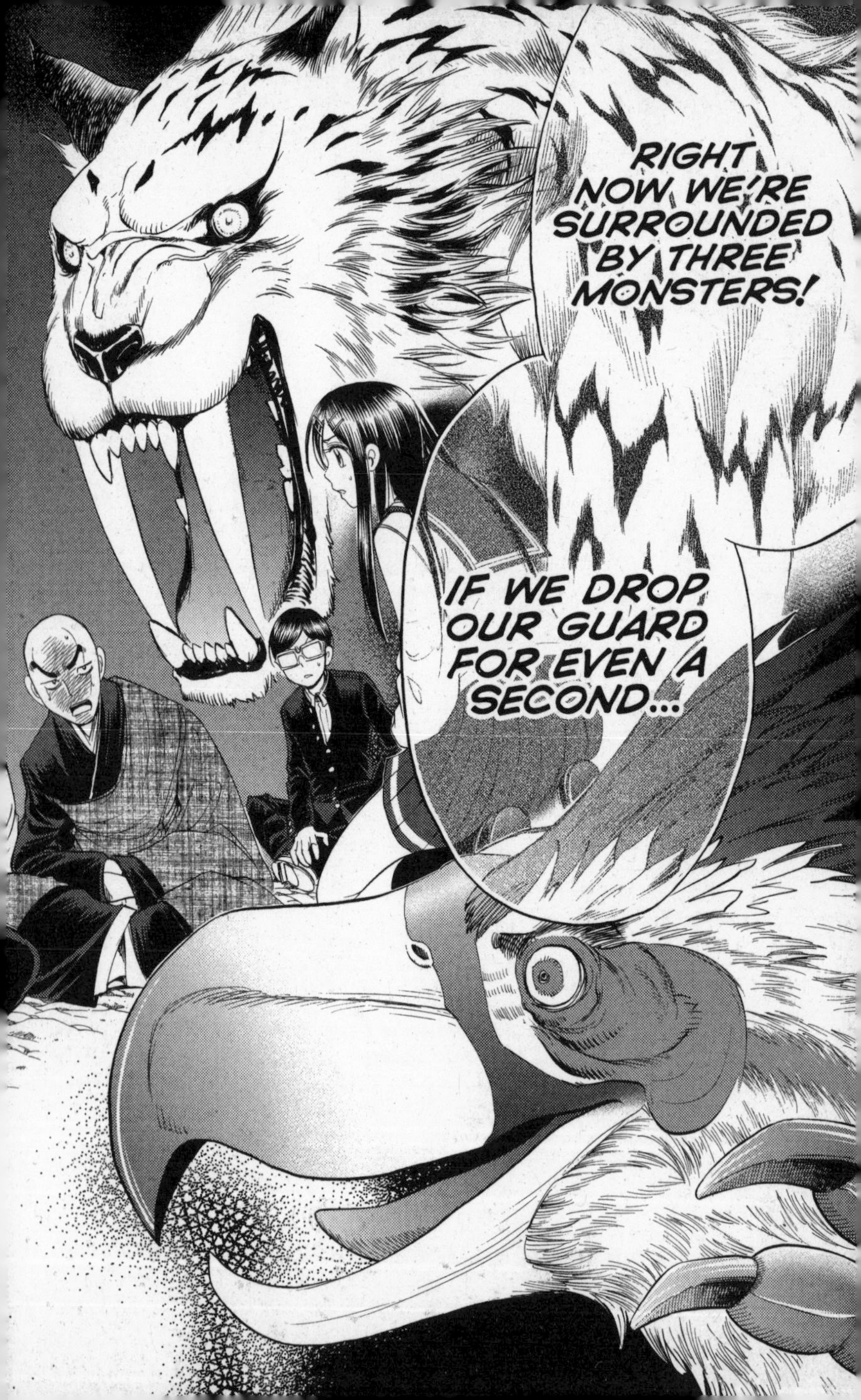
RIGHT NOW WE'RE SURROUNDED BY THREE MONSTERS!
IF WE DROP OUR GUARD FOR EVEN A SECOND...

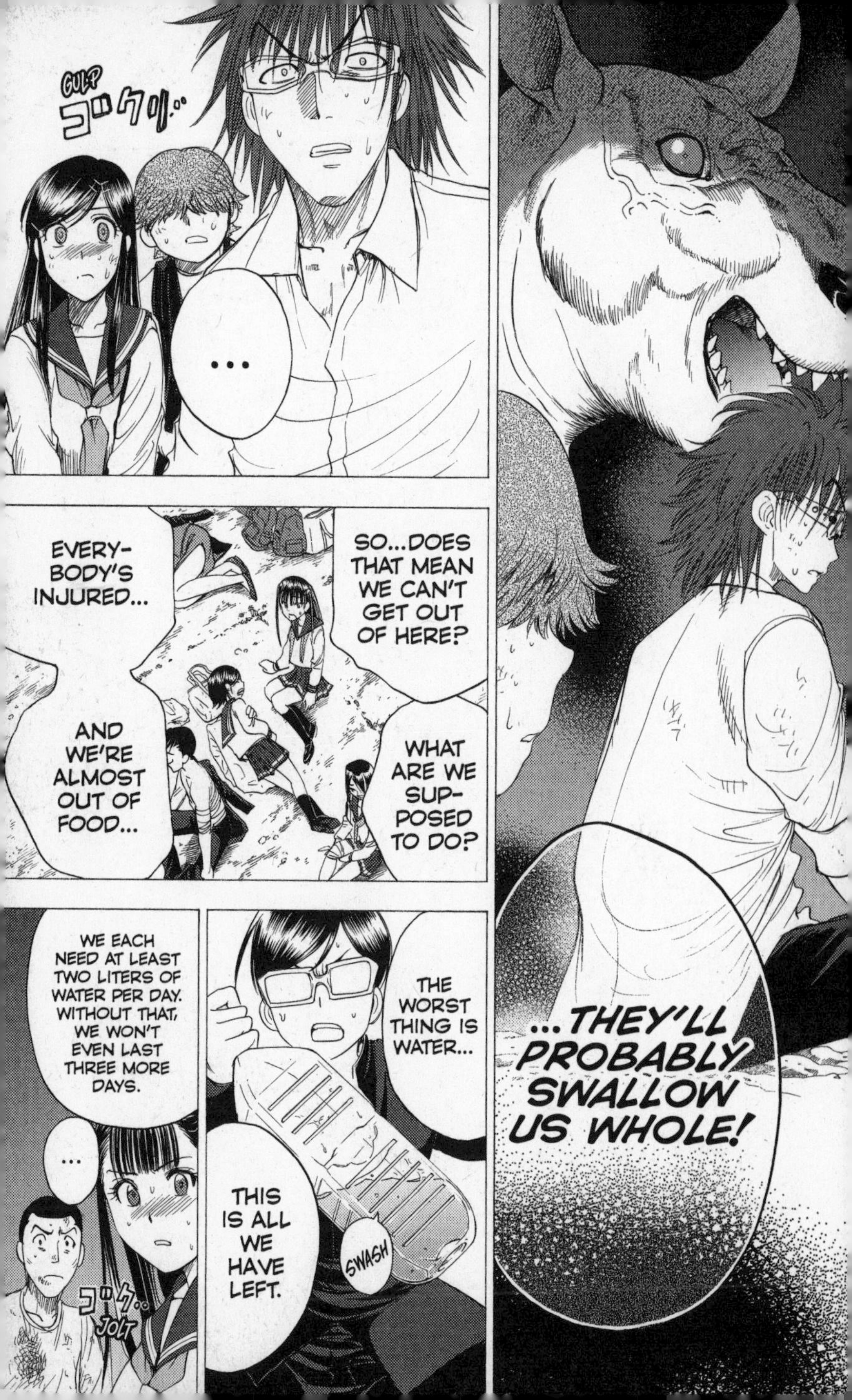
...THEY'LL PROBABLY SWALLOW US WHOLE!
GULP
ゴクリ..
...
SO...DOES THAT MEAN WE CAN'T GET OUT OF HERE?
EVERY-BODY'S INJURED...
WHAT ARE WE SUP-POSED TO DO?
AND WE'RE ALMOST OUT OF FOOD...
THE WORST THING IS WATER...
THIS IS ALL WE HAVE LEFT.
SWASH
WE EACH NEED AT LEAST TWO LITERS OF WATER PER DAY. WITHOUT THAT, WE WON'T EVEN LAST THREE MORE DAYS.
...
ゴクッ..
JOLT

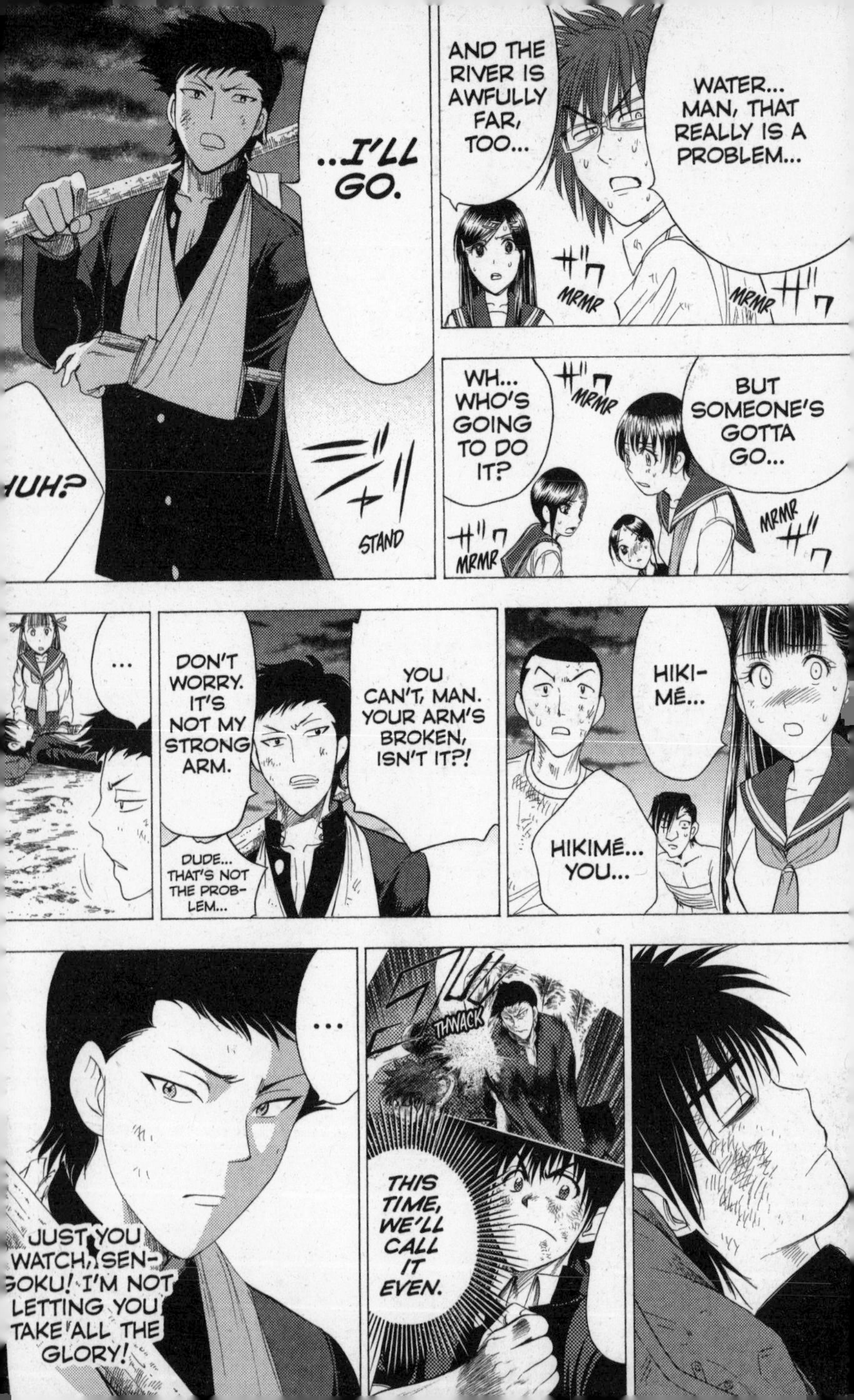
WATER... MAN, THAT REALLY IS A PROBLEM...
AND THE RIVER IS AWFULLY FAR, TOO...
MRMR
MRMR
BUT SOMEONE'S GOTTA GO...
WH... WHO'S GOING TO DO IT?
MRMR
MRMR
MRMR
...I'LL GO.
HUH?
STAND
HIKI-MÉ...
HIKIMÉ... YOU...
YOU CAN'T, MAN. YOUR ARM'S BROKEN, ISN'T IT?!
DON'T WORRY. IT'S NOT MY STRONG ARM.
DUDE... THAT'S NOT THE PROB-LEM...
...
THWACK
THIS TIME, WE'LL CALL IT EVEN.
...
JUST YOU WATCH, SEN-GOKU! I'M NOT LETTING YOU TAKE ALL THE GLORY!

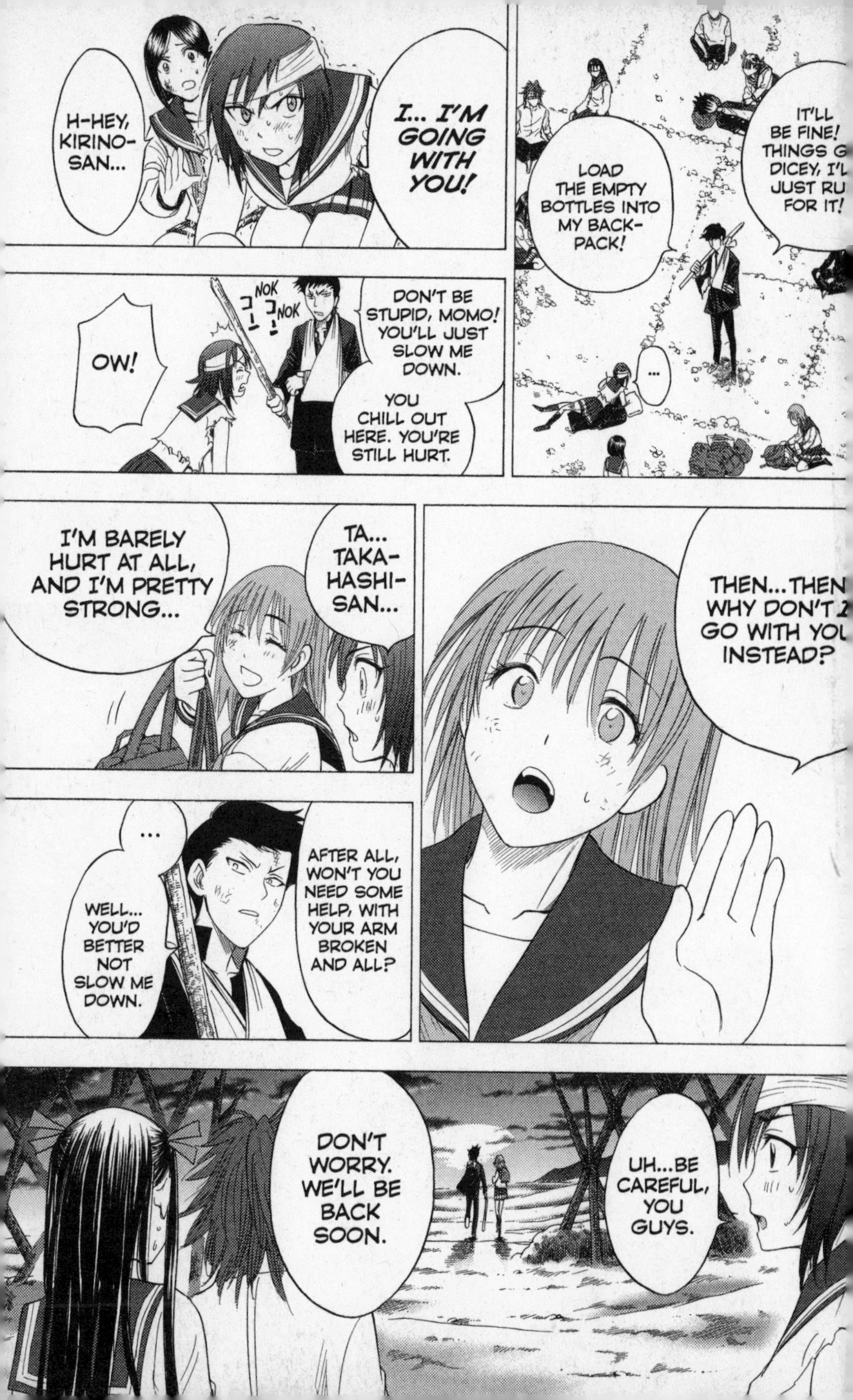
IT'LL BE FINE! THINGS G DICEY, I'L JUST RU FOR IT!
LOAD THE EMPTY BOTTLES INTO MY BACK-PACK!
...
I... I'M GOING WITH YOU!
H-HEY, KIRINO-SAN...
DON'T BE STUPID, MOMO! YOU'LL JUST SLOW ME DOWN.
YOU CHILL OUT HERE. YOU'RE STILL HURT.
NOK
NOK
OW!
THEN...THEN WHY DON'T GO WITH YO INSTEAD?
TA... TAKA-HASHI-SAN...
I'M BARELY HURT AT ALL, AND I'M PRETTY STRONG...
AFTER ALL, WON'T YOU NEED SOME HELP, WITH YOUR ARM BROKEN AND ALL?
...
WELL... YOU'D BETTER NOT SLOW ME DOWN.
UH...BE CAREFUL, YOU GUYS.
DON'T WORRY. WE'LL BE BACK SOON.

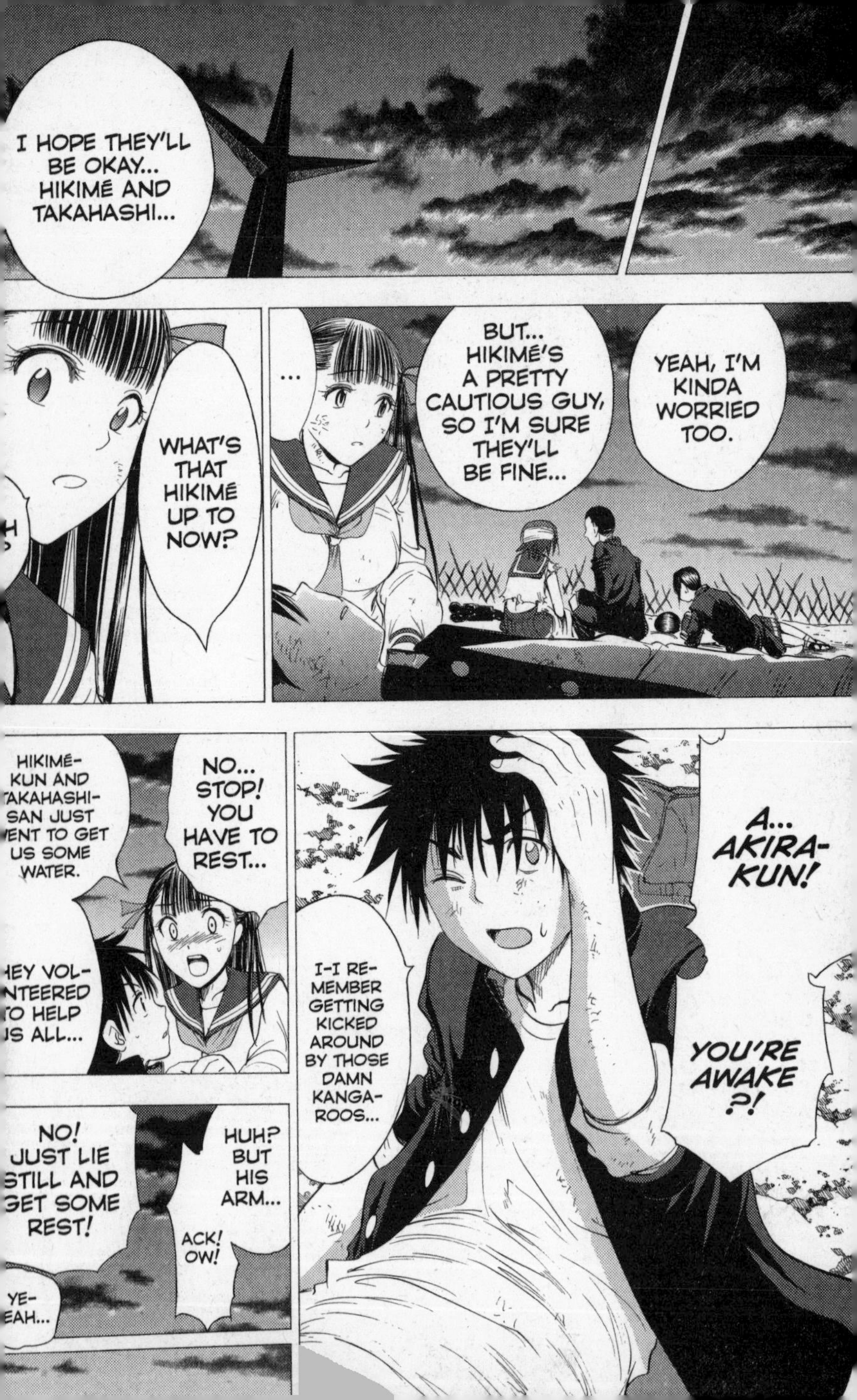
I HOPE THEY'LL BE OKAY... HIKIMÉ AND TAKAHASHI...
YEAH, I'M KINDA WORRIED TOO.
BUT... HIKIMÉ'S A PRETTY CAUTIOUS GUY, SO I'M SURE THEY'LL BE FINE...
...
WHAT'S THAT HIKIMÉ UP TO NOW?
A... AKIRA-KUN!
YOU'RE AWAKE ?!
I-I RE-MEMBER GETTING KICKED AROUND BY THOSE DAMN KANGA-ROOS...
NO... STOP! YOU HAVE TO REST...
HIKIMÉ-KUN AND AKAHASHI-SAN JUST ENT TO GET US SOME WATER.
HEY VOL-NTEERED O HELP S ALL...
HUH? BUT HIS ARM...
NO! JUST LIE STILL AND GET SOME REST!
ACK! OW!
YE-EAH...

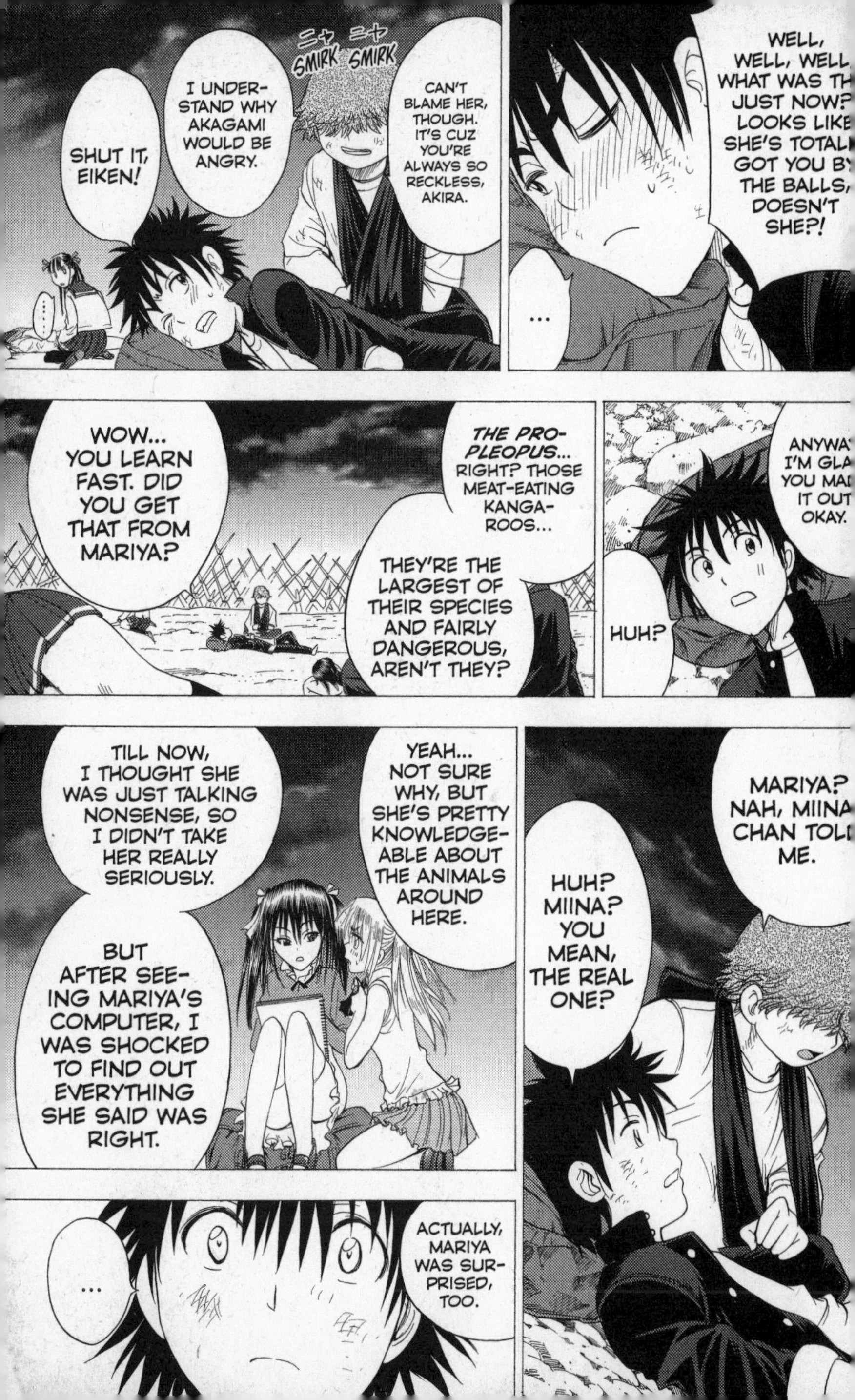
WELL, WELL, WELL WHAT WAS TH JUST NOW? LOOKS LIKE SHE'S TOTALL GOT YOU BY THE BALLS, DOESN'T SHE?!
...
ニャ ニヤ SMIRK SMIRK
CAN'T BLAME HER, THOUGH. IT'S CUZ YOU'RE ALWAYS SO RECKLESS, AKIRA.
I UNDER-STAND WHY AKAGAMI WOULD BE ANGRY.
SHUT IT, EIKEN!
...
ANYWA I'M GLA YOU MA IT OUT OKAY.
HUH?
THE PRO-PLEOPUS... RIGHT? THOSE MEAT-EATING KANGA-ROOS...
THEY'RE THE LARGEST OF THEIR SPECIES AND FAIRLY DANGEROUS, AREN'T THEY?
WOW... YOU LEARN FAST. DID YOU GET THAT FROM MARIYA?
MARIYA? NAH, MIINA CHAN TOL ME.
HUH? MIINA? YOU MEAN, THE REAL ONE?
YEAH... NOT SURE WHY, BUT SHE'S PRETTY KNOWLEDGE-ABLE ABOUT THE ANIMALS AROUND HERE.
TILL NOW, I THOUGHT SHE WAS JUST TALKING NONSENSE, SO I DIDN'T TAKE HER REALLY SERIOUSLY.
BUT AFTER SEE-ING MARIYA'S COMPUTER, I WAS SHOCKED TO FIND OUT EVERYTHING SHE SAID WAS RIGHT.
ACTUALLY, MARIYA WAS SUR-PRISED, TOO.
...

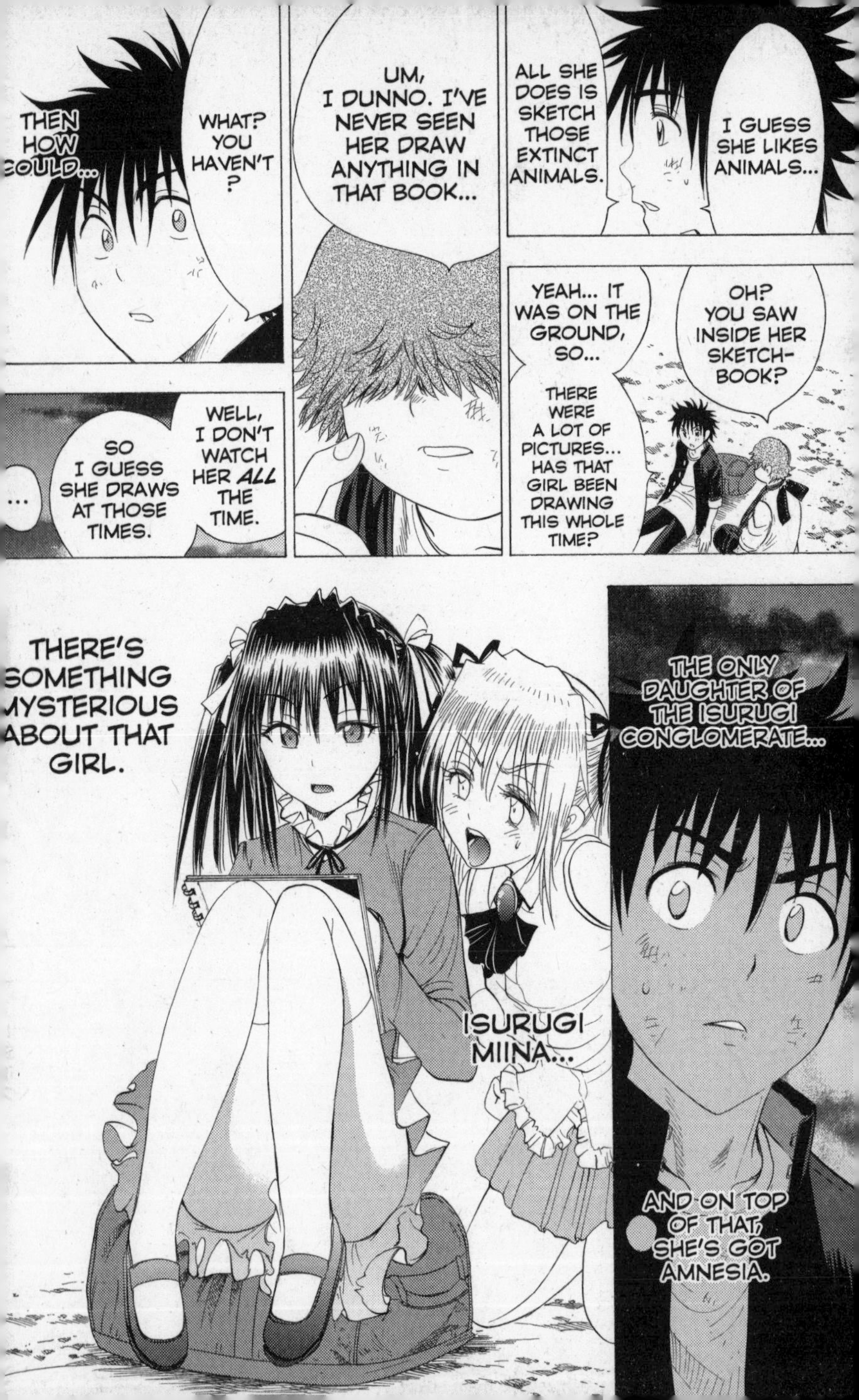
I GUESS SHE LIKES ANIMALS...
ALL SHE DOES IS SKETCH THOSE EXTINCT ANIMALS.
OH? YOU SAW INSIDE HER SKETCH-BOOK?
YEAH... IT WAS ON THE GROUND, SO...
THERE WERE A LOT OF PICTURES... HAS THAT GIRL BEEN DRAWING THIS WHOLE TIME?
UM, I DUNNO. I'VE NEVER SEEN HER DRAW ANYTHING IN THAT BOOK...
WHAT? YOU HAVEN'T?
THEN HOW COULD...
WELL, I DON'T WATCH HER *ALL* THE TIME.
SO I GUESS SHE DRAWS AT THOSE TIMES.
...
THE ONLY DAUGHTER OF THE ISURUGI CONGLOMERATE...
AND ON TOP OF THAT, SHE'S GOT AMNESIA.
ISURUGI MIINA...
THERE'S SOMETHING MYSTERIOUS ABOUT THAT GIRL.

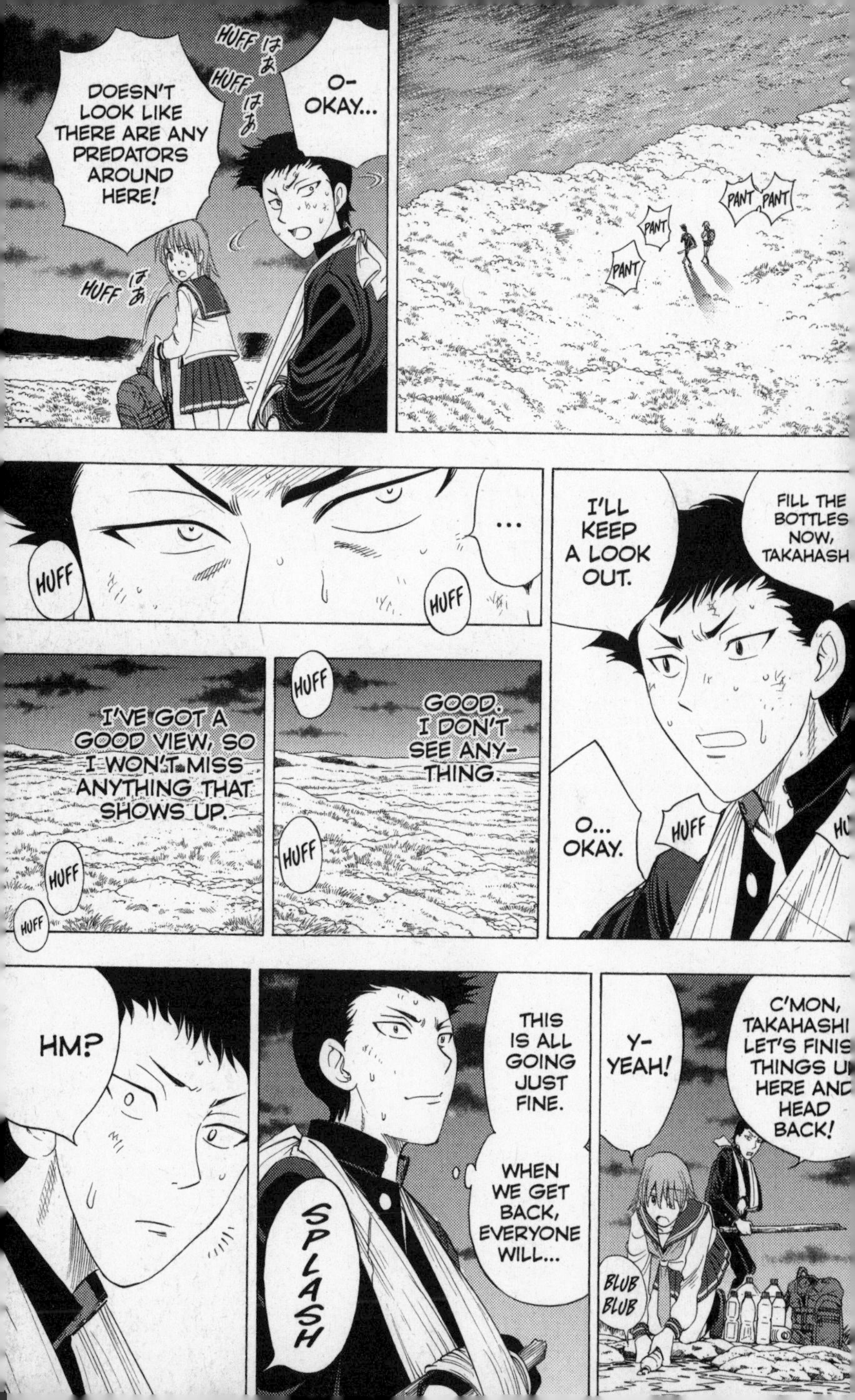
PANT
PANT
PANT
PANT
O-OKAY...
HUFF はあ
HUFF はあ
DOESN'T LOOK LIKE THERE ARE ANY PREDATORS AROUND HERE!
HUFF はあ
FILL THE BOTTLES NOW, TAKAHASH
I'LL KEEP A LOOK OUT.
O... OKAY.
HUFF
HU
...
HUFF
HUFF
HUFF
GOOD. I DON'T SEE ANY-THING.
HUFF
I'VE GOT A GOOD VIEW, SO I WON'T MISS ANYTHING THAT SHOWS UP.
HUFF
HUFF
C'MON, TAKAHASHI LET'S FINIS THINGS U HERE AND HEAD BACK!
Y- YEAH!
BLUB BLUB
THIS IS ALL GOING JUST FINE.
WHEN WE GET BACK, EVERYONE WILL...
SPLASH
HM?

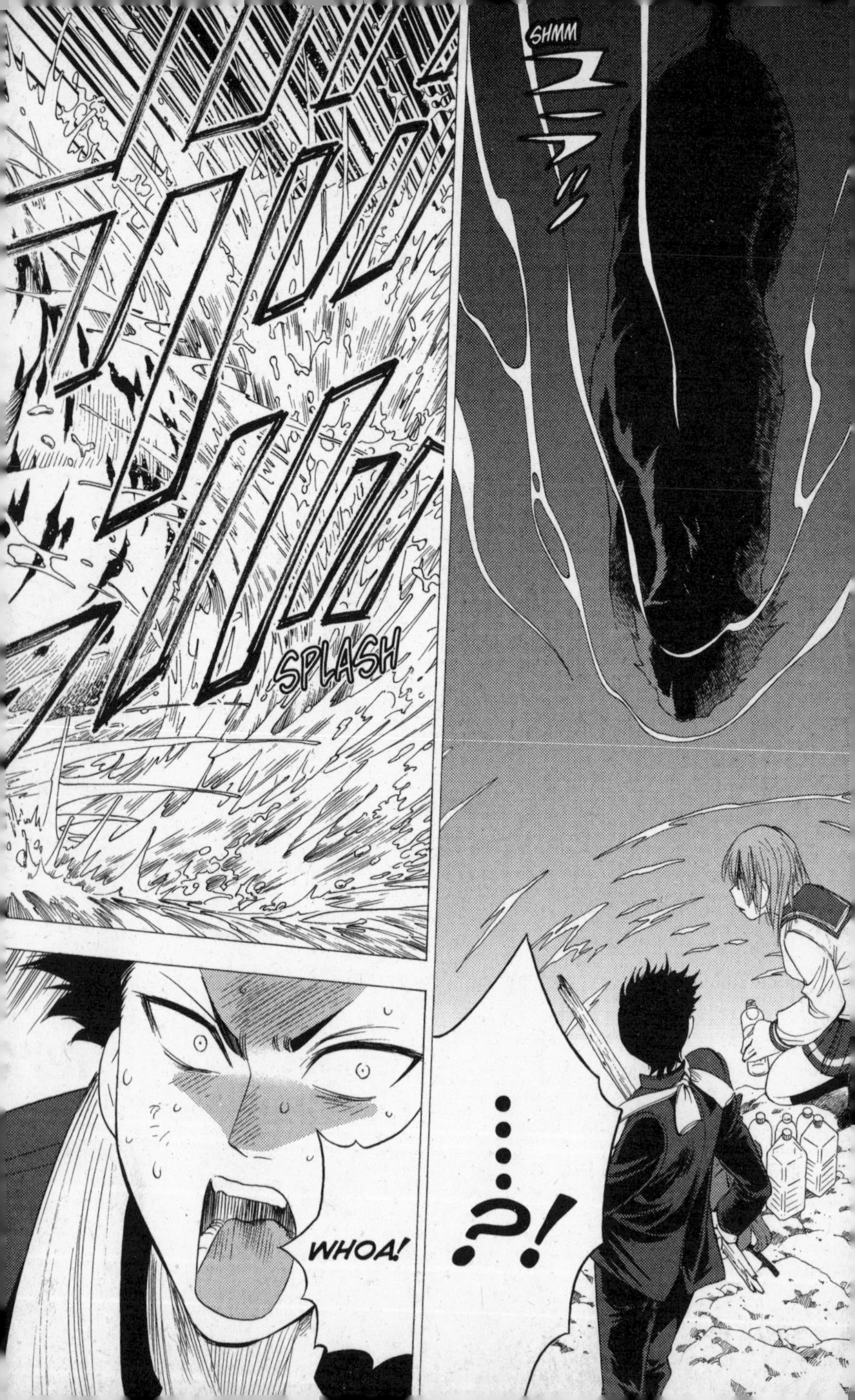
SHMM
SPLASH
...?!
WHOA!

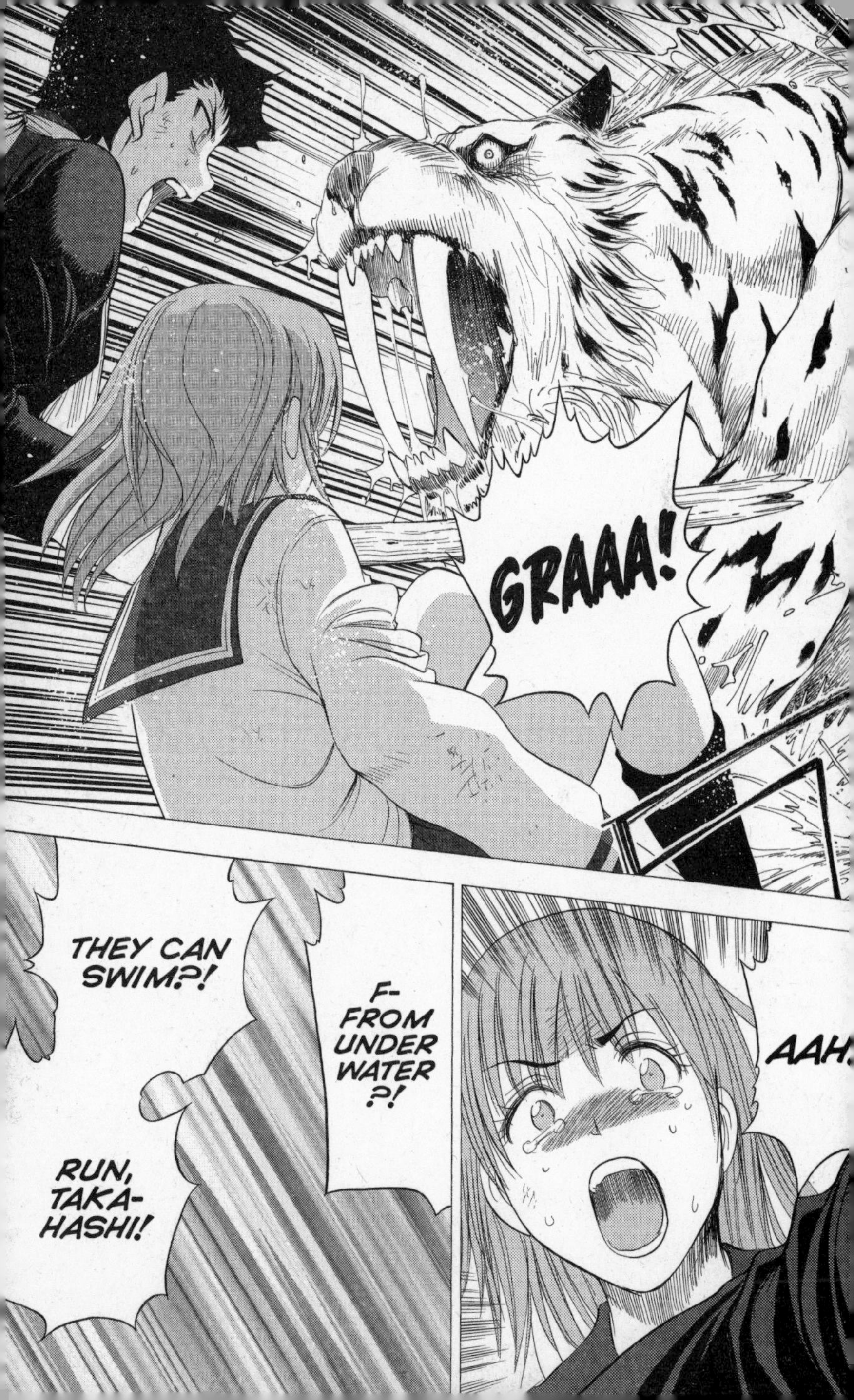
GRAAA!
AAH!
F-FROM UNDER WATER?!
THEY CAN SWIM?!
RUN, TAKA-HASHI!

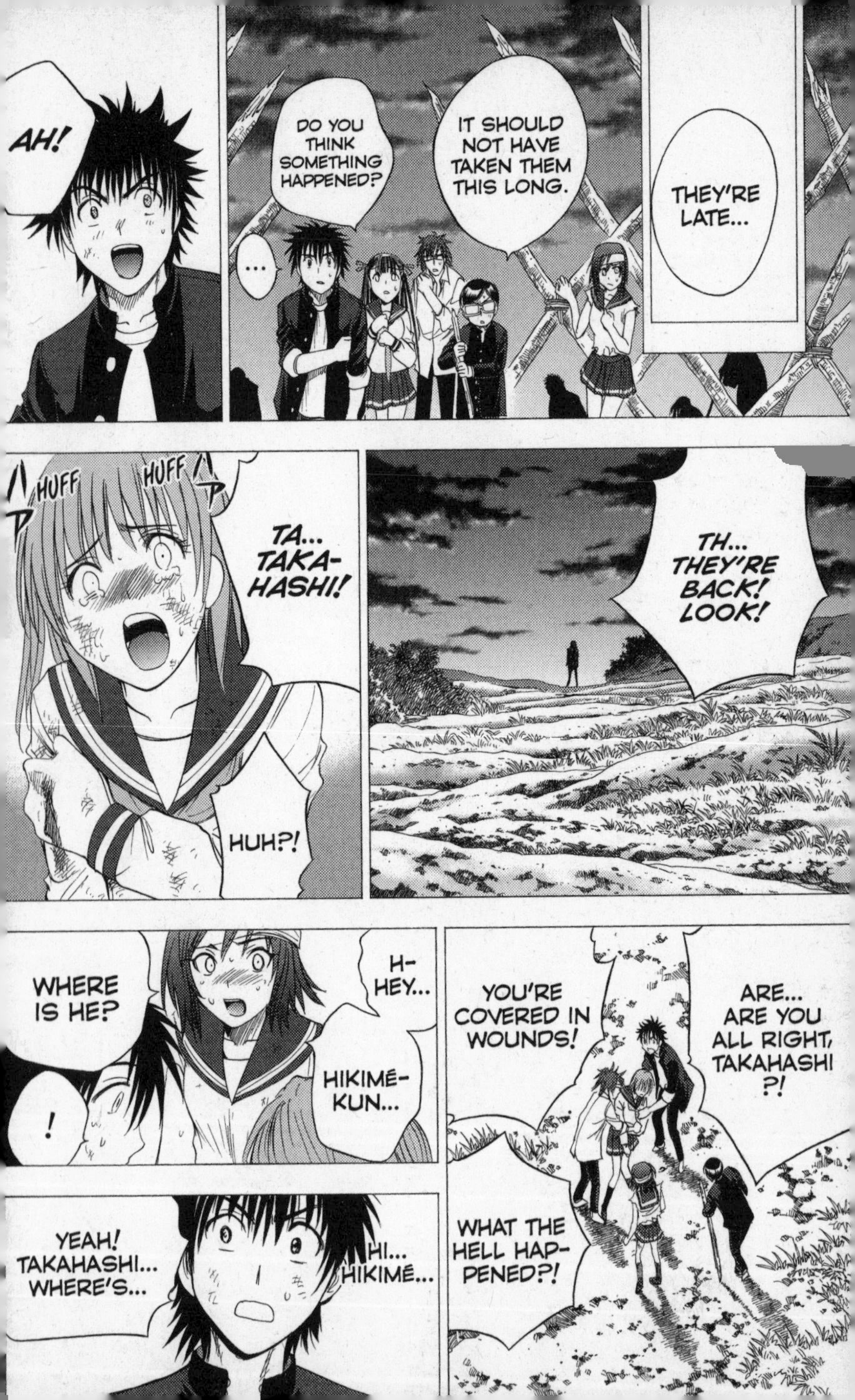
THEY'RE LATE...
IT SHOULD NOT HAVE TAKEN THEM THIS LONG.
DO YOU THINK SOMETHING HAPPENED?
....
AH!
TH... THEY'RE BACK! LOOK!
HUFF
HUFF
TA... TAKA-HASHI!
HUH?!
ARE... ARE YOU ALL RIGHT, TAKAHASHI?!
YOU'RE COVERED IN WOUNDS!
WHAT THE HELL HAP-PENED?!
H-HEY...
HIKIMÉ-KUN...
WHERE IS HE?
!
HI... HIKIMÉ...
YEAH! TAKAHASHI... WHERE'S...

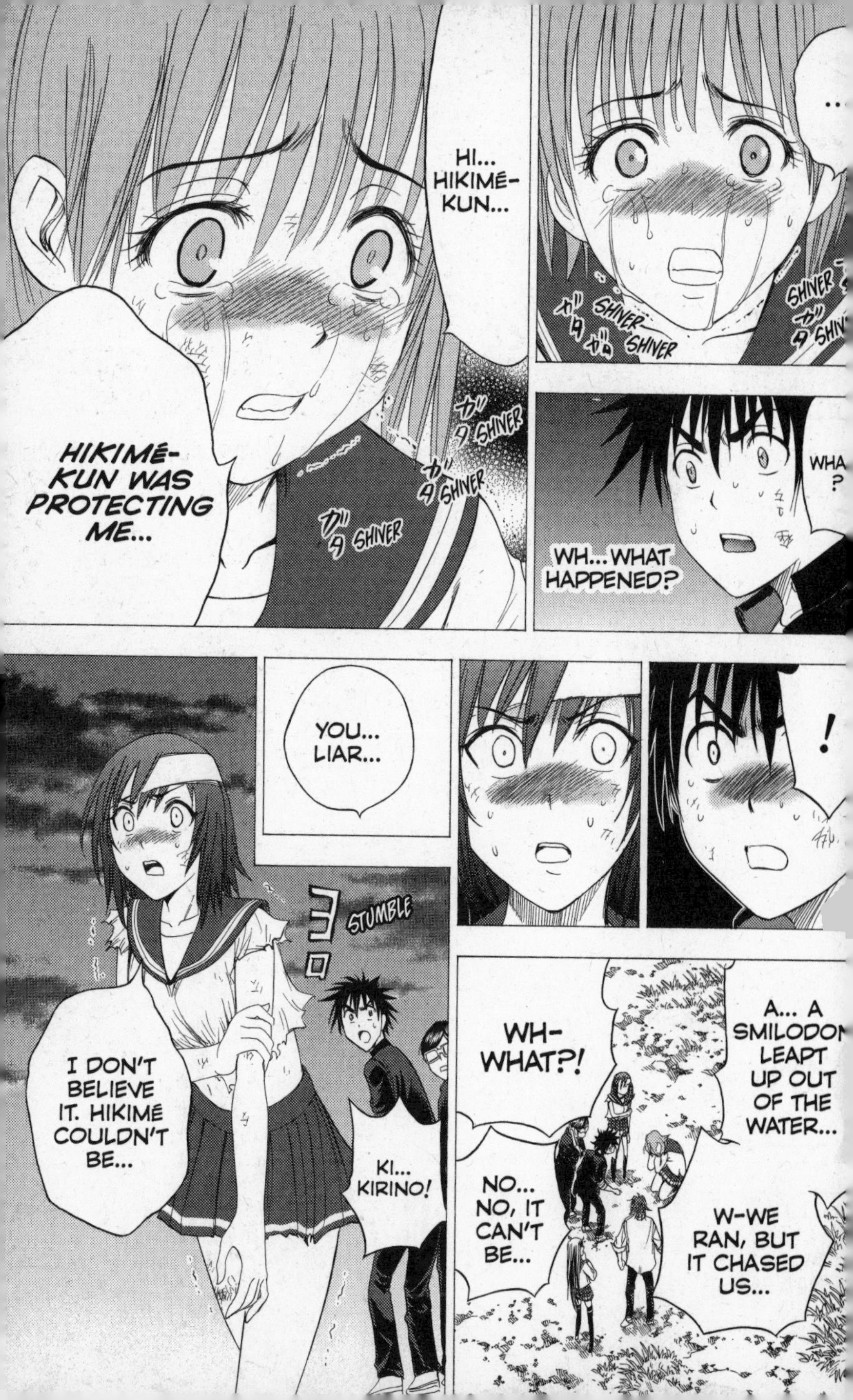
...
SHIVER
SHIVER
SHIVER
SHIVER
WHA ?
WH... WHAT HAPPENED?
HI... HIKIME-KUN...
SHIVER
SHIVER
SHIVER
HIKIME-KUN WAS PROTECTING ME...
!
YOU... LIAR...
A... A SMILODON LEAPT UP OUT OF THE WATER...
WH-WHAT?!
W-WE RAN, BUT IT CHASED US...
NO... NO, IT CAN'T BE...
STUMBLE
KI... KIRINO!
I DON'T BELIEVE IT. HIKIME COULDN'T BE...

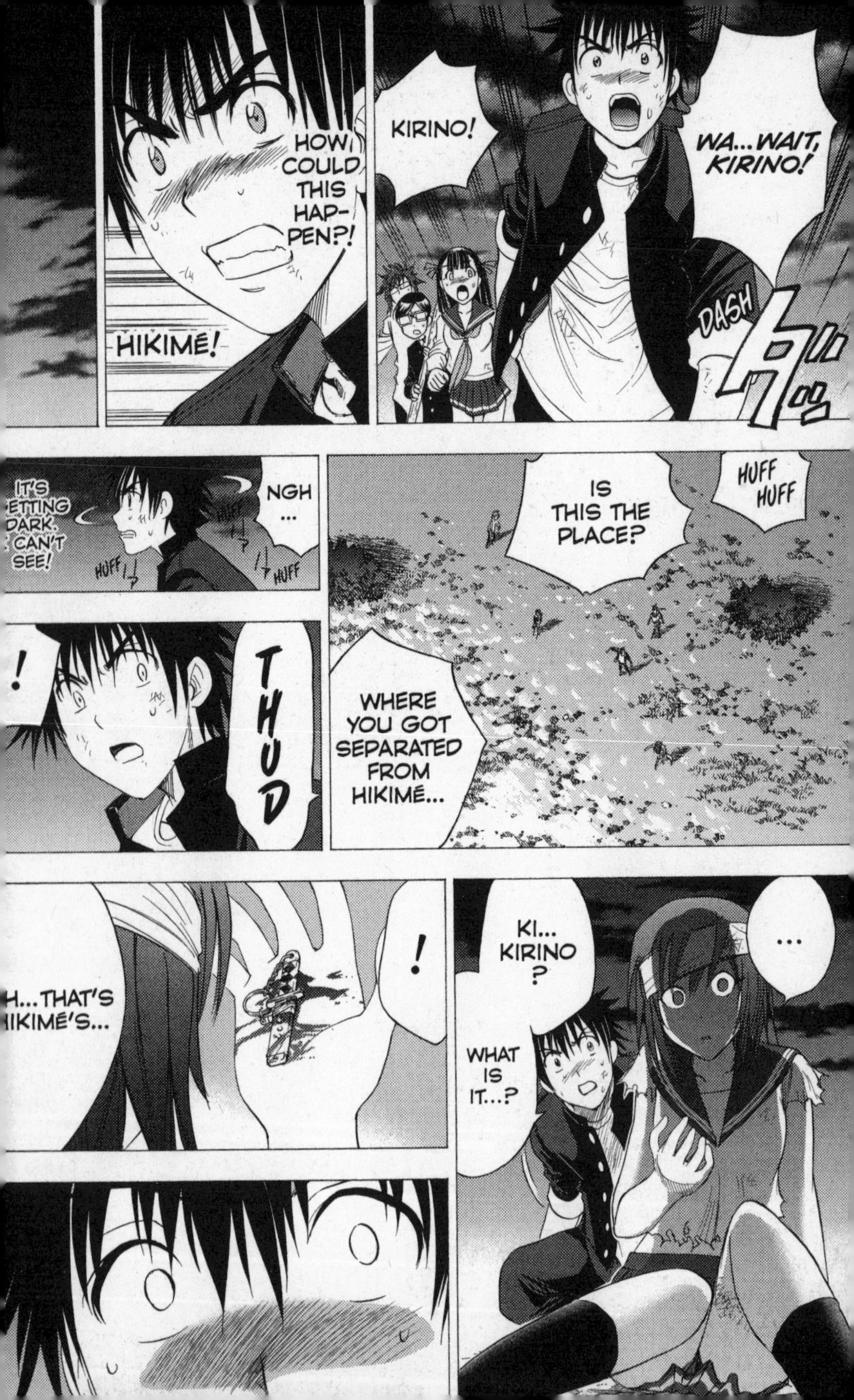

WA...WAIT, KIRINO!
KIRINO!
DASH
HOW COULD THIS HAP-PEN?!
HIKIMÉ!
HUFF HUFF
IS THIS THE PLACE?
WHERE YOU GOT SEPARATED FROM HIKIMÉ...
NGH ...
IT'S ETTING DARK. CAN'T SEE!
HUFF HUFF HUFF
THUD
!
...
KI... KIRINO?
WHAT IS IT...?
!
H...THAT'S IKIMÉ'S...

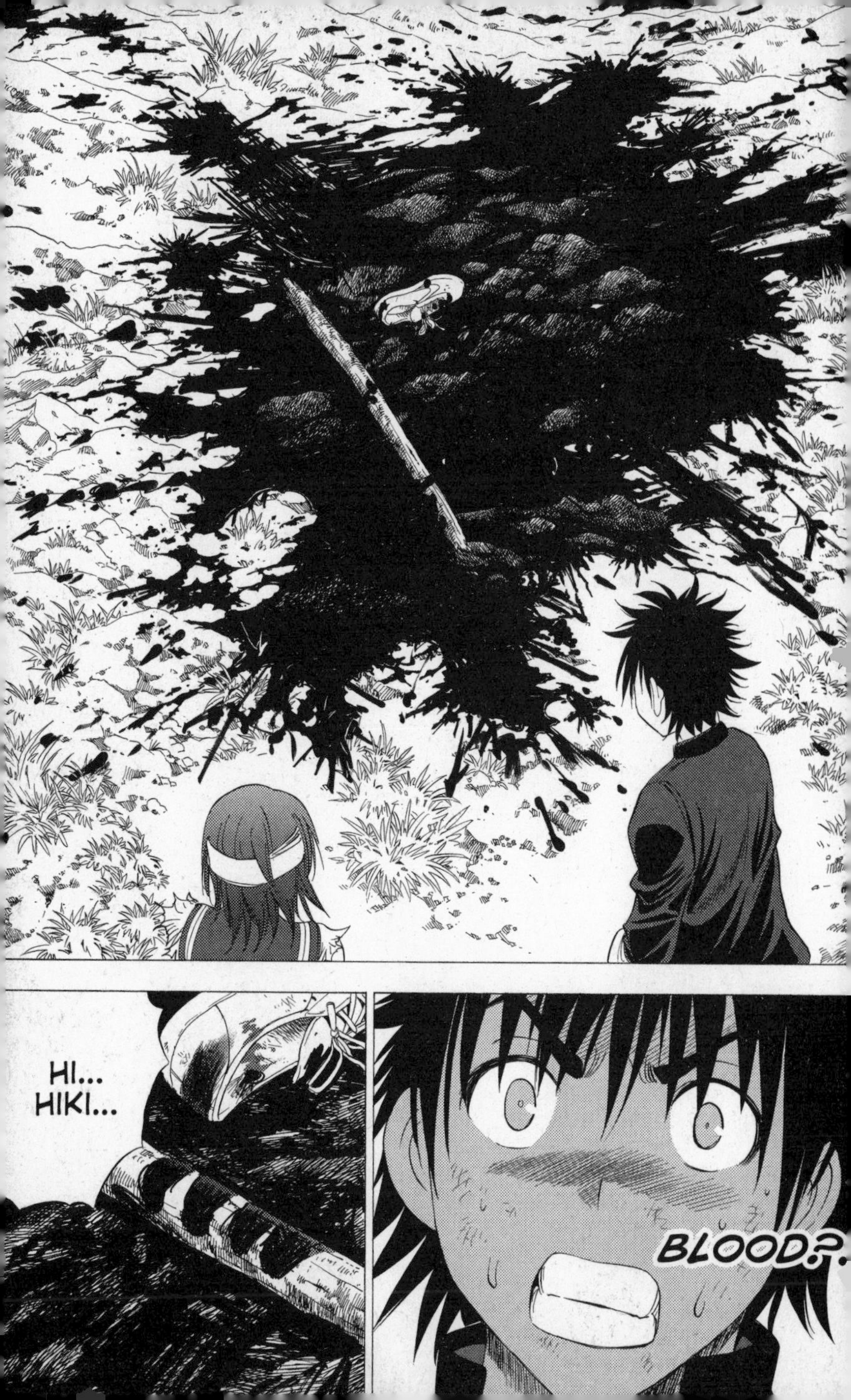
BLOOD?.
HI...
HIKI...

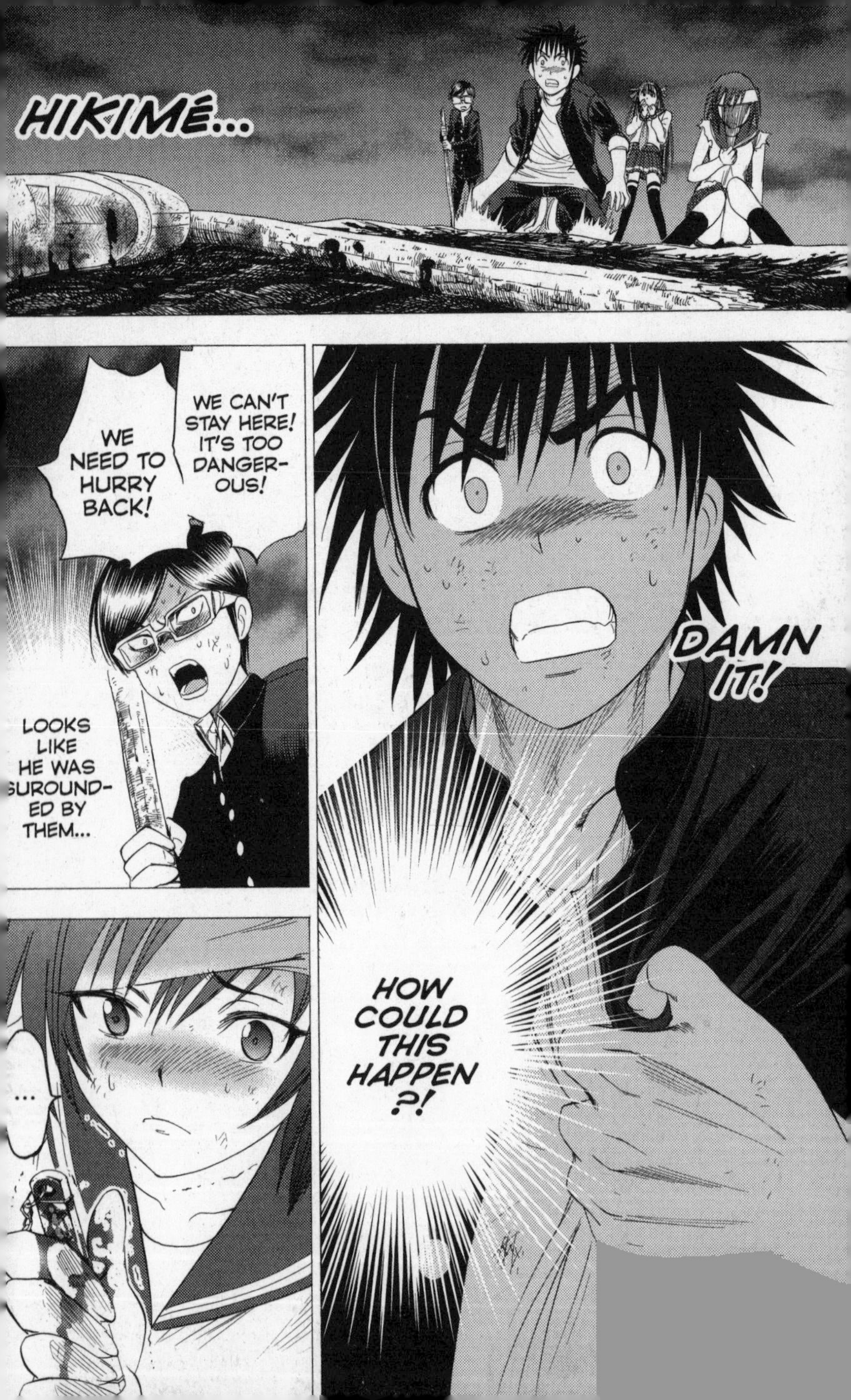
HIKIMÉ...
DAMN IT!
HOW COULD THIS HAPPEN ?!
WE CAN'T STAY HERE! IT'S TOO DANGER-OUS!
WE NEED TO HURRY BACK!
LOOKS LIKE HE WAS SUROUND-ED BY THEM...
...

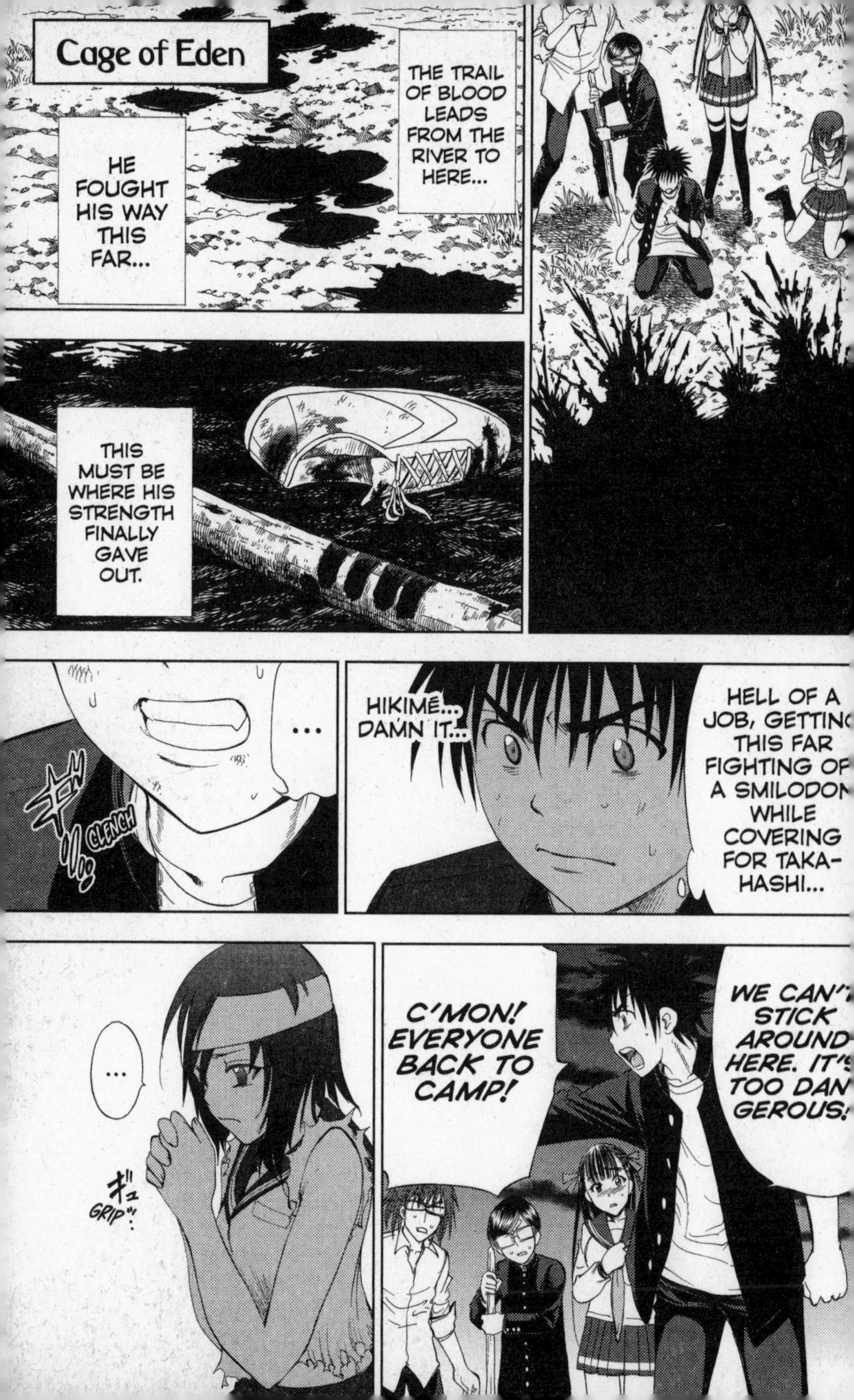
THE TRAIL OF BLOOD LEADS FROM THE RIVER TO HERE...
HE FOUGHT HIS WAY THIS FAR...
THIS MUST BE WHERE HIS STRENGTH FINALLY GAVE OUT.
HELL OF A JOB, GETTING THIS FAR FIGHTING OFF A SMILODON WHILE COVERING FOR TAKA-HASHI...
HIKIME... DAMN IT...
...
CLENCH
WE CAN'T STICK AROUND HERE. IT'S TOO DAN-GEROUS!
C'MON! EVERYONE BACK TO CAMP!
...
GRIP

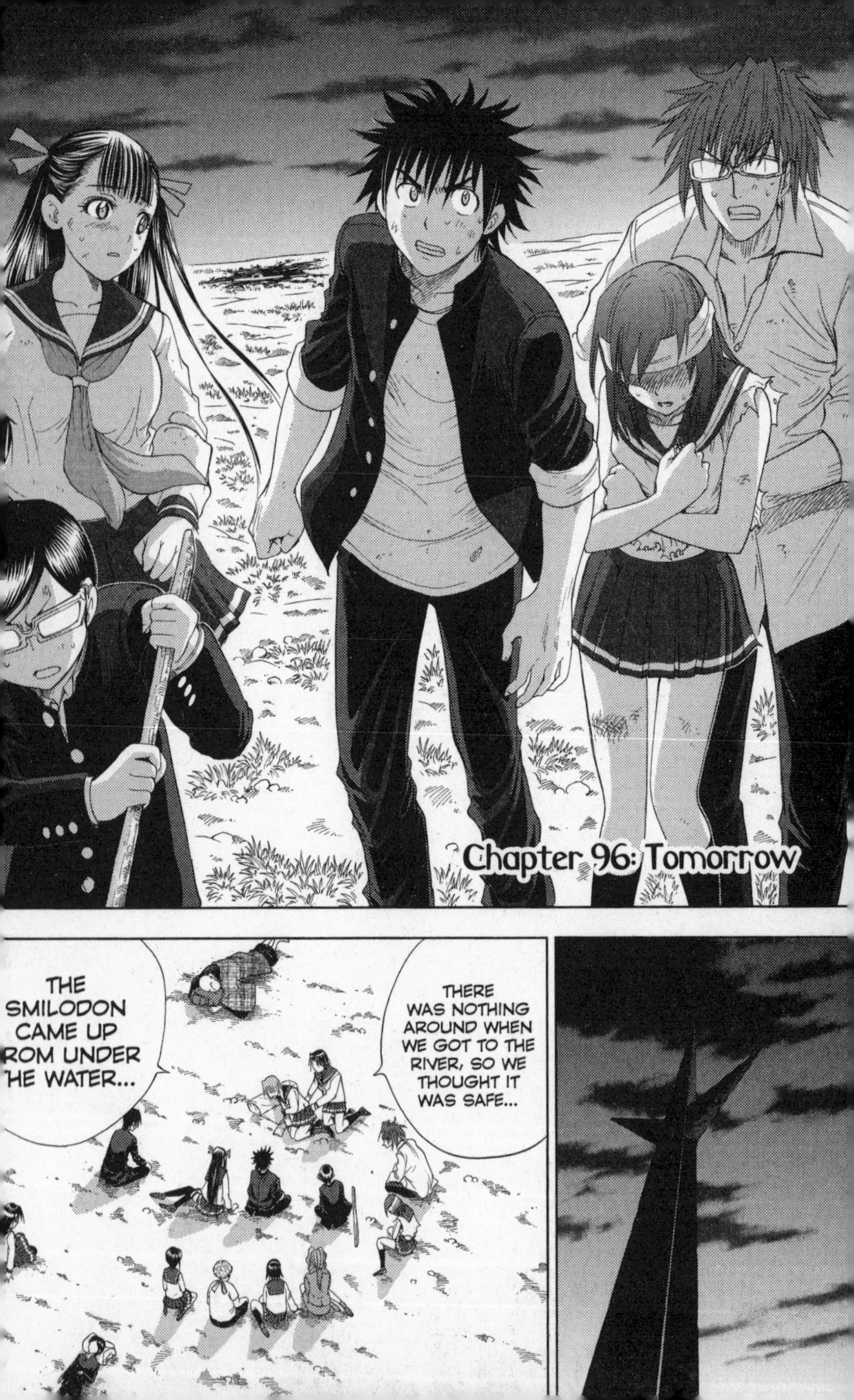
Chapter 96: Tomorrow
THERE WAS NOTHING AROUND WHEN WE GOT TO THE RIVER, SO WE THOUGHT IT WAS SAFE...
THE SMILODON CAME UP ROM UNDER HE WATER...

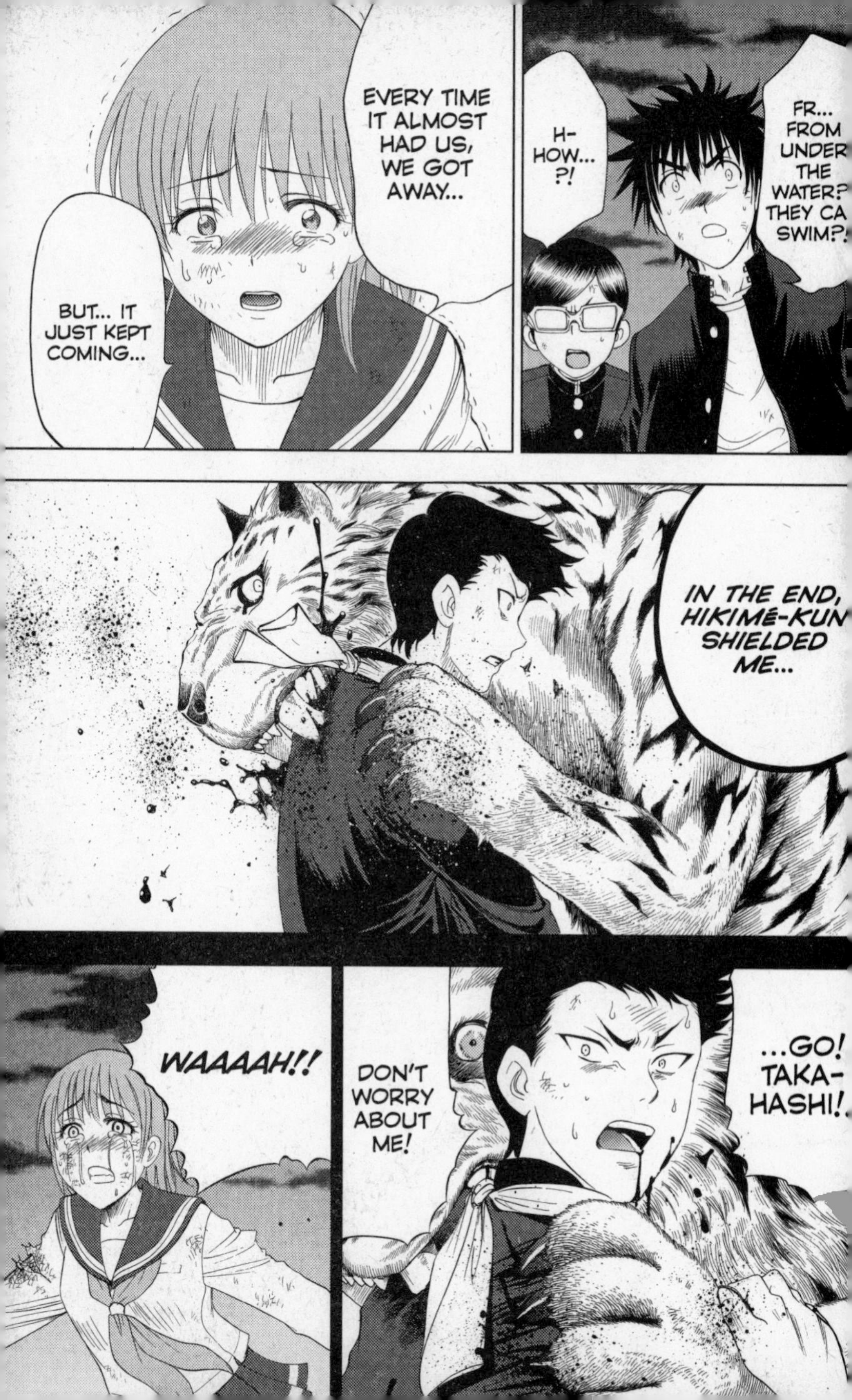
FR... FROM UNDER THE WATER? THEY CA SWIM?!
H- HOW... ?!
EVERY TIME IT ALMOST HAD US, WE GOT AWAY...
BUT... IT JUST KEPT COMING...
IN THE END, HIKIMÉ-KUN SHIELDED ME...
...GO! TAKA-HASHI!
DON'T WORRY ABOUT ME!
WAAAAH!!

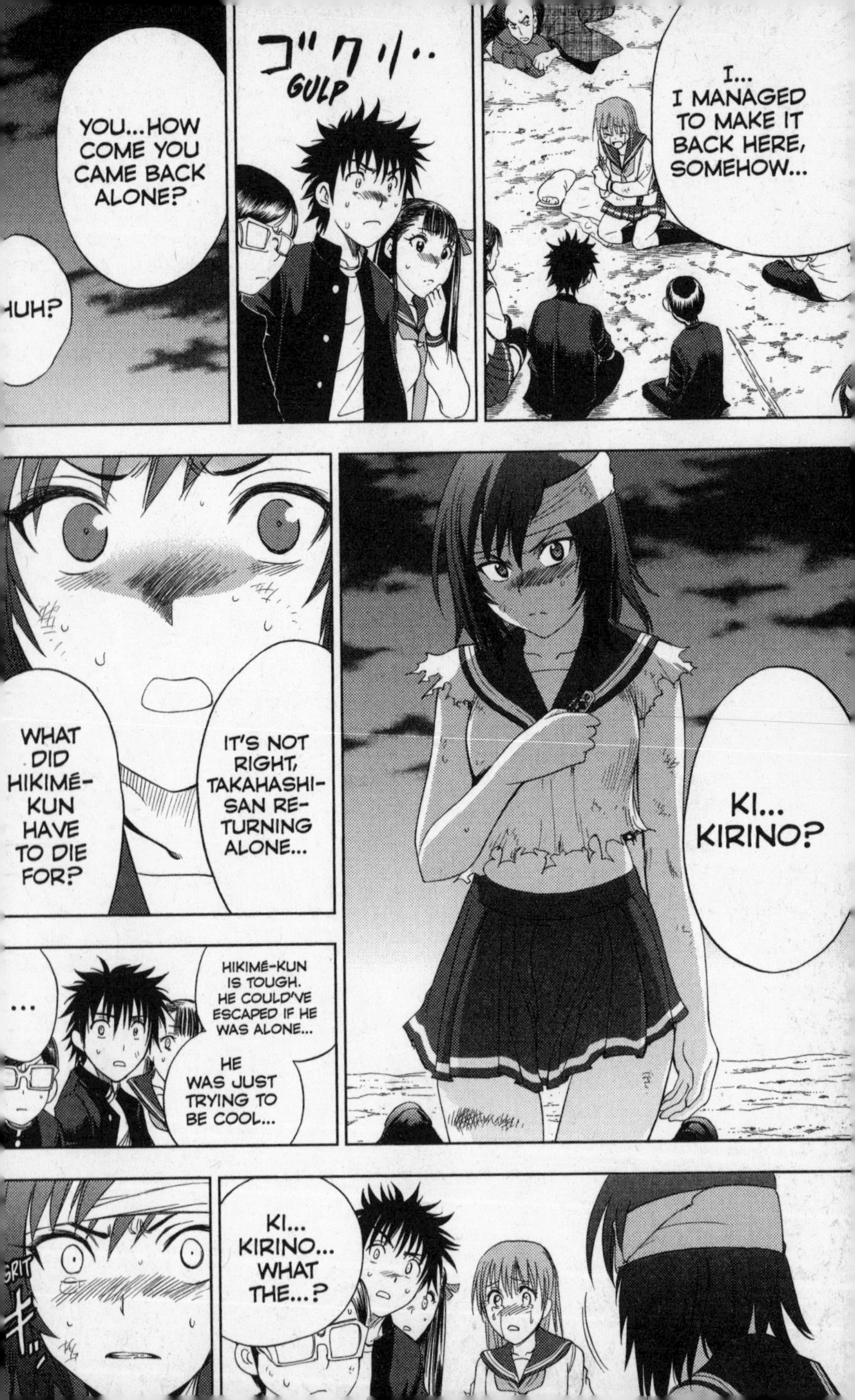
I... I MANAGED TO MAKE IT BACK HERE, SOMEHOW...
ゴクリ‥
GULP
YOU...HOW COME YOU CAME BACK ALONE?
HUH?
KI... KIRINO?
IT'S NOT RIGHT, TAKAHASHI-SAN RE-TURNING ALONE...
WHAT DID HIKIMÉ-KUN HAVE TO DIE FOR?
HIKIMÉ-KUN IS TOUGH. HE COULD'VE ESCAPED IF HE WAS ALONE...
HE WAS JUST TRYING TO BE COOL...
...
KI... KIRINO... WHAT THE...?
GRIT

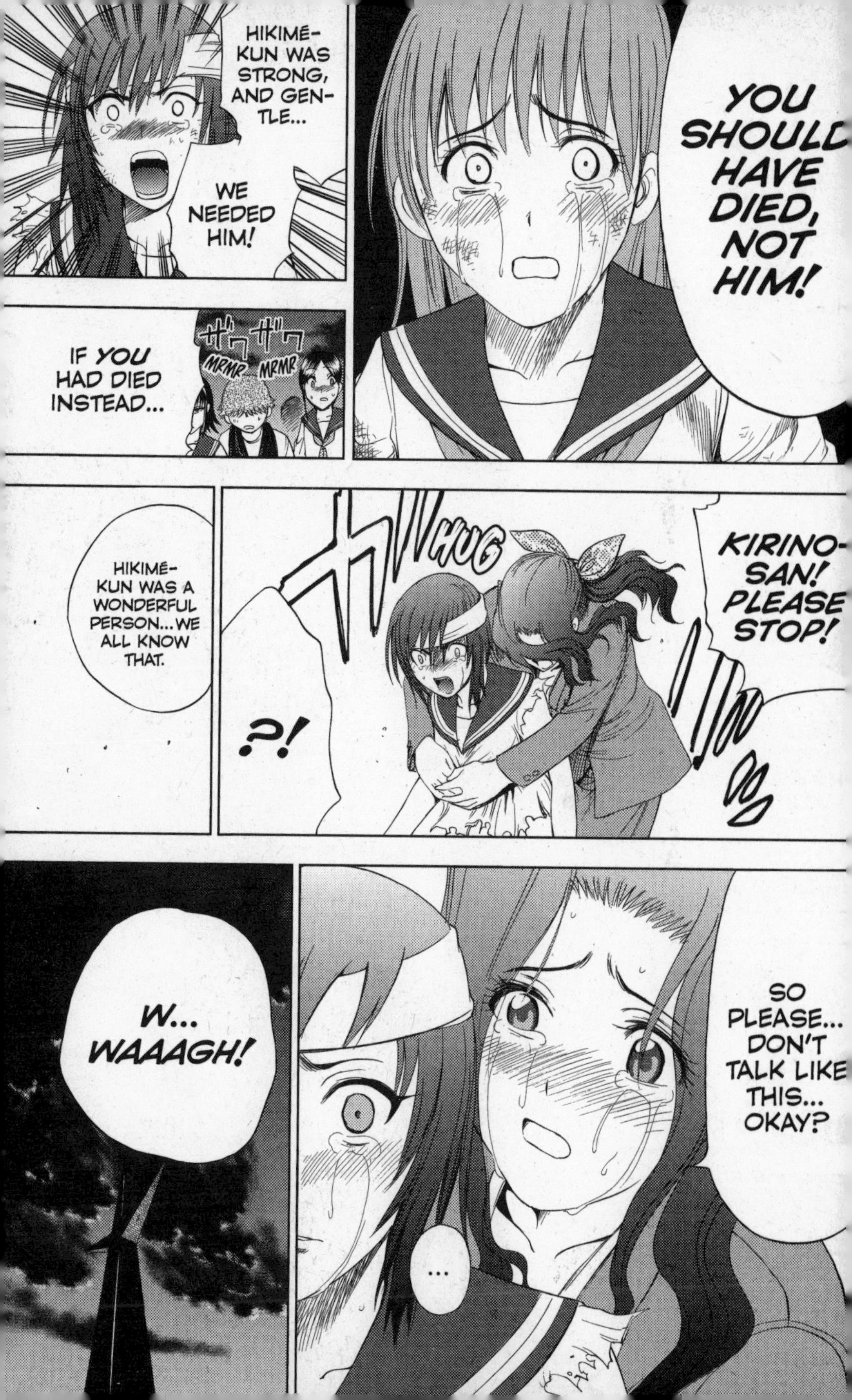
YOU SHOULD HAVE DIED, NOT HIM!
HIKIMÉ-KUN WAS STRONG, AND GENTLE...
WE NEEDED HIM!
ザワザワ
MRMR MRMR
IF YOU HAD DIED INSTEAD...
KIRINO-SAN! PLEASE STOP!
HUG
?!
HIKIMÉ-KUN WAS A WONDERFUL PERSON...WE ALL KNOW THAT.
SO PLEASE... DON'T TALK LIKE THIS... OKAY?
...
W... WAAAGH!

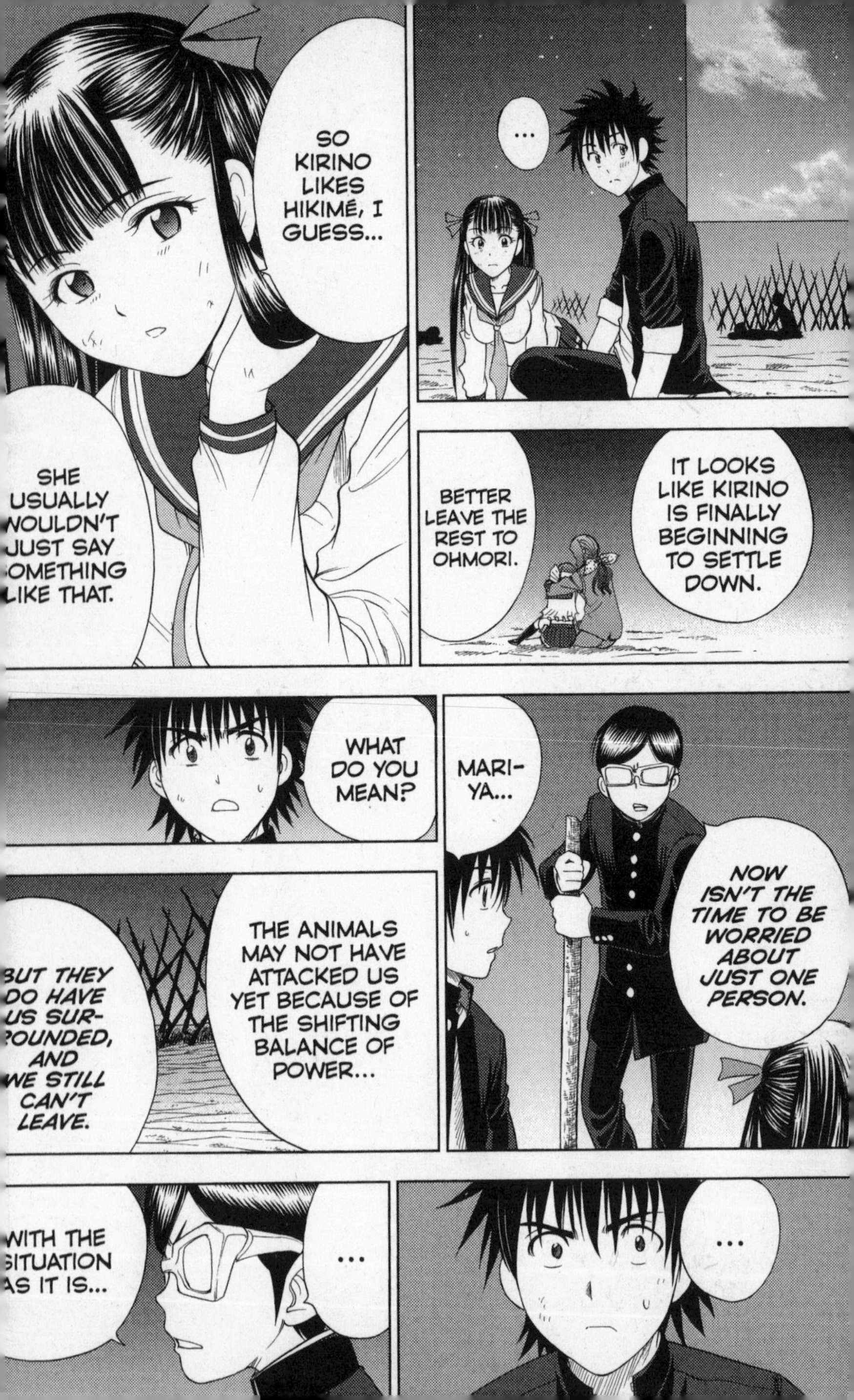
...
IT LOOKS LIKE KIRINO IS FINALLY BEGINNING TO SETTLE DOWN.
BETTER LEAVE THE REST TO OHMORI.
SO KIRINO LIKES HIKIMÉ, I GUESS...
SHE USUALLY WOULDN'T JUST SAY SOMETHING LIKE THAT.
MARI-YA...
NOW ISN'T THE TIME TO BE WORRIED ABOUT JUST ONE PERSON.
WHAT DO YOU MEAN?
THE ANIMALS MAY NOT HAVE ATTACKED US YET BECAUSE OF THE SHIFTING BALANCE OF POWER...
BUT THEY DO HAVE US SURROUNDED, AND WE STILL CAN'T LEAVE.
...
...
WITH THE SITUATION AS IT IS...

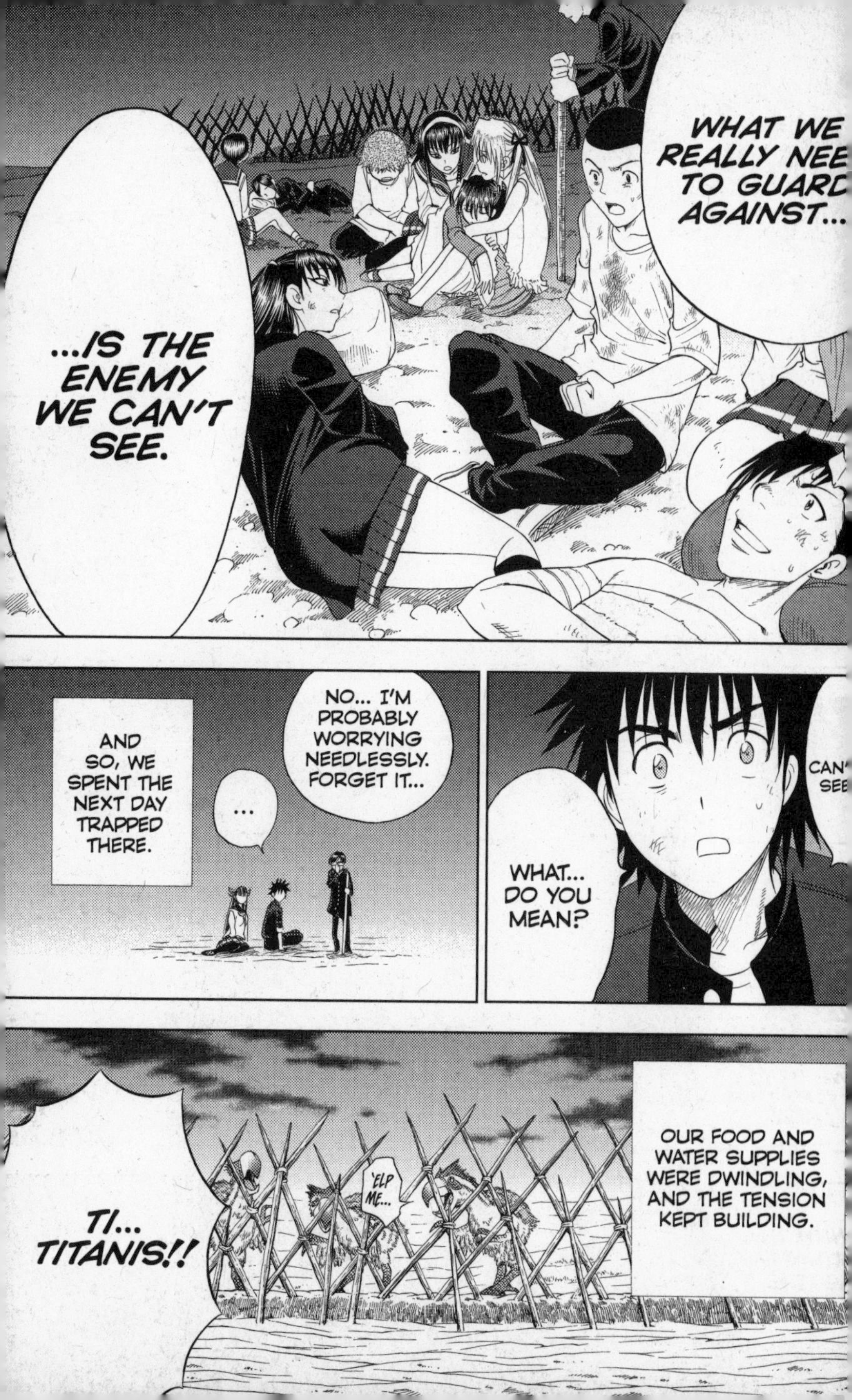
WHAT WE REALLY NEE TO GUARD AGAINST...
...IS THE ENEMY WE CAN'T SEE.
CAN' SEE
WHAT... DO YOU MEAN?
NO... I'M PROBABLY WORRYING NEEDLESSLY. FORGET IT...
...
AND SO, WE SPENT THE NEXT DAY TRAPPED THERE.
OUR FOOD AND WATER SUPPLIES WERE DWINDLING, AND THE TENSION KEPT BUILDING.
'ELP ME...
TI... TITANIS!!

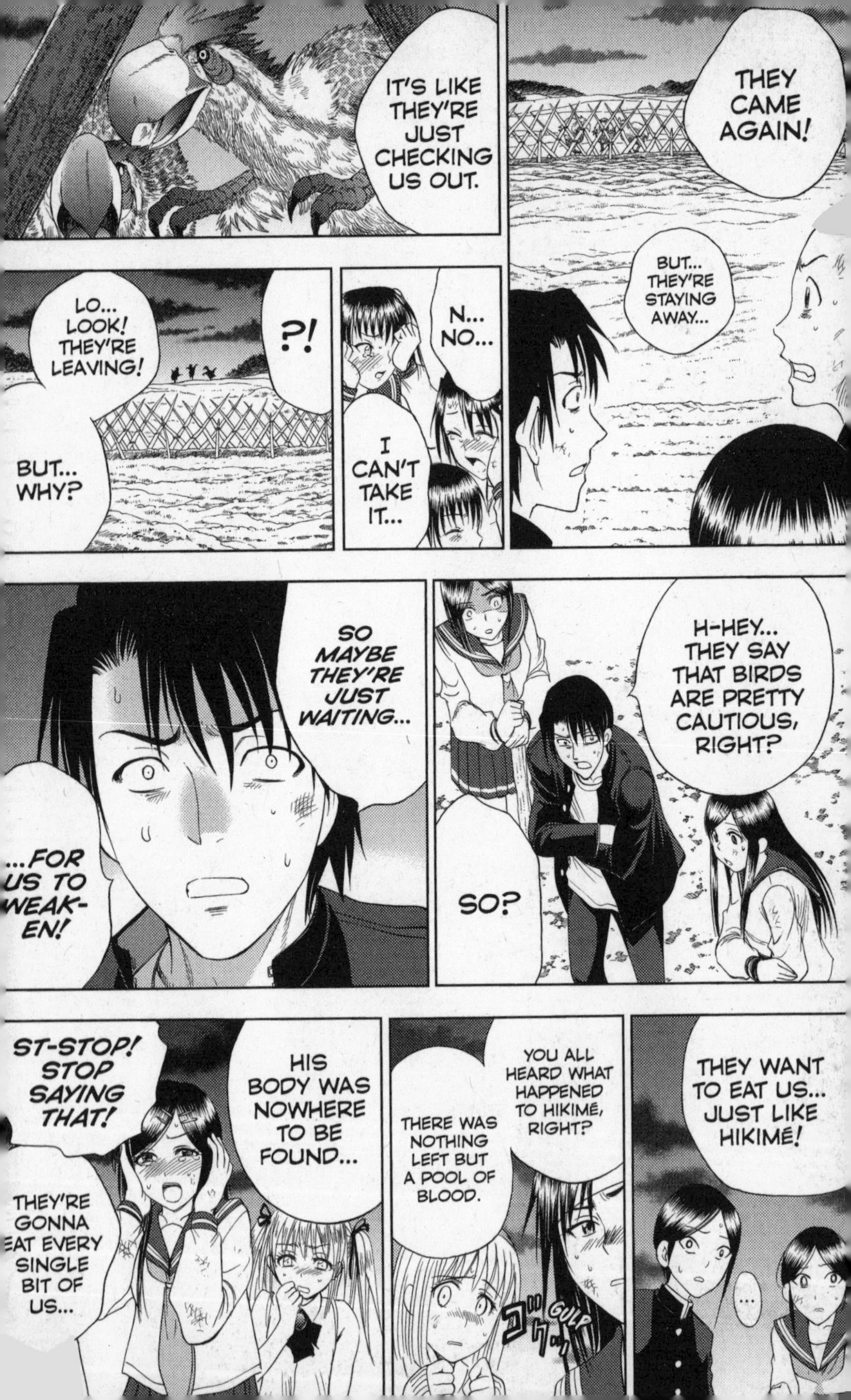
THEY CAME AGAIN!
BUT... THEY'RE STAYING AWAY...
IT'S LIKE THEY'RE JUST CHECKING US OUT.
N... NO...
I CAN'T TAKE IT...
LO... LOOK! THEY'RE LEAVING!
?!
BUT... WHY?
H-HEY... THEY SAY THAT BIRDS ARE PRETTY CAUTIOUS, RIGHT?
SO?
SO MAYBE THEY'RE JUST WAITING...
...FOR US TO WEAKEN!
THEY WANT TO EAT US... JUST LIKE HIKIMÉ!
...
YOU ALL HEARD WHAT HAPPENED TO HIKIMÉ, RIGHT?
THERE WAS NOTHING LEFT BUT A POOL OF BLOOD.
GULP
HIS BODY WAS NOWHERE TO BE FOUND...
ST-STOP! STOP SAYING THAT!
THEY'RE GONNA EAT EVERY SINGLE BIT OF US...

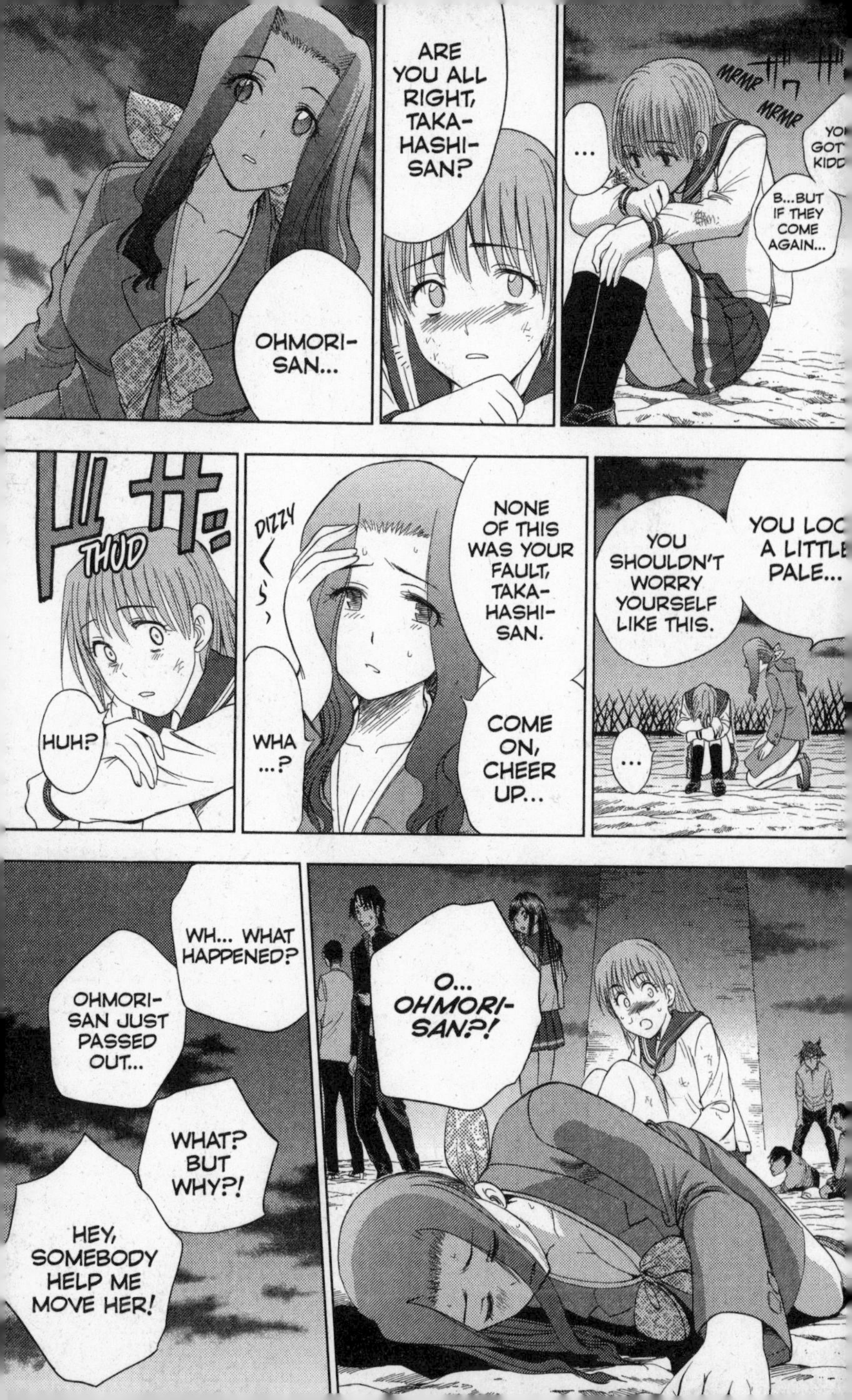
MRMR
MRMR
YO GOT KIDD
B...BUT IF THEY COME AGAIN...
...
ARE YOU ALL RIGHT, TAKA-HASHI-SAN?
OHMORI-SAN...
YOU LOC A LITTLE PALE...
YOU SHOULDN'T WORRY YOURSELF LIKE THIS.
...
NONE OF THIS WAS YOUR FAULT, TAKA-HASHI-SAN.
COME ON, CHEER UP...
DIZZY
WHA ...?
THUD
HUH?
O... OHMORI-SAN?!
WH... WHAT HAPPENED?
OHMORI-SAN JUST PASSED OUT...
WHAT? BUT WHY?!
HEY, SOMEBODY HELP ME MOVE HER!

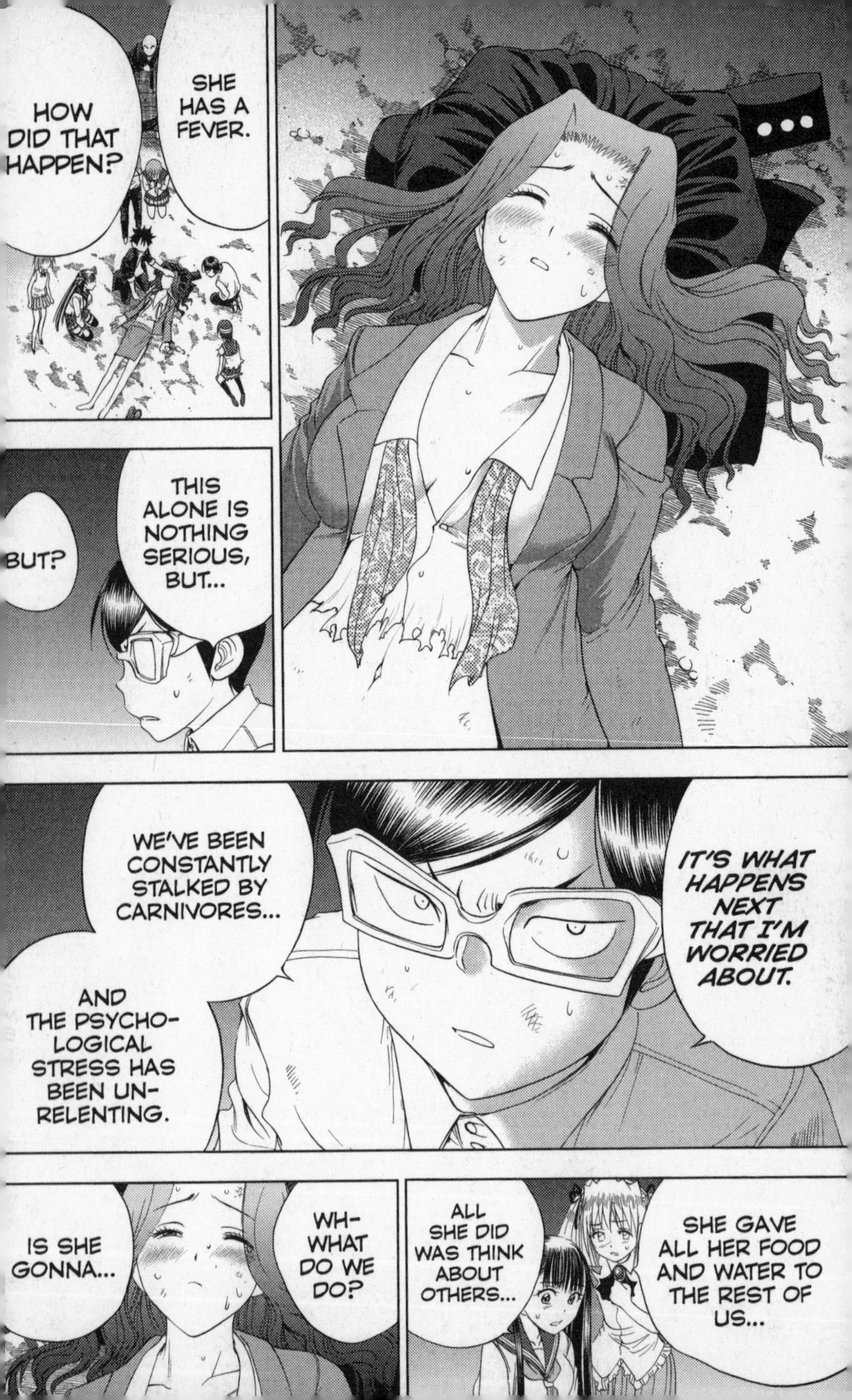
...
SHE HAS A FEVER.
HOW DID THAT HAPPEN?
THIS ALONE IS NOTHING SERIOUS, BUT...
BUT?
IT'S WHAT HAPPENS NEXT THAT I'M WORRIED ABOUT.
WE'VE BEEN CONSTANTLY STALKED BY CARNIVORES...
AND THE PSYCHOLOGICAL STRESS HAS BEEN UNRELENTING.
SHE GAVE ALL HER FOOD AND WATER TO THE REST OF US...
ALL SHE DID WAS THINK ABOUT OTHERS...
WH-WHAT DO WE DO?
IS SHE GONNA...

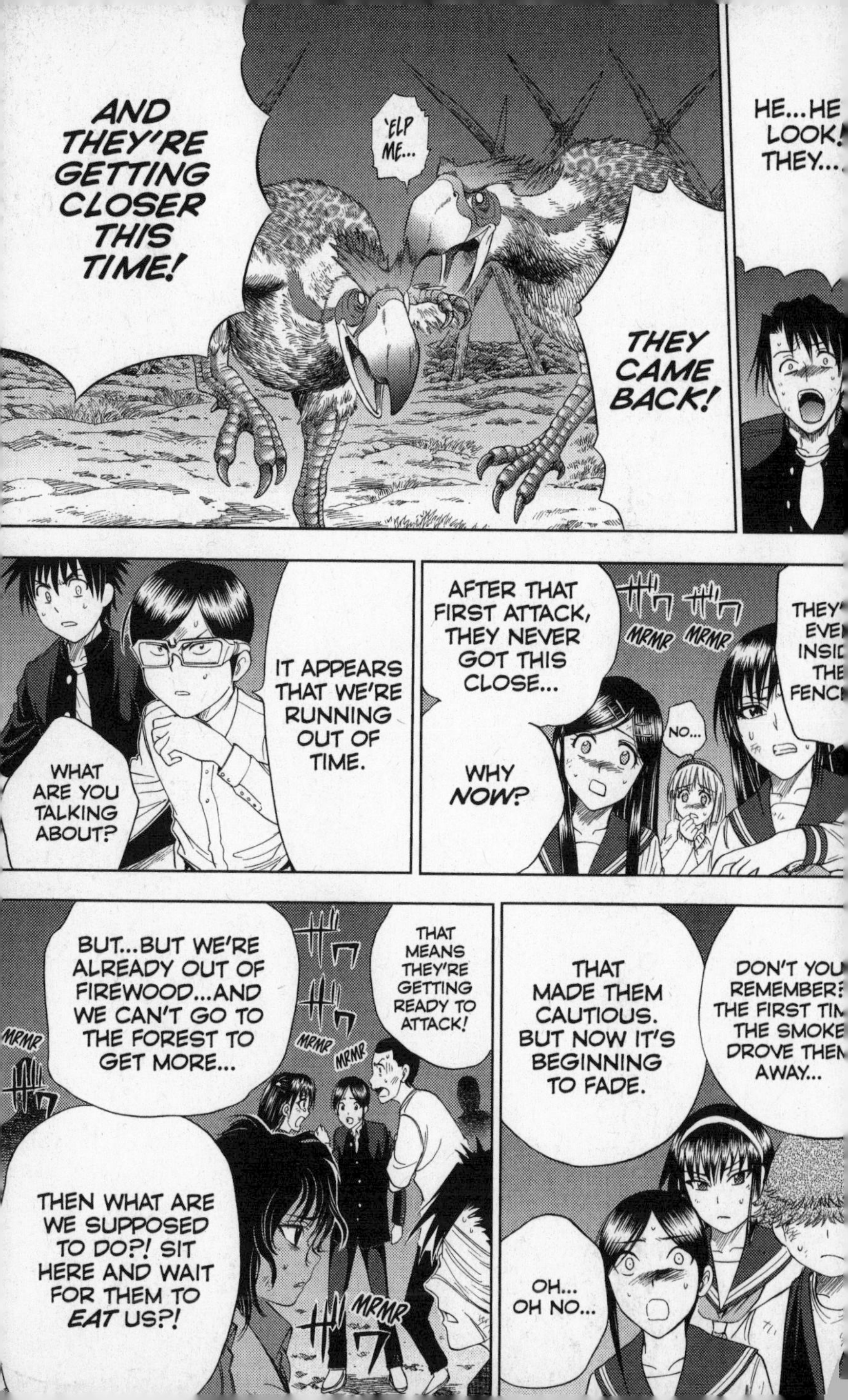
HE...HE LOOK! THEY...
'ELP ME...
AND THEY'RE GETTING CLOSER THIS TIME!
THEY CAME BACK!
THEY' EVE INSID THE FENC
MRMR MRMR
AFTER THAT FIRST ATTACK, THEY NEVER GOT THIS CLOSE...
NO...
WHY *NOW*?
IT APPEARS THAT WE'RE RUNNING OUT OF TIME.
WHAT ARE YOU TALKING ABOUT?
DON'T YOU REMEMBER? THE FIRST TIM THE SMOKE DROVE THEM AWAY...
THAT MADE THEM CAUTIOUS. BUT NOW IT'S BEGINNING TO FADE.
OH... OH NO...
THAT MEANS THEY'RE GETTING READY TO ATTACK!
MRMR MRMR
BUT...BUT WE'RE ALREADY OUT OF FIREWOOD...AND WE CAN'T GO TO THE FOREST TO GET MORE...
MRMR
THEN WHAT ARE WE SUPPOSED TO DO?! SIT HERE AND WAIT FOR THEM TO *EAT* US?!
MRMR

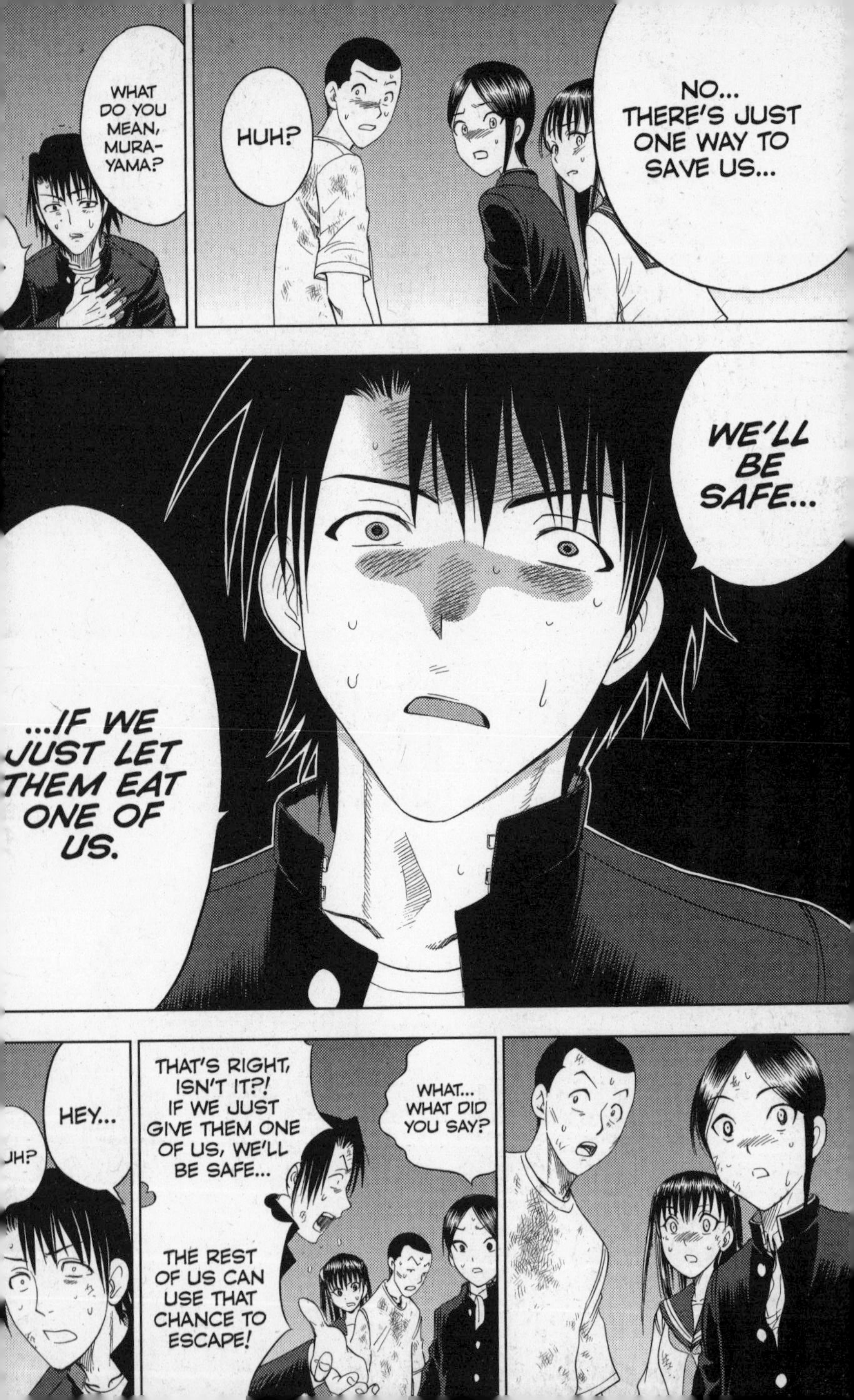
NO... THERE'S JUST ONE WAY TO SAVE US...
HUH?
WHAT DO YOU MEAN, MURA-YAMA?
WE'LL BE SAFE...
...IF WE JUST LET THEM EAT ONE OF US.
WHAT... WHAT DID YOU SAY?
THAT'S RIGHT, ISN'T IT?! IF WE JUST GIVE THEM ONE OF US, WE'LL BE SAFE...
THE REST OF US CAN USE THAT CHANCE TO ESCAPE!
HEY...

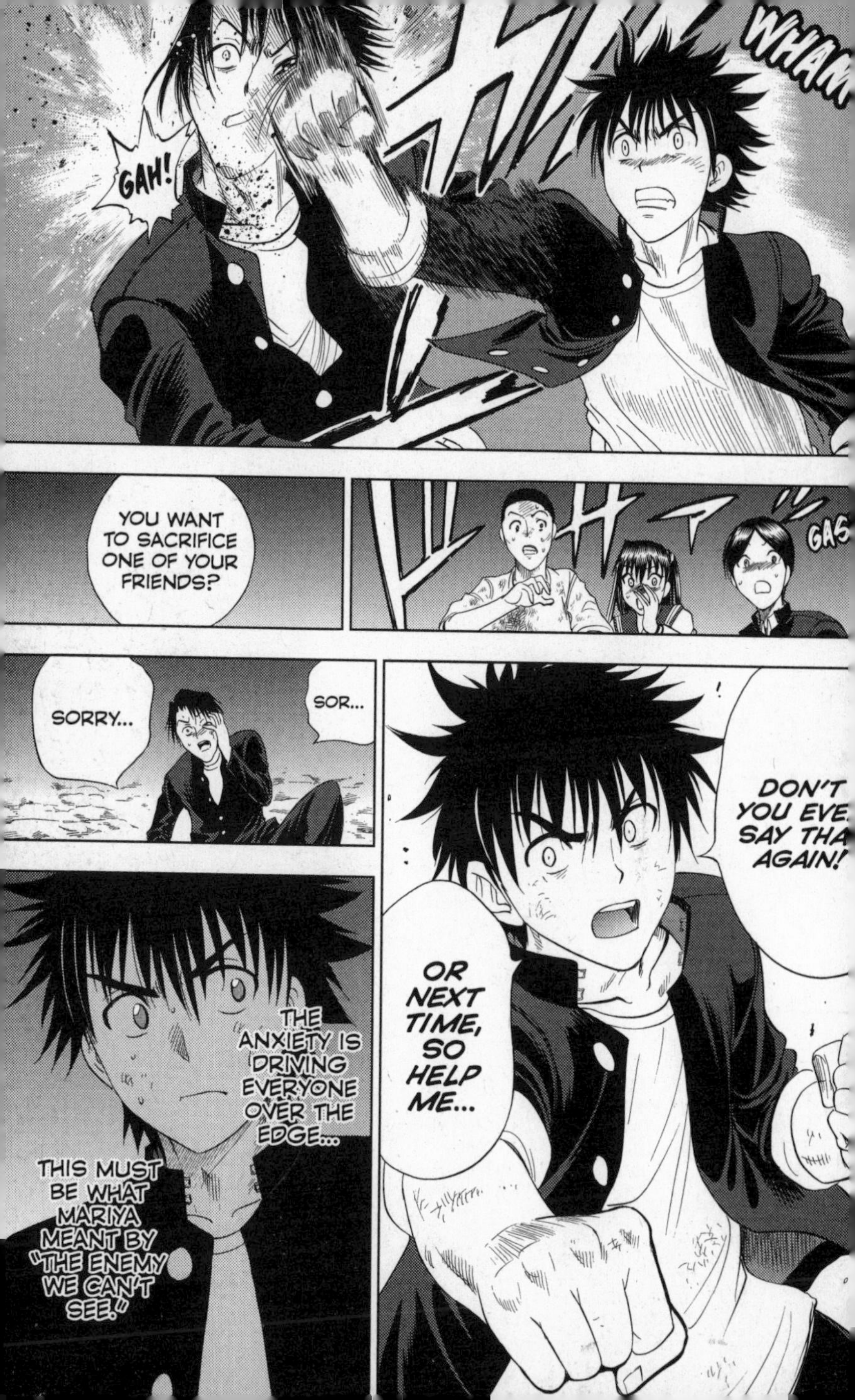
WHAM
GAH!
GAS
YOU WANT TO SACRIFICE ONE OF YOUR FRIENDS?
!
DON'T YOU EVE SAY THA AGAIN!
OR NEXT TIME, SO HELP ME...
SOR...
SORRY...
THE ANXIETY IS DRIVING EVERYONE OVER THE EDGE...
THIS MUST BE WHAT MARIYA MEANT BY "THE ENEMY WE CAN'T SEE."

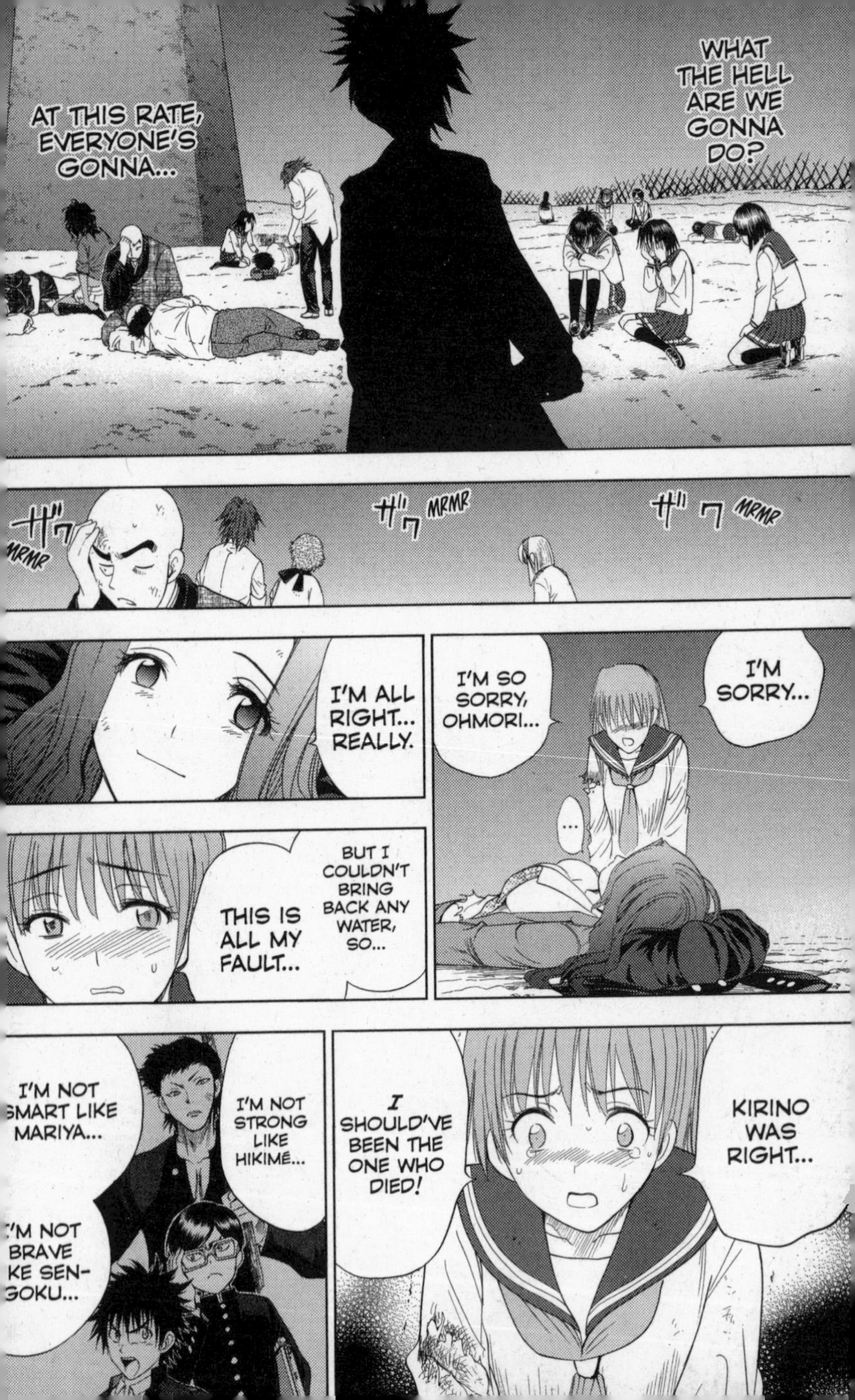

WHAT THE HELL ARE WE GONNA DO?
AT THIS RATE, EVERYONE'S GONNA...
ザワ MRMR
ザワ MRMR
ザワ MRMR
I'M SORRY...
I'M SO SORRY, OHMORI...
...
I'M ALL RIGHT... REALLY.
BUT I COULDN'T BRING BACK ANY WATER, SO...
THIS IS ALL MY FAULT...
KIRINO WAS RIGHT...
I SHOULD'VE BEEN THE ONE WHO DIED!
I'M NOT STRONG LIKE HIKIMÉ...
I'M NOT SMART LIKE MARIYA...
'M NOT BRAVE KE SEN-GOKU...

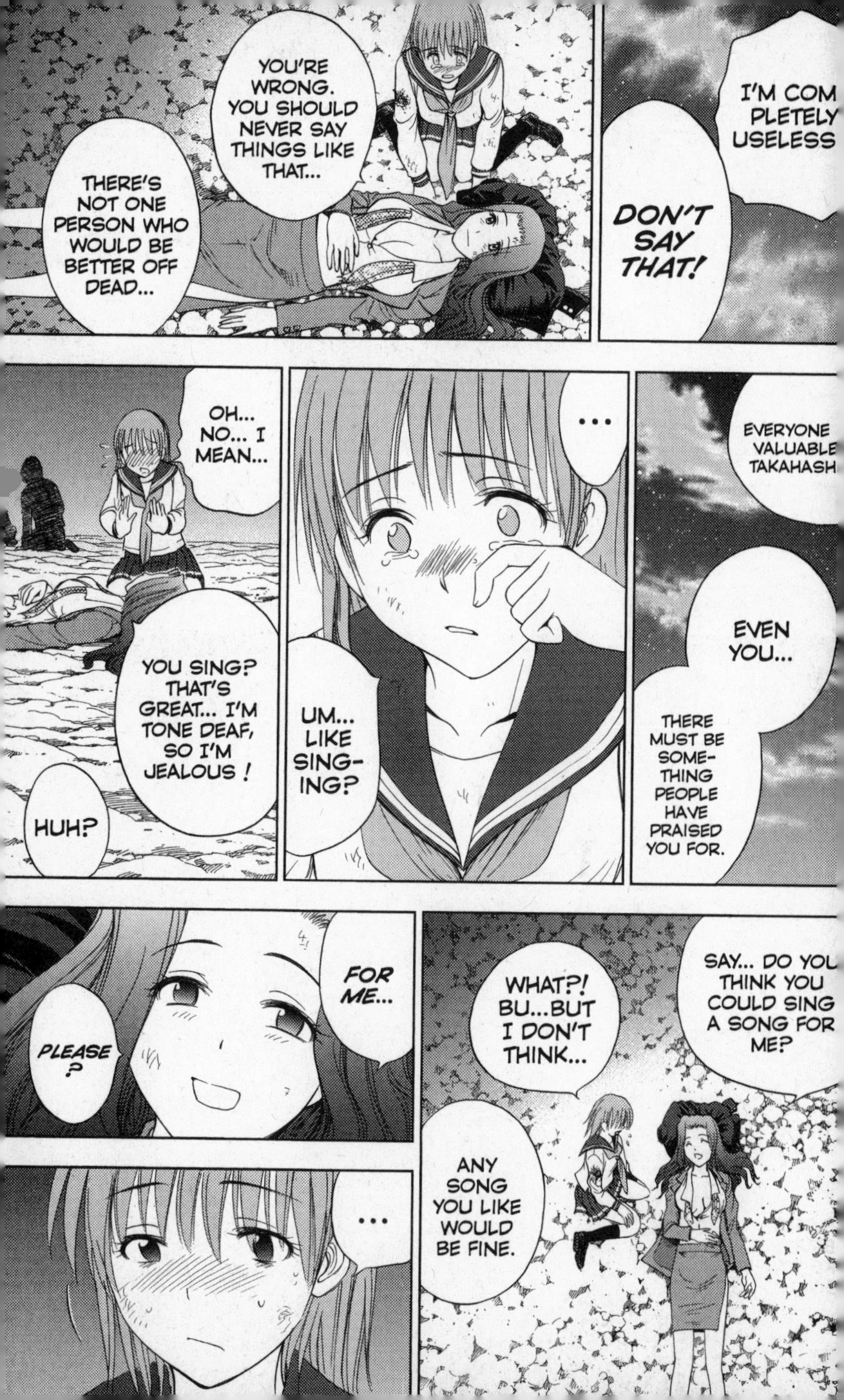

I'M COMPLETELY USELESS
DON'T SAY THAT!
YOU'RE WRONG. YOU SHOULD NEVER SAY THINGS LIKE THAT...
THERE'S NOT ONE PERSON WHO WOULD BE BETTER OFF DEAD...
EVERYONE VALUABLE TAKAHASH
EVEN YOU...
THERE MUST BE SOMETHING PEOPLE HAVE PRAISED YOU FOR.
...
UM... LIKE SINGING?
OH... NO... I MEAN...
YOU SING? THAT'S GREAT... I'M TONE DEAF, SO I'M JEALOUS !
HUH?
SAY... DO YOU THINK YOU COULD SING A SONG FOR ME?
WHAT?! BU...BUT I DON'T THINK...
ANY SONG YOU LIKE WOULD BE FINE.
FOR ME...
PLEASE ?
...

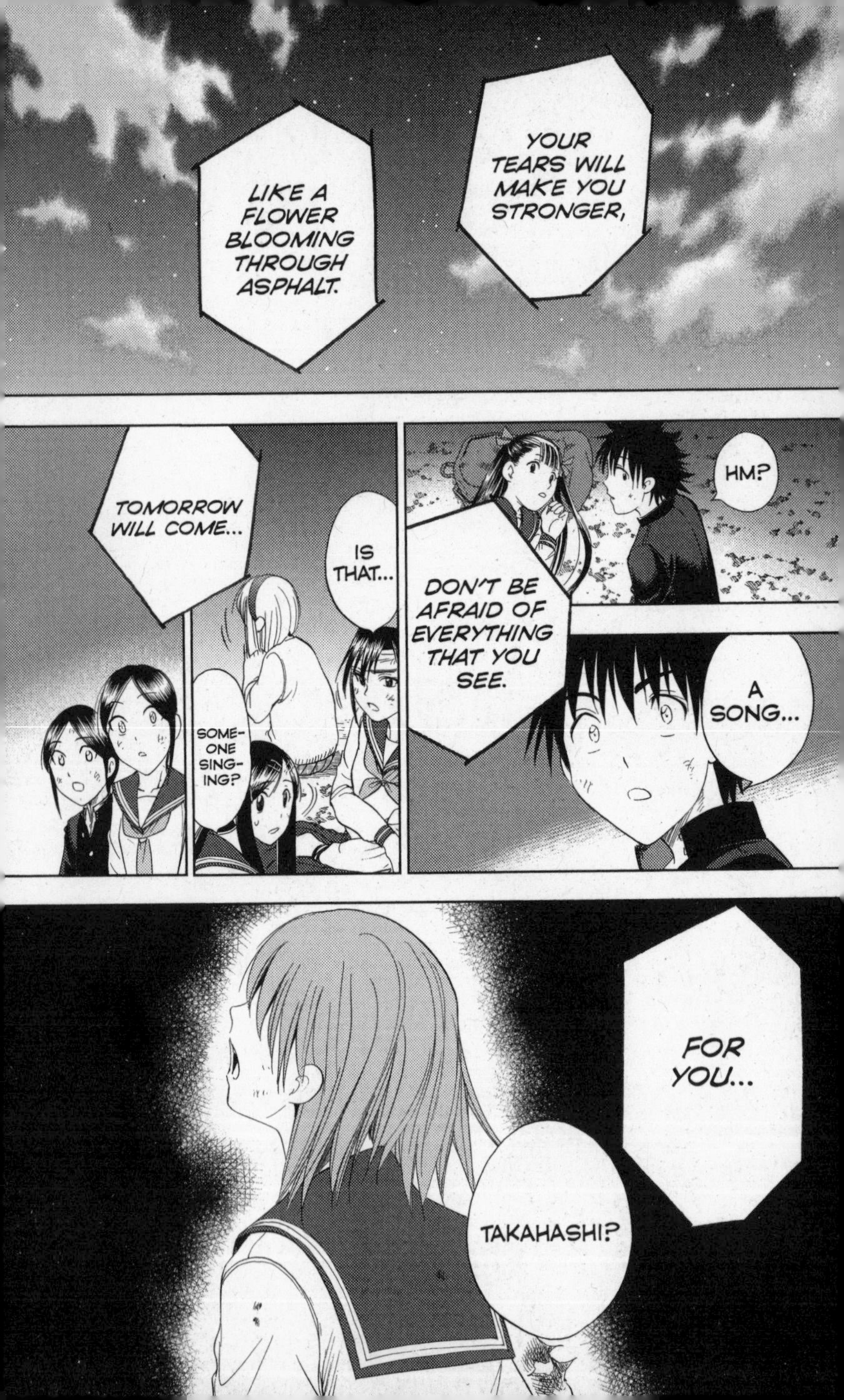
YOUR TEARS WILL MAKE YOU STRONGER,
LIKE A FLOWER BLOOMING THROUGH ASPHALT.
HM?
DON'T BE AFRAID OF EVERYTHING THAT YOU SEE.
A SONG...
IS THAT...
SOME-ONE SING-ING?
TOMORROW WILL COME...
FOR YOU...
TAKAHASHI?

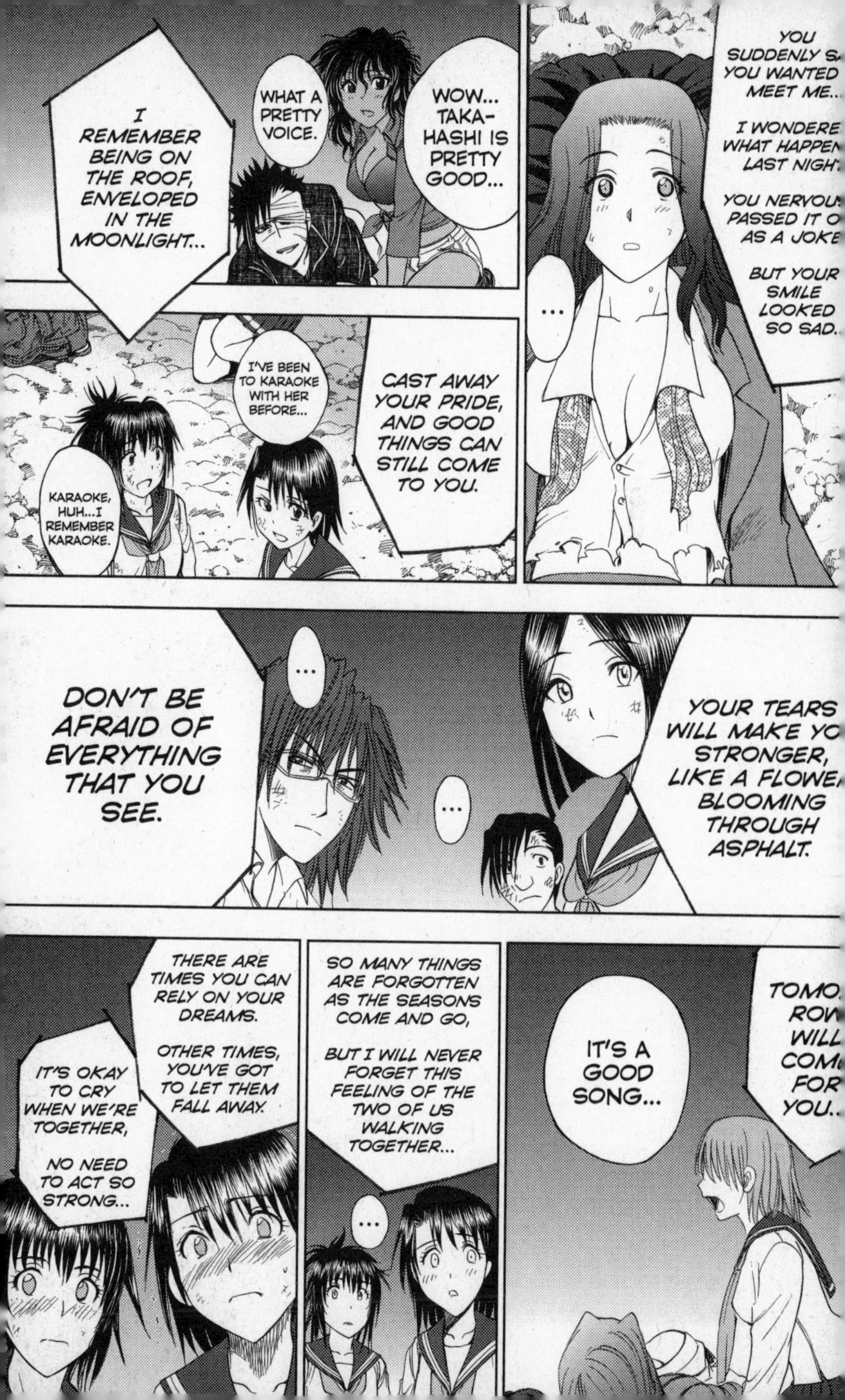
YOU SUDDENLY SA YOU WANTED MEET ME...
I WONDERE WHAT HAPPEN LAST NIGHT
YOU NERVOU PASSED IT O AS A JOKE
BUT YOUR SMILE LOOKED SO SAD..
...
WOW... TAKA-HASHI IS PRETTY GOOD...
WHAT A PRETTY VOICE.
I REMEMBER BEING ON THE ROOF, ENVELOPED IN THE MOONLIGHT...
CAST AWAY YOUR PRIDE, AND GOOD THINGS CAN STILL COME TO YOU.
I'VE BEEN TO KARAOKE WITH HER BEFORE...
KARAOKE, HUH...I REMEMBER KARAOKE.
YOUR TEARS WILL MAKE YO STRONGER, LIKE A FLOWE BLOOMING THROUGH ASPHALT.
...
...
DON'T BE AFRAID OF EVERYTHING THAT YOU SEE.
TOMO ROW WILL COM FOR YOU..
IT'S A GOOD SONG...
SO MANY THINGS ARE FORGOTTEN AS THE SEASONS COME AND GO,
BUT I WILL NEVER FORGET THIS FEELING OF THE TWO OF US WALKING TOGETHER...
...
THERE ARE TIMES YOU CAN RELY ON YOUR DREAMS.
OTHER TIMES, YOU'VE GOT TO LET THEM FALL AWAY.
IT'S OKAY TO CRY WHEN WE'RE TOGETHER,
NO NEED TO ACT SO STRONG...

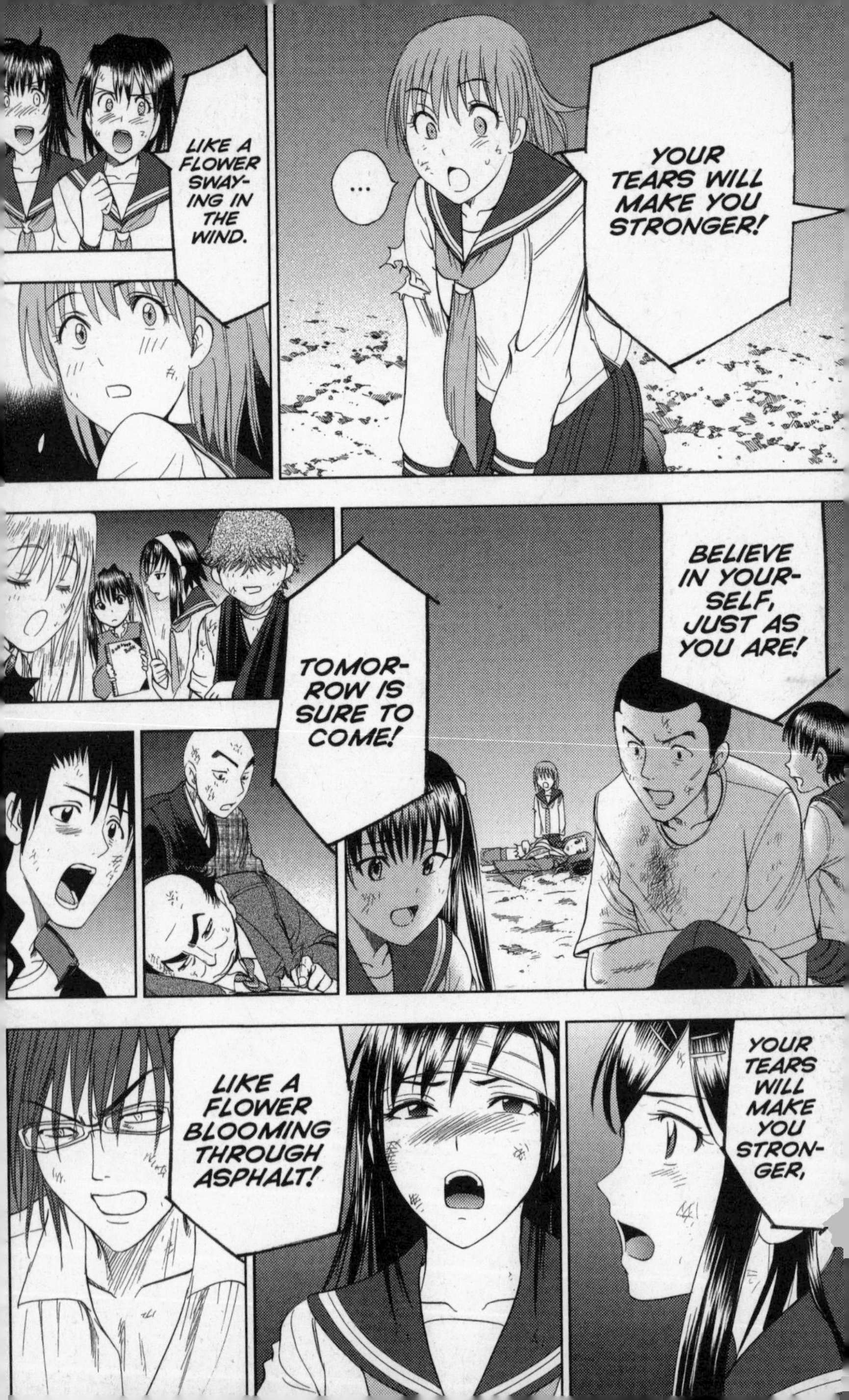
YOUR TEARS WILL MAKE YOU STRONGER!
...
LIKE A FLOWER SWAY-ING IN THE WIND.
BELIEVE IN YOUR-SELF, JUST AS YOU ARE!
TOMOR-ROW IS SURE TO COME!
YOUR TEARS WILL MAKE YOU STRON-GER,
LIKE A FLOWER BLOOMING THROUGH ASPHALT!

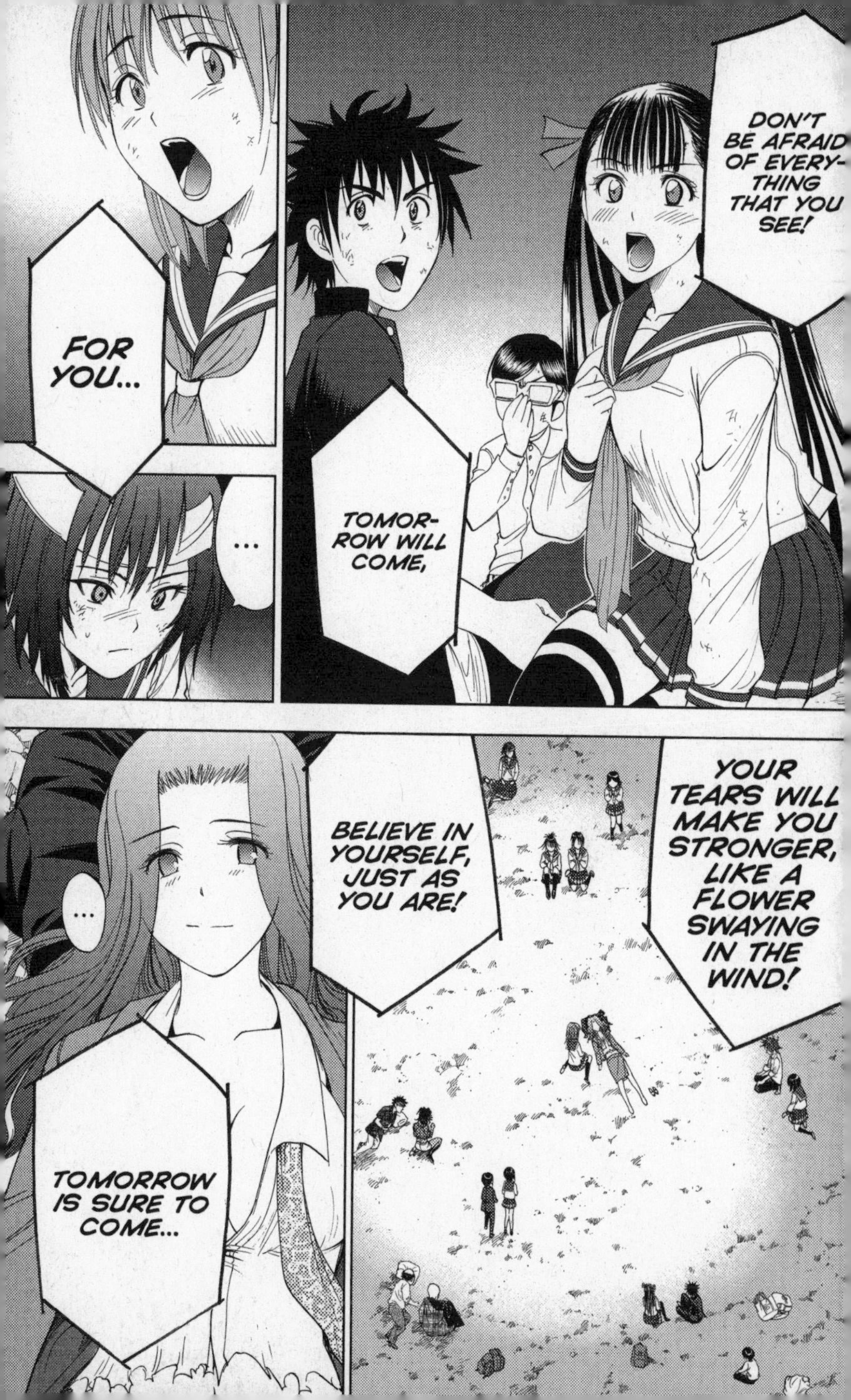
DON'T BE AFRAID OF EVERYTHING THAT YOU SEE!
TOMORROW WILL COME,
FOR YOU...
...
YOUR TEARS WILL MAKE YOU STRONGER, LIKE A FLOWER SWAYING IN THE WIND!
BELIEVE IN YOURSELF, JUST AS YOU ARE!
...
TOMORROW IS SURE TO COME...

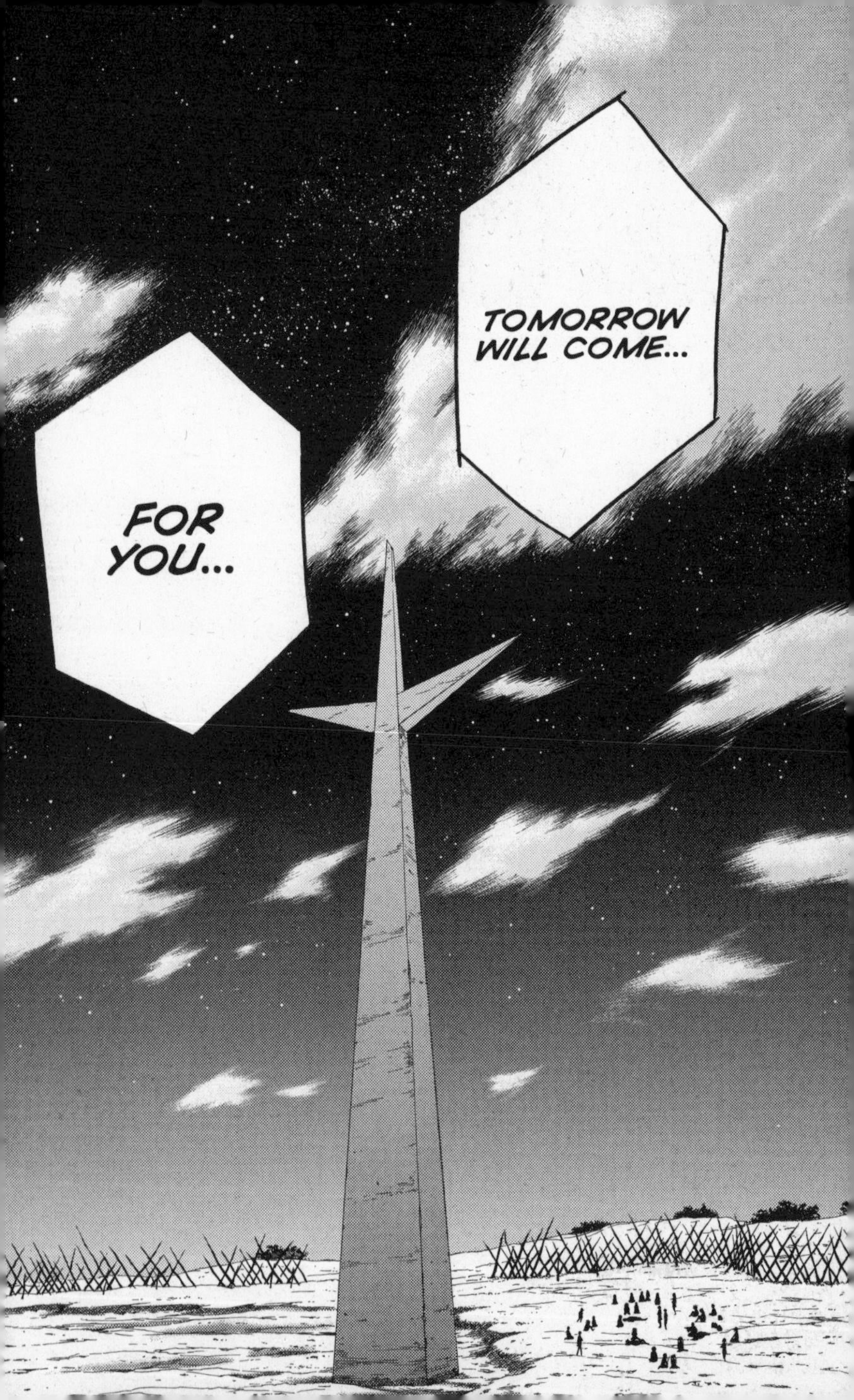
TOMORROW WILL COME...
FOR YOU...

Chapter 97: Truth or Nonsense

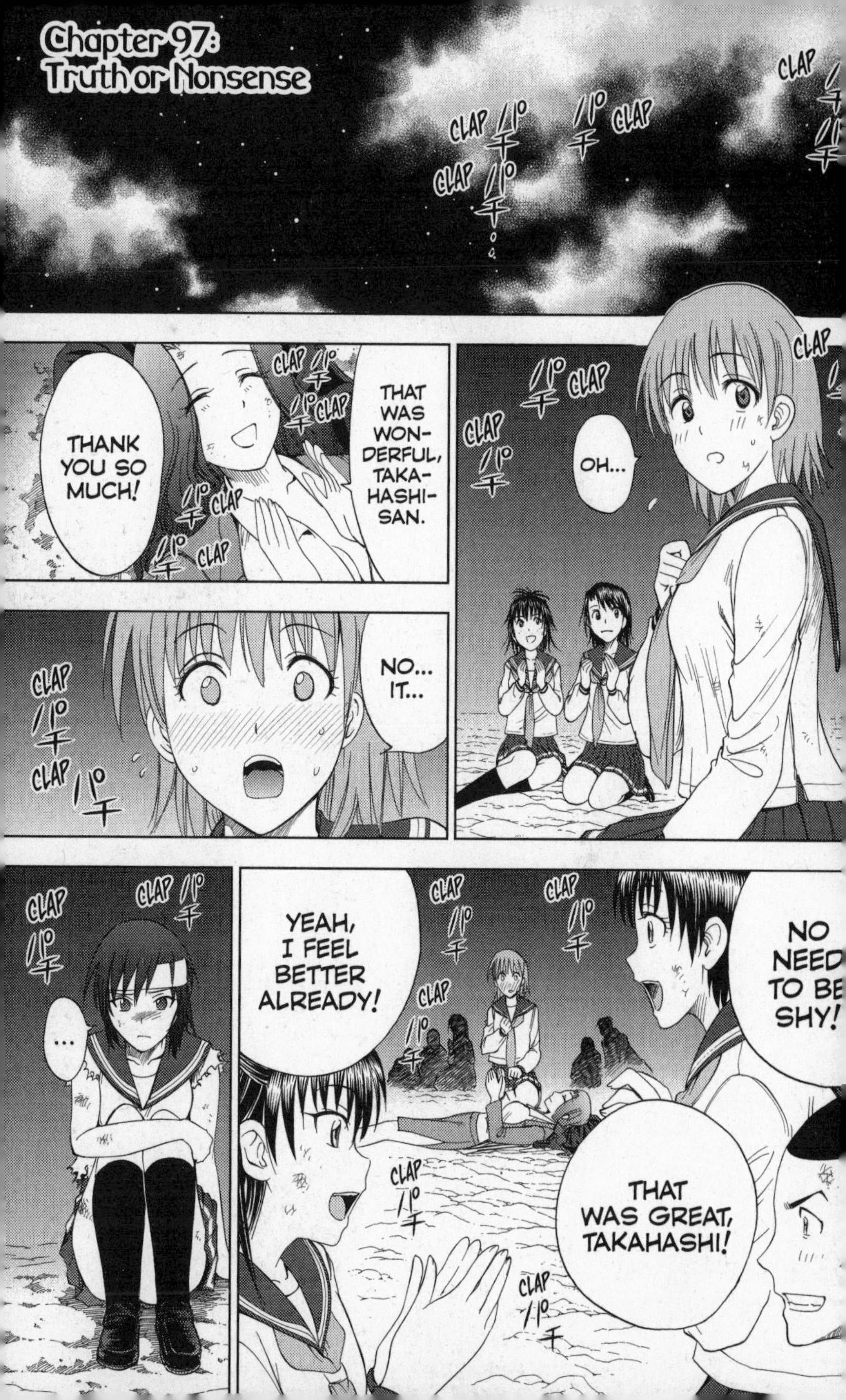
CLAP パチ
CLAP パチ
CLAP パチ
CLAP パチ
CLAP
OH...
CLAP パチ
CLAP パチ
THAT WAS WONDERFUL, TAKAHASHI-SAN.
CLAP パチ
CLAP パチ
THANK YOU SO MUCH!
CLAP パチ
CLAP パチ
NO... IT...
CLAP パチ
CLAP パチ
NO NEED TO BE SHY!
THAT WAS GREAT, TAKAHASHI!
CLAP パチ
CLAP パチ
CLAP パチ
CLAP パチ
YEAH, I FEEL BETTER ALREADY!
CLAP パチ
CLAP パチ
CLAP パチ
...

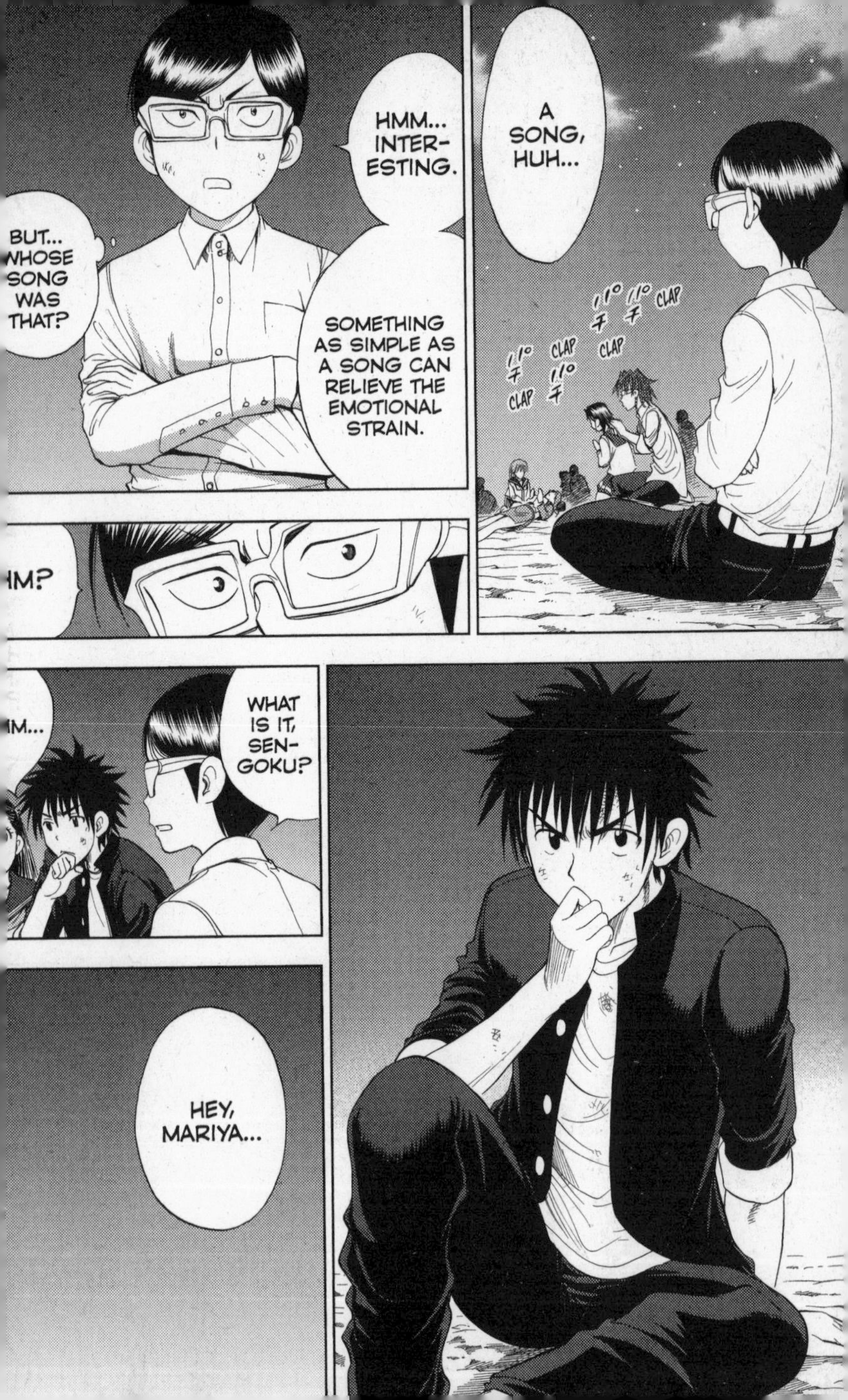
A SONG, HUH...
パチ パチ CLAP
パチ CLAP パチ CLAP
CLAP
HMM... INTERESTING.
SOMETHING AS SIMPLE AS A SONG CAN RELIEVE THE EMOTIONAL STRAIN.
BUT... WHOSE SONG WAS THAT?
HM?
WHAT IS IT, SEN-GOKU?
HEY, MARIYA...

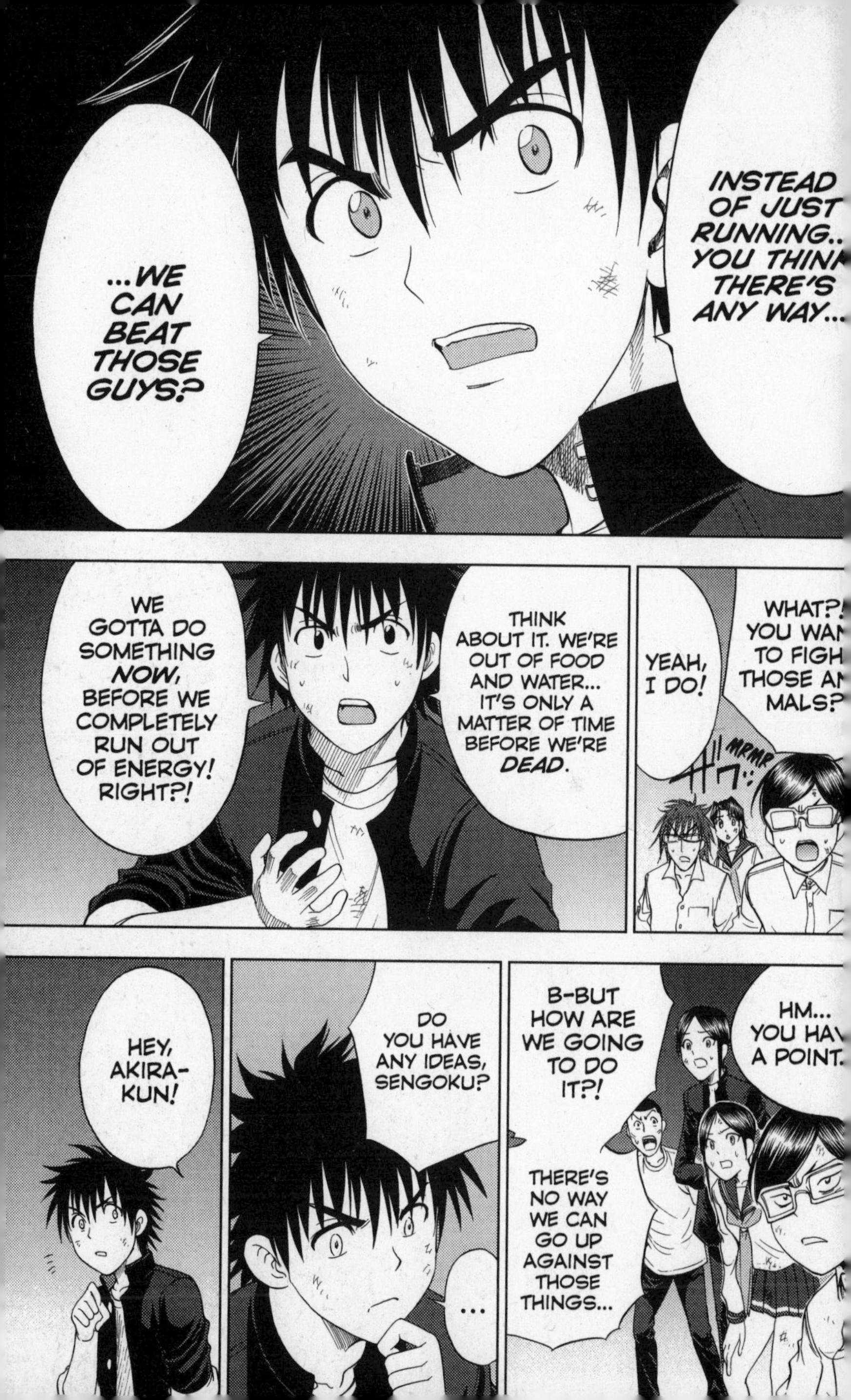
INSTEAD OF JUST RUNNING.. YOU THIN THERE'S ANY WAY...
...WE CAN BEAT THOSE GUYS?
WHAT?! YOU WAN TO FIGH THOSE AN MALS?
MRMP
YEAH, I DO!
THINK ABOUT IT. WE'RE OUT OF FOOD AND WATER... IT'S ONLY A MATTER OF TIME BEFORE WE'RE DEAD.
WE GOTTA DO SOMETHING NOW, BEFORE WE COMPLETELY RUN OUT OF ENERGY! RIGHT?!
HM... YOU HAV A POINT.
B-BUT HOW ARE WE GOING TO DO IT?!
THERE'S NO WAY WE CAN GO UP AGAINST THOSE THINGS...
DO YOU HAVE ANY IDEAS, SENGOKU?
...
HEY, AKIRA-KUN!

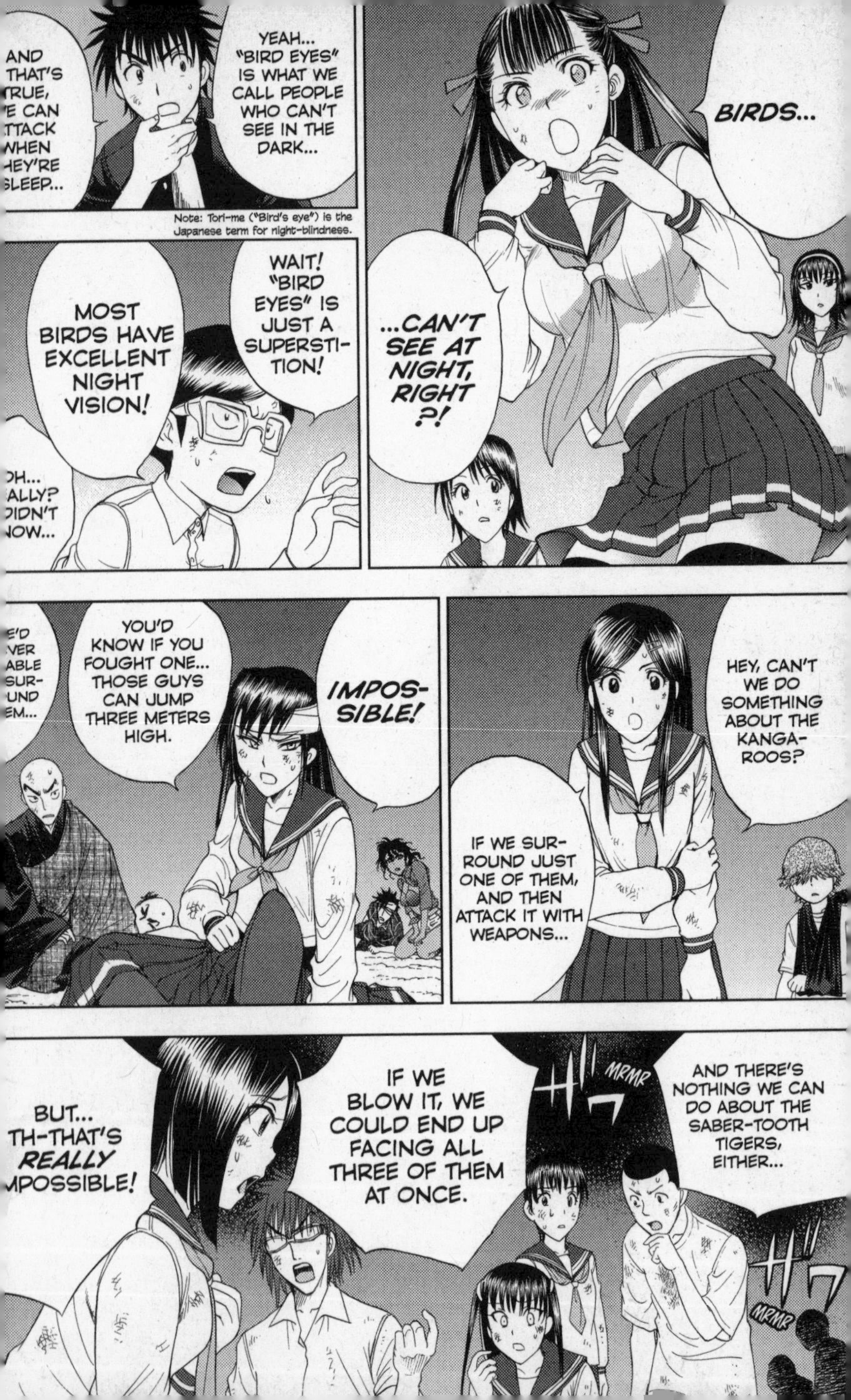
BIRDS...
...CAN'T SEE AT NIGHT, RIGHT?!
YEAH... "BIRD EYES" IS WHAT WE CALL PEOPLE WHO CAN'T SEE IN THE DARK...
AND THAT'S TRUE, E CAN TTACK WHEN HEY'RE SLEEP...
Note: Tori-me ("Bird's eye") is the Japanese term for night-blindness.
WAIT! "BIRD EYES" IS JUST A SUPERSTITION!
MOST BIRDS HAVE EXCELLENT NIGHT VISION!
OH... ALLY? DIDN'T NOW...
HEY, CAN'T WE DO SOMETHING ABOUT THE KANGAROOS?
IF WE SURROUND JUST ONE OF THEM, AND THEN ATTACK IT WITH WEAPONS...
IMPOSSIBLE!
YOU'D KNOW IF YOU FOUGHT ONE... THOSE GUYS CAN JUMP THREE METERS HIGH.
E'D VER ABLE SUR- UND EM...
AND THERE'S NOTHING WE CAN DO ABOUT THE SABER-TOOTH TIGERS, EITHER...
MRMR
IF WE BLOW IT, WE COULD END UP FACING ALL THREE OF THEM AT ONCE.
BUT... TH-THAT'S REALLY MPOSSIBLE!
MRMR

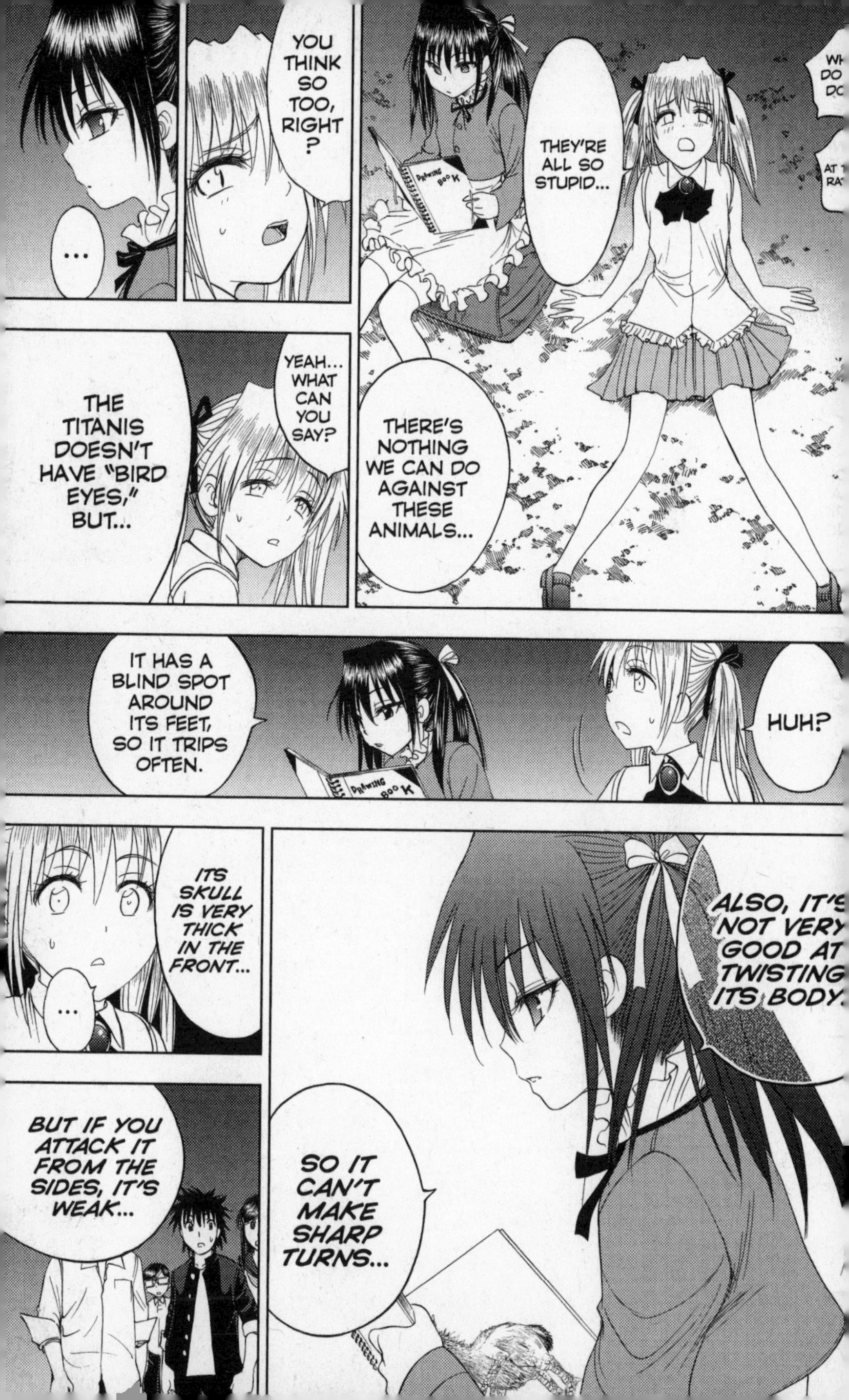
THEY'RE ALL SO STUPID...
DRAWING BOOK
THERE'S NOTHING WE CAN DO AGAINST THESE ANIMALS...
YOU THINK SO TOO, RIGHT?
...
YEAH... WHAT CAN YOU SAY?
THE TITANIS DOESN'T HAVE "BIRD EYES," BUT...
HUH?
IT HAS A BLIND SPOT AROUND ITS FEET, SO IT TRIPS OFTEN.
DRAWING BOOK
ALSO, IT'S NOT VERY GOOD AT TWISTING ITS BODY.
SO IT CAN'T MAKE SHARP TURNS...
ITS SKULL IS VERY THICK IN THE FRONT...
...
BUT IF YOU ATTACK IT FROM THE SIDES, IT'S WEAK...

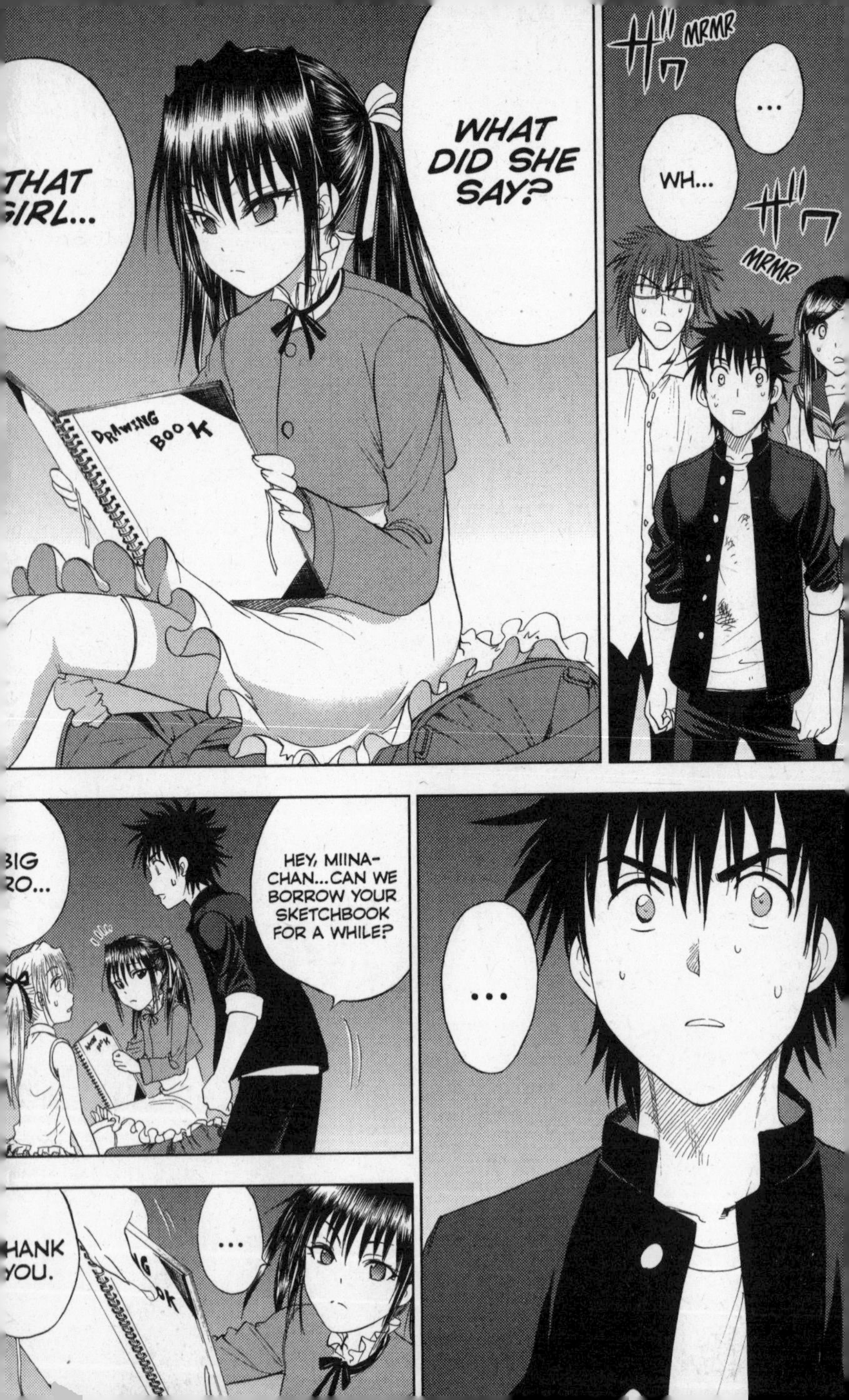
ザワ
MRMR
...
WH...
ザワ
MRMR
WHAT DID SHE SAY?
THAT GIRL...
DRAWING BOOK
...
HEY, MIINA-CHAN...CAN WE BORROW YOUR SKETCHBOOK FOR A WHILE?
BIG RO...
...
HANK YOU.

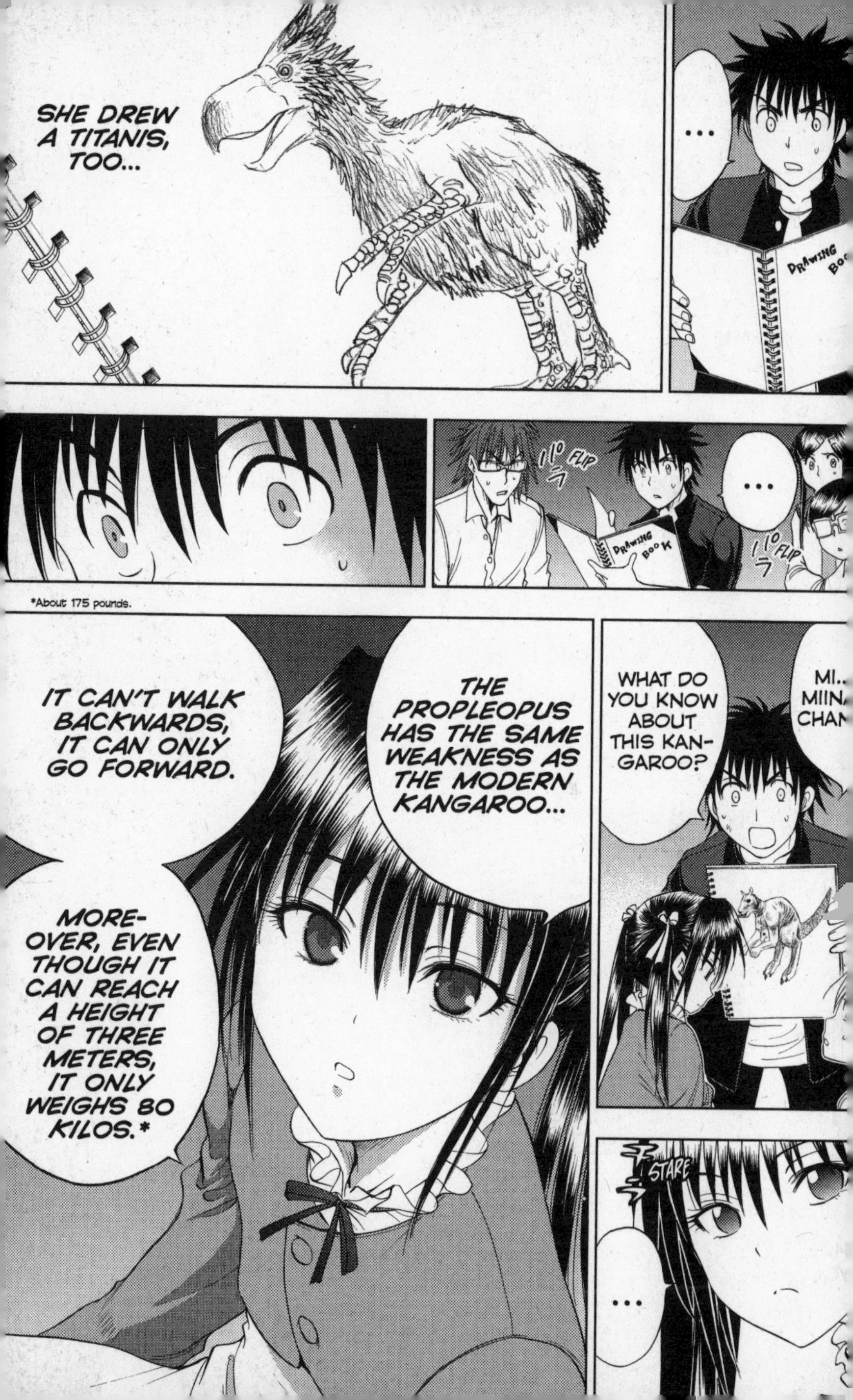
...
DRAWING BOOK
SHE DREW A TITANIS, TOO...
FLIP
...
FLIP
DRAWING BOOK
MI.. MIINA CHAN
WHAT DO YOU KNOW ABOUT THIS KAN-GAROO?
THE PROPLEOPUS HAS THE SAME WEAKNESS AS THE MODERN KANGAROO...
IT CAN'T WALK BACKWARDS, IT CAN ONLY GO FORWARD.
MORE-OVER, EVEN THOUGH IT CAN REACH A HEIGHT OF THREE METERS, IT ONLY WEIGHS 80 KILOS.*
STARE
...

*About 175 pounds.

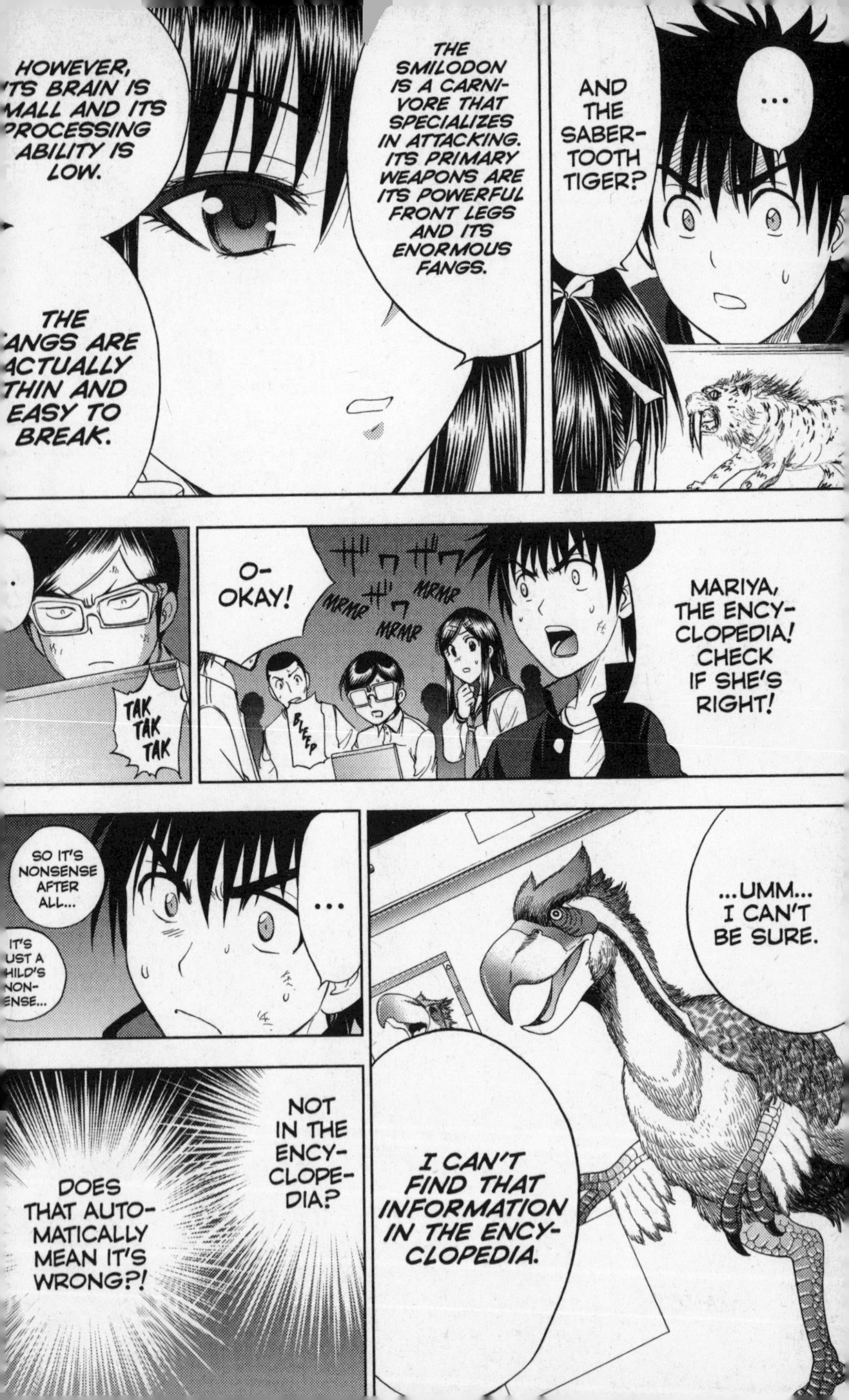
...
AND THE SABER-TOOTH TIGER?
THE SMILODON IS A CARNIVORE THAT SPECIALIZES IN ATTACKING. ITS PRIMARY WEAPONS ARE ITS POWERFUL FRONT LEGS AND ITS ENORMOUS FANGS.
HOWEVER, 'TS BRAIN IS MALL AND ITS PROCESSING ABILITY IS LOW.
THE ANGS ARE ACTUALLY THIN AND EASY TO BREAK.
MARIYA, THE ENCYCLOPEDIA! CHECK IF SHE'S RIGHT!
O-OKAY!
MRMR
MRMR
MRMR
BLEEP
TAK TAK TAK
...UMM... I CAN'T BE SURE.
I CAN'T FIND THAT INFORMATION IN THE ENCYCLOPEDIA.
...
SO IT'S NONSENSE AFTER ALL...
IT'S UST A HILD'S NON-ENSE...
NOT IN THE ENCYCLOPEDIA?
DOES THAT AUTOMATICALLY MEAN IT'S WRONG?!

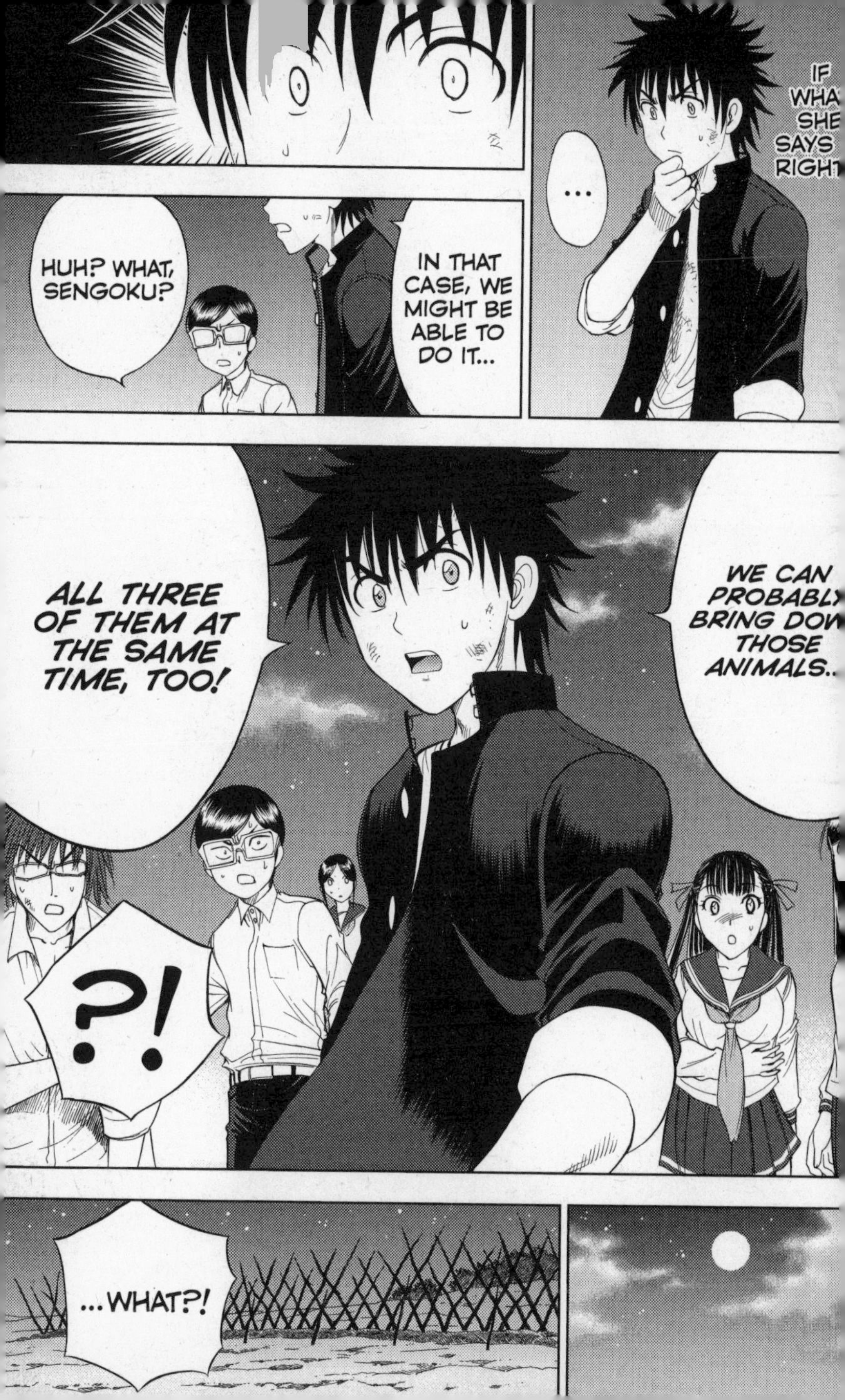
IF WHA SHE SAYS RIGHT
...
IN THAT CASE, WE MIGHT BE ABLE TO DO IT...
HUH? WHAT, SENGOKU?
WE CAN PROBABL BRING DOW THOSE ANIMALS..
ALL THREE OF THEM AT THE SAME TIME, TOO!
?!
...WHAT?!

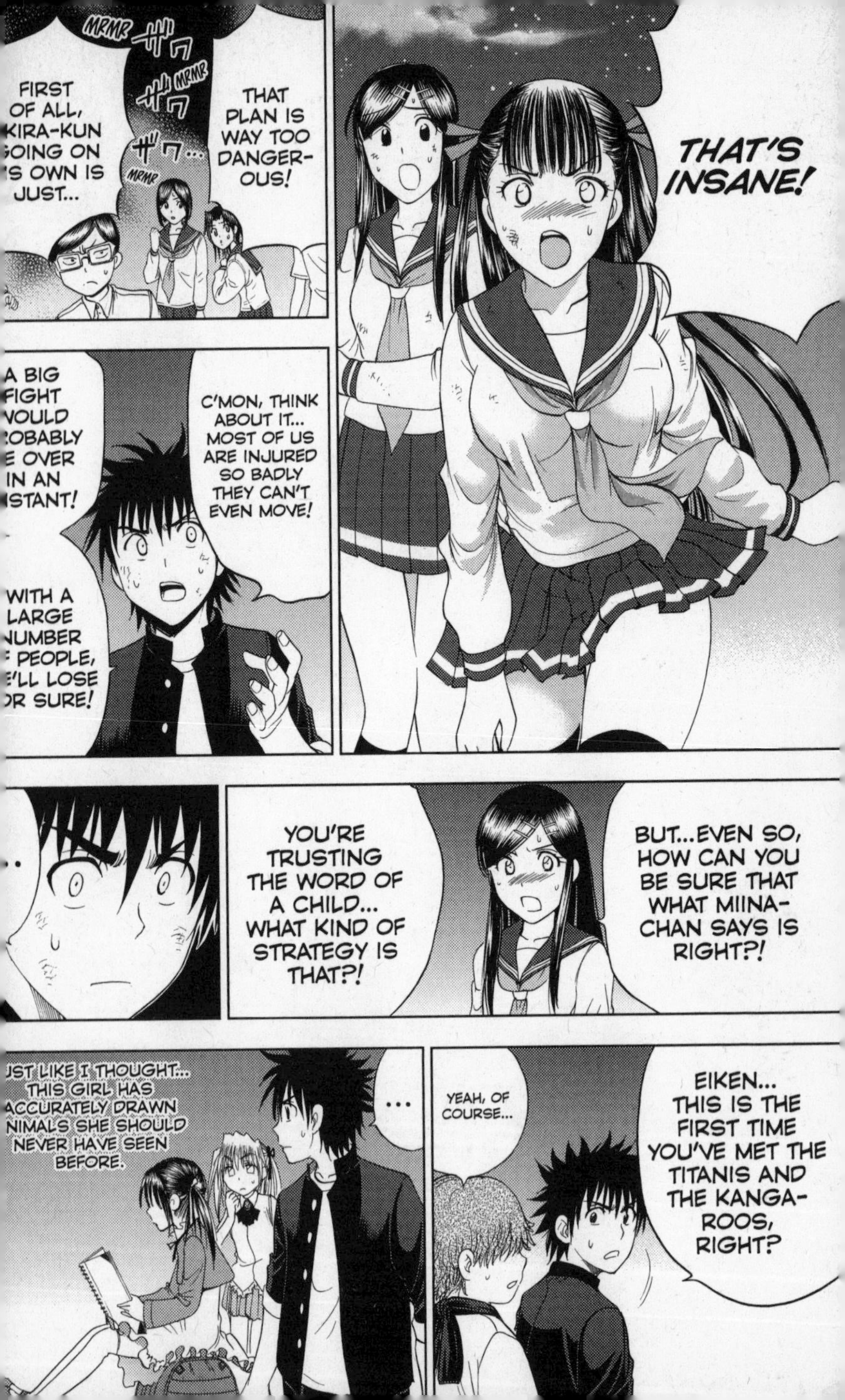
THAT'S INSANE!
THAT PLAN IS WAY TOO DANGER-OUS!
FIRST OF ALL, KIRA-KUN GOING ON 'S OWN IS JUST...
MRMR ザワ
ザワ MRMR
ザワ...
MRMR
C'MON, THINK ABOUT IT... MOST OF US ARE INJURED SO BADLY THEY CAN'T EVEN MOVE!
A BIG FIGHT WOULD OBABLY E OVER IN AN STANT!
WITH A LARGE NUMBER F PEOPLE, E'LL LOSE OR SURE!
BUT...EVEN SO, HOW CAN YOU BE SURE THAT WHAT MIINA-CHAN SAYS IS RIGHT?!
YOU'RE TRUSTING THE WORD OF A CHILD... WHAT KIND OF STRATEGY IS THAT?!
EIKEN... THIS IS THE FIRST TIME YOU'VE MET THE TITANIS AND THE KANGA-ROOS, RIGHT?
YEAH, OF COURSE...
...
UST LIKE I THOUGHT... THIS GIRL HAS ACCURATELY DRAWN NIMALS SHE SHOULD NEVER HAVE SEEN BEFORE.

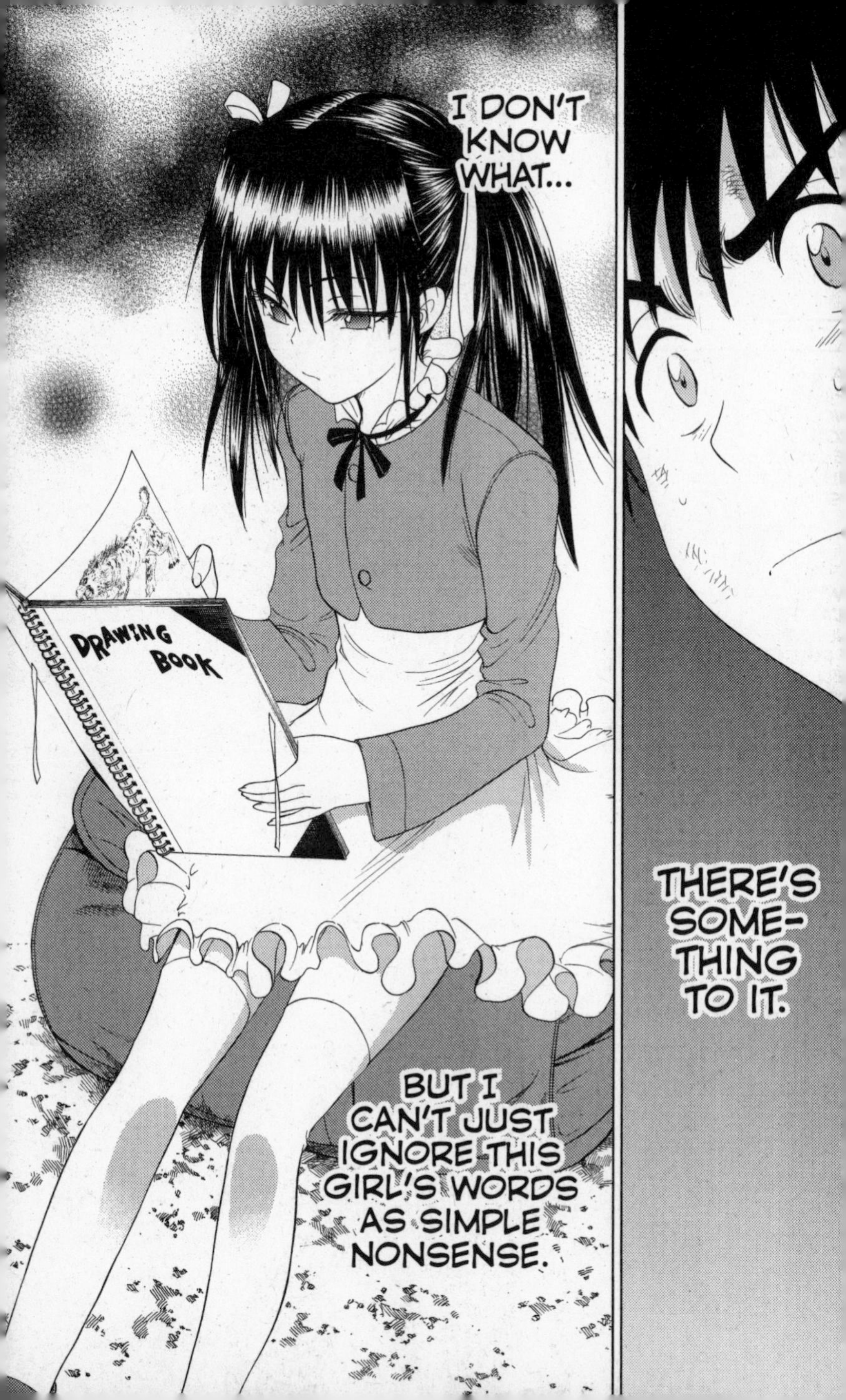
THERE'S SOME-THING TO IT.
I DON'T KNOW WHAT...
BUT I CAN'T JUST IGNORE THIS GIRL'S WORDS AS SIMPLE NONSENSE.
DRAWING BOOK

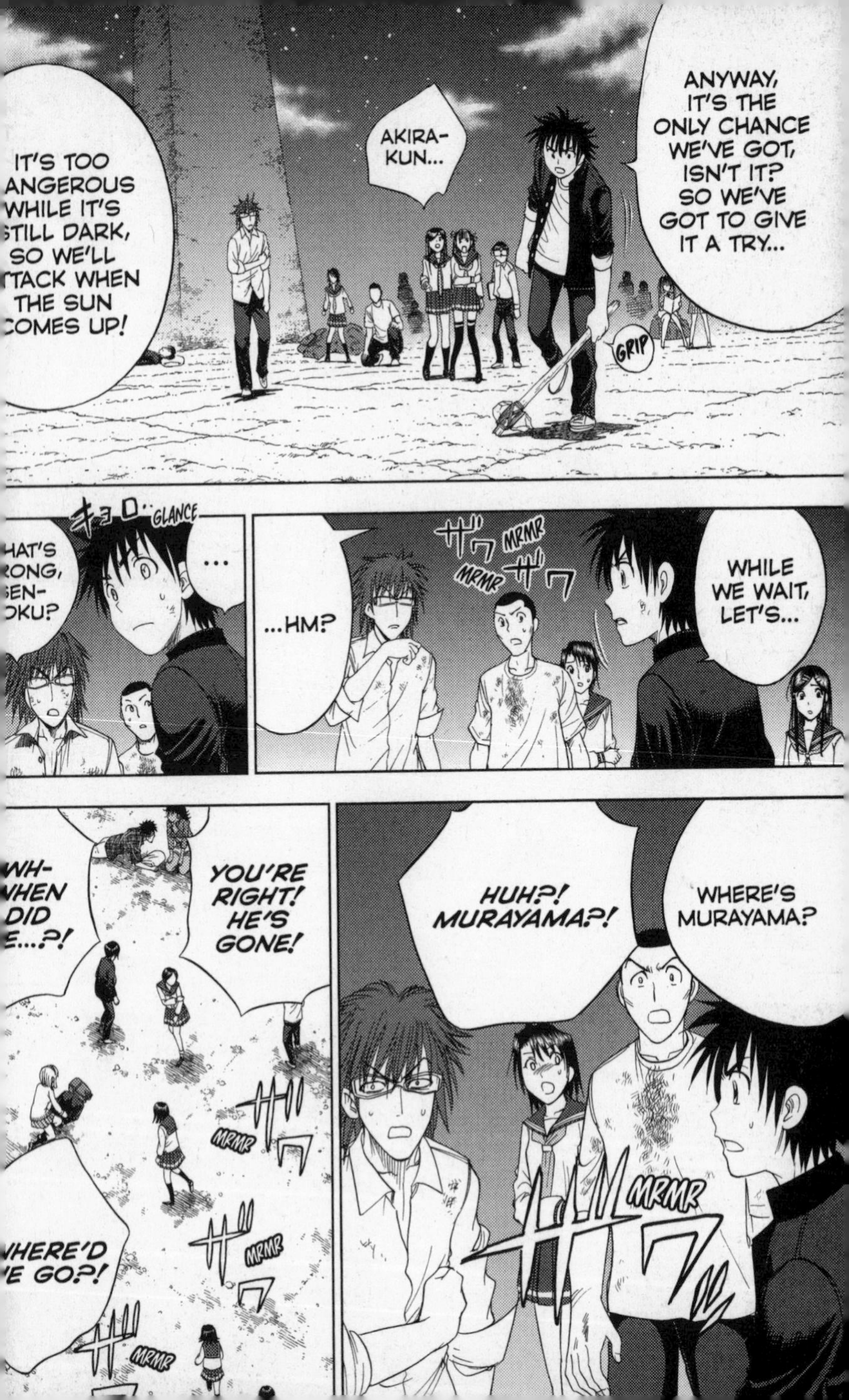
ANYWAY, IT'S THE ONLY CHANCE WE'VE GOT, ISN'T IT? SO WE'VE GOT TO GIVE IT A TRY...
GRIP
AKIRA-KUN...
IT'S TOO ANGEROUS WHILE IT'S STILL DARK, SO WE'LL TTACK WHEN THE SUN COMES UP!
WHILE WE WAIT, LET'S...
ザワ MRMR
MRMR ザワ
...HM?
...
キョロ.. GLANCE
HAT'S RONG, SEN- OKU?
WHERE'S MURAYAMA?
HUH?! MURAYAMA?!
ザワ MRMR
YOU'RE RIGHT! HE'S GONE!
WH- WHEN DID E...?!
ザワ MRMR
ザワ MRMR
WHERE'D E GO?!
ザ MRMR

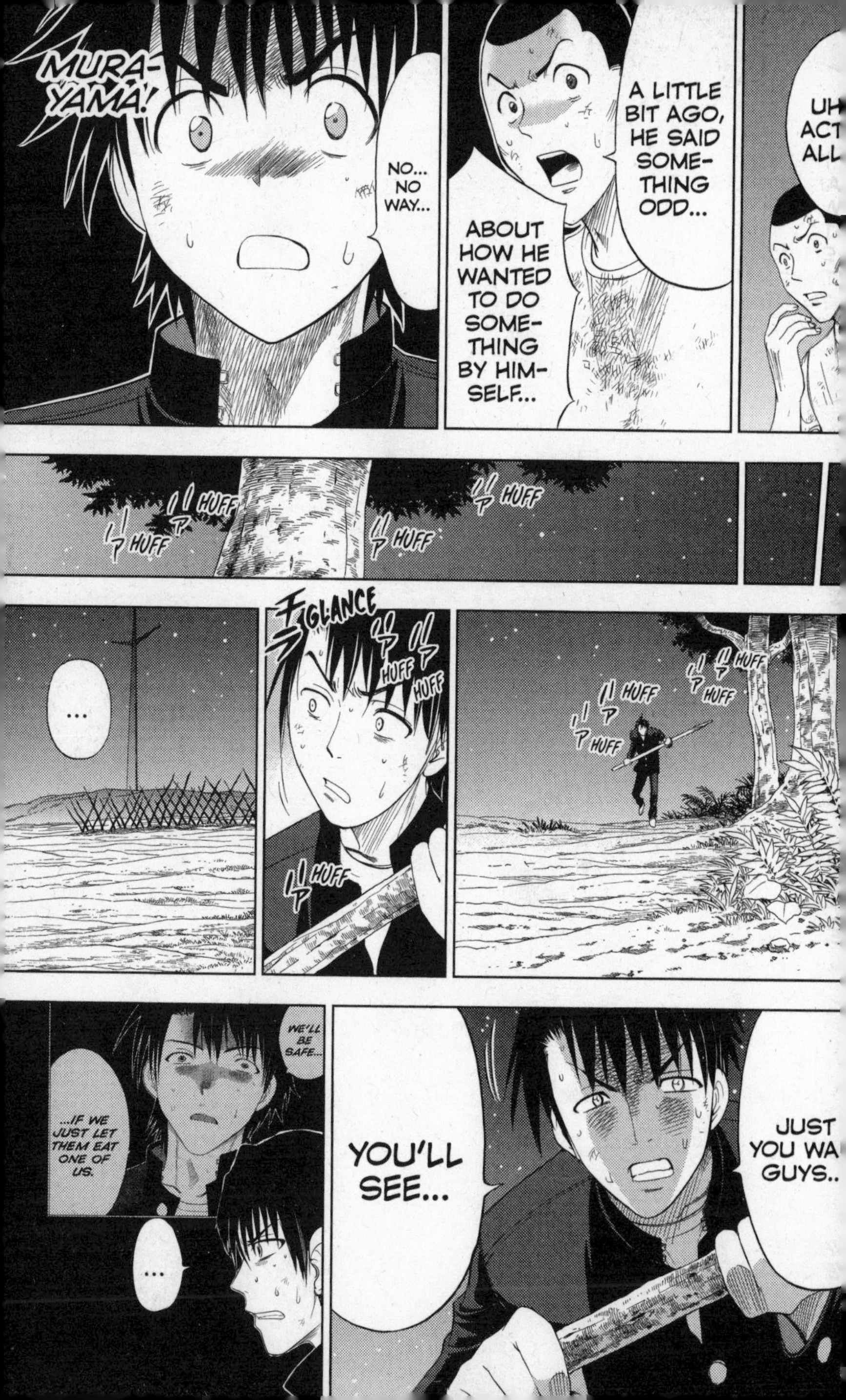
UH
ACT
ALL
A LITTLE BIT AGO, HE SAID SOME-THING ODD...
ABOUT HOW HE WANTED TO DO SOME-THING BY HIM-SELF...
NO... NO WAY...
MURA-YAMA!
HUFF
HUFF
HUFF
HUFF
HUFF
HUFF
HUFF
HUFF
GLANCE
HUFF
HUFF
HUFF
...
JUST YOU WA
GUYS..
YOU'LL SEE...
WE'LL BE SAFE...
...IF WE JUST LET THEM EAT ONE OF US.
...

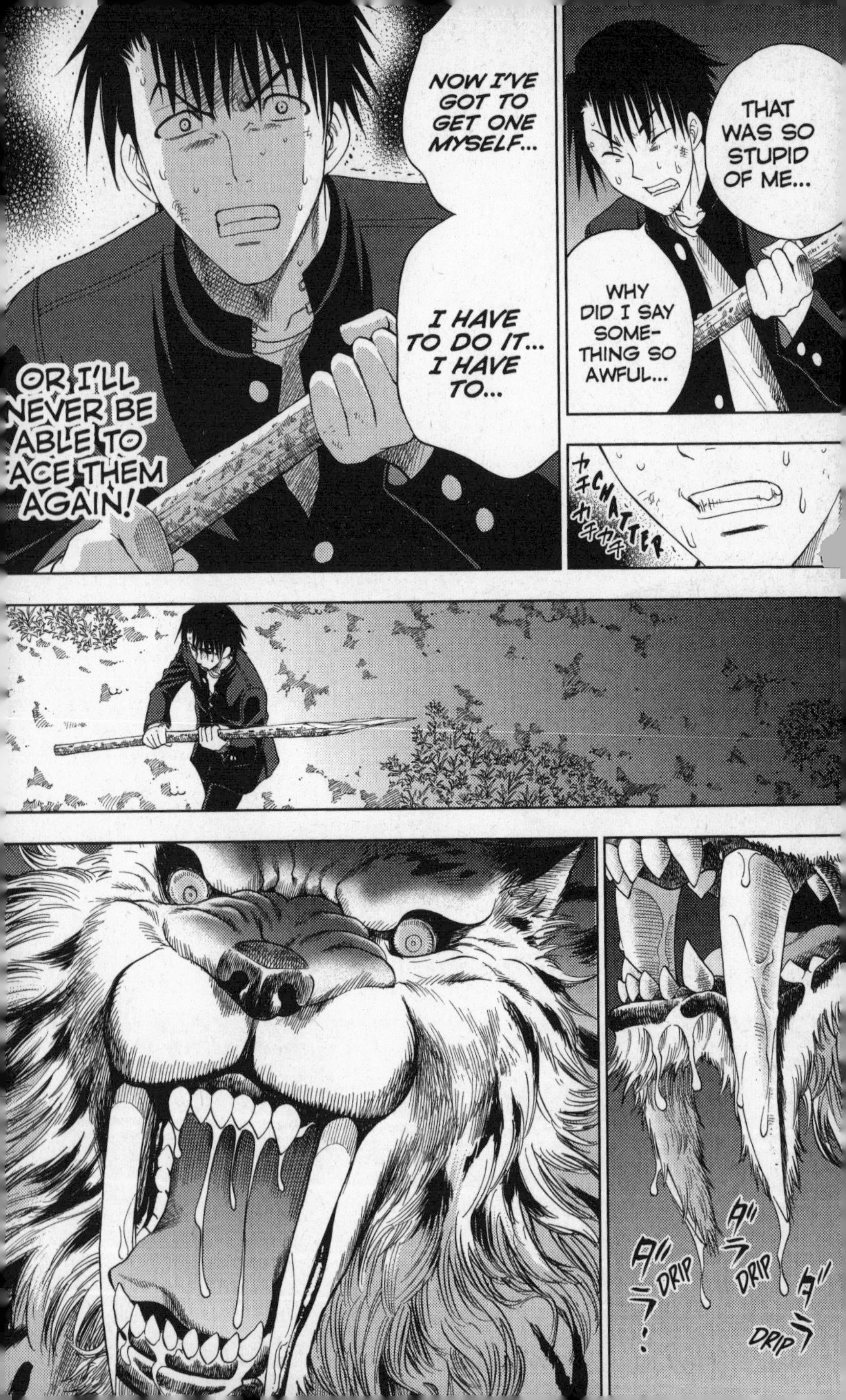
THAT WAS SO STUPID OF ME...
WHY DID I SAY SOME-THING SO AWFUL...
CHATTER
NOW I'VE GOT TO GET ONE MYSELF...
I HAVE TO DO IT... I HAVE TO...
OR I'LL NEVER BE ABLE TO ACE THEM AGAIN!
DRIP
DRIP
DRIP

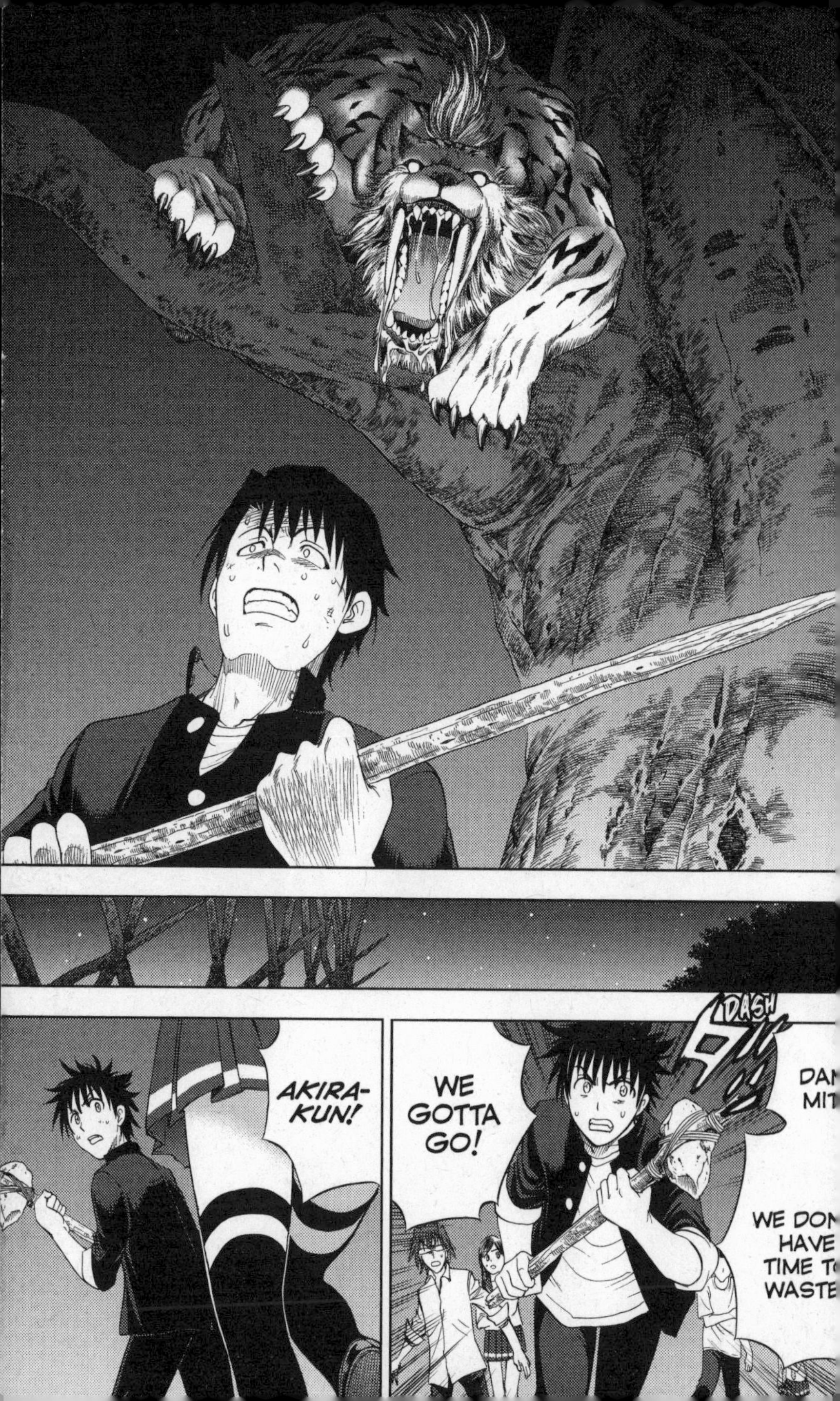
DASH
DAN
MIT
WE DON
HAVE
TIME T
WASTE
WE GOTTA GO!
AKIRA-KUN!

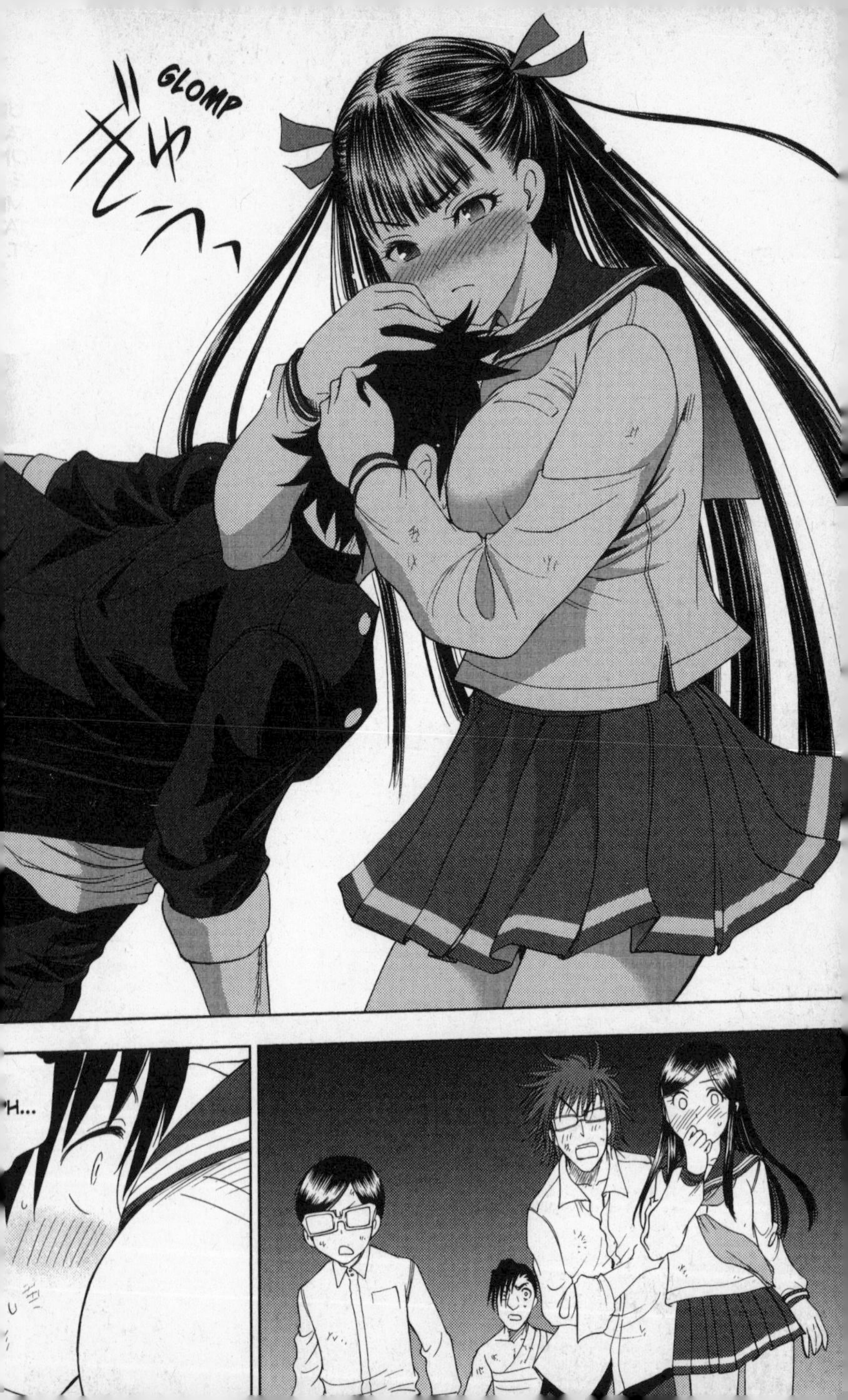

ぎゅ〜
GLOMP
H...

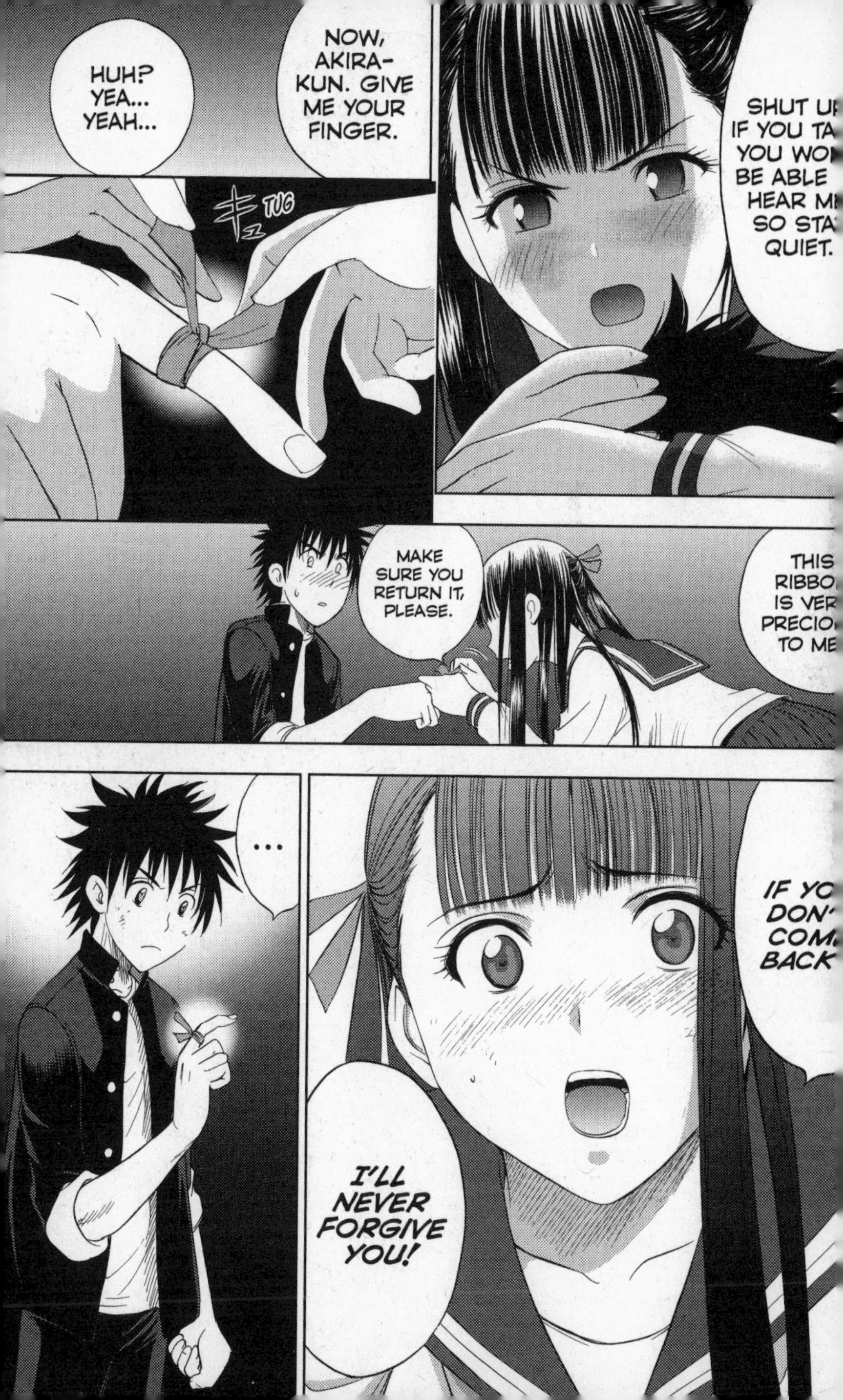
SHUT U IF YOU TA YOU WO BE ABLE HEAR M SO STA QUIET.
NOW, AKIRA-KUN. GIVE ME YOUR FINGER.
HUH? YEA... YEAH...
キュ TUG
THIS RIBBO IS VER PRECIO TO ME
MAKE SURE YOU RETURN IT, PLEASE.
IF YO DON' COM BACK
I'LL NEVER FORGIVE YOU!
...

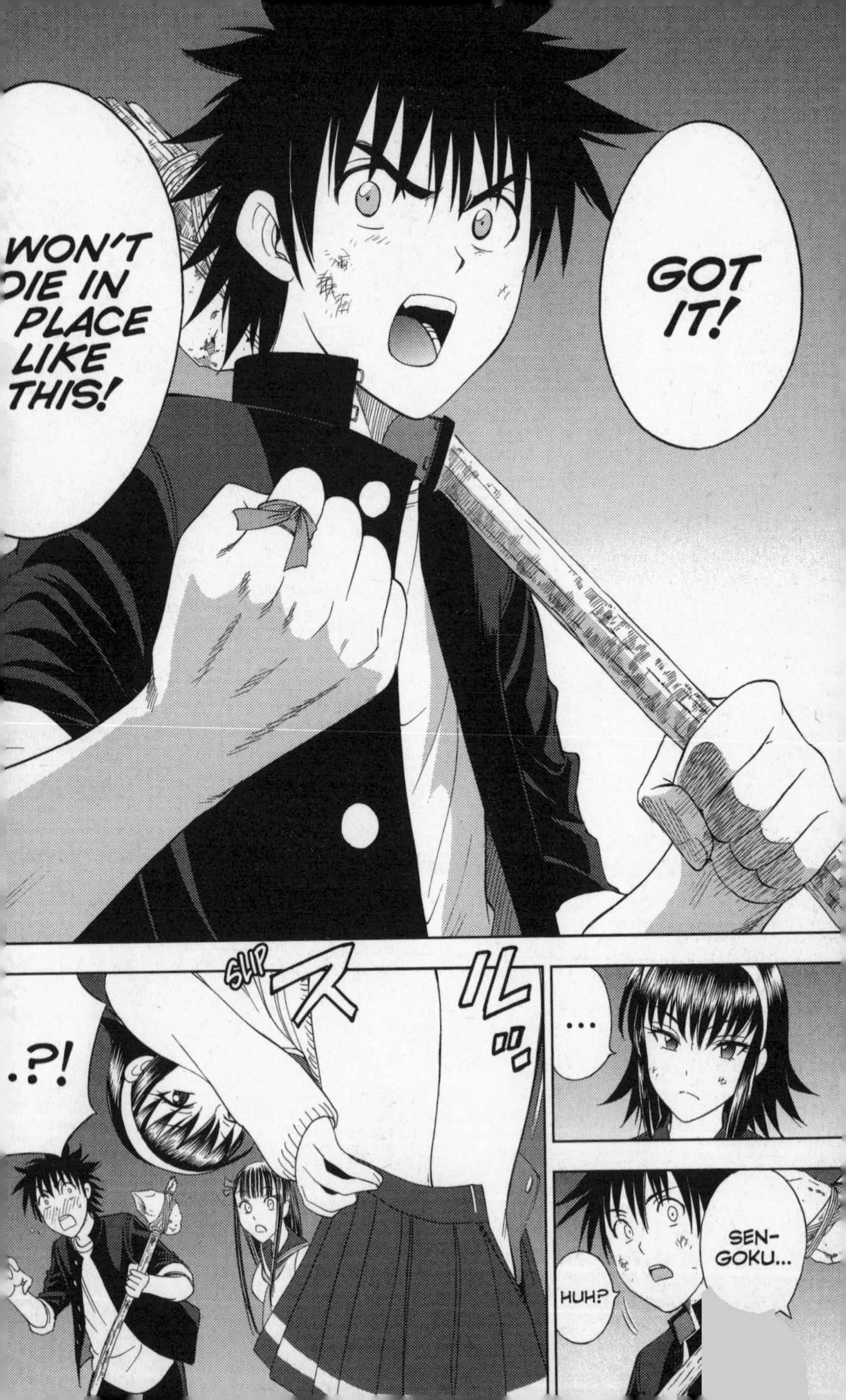

GOT IT!
WON'T DIE IN PLACE LIKE THIS!
...
SEN-GOKU...
HUH?
SLIP
スル
.?!

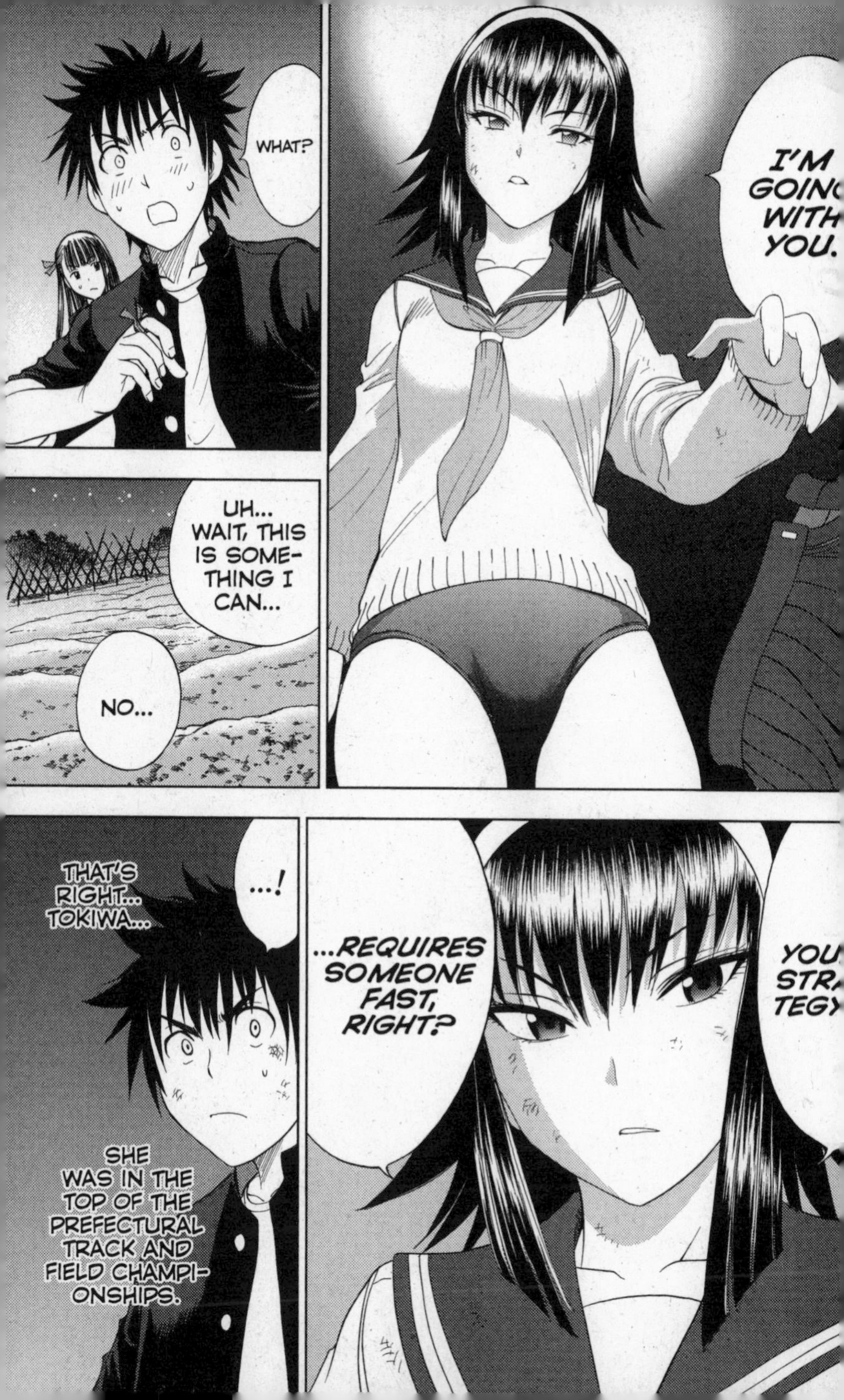
I'M GOIN WITH YOU.
WHAT?
UH... WAIT, THIS IS SOME-THING I CAN...
NO...
YOU STRA TEGY
...REQUIRES SOMEONE FAST, RIGHT?
...!
THAT'S RIGHT... TOKIWA...
SHE WAS IN THE TOP OF THE PREFECTURAL TRACK AND FIELD CHAMPI-ONSHIPS.

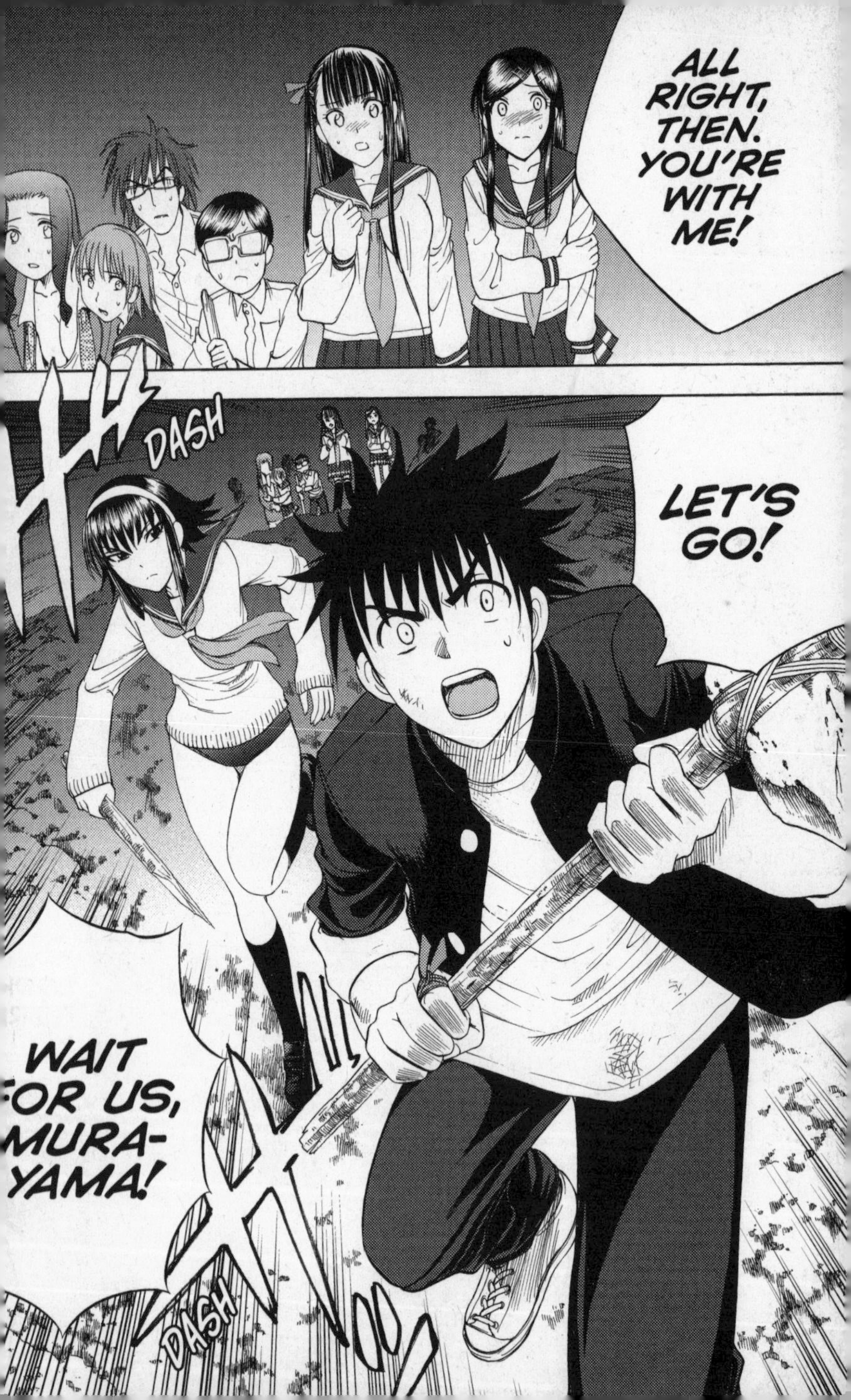

ALL RIGHT, THEN. YOU'RE WITH ME!
LET'S GO!
DASH
WAIT FOR US, MURA-YAMA!
DASH

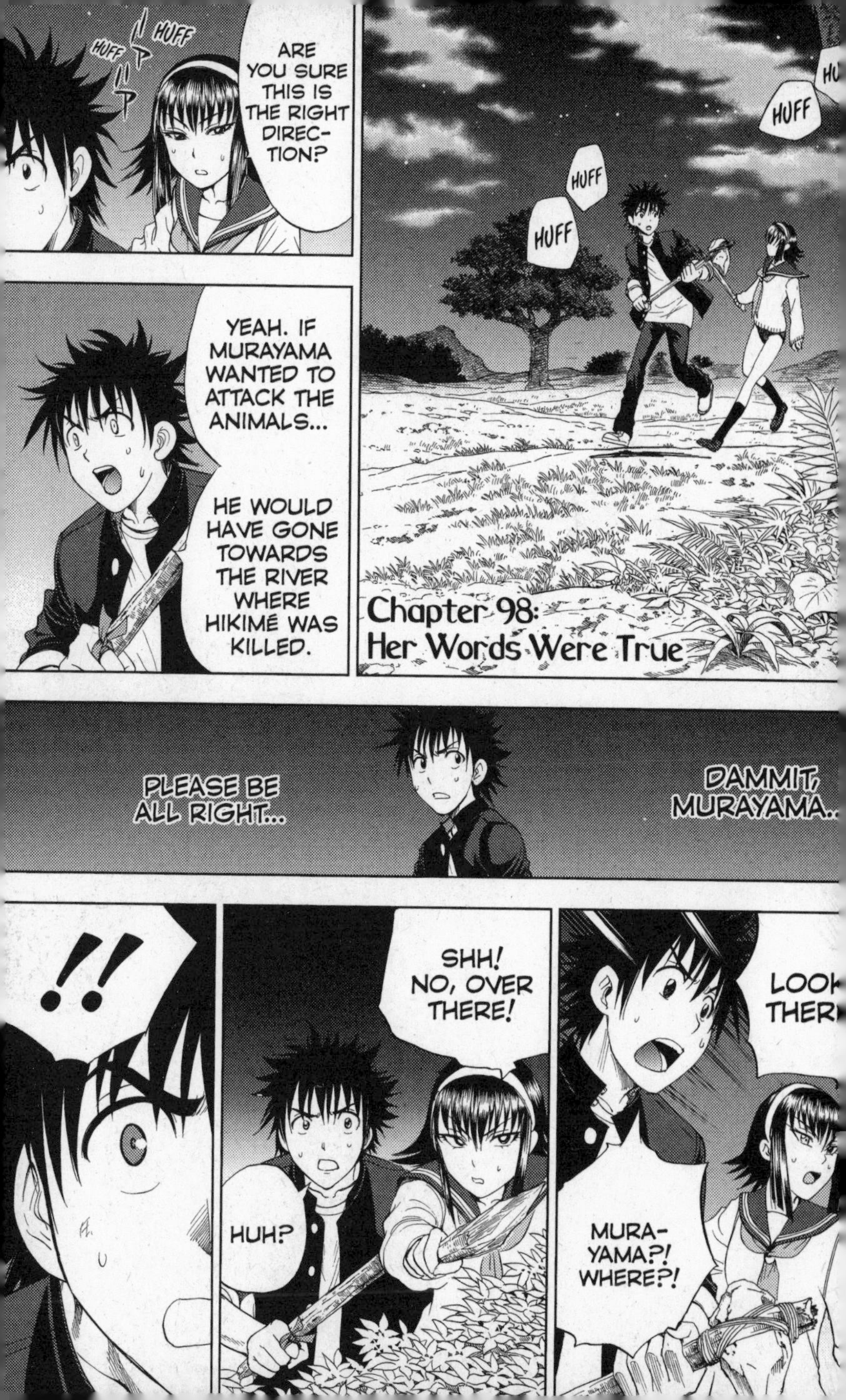
HU
HUFF
HUFF
HUFF
Chapter 98:
Her Words Were True
HUFF
HUFF
ARE YOU SURE THIS IS THE RIGHT DIREC-TION?
YEAH. IF MURAYAMA WANTED TO ATTACK THE ANIMALS...
HE WOULD HAVE GONE TOWARDS THE RIVER WHERE HIKIMÉ WAS KILLED.
DAMMIT, MURAYAMA...
PLEASE BE ALL RIGHT...
LOOK THER
MURA-YAMA?! WHERE?!
SHH! NO, OVER THERE!
HUH?
!!

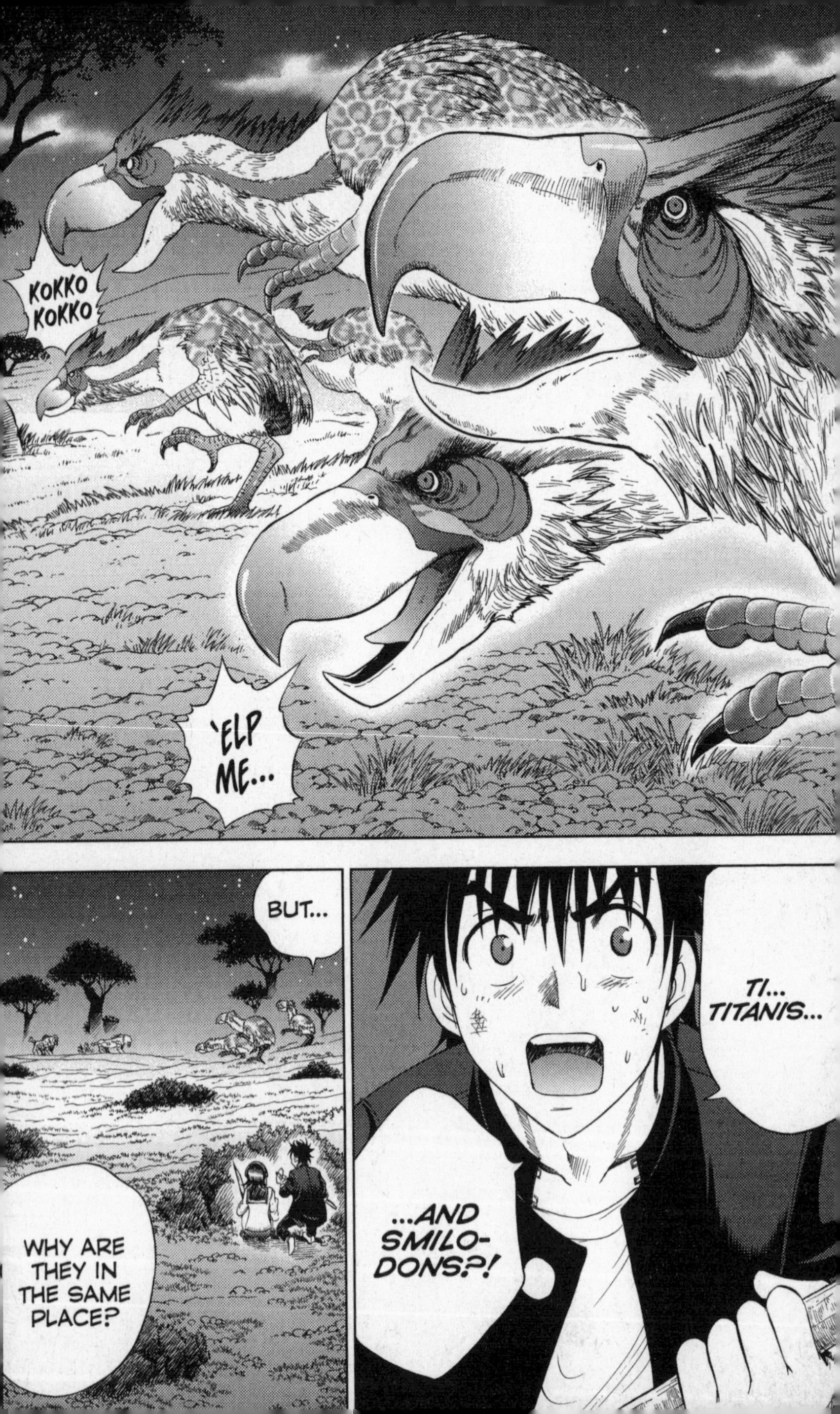
KOKKO KOKKO
'ELP ME...
TI... TITANIS...
...AND SMILO-DONS?!
BUT...
WHY ARE THEY IN THE SAME PLACE?

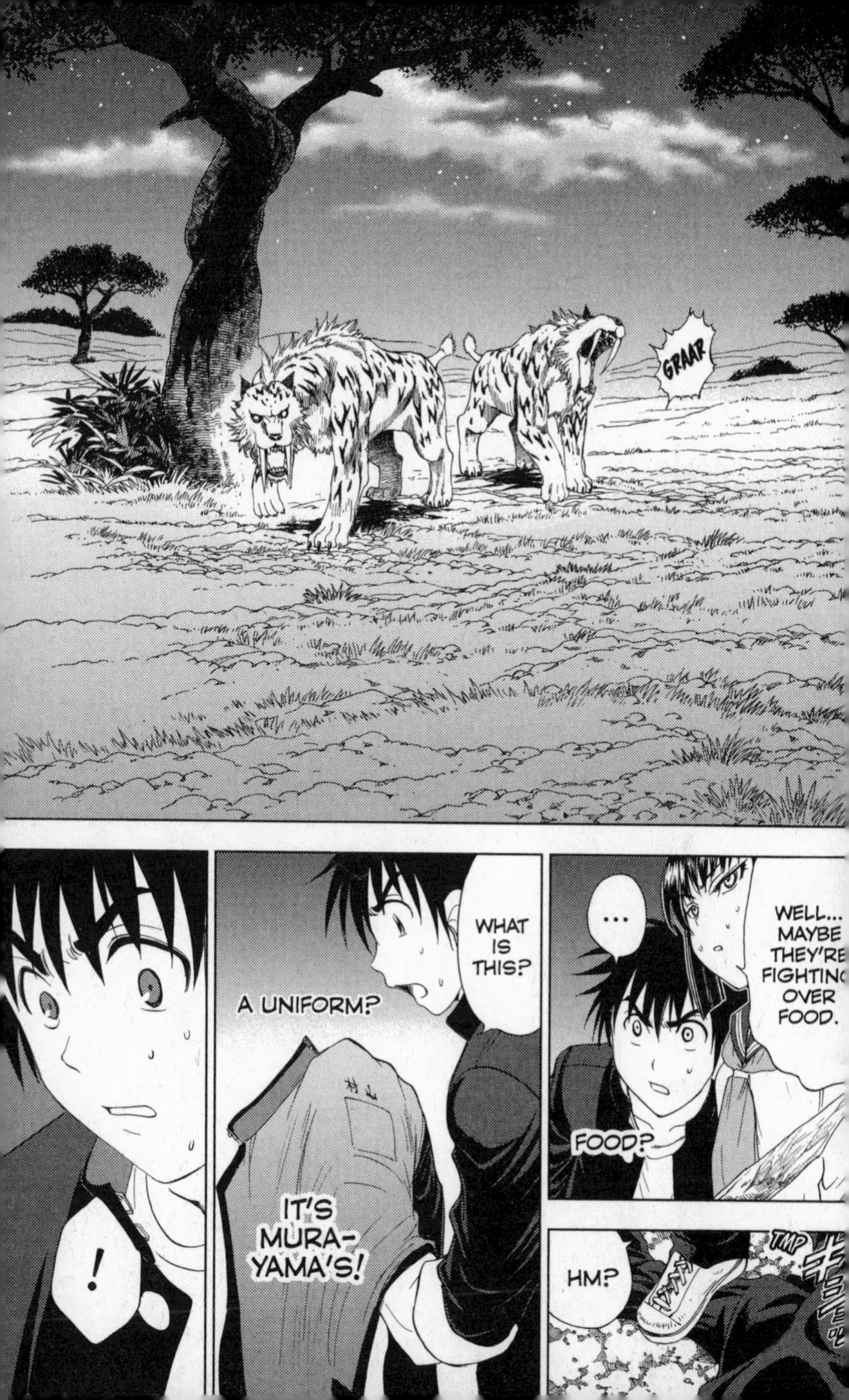
GRAAR
WELL... MAYBE THEY'RE FIGHTING OVER FOOD.
...
FOOD?
TMP
HM?
WHAT IS THIS?
A UNIFORM?
IT'S MURA-YAMA'S!
!

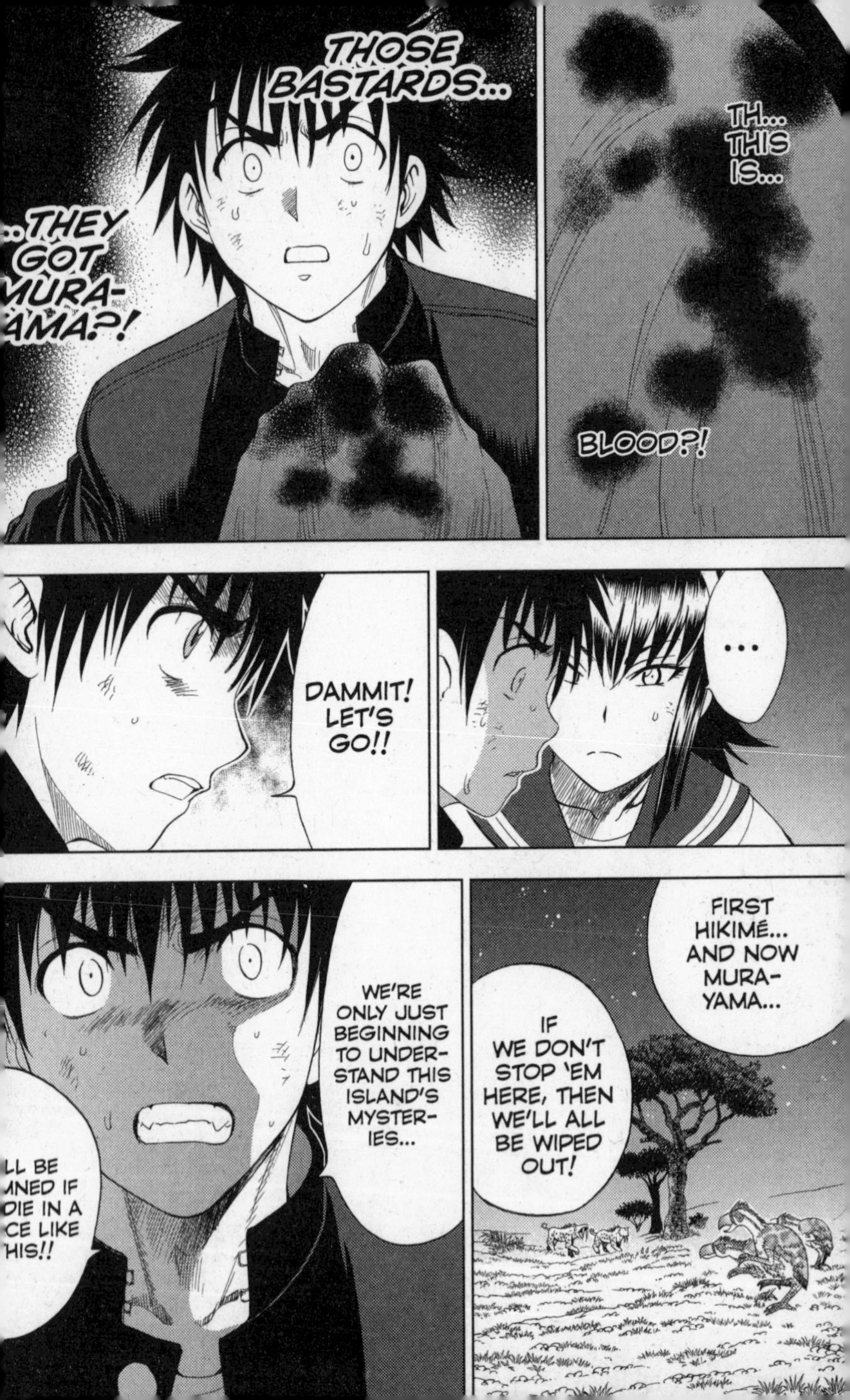
TH... THIS IS...
BLOOD?!
THOSE BASTARDS...
...THEY GOT MURA-AMA?!
...
DAMMIT! LET'S GO!!
FIRST HIKIME... AND NOW MURA-YAMA...
IF WE DON'T STOP 'EM HERE, THEN WE'LL ALL BE WIPED OUT!
WE'RE ONLY JUST BEGINNING TO UNDER-STAND THIS ISLAND'S MYSTER-IES...
LL BE MNED IF DIE IN A CE LIKE HIS!!

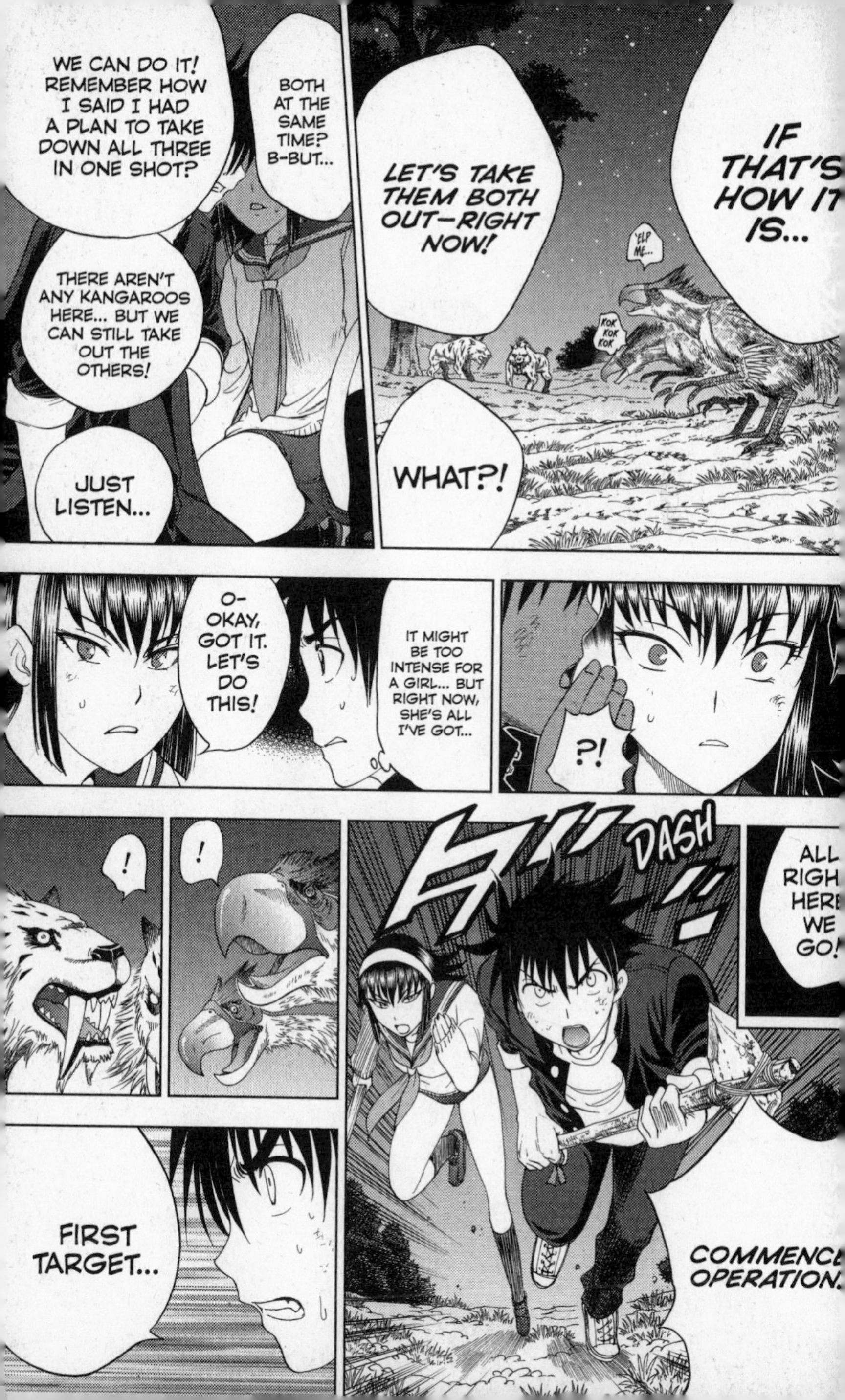
IF THAT'S HOW IT IS...
LET'S TAKE THEM BOTH OUT—RIGHT NOW!
'ELP ME...
KOK KOK KOK
WHAT?!
BOTH AT THE SAME TIME? B-BUT...
WE CAN DO IT! REMEMBER HOW I SAID I HAD A PLAN TO TAKE DOWN ALL THREE IN ONE SHOT?
THERE AREN'T ANY KANGAROOS HERE... BUT WE CAN STILL TAKE OUT THE OTHERS!
JUST LISTEN...
?!
IT MIGHT BE TOO INTENSE FOR A GIRL... BUT RIGHT NOW, SHE'S ALL I'VE GOT...
O-OKAY, GOT IT. LET'S DO THIS!
ALL RIGH HERE WE GO!
DASH
COMMENCE OPERATION.
!
!
FIRST TARGET...

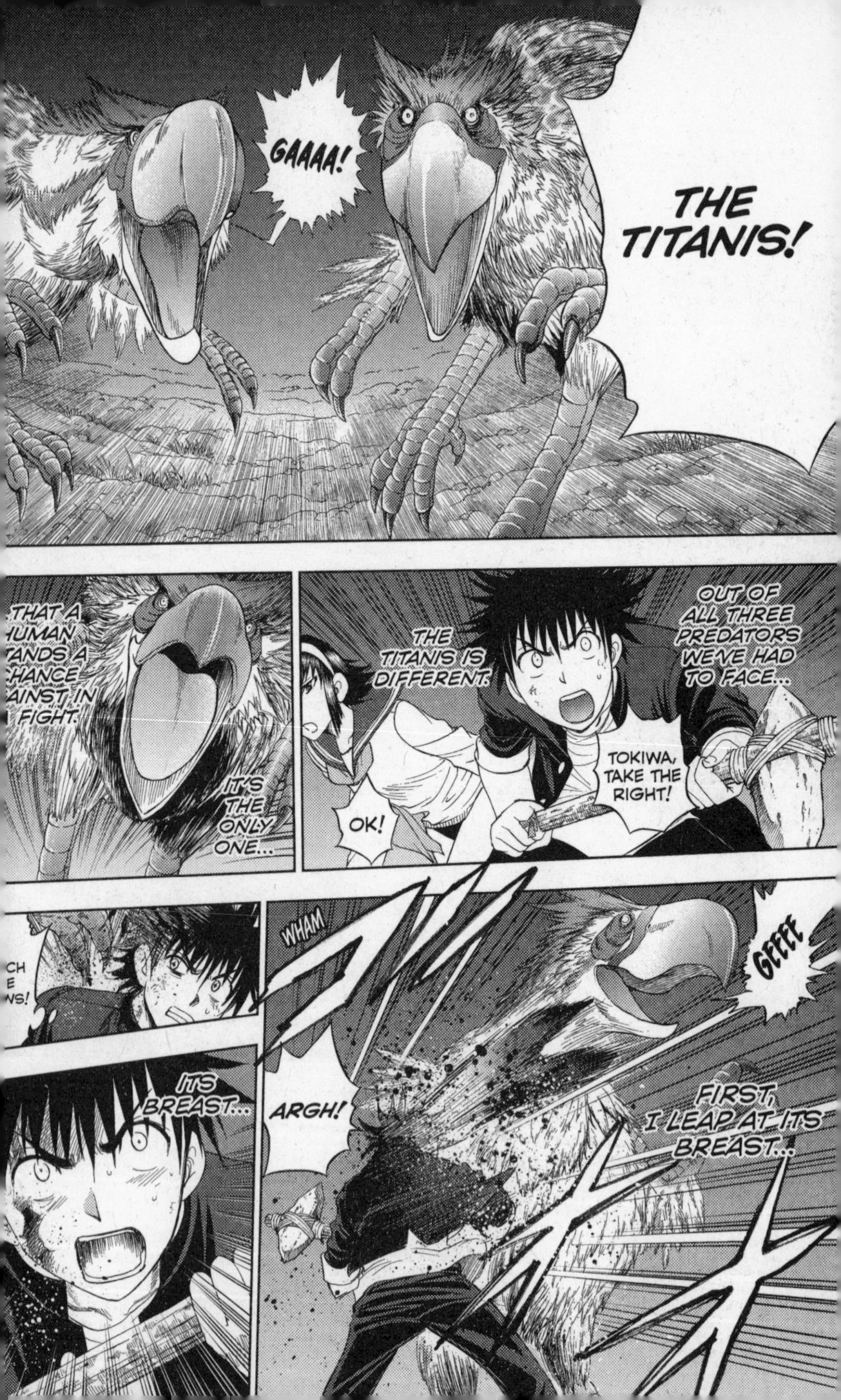
THE TITANIS!
GAAAA!
OUT OF ALL THREE PREDATORS WE'VE HAD TO FACE...
THE TITANIS IS DIFFERENT.
TOKIWA, TAKE THE RIGHT!
OK!
IT'S THE ONLY ONE...
THAT A HUMAN TANDS A HANCE AINST IN FIGHT.
GEEEE
WHAM
FIRST, I LEAP AT ITS BREAST...
ARGH!
CH E WS!
ITS BREAST...

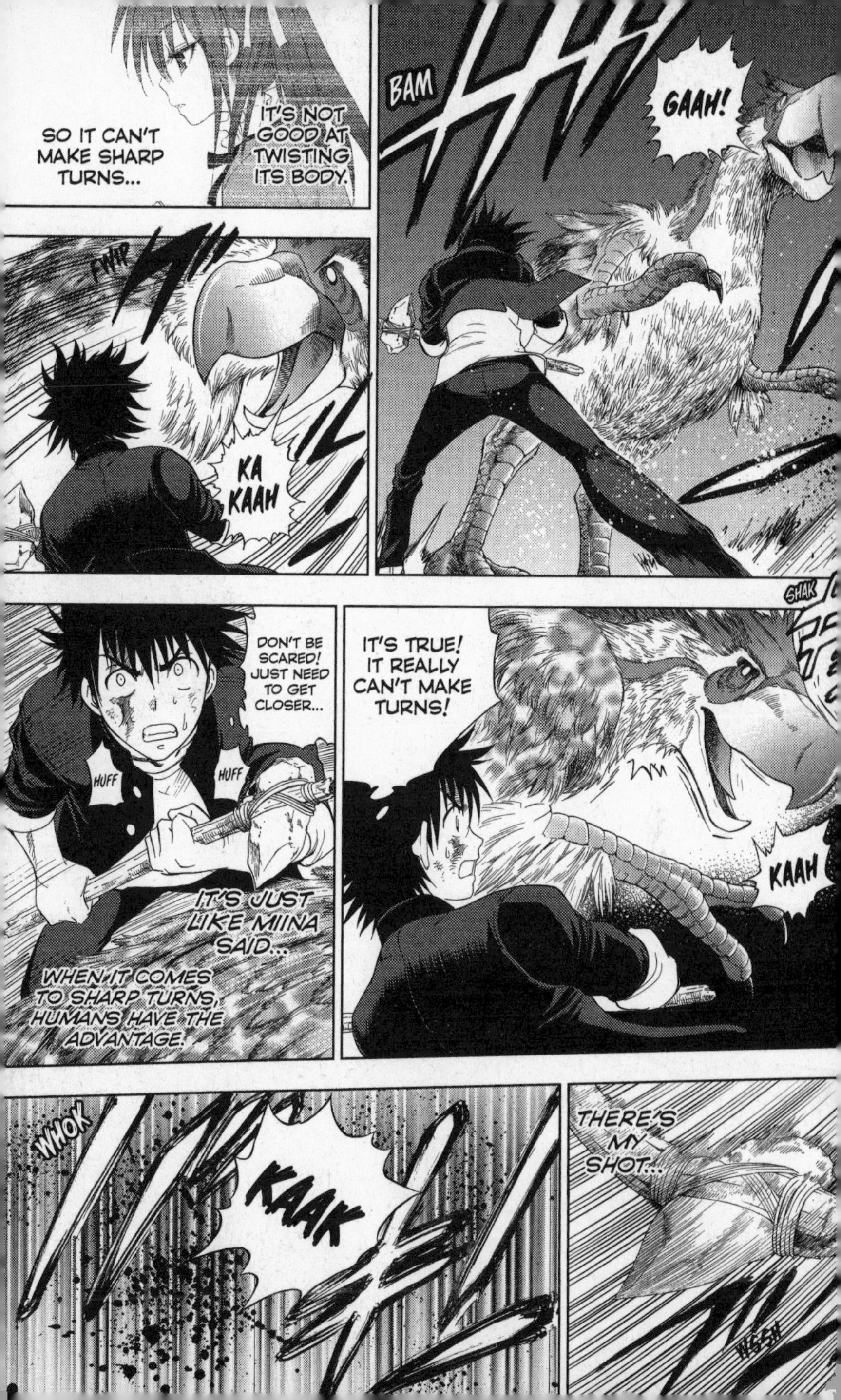
GAAH!
BAM
IT'S NOT GOOD AT TWISTING ITS BODY.
SO IT CAN'T MAKE SHARP TURNS...
FWIP
KA KAAH
SHAK
IT'S TRUE! IT REALLY CAN'T MAKE TURNS!
KAAH
DON'T BE SCARED! JUST NEED TO GET CLOSER...
HUFF
HUFF
IT'S JUST LIKE MIINA SAID...
WHEN IT COMES TO SHARP TURNS, HUMANS HAVE THE ADVANTAGE.
THERE'S MY SHOT...
WSSH
WHOK
KAAK

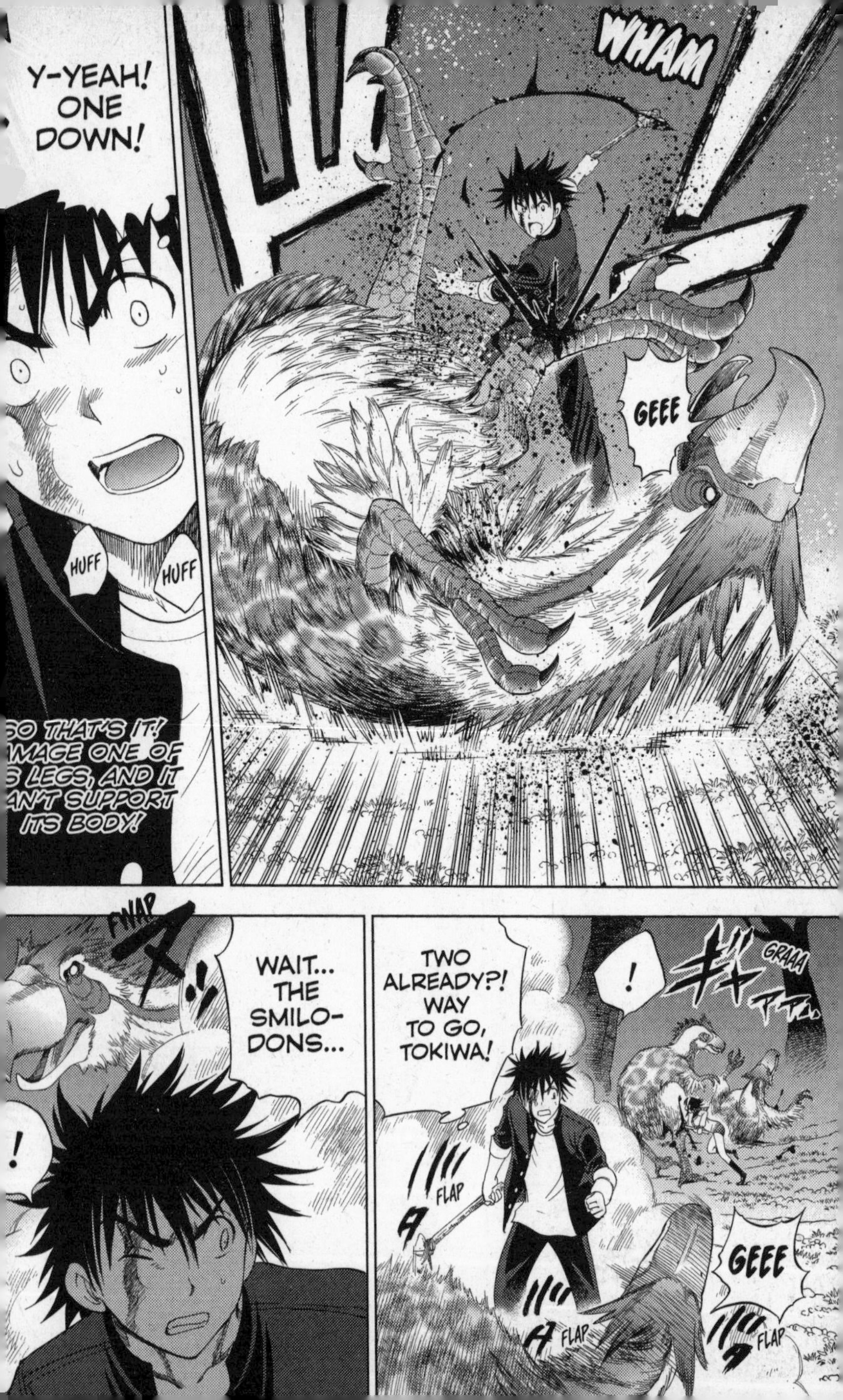
WHAM
GEEE
Y-YEAH! ONE DOWN!
HUFF
HUFF
SO THAT'S IT! AMAGE ONE OF S LEGS, AND IT AN'T SUPPORT ITS BODY!
!
GRAAA
TWO ALREADY?! WAY TO GO, TOKIWA!
FLAP
GEEE
FLAP
FLAP
FWAP
WAIT... THE SMILO-DONS...
!

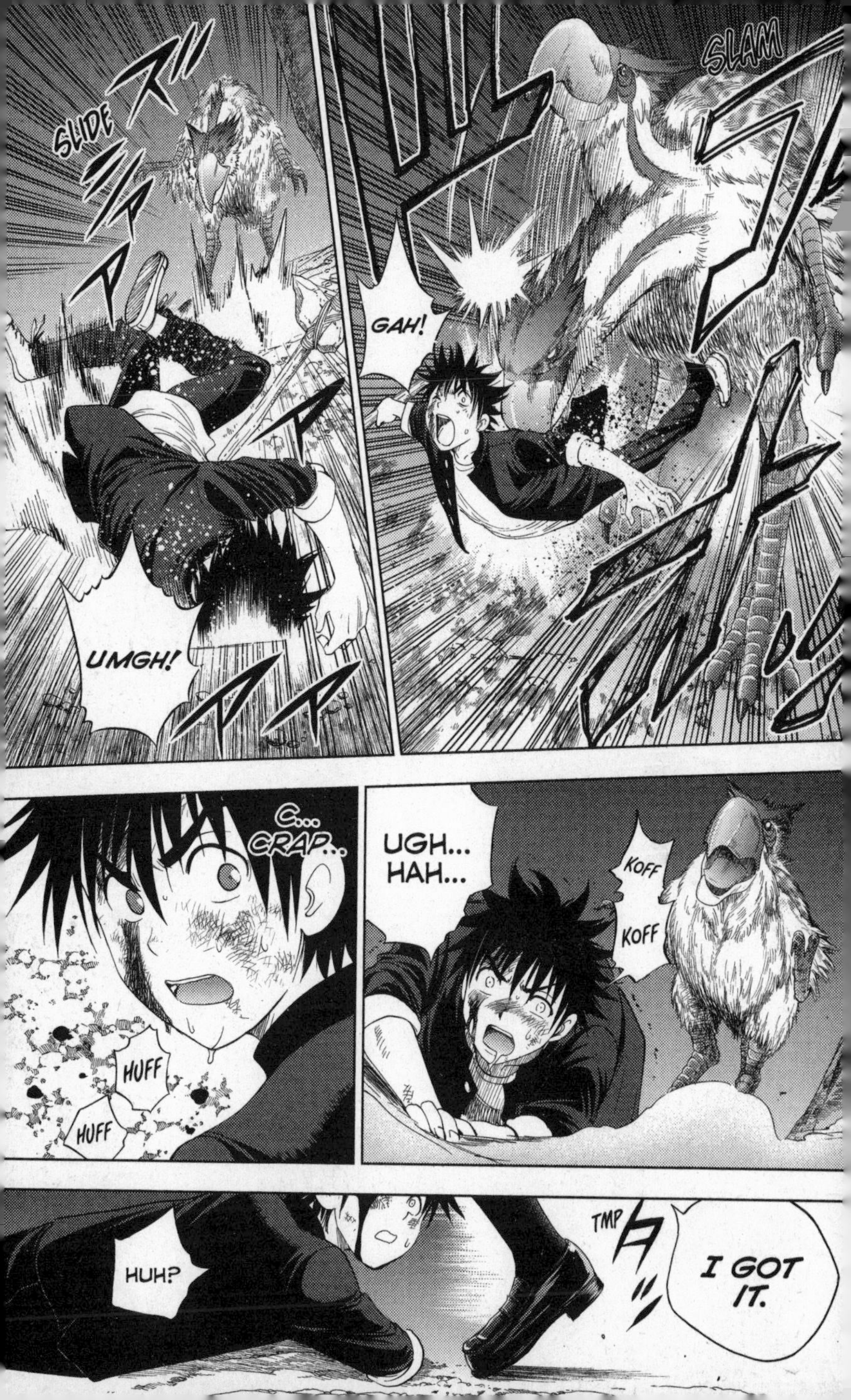
SLAM
GAH!
SLIDE
UMGH!
UGH... HAH...
KOFF
KOFF
C... CRAP...
HUFF
HUFF
TMP
I GOT IT.
HUH?

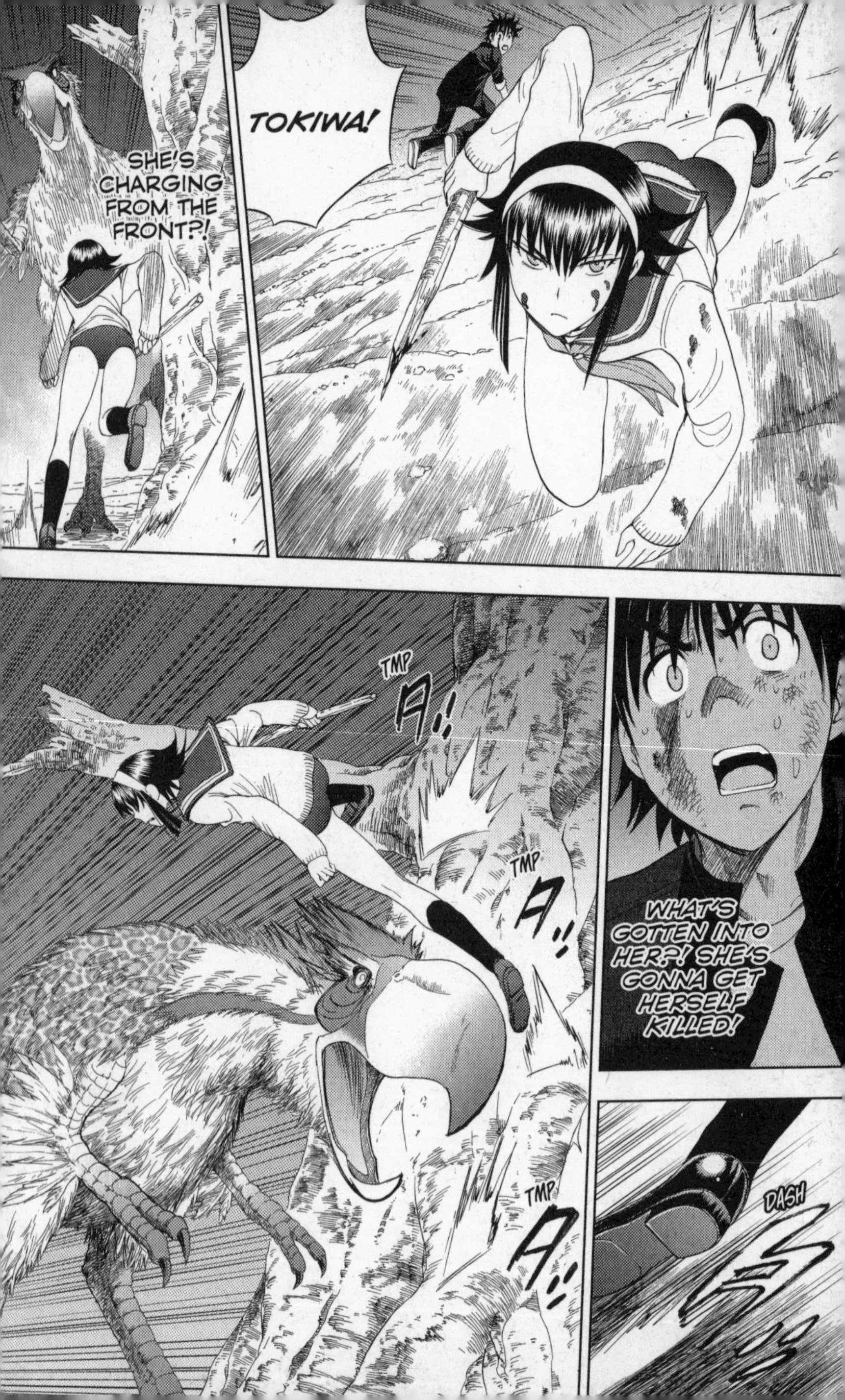
TOKIWA!
SHE'S CHARGING FROM THE FRONT?!
WHAT'S GOTTEN INTO HER?! SHE'S GONNA GET HERSELF KILLED!
DASH
TMP
TMP
TMP

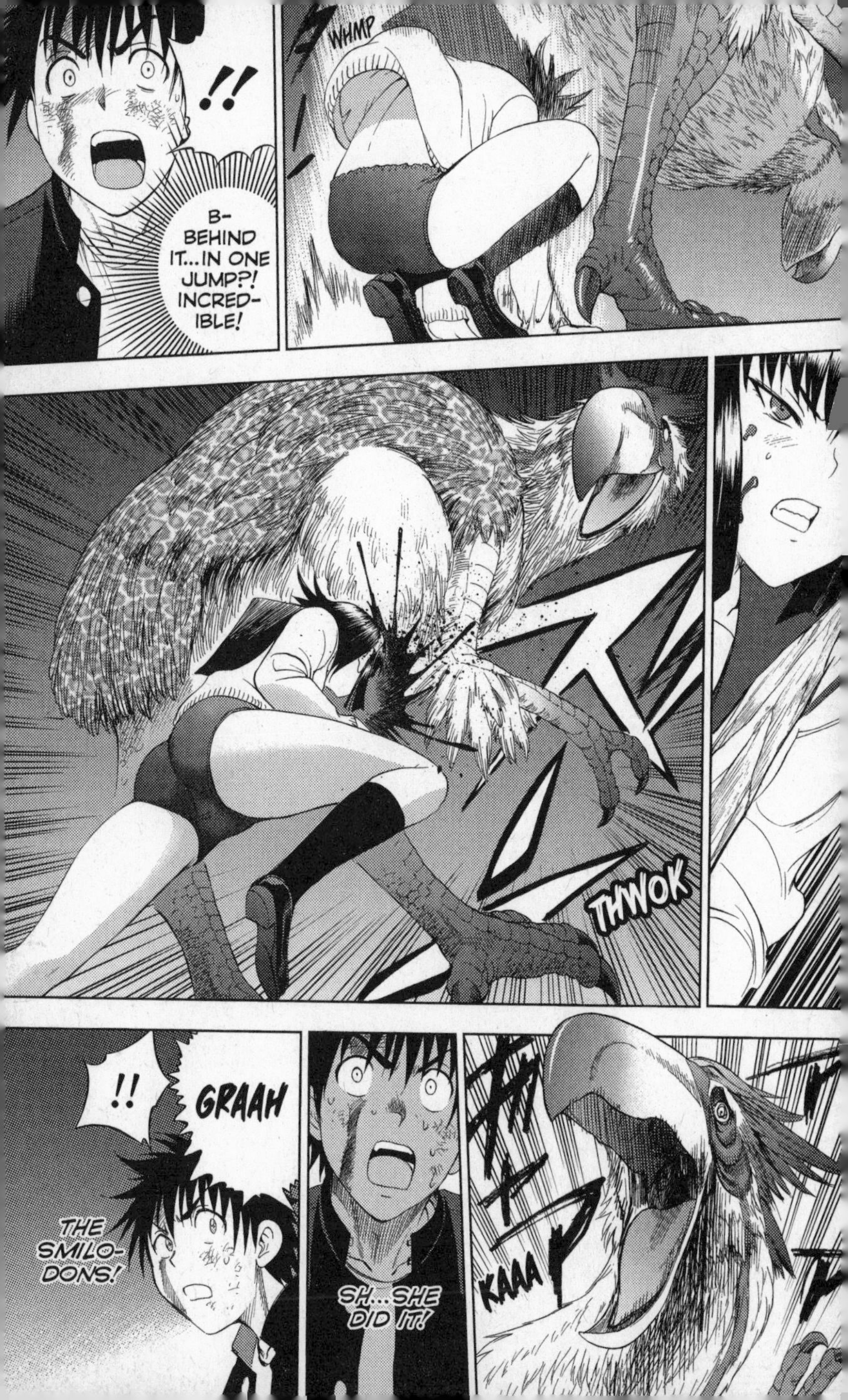
WHMP
!!
B-BEHIND IT...IN ONE JUMP?! INCREDIBLE!
THWOK
KAAA
SH...SHE DID IT!
!!
GRAAH
THE SMILO-DONS!

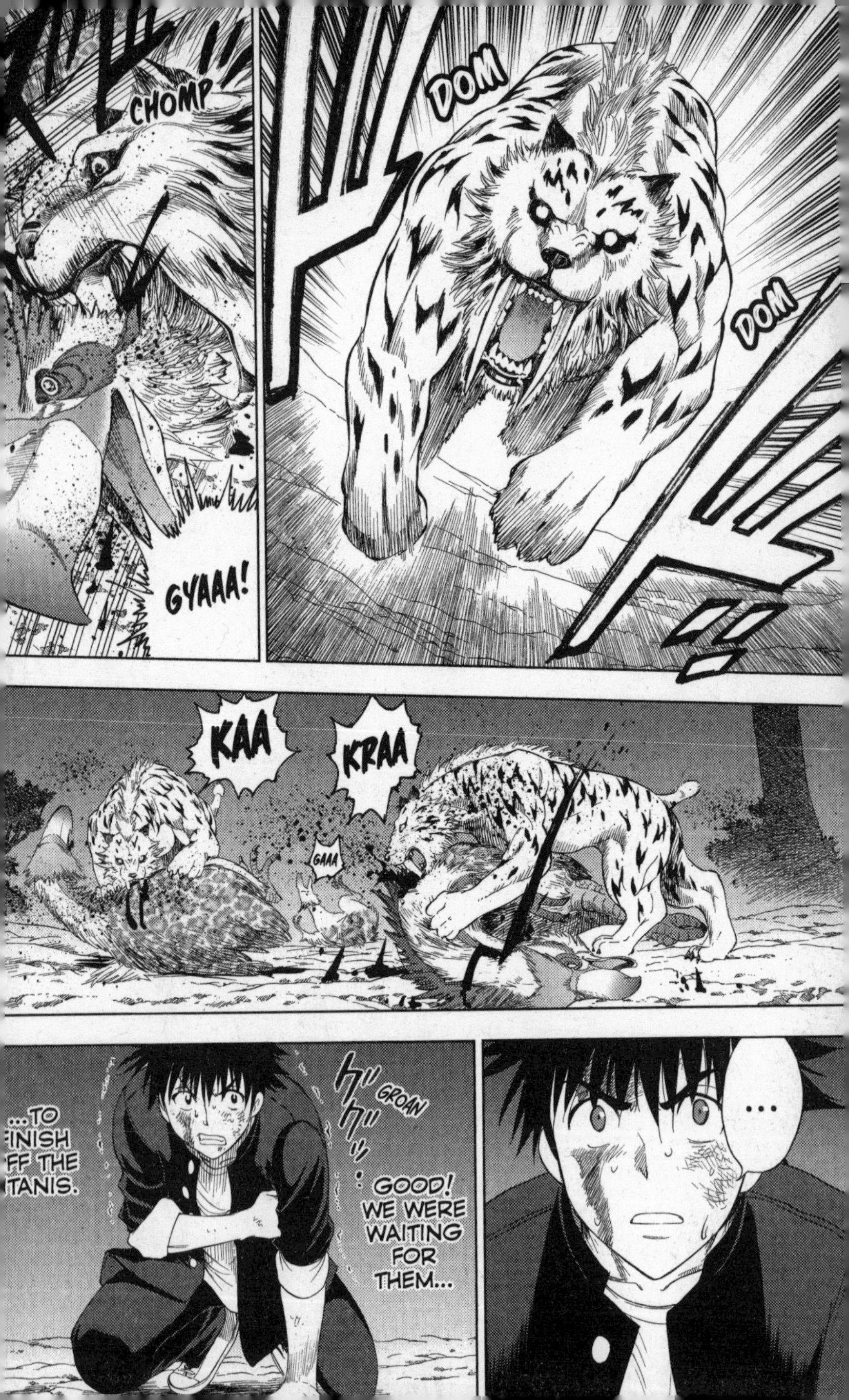
DOM
DOM
CHOMP
GYAAA!
KRAA
KAA
GAAA
...
GROAN
...TO FINISH FF THE TANIS.
GOOD! WE WERE WAITING FOR THEM...

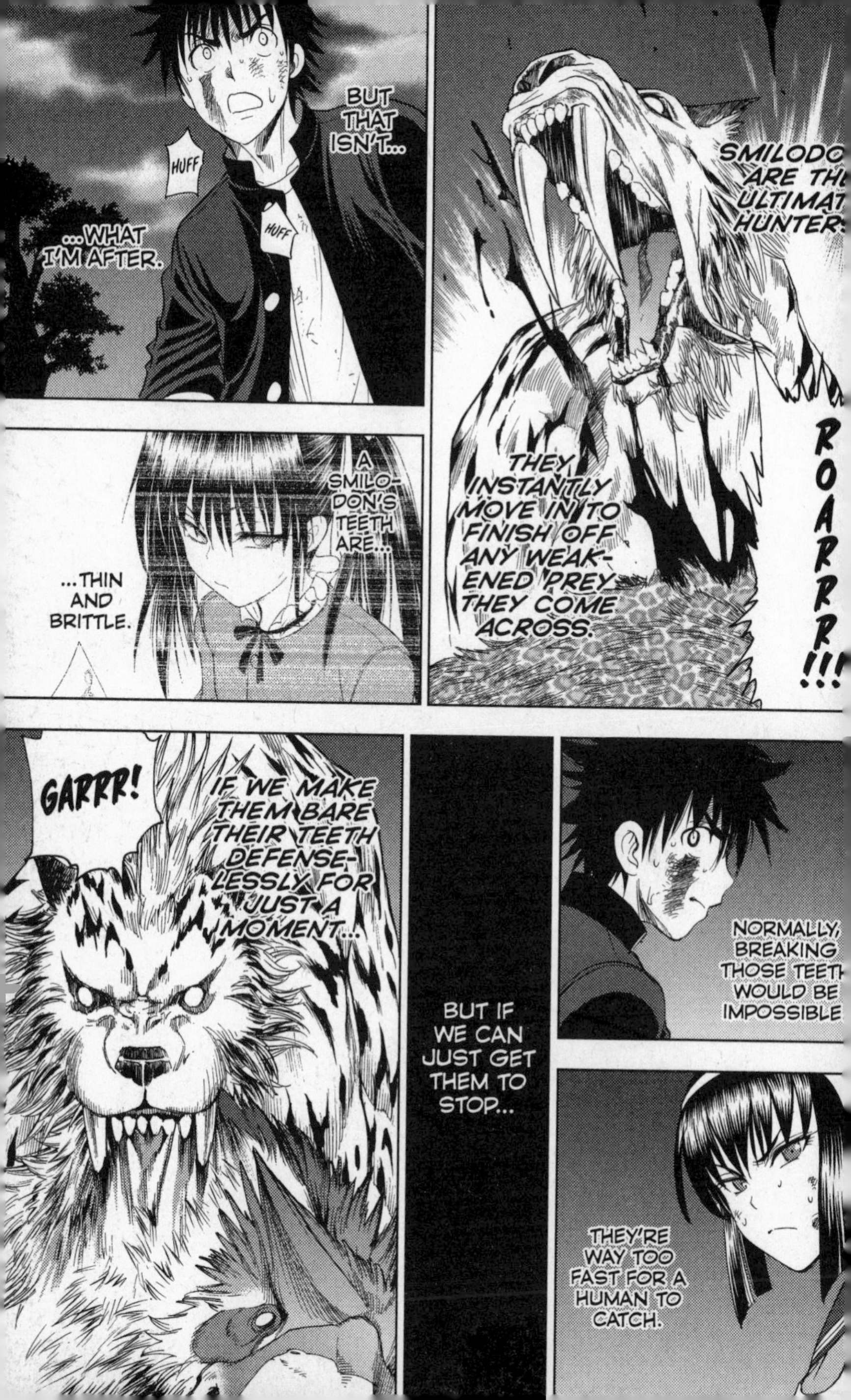
SMILODO ARE TH ULTIMAT HUNTER
THEY INSTANTLY MOVE IN TO FINISH OFF ANY WEAK-ENED PREY THEY COME ACROSS.
ROARRRR!!!
BUT THAT ISN'T...
HUFF
HUFF
...WHAT I'M AFTER.
A SMILO-DON'S TEETH ARE...
...THIN AND BRITTLE.
NORMALLY, BREAKING THOSE TEETH WOULD BE IMPOSSIBLE.
THEY'RE WAY TOO FAST FOR A HUMAN TO CATCH.
BUT IF WE CAN JUST GET THEM TO STOP...
IF WE MAKE THEM BARE THEIR TEETH DEFENSE-LESSLY FOR JUST A MOMENT...
GARRR!

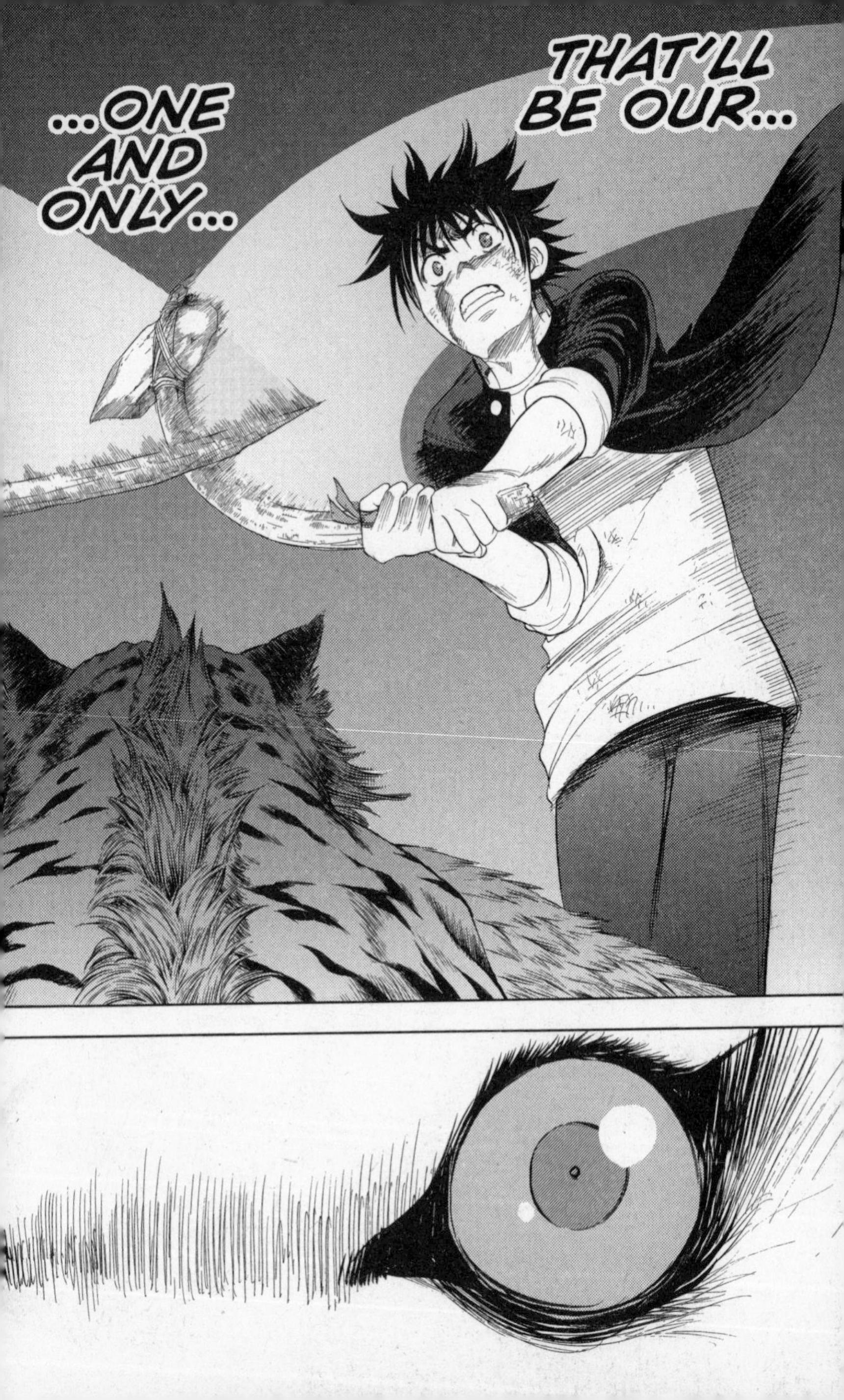
THAT'LL BE OUR...
...ONE AND ONLY...

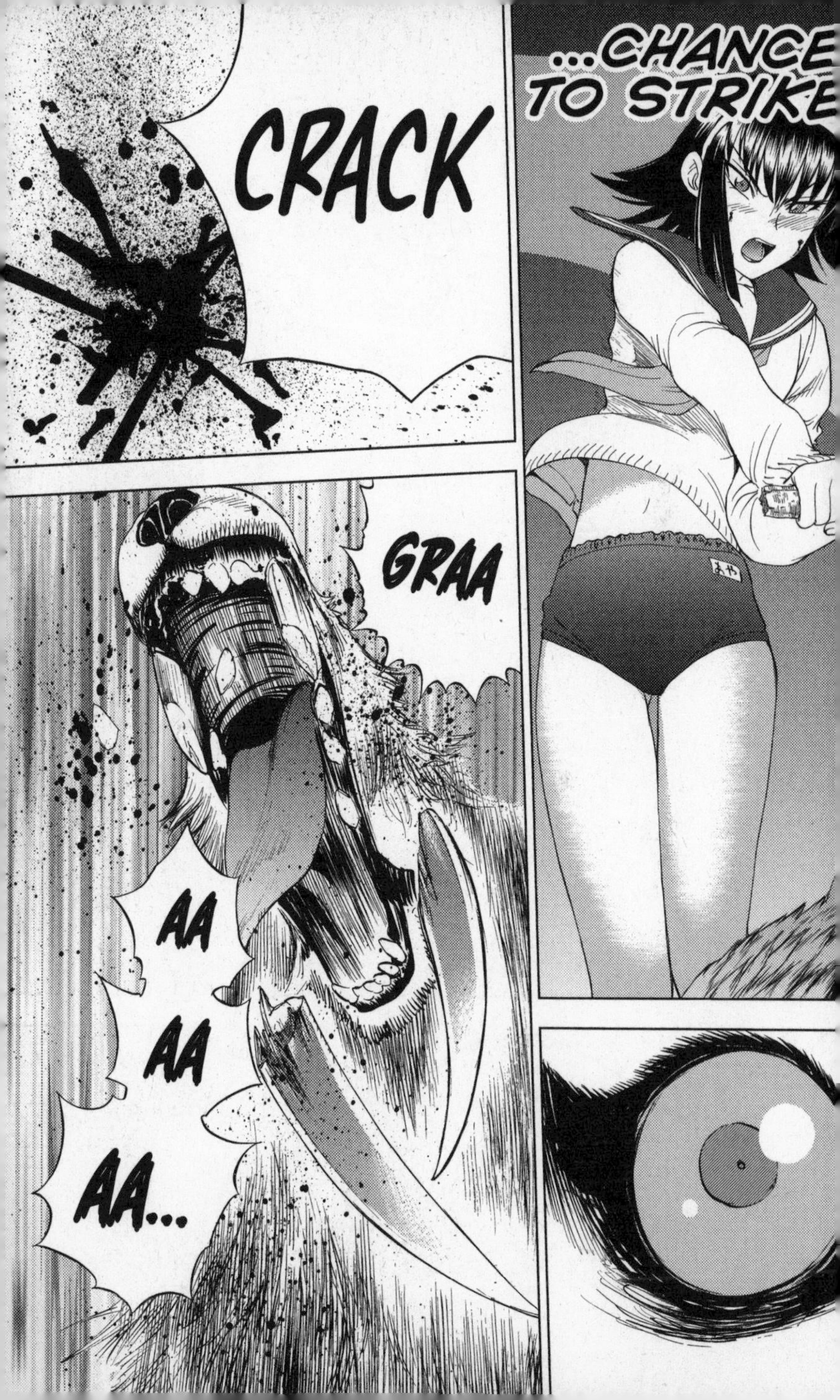
...CHANCE TO STRIKE
あや
CRACK
GRAA
AA
AA
AA...

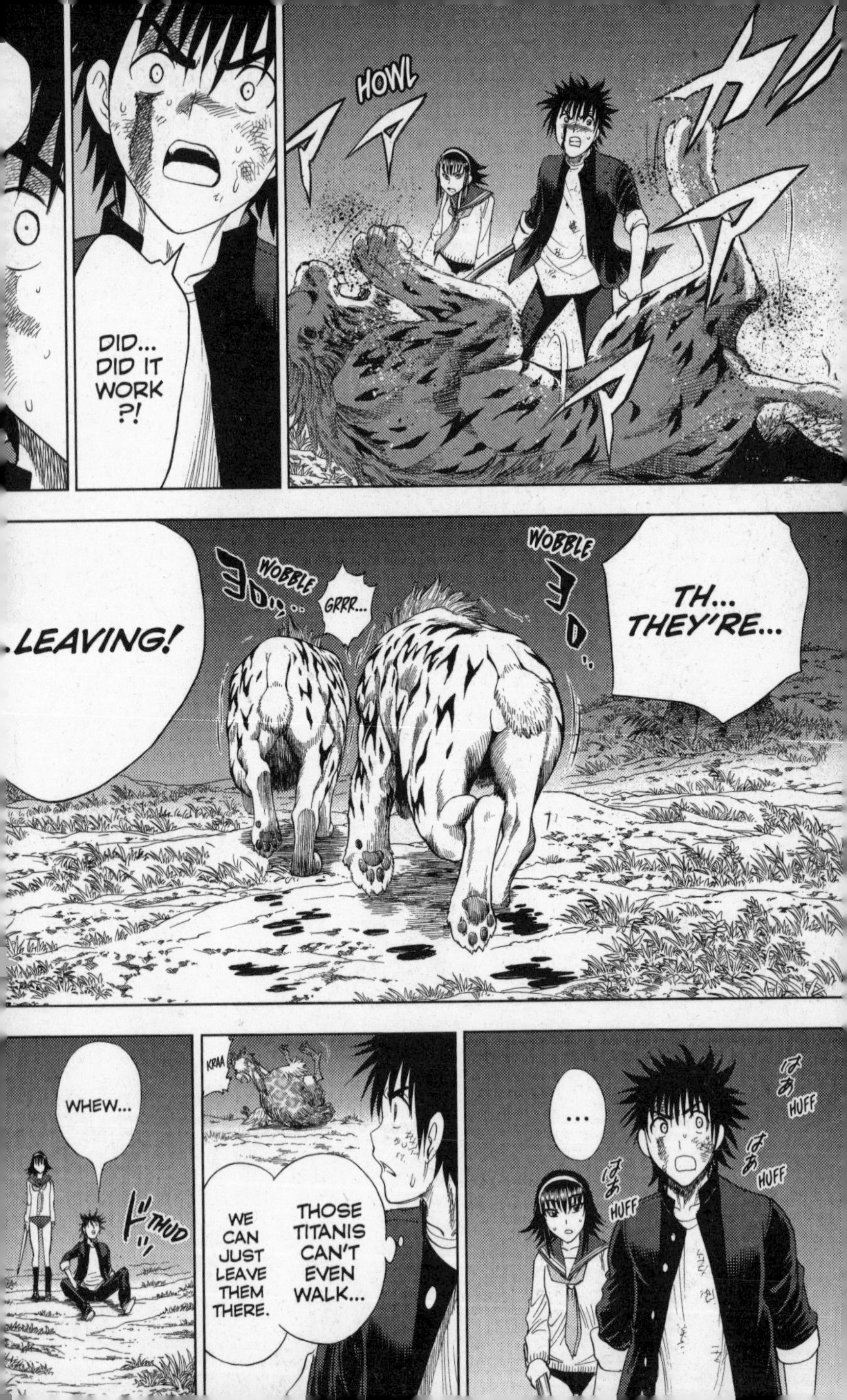
HOWL
DID... DID IT WORK?!
TH... THEY'RE...
WOBBLE
GRRR...
WOBBLE
.LEAVING!
HUFF
HUFF
HUFF
...
THOSE TITANIS CAN'T EVEN WALK...
WE CAN JUST LEAVE THEM THERE.
KRAA
WHEW...
THUD

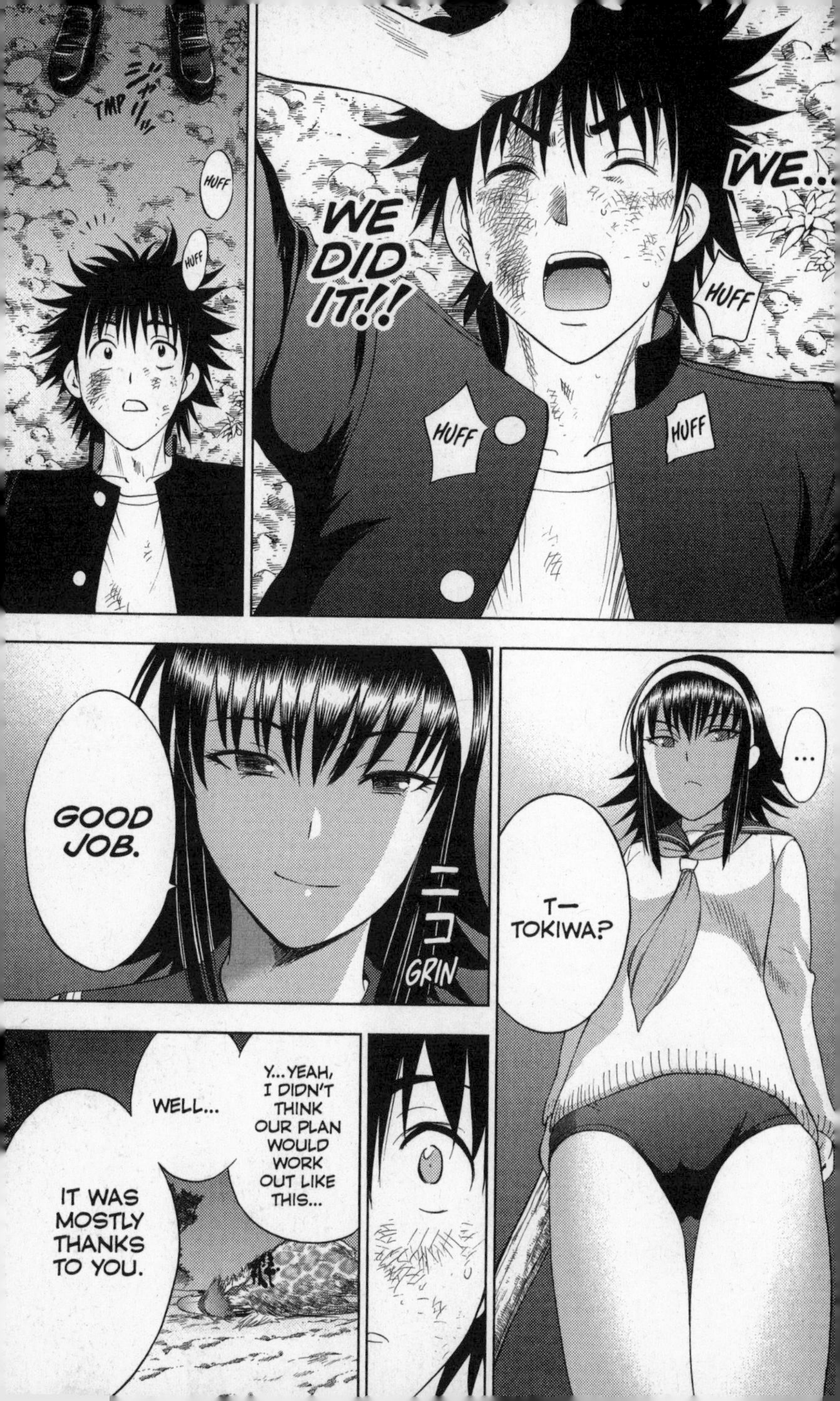
WE...
HUFF
WE DID IT!!
HUFF
HUFF
TMP
HUFF
HUFF
...
T— TOKIWA?
GOOD JOB.
ニコ
GRIN
Y...YEAH, I DIDN'T THINK OUR PLAN WOULD WORK OUT LIKE THIS...
WELL...
IT WAS MOSTLY THANKS TO YOU.

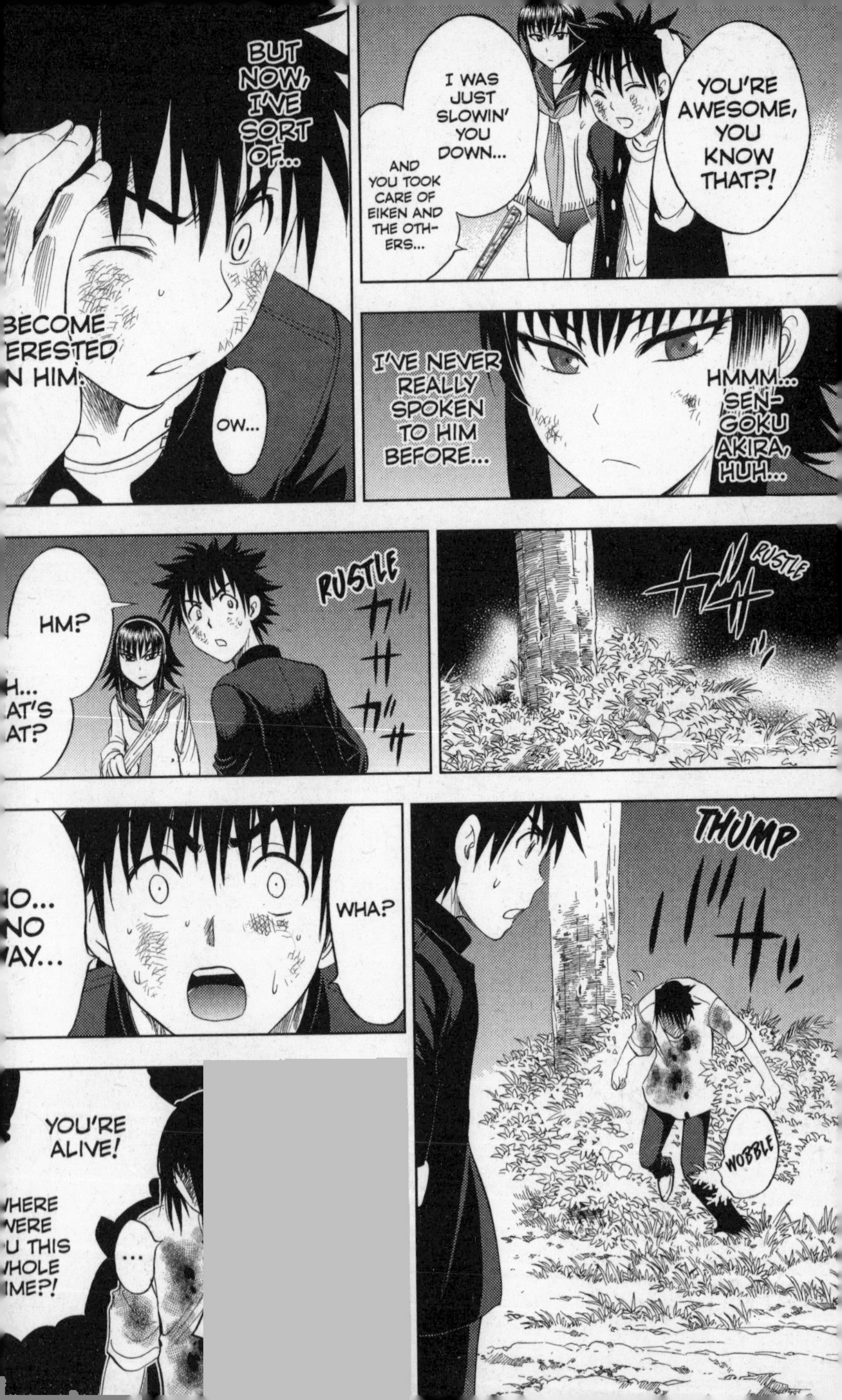
YOU'RE AWESOME, YOU KNOW THAT?!
I WAS JUST SLOWIN' YOU DOWN...
AND YOU TOOK CARE OF EIKEN AND THE OTH-ERS...
HMMM... SEN-GOKU AKIRA, HUH...
I'VE NEVER REALLY SPOKEN TO HIM BEFORE...
BUT NOW, I'VE SORT OF...
BECOME ERESTED N HIM.
OW...
RUSTLE
RUSTLE
HM?
H... AT'S AT?
THUMP
WOBBLE
WHA?
O... NO AY...
YOU'RE ALIVE!
HERE VERE U THIS VHOLE IME?!
...

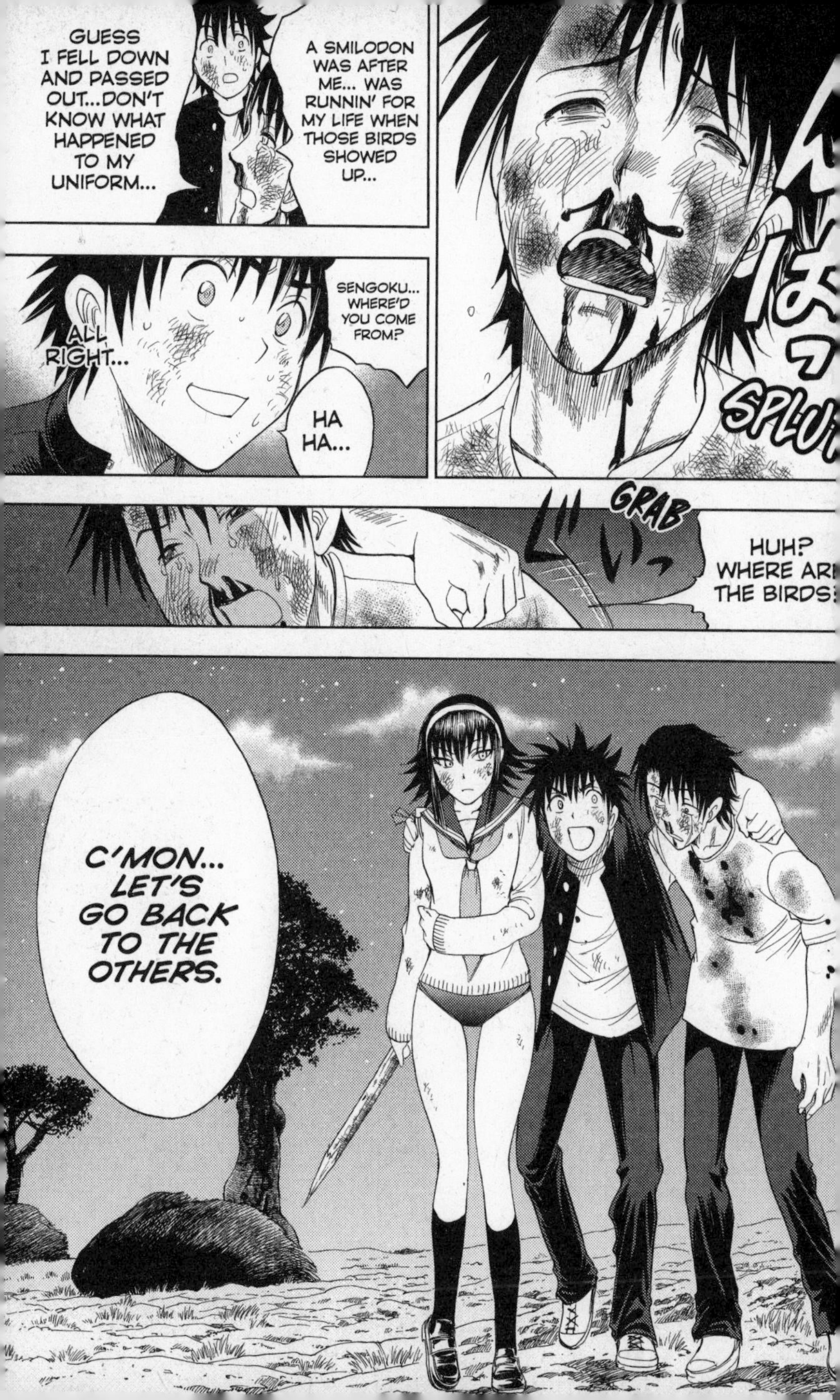
SPLU
A SMILODON WAS AFTER ME... WAS RUNNIN' FOR MY LIFE WHEN THOSE BIRDS SHOWED UP...
GUESS I FELL DOWN AND PASSED OUT...DON'T KNOW WHAT HAPPENED TO MY UNIFORM...
SENGOKU... WHERE'D YOU COME FROM?
HA HA...
ALL RIGHT...
HUH? WHERE ARE THE BIRDS
GRAB
C'MON... LET'S GO BACK TO THE OTHERS.

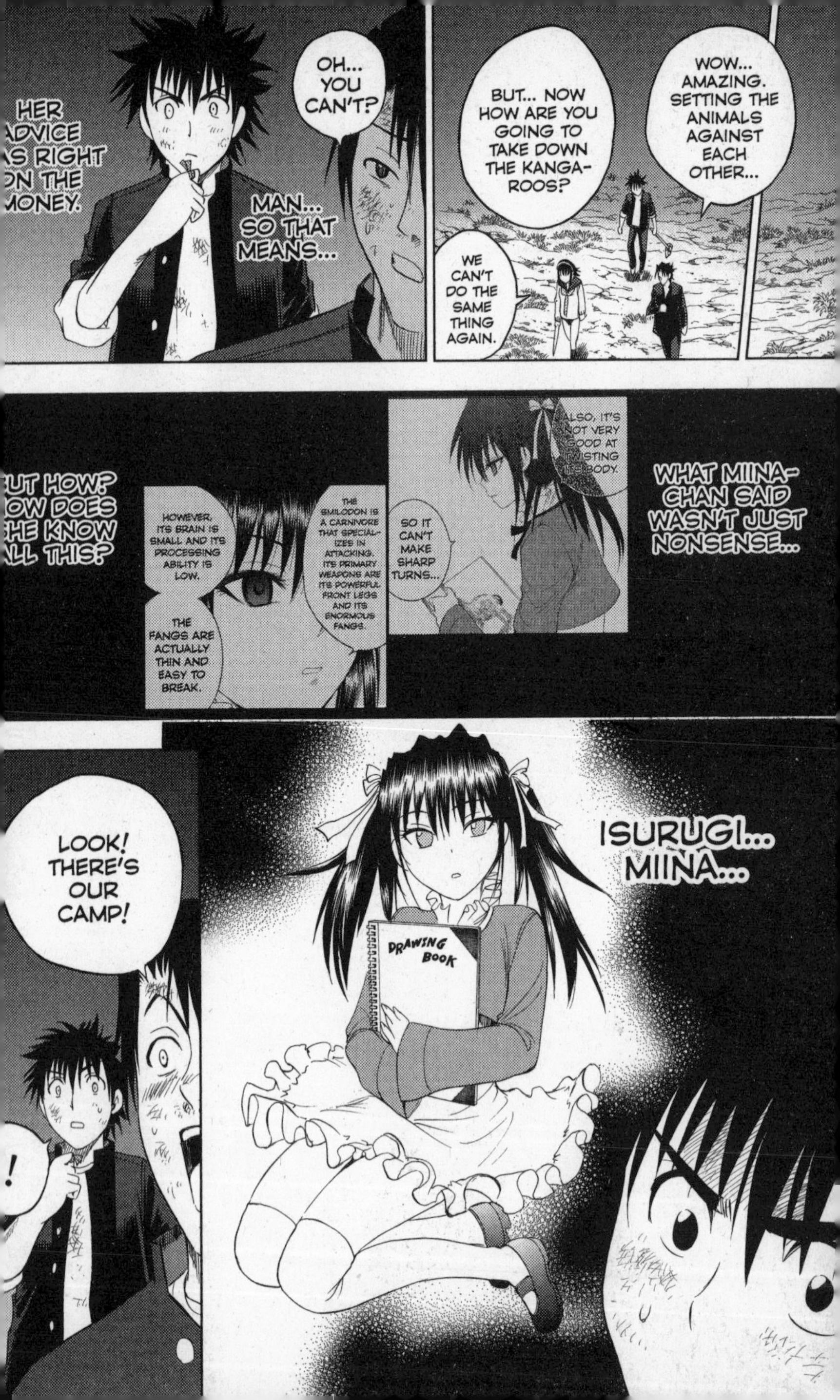
WOW... AMAZING. SETTING THE ANIMALS AGAINST EACH OTHER...
BUT... NOW HOW ARE YOU GOING TO TAKE DOWN THE KANGA-ROOS?
WE CAN'T DO THE SAME THING AGAIN.
OH... YOU CAN'T?
MAN... SO THAT MEANS...
HER ADVICE AS RIGHT ON THE MONEY.
WHAT MIINA-CHAN SAID WASN'T JUST NONSENSE...
ALSO, IT'S NOT VERY GOOD AT TWISTING ITS BODY.
SO IT CAN'T MAKE SHARP TURNS...
THE SMILODON IS A CARNIVORE THAT SPECIAL-IZES IN ATTACKING. ITS PRIMARY WEAPONS ARE ITS POWERFUL FRONT LEGS AND ITS ENORMOUS FANGS.
HOWEVER, ITS BRAIN IS SMALL AND ITS PROCESSING ABILITY IS LOW.
THE FANGS ARE ACTUALLY THIN AND EASY TO BREAK.
UT HOW? OW DOES HE KNOW LL THIS?
ISURUGI... MIINA...
DRAWING BOOK
LOOK! THERE'S OUR CAMP!
!

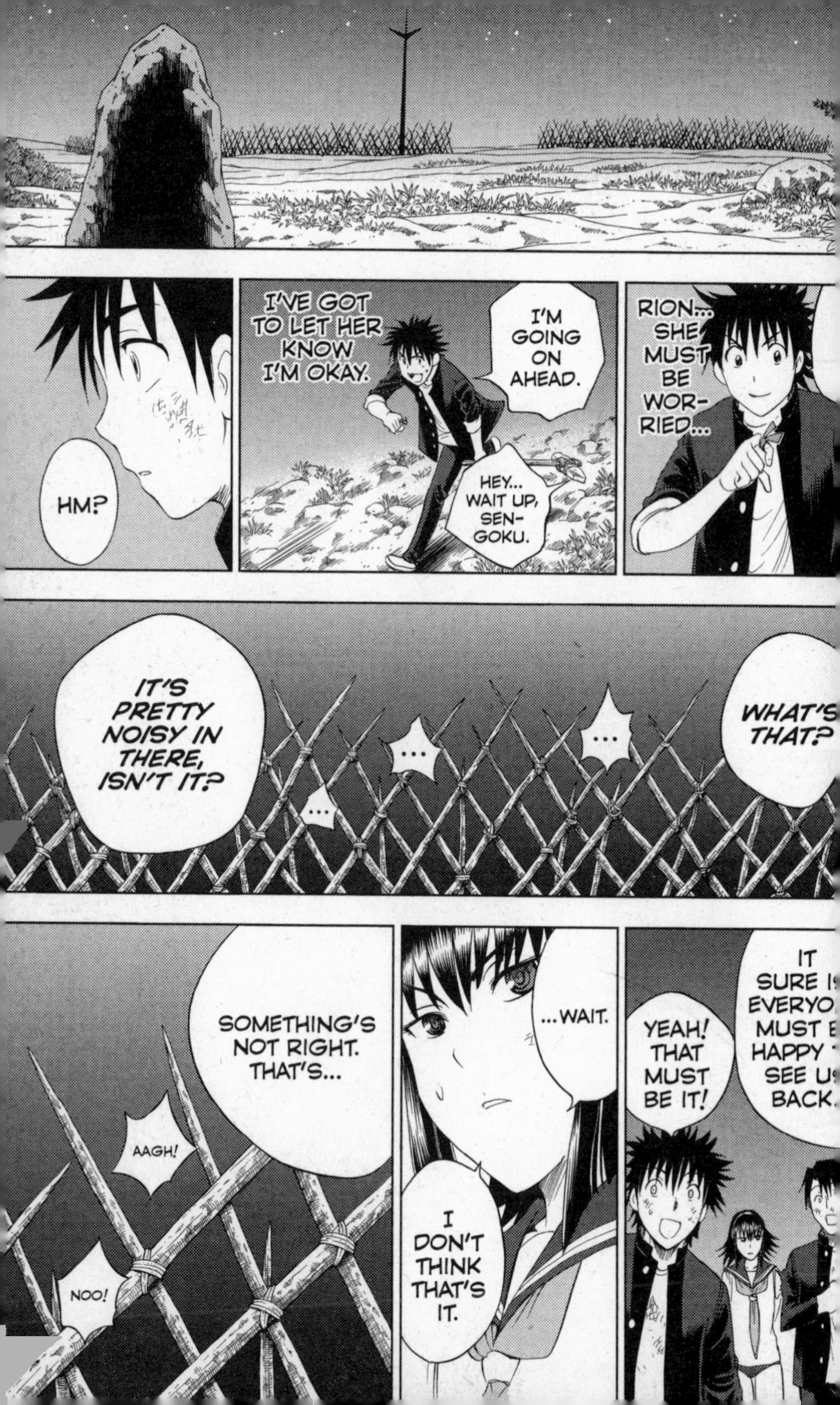
RION... SHE MUST BE WOR-RIED...
I'M GOING ON AHEAD.
I'VE GOT TO LET HER KNOW I'M OKAY.
HEY... WAIT UP, SEN-GOKU.
HM?
WHAT'S THAT?
...
...
...
IT'S PRETTY NOISY IN THERE, ISN'T IT?
IT SURE I EVERYO MUST B HAPPY T SEE U BACK.
YEAH! THAT MUST BE IT!
...WAIT.
I DON'T THINK THAT'S IT.
SOMETHING'S NOT RIGHT. THAT'S...
AAGH!
NOO!

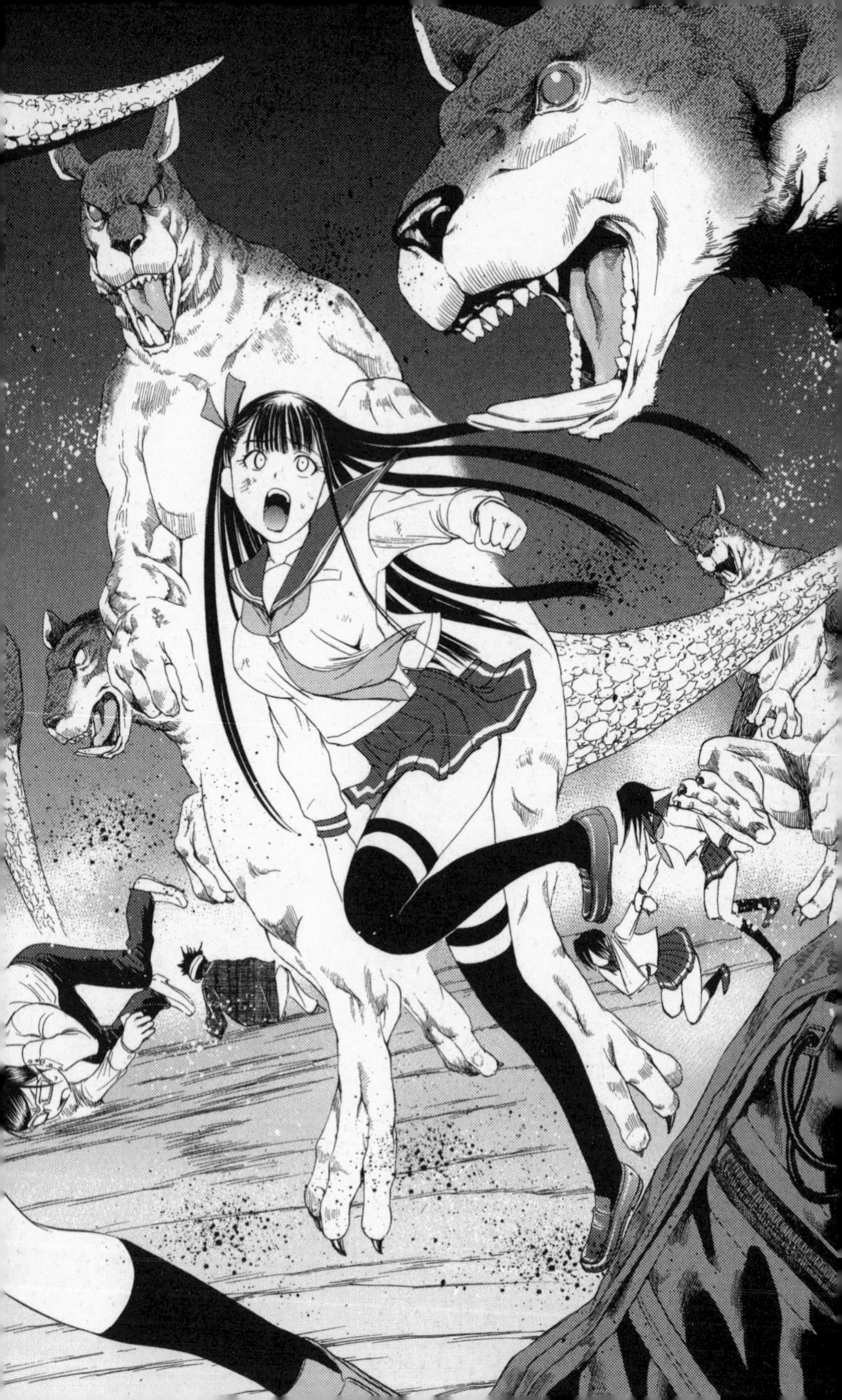

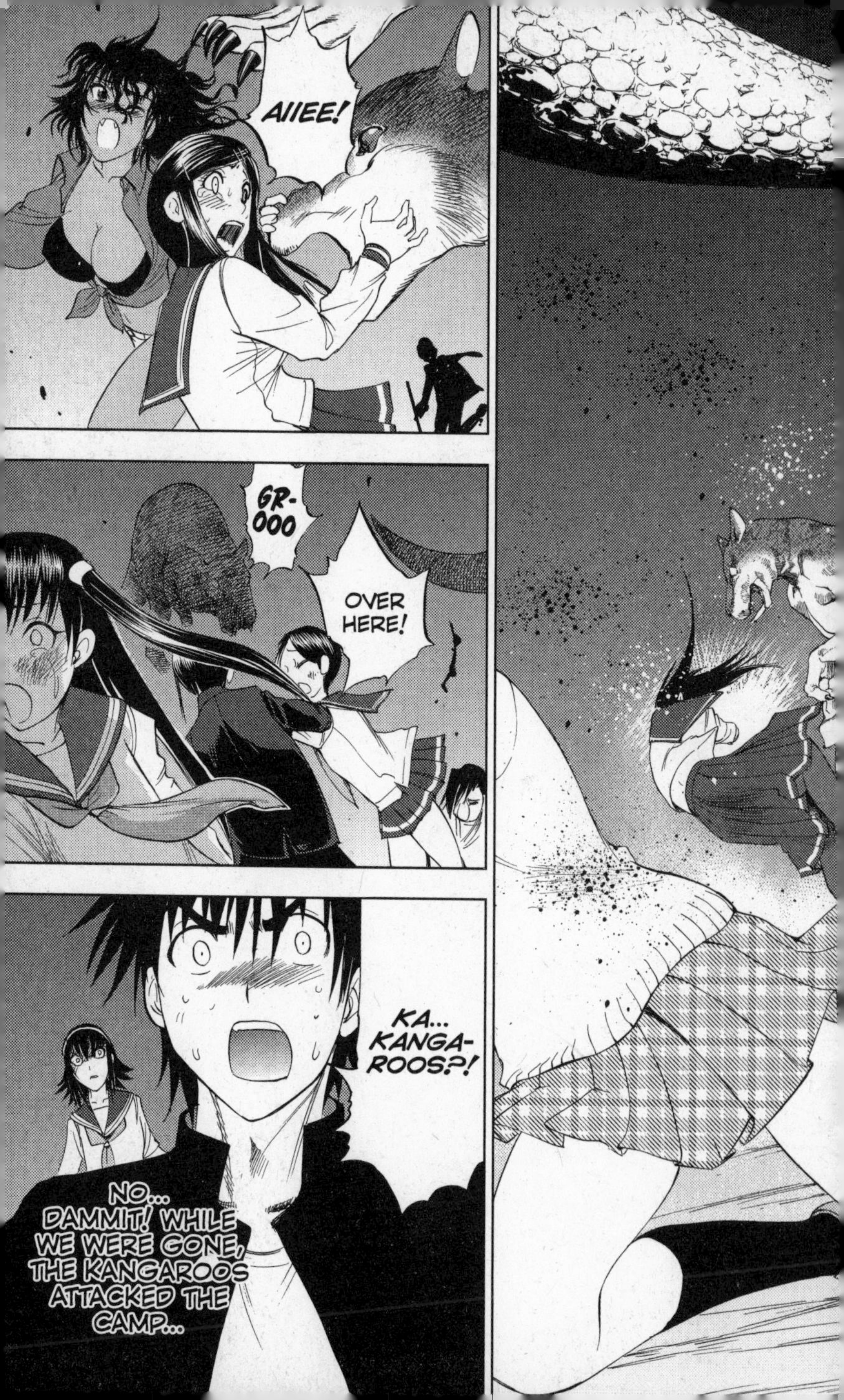
AIIEE!
GR-OOO
OVER HERE!
KA... KANGA-ROOS?!
NO... DAMMIT! WHILE WE WERE GONE, THE KANGAROOS ATTACKED THE CAMP...

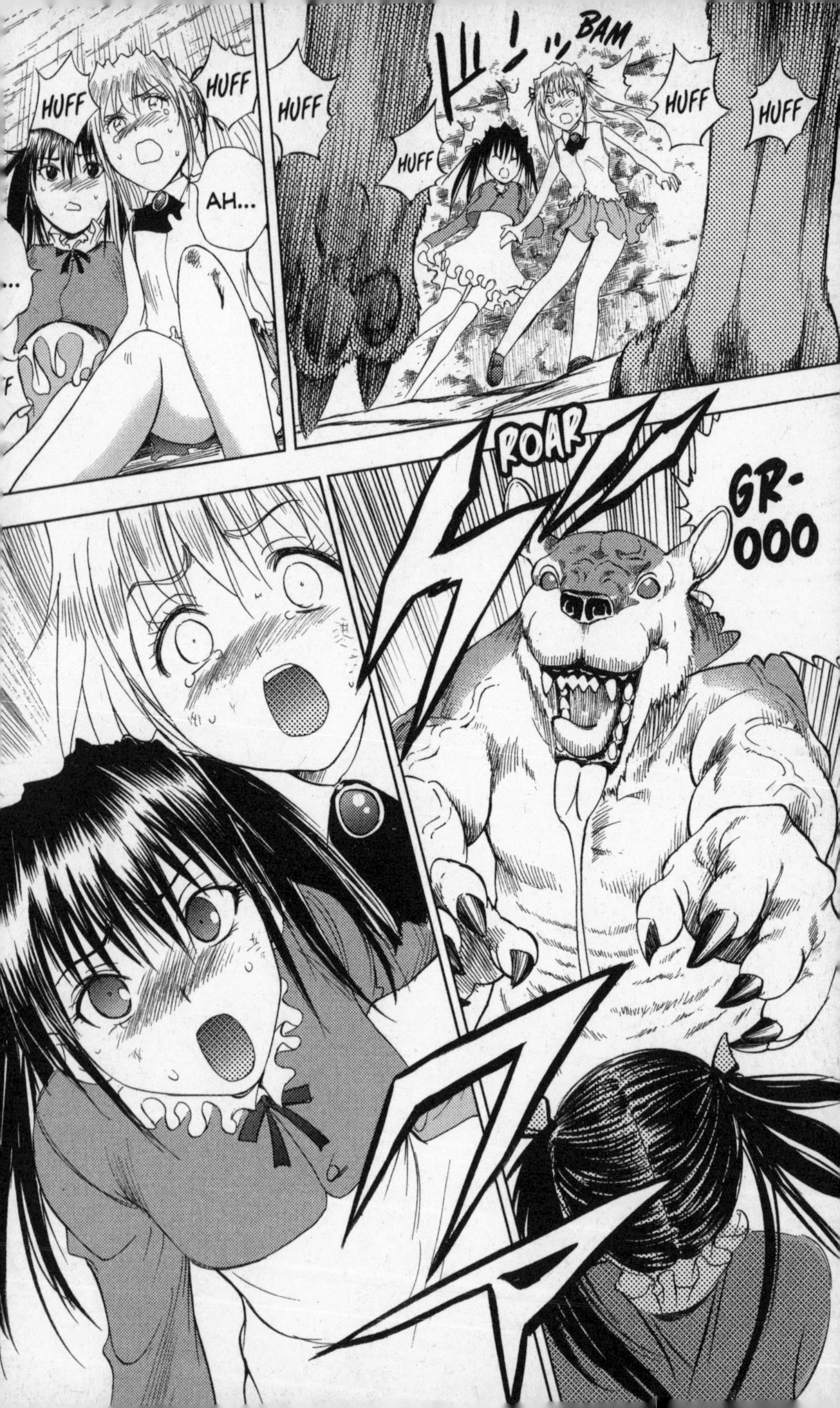
HUFF
HUFF
BAM
HUFF
HUFF
HUFF
HUFF
AH...
GR-OOO
ROAR

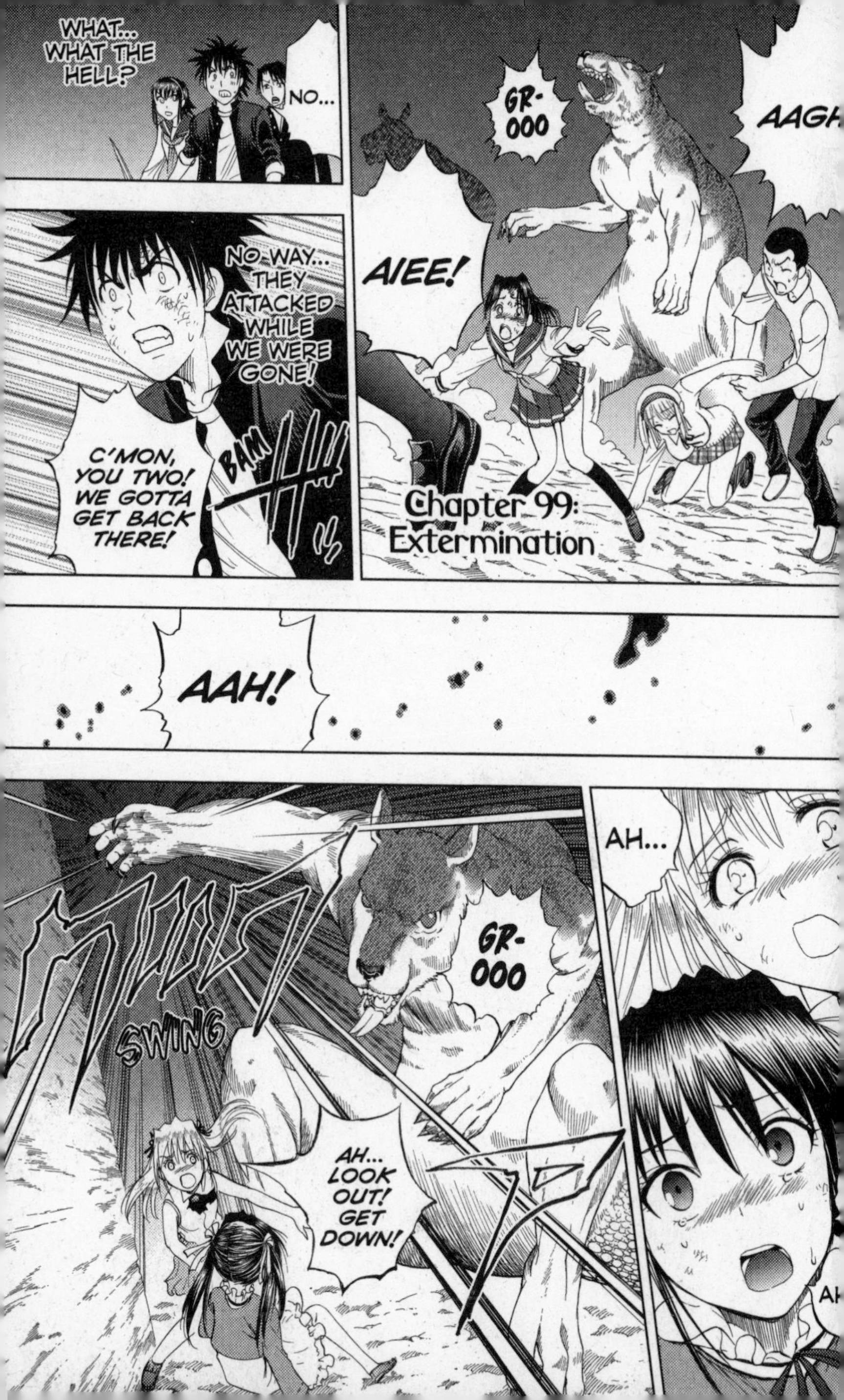
AAGH
GR-OOO
AIEE!
Chapter 99: Extermination
WHAT... WHAT THE HELL?
NO...
NO WAY... THEY ATTACKED WHILE WE WERE GONE!
BAM
C'MON, YOU TWO! WE GOTTA GET BACK THERE!
AAH!
AH...
GR-OOO
SWING
AH... LOOK OUT! GET DOWN!

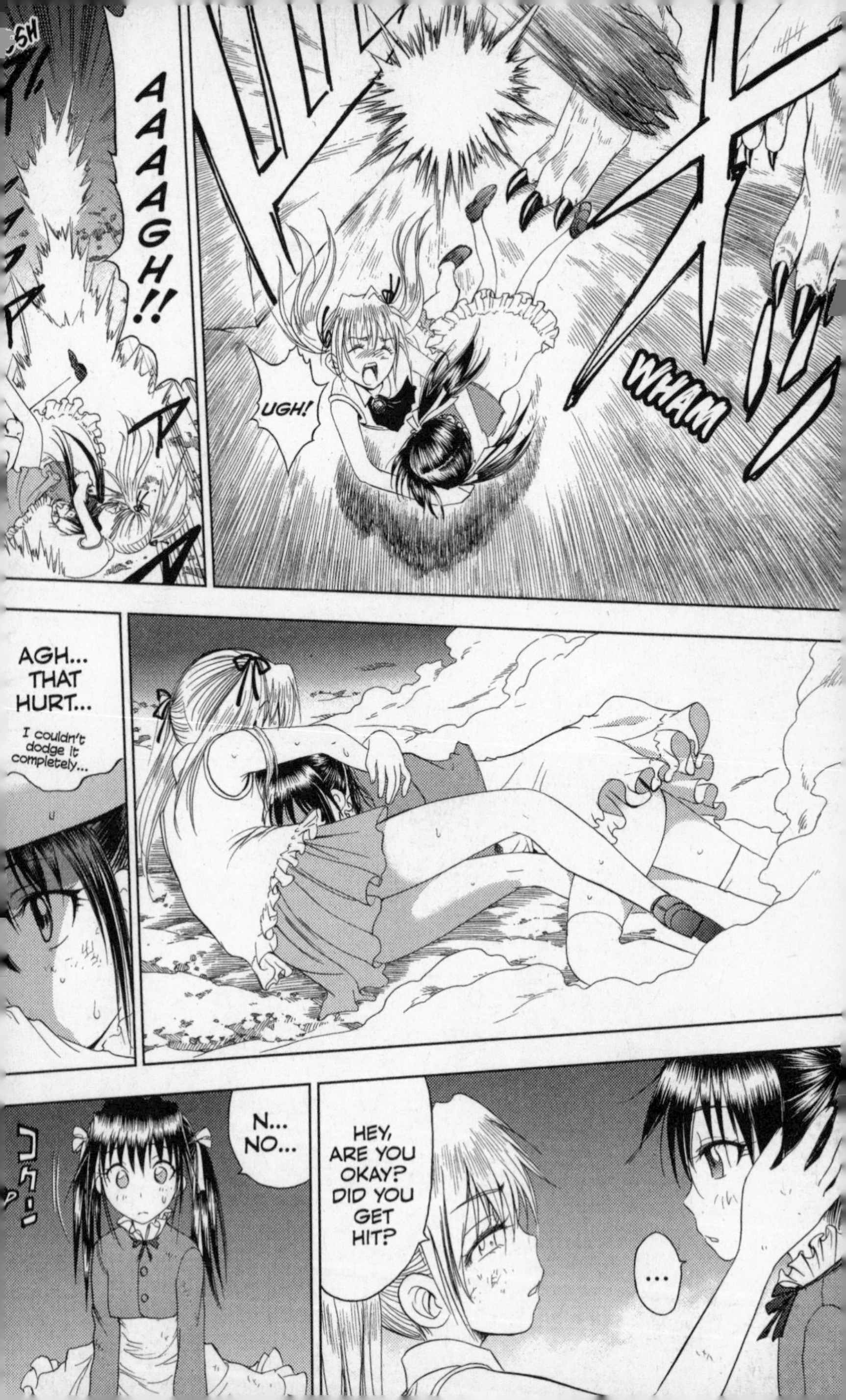
WHAM
UGH!
AAAAAGH!!
AGH... THAT HURT...
I couldn't dodge it completely...
HEY, ARE YOU OKAY? DID YOU GET HIT?
...
N... NO...

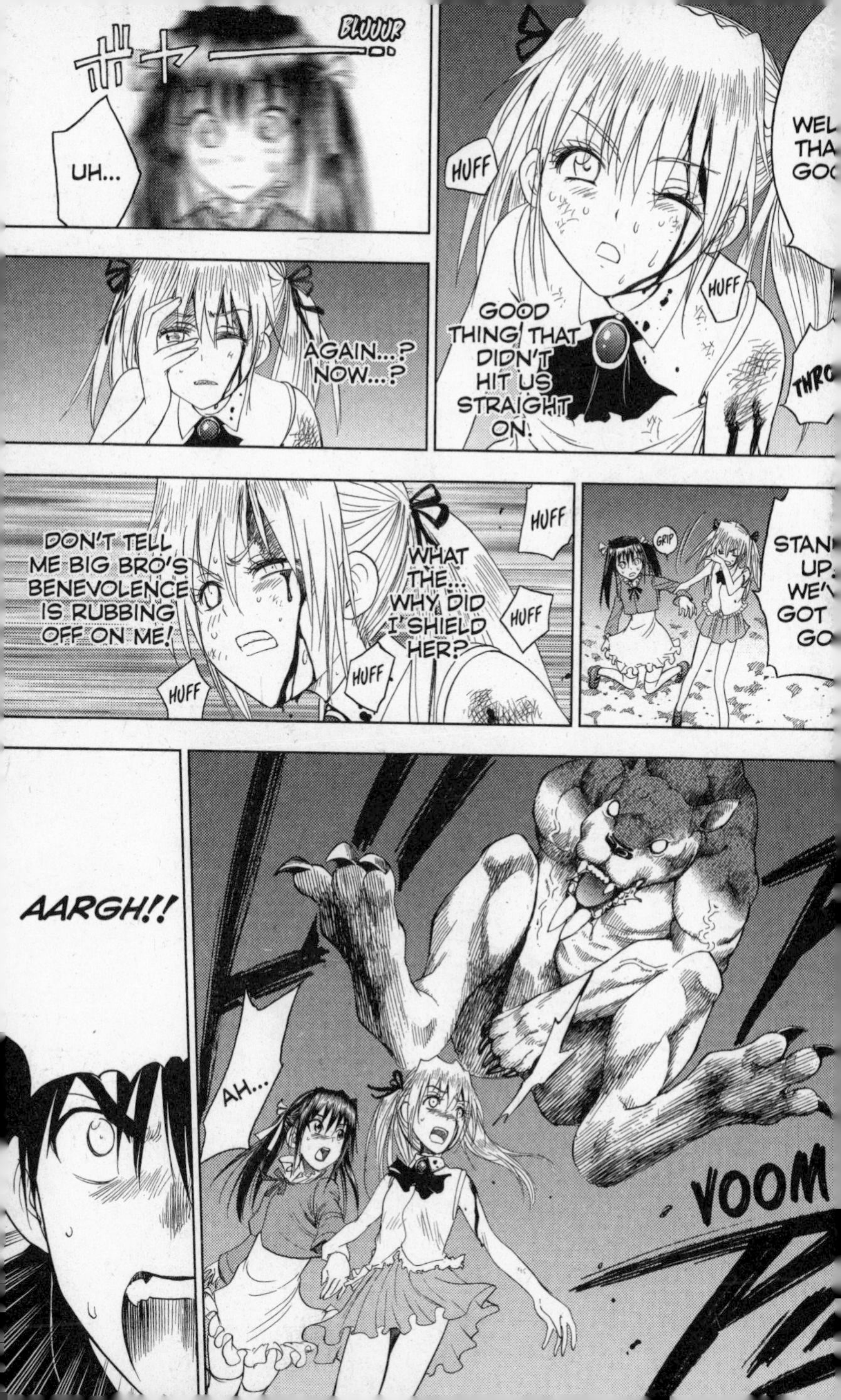

WEL THA GOO
HUFF
GOOD THING THAT DIDN'T HIT US STRAIGHT ON.
HUFF
THRO
ボヤー
BLUUUR
UH...
AGAIN...? NOW...?
STAN UP. WE'V GOT GO
GRIP
HUFF
WHAT THE... WHY DID I SHIELD HER?
HUFF
DON'T TELL ME BIG BRO'S BENEVOLENCE IS RUBBING OFF ON ME!
HUFF
HUFF
AH...
VOOM
AARGH!!

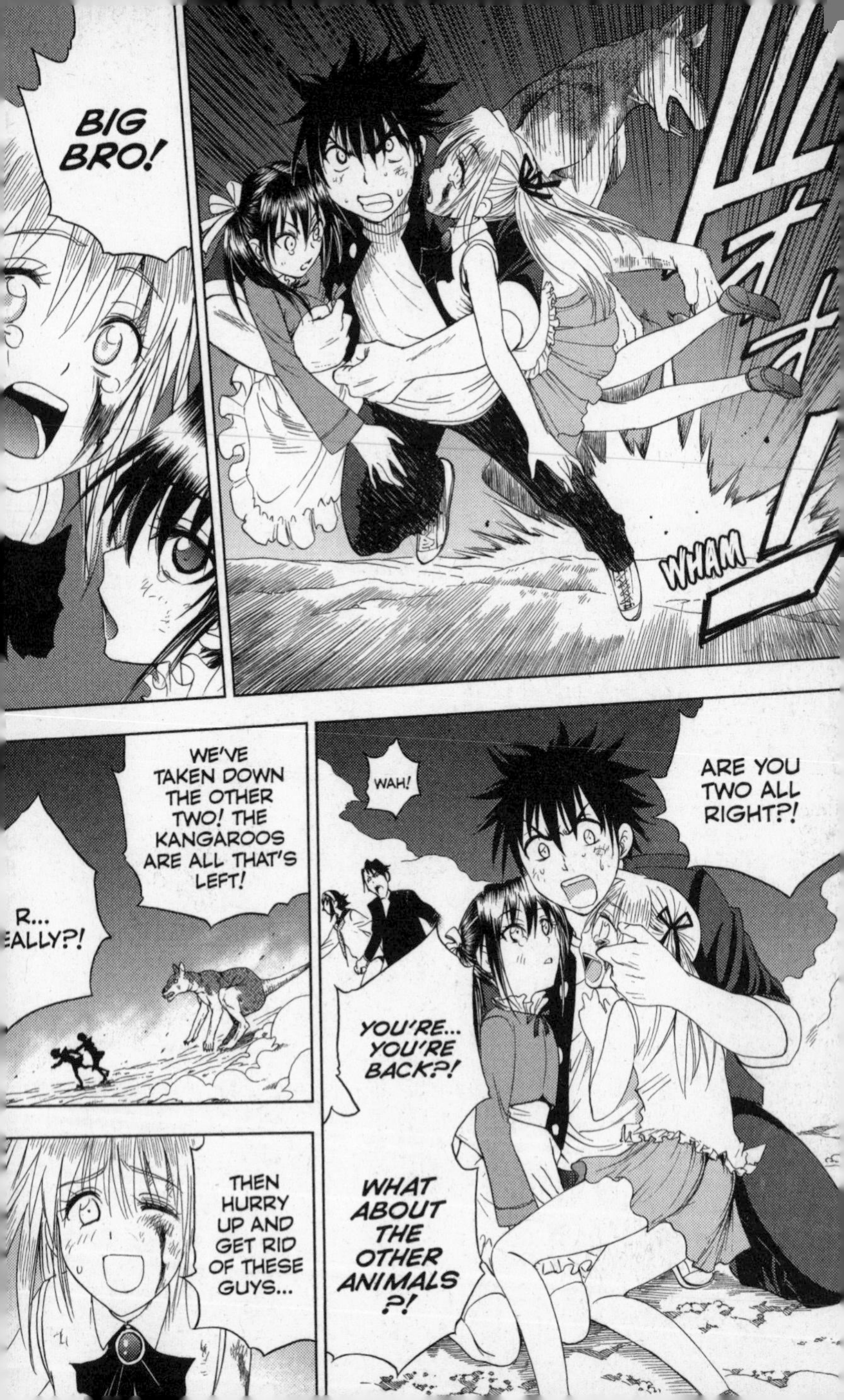
WHAM
BIG BRO!
ARE YOU TWO ALL RIGHT?!
WAH!
YOU'RE... YOU'RE BACK?!
WHAT ABOUT THE OTHER ANIMALS?!
WE'VE TAKEN DOWN THE OTHER TWO! THE KANGAROOS ARE ALL THAT'S LEFT!
R... EALLY?!
THEN HURRY UP AND GET RID OF THESE GUYS...

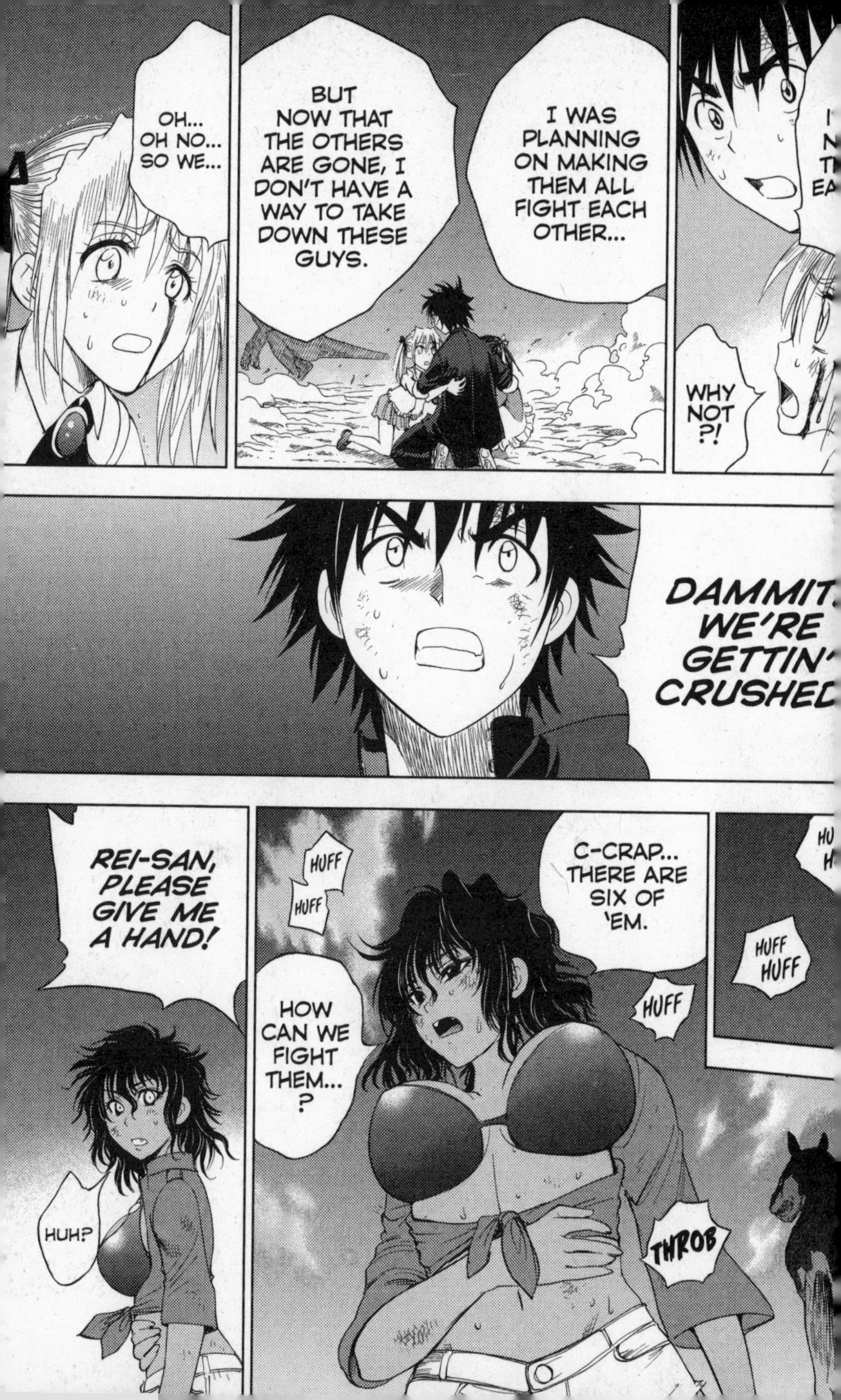
WHY NOT ?!
I WAS PLANNING ON MAKING THEM ALL FIGHT EACH OTHER...
BUT NOW THAT THE OTHERS ARE GONE, I DON'T HAVE A WAY TO TAKE DOWN THESE GUYS.
OH... OH NO... SO WE...
DAMMIT WE'RE GETTIN' CRUSHED
HUFF HUFF
C-CRAP... THERE ARE SIX OF 'EM.
HUFF
HUFF
HUFF
HOW CAN WE FIGHT THEM...?
THROB
REI-SAN, PLEASE GIVE ME A HAND!
HUH?

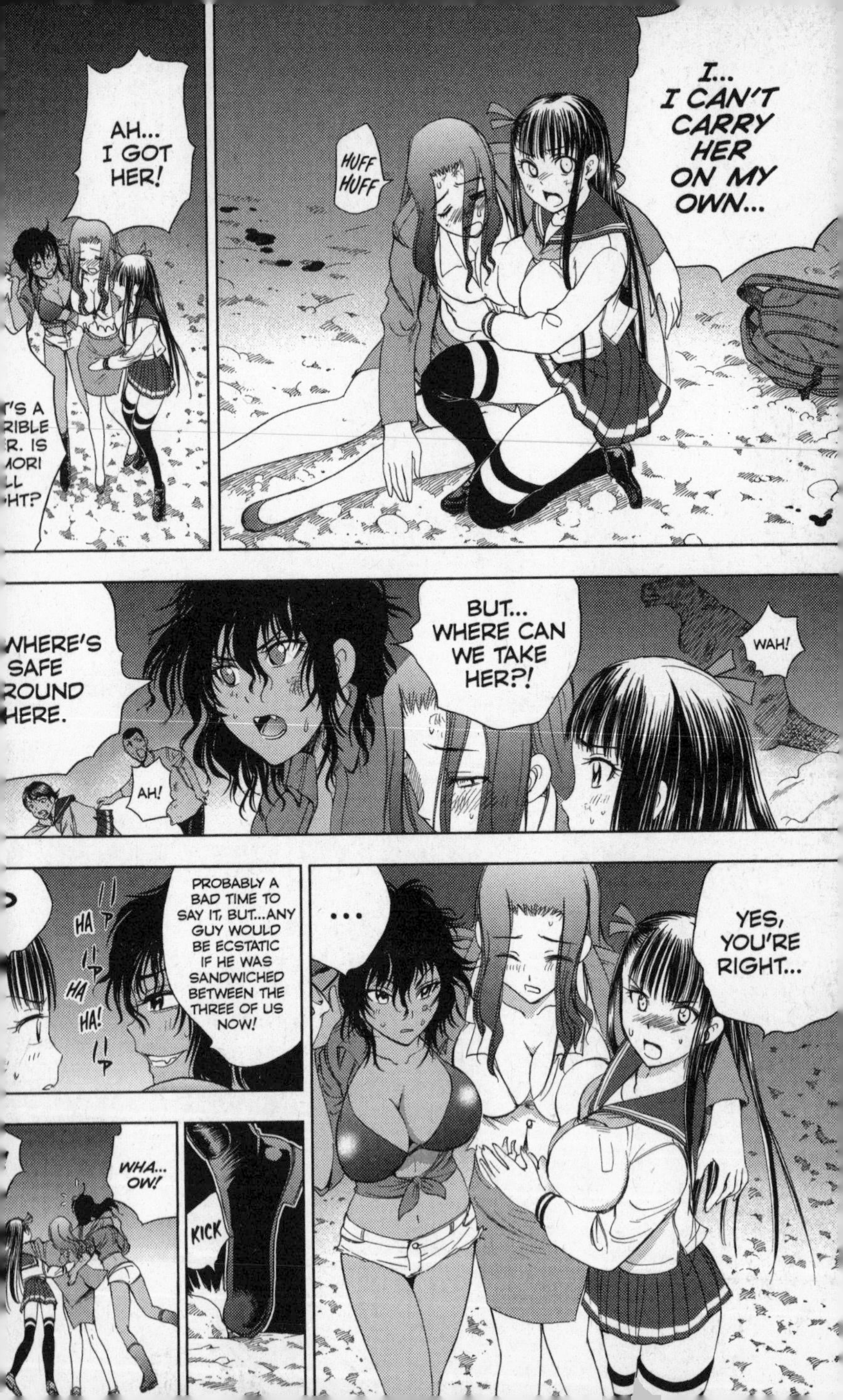
I... I CAN'T CARRY HER ON MY OWN...
HUFF HUFF
AH... I GOT HER!
T'S A RIBLE R. IS MORI LL HT?
WAH!
BUT... WHERE CAN WE TAKE HER?!
WHERE'S SAFE ROUND HERE.
AH!
YES, YOU'RE RIGHT...
...
PROBABLY A BAD TIME TO SAY IT, BUT...ANY GUY WOULD BE ECSTATIC IF HE WAS SANDWICHED BETWEEN THE THREE OF US NOW!
HA HA HA!
KICK
WHA... OW!

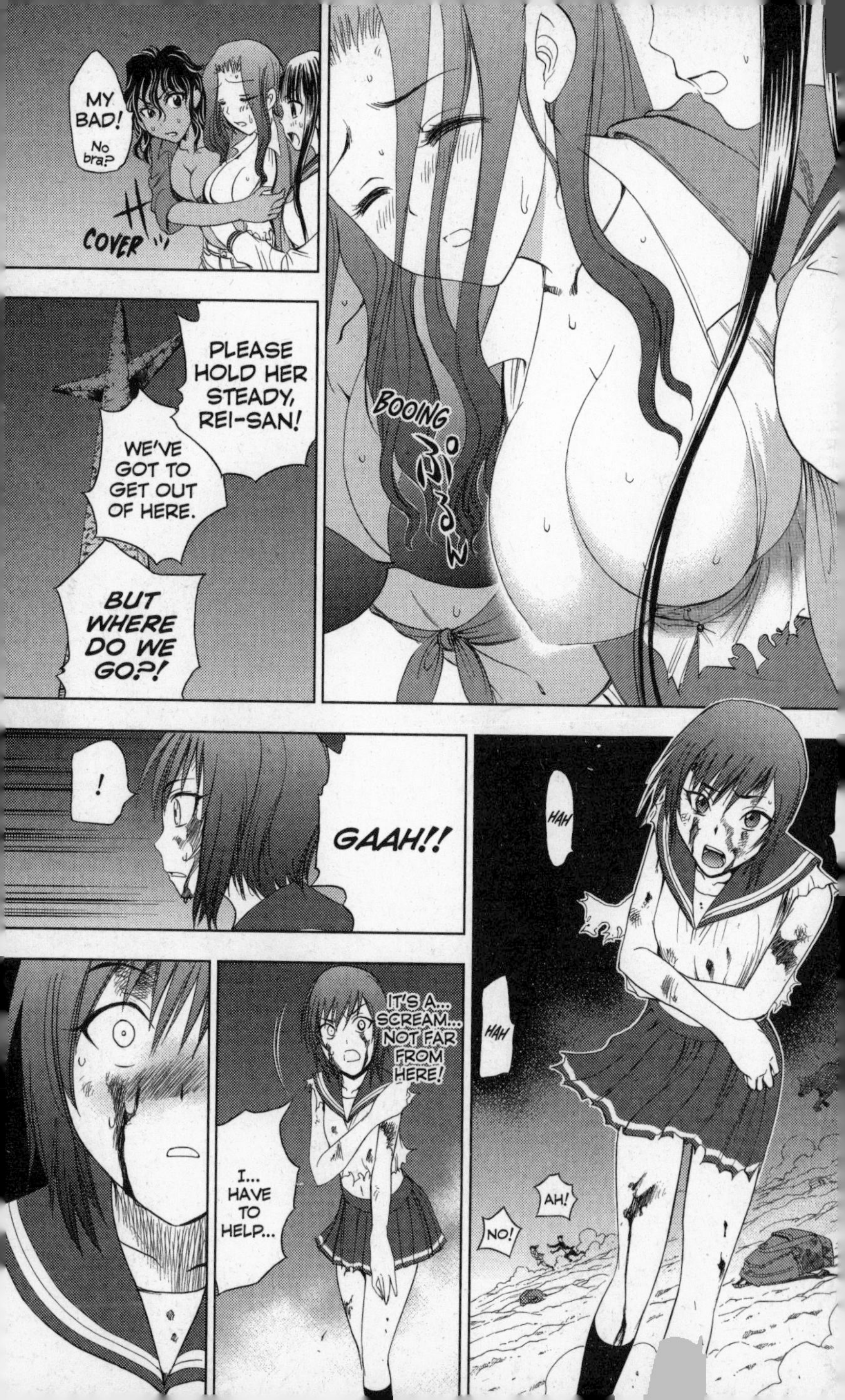

BOOING
MY BAD!
No bra?
COVER
PLEASE HOLD HER STEADY, REI-SAN!
WE'VE GOT TO GET OUT OF HERE.
BUT WHERE DO WE GO?!
HAH
HAH
AH!
NO!
!
GAAH!!
IT'S A... SCREAM... NOT FAR FROM HERE!
I... HAVE TO HELP...

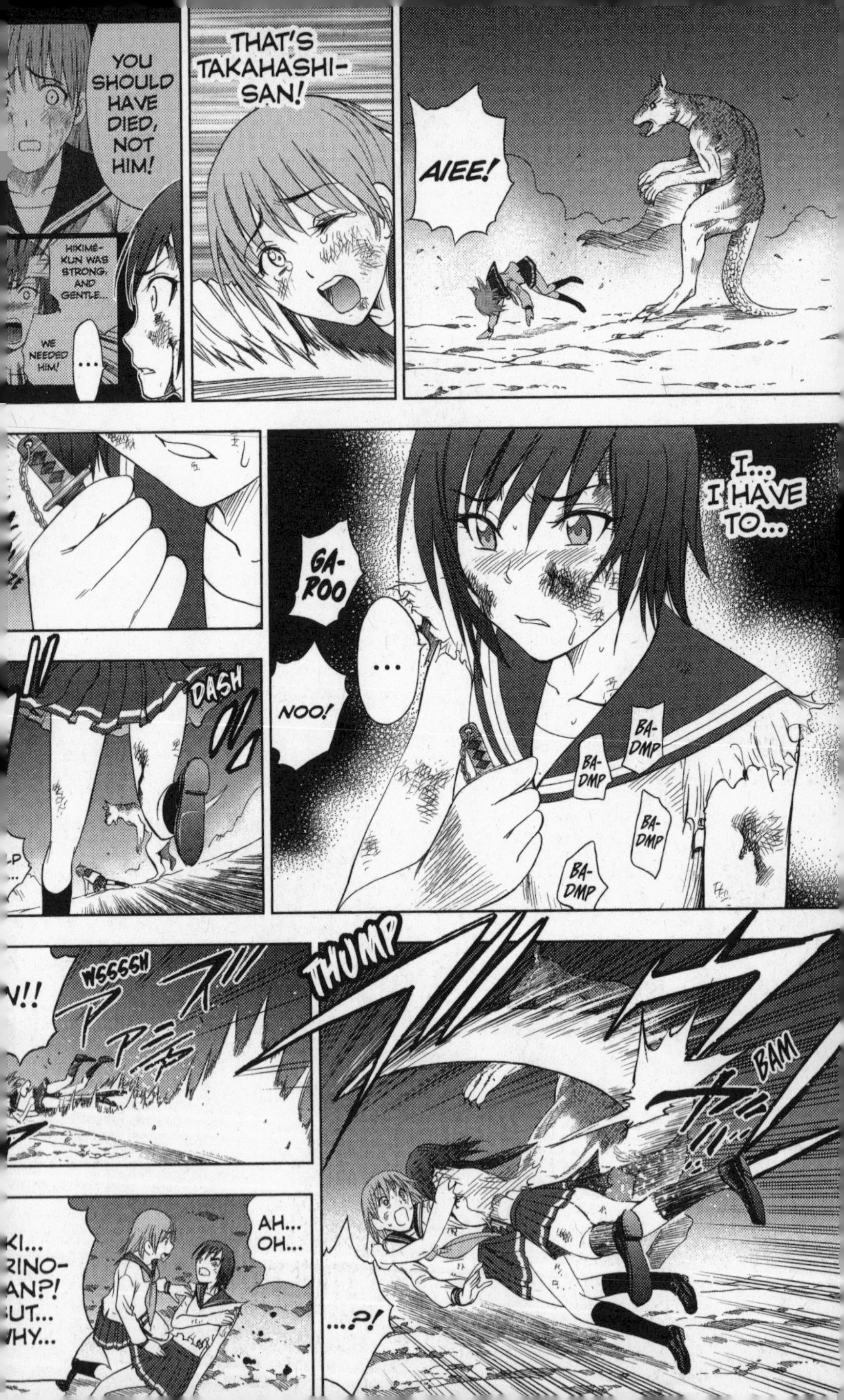
AIEE!
THAT'S TAKAHASHI-SAN!
YOU SHOULD HAVE DIED, NOT HIM!
HIKIME-KUN WAS STRONG, AND GENTLE...
WE NEEDED HIM!
...
I... I HAVE TO...
GA-ROO
...
NOO!
BA-DMP
BA-DMP
BA-DMP
BA-DMP
DASH
THUMP
BAM
...?!
WSSSSH
AH... OH...

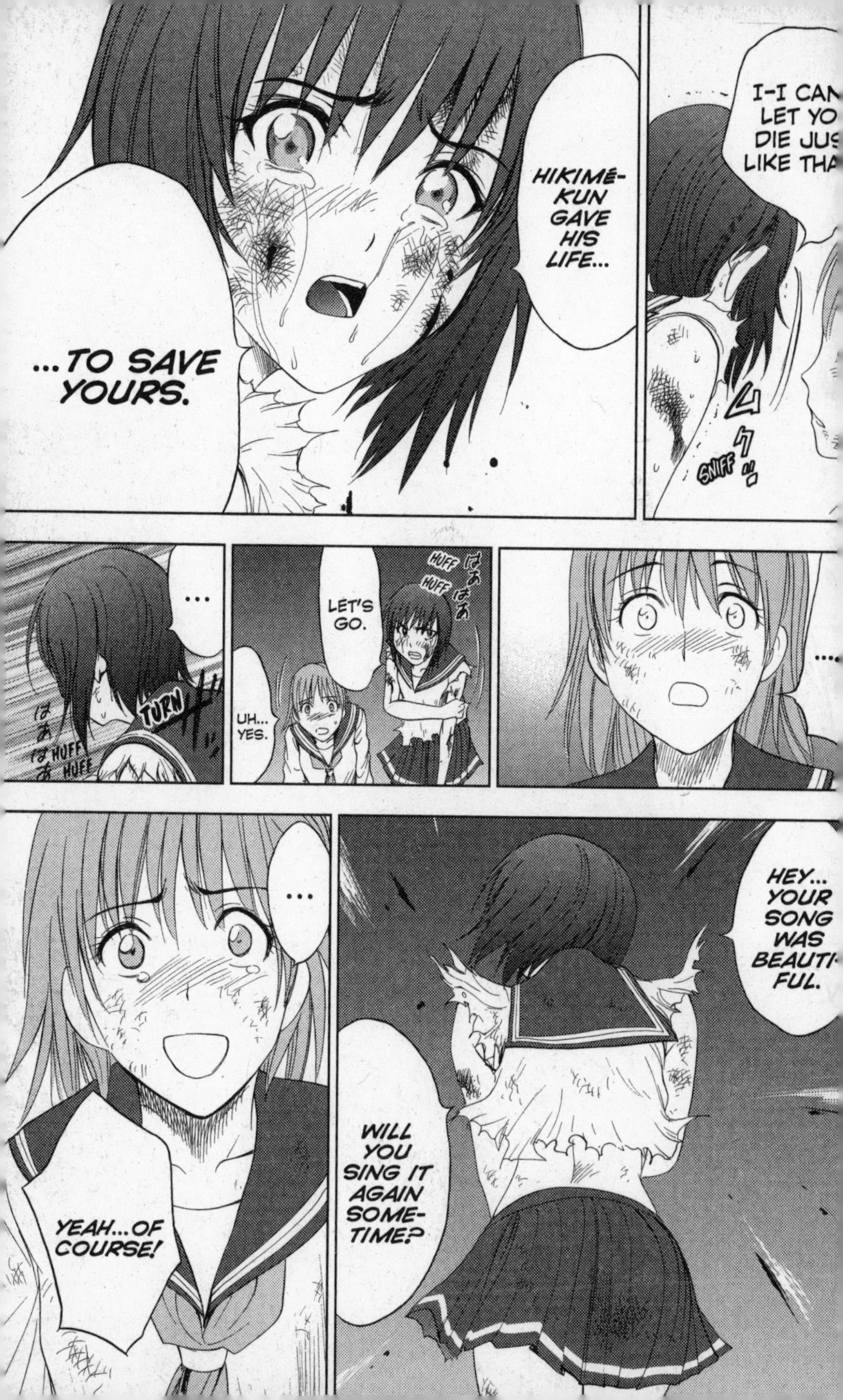

I-I CAN
LET YO
DIE JUS
LIKE THA
SNIFF
HIKIMÉ-KUN GAVE HIS LIFE...
...TO SAVE YOURS.
....
HUFF HUFF
LET'S GO.
UH... YES.
...
TURN
HUFF HUFF
HEY... YOUR SONG WAS BEAUTIFUL.
WILL YOU SING IT AGAIN SOMETIME?
...
YEAH...OF COURSE!

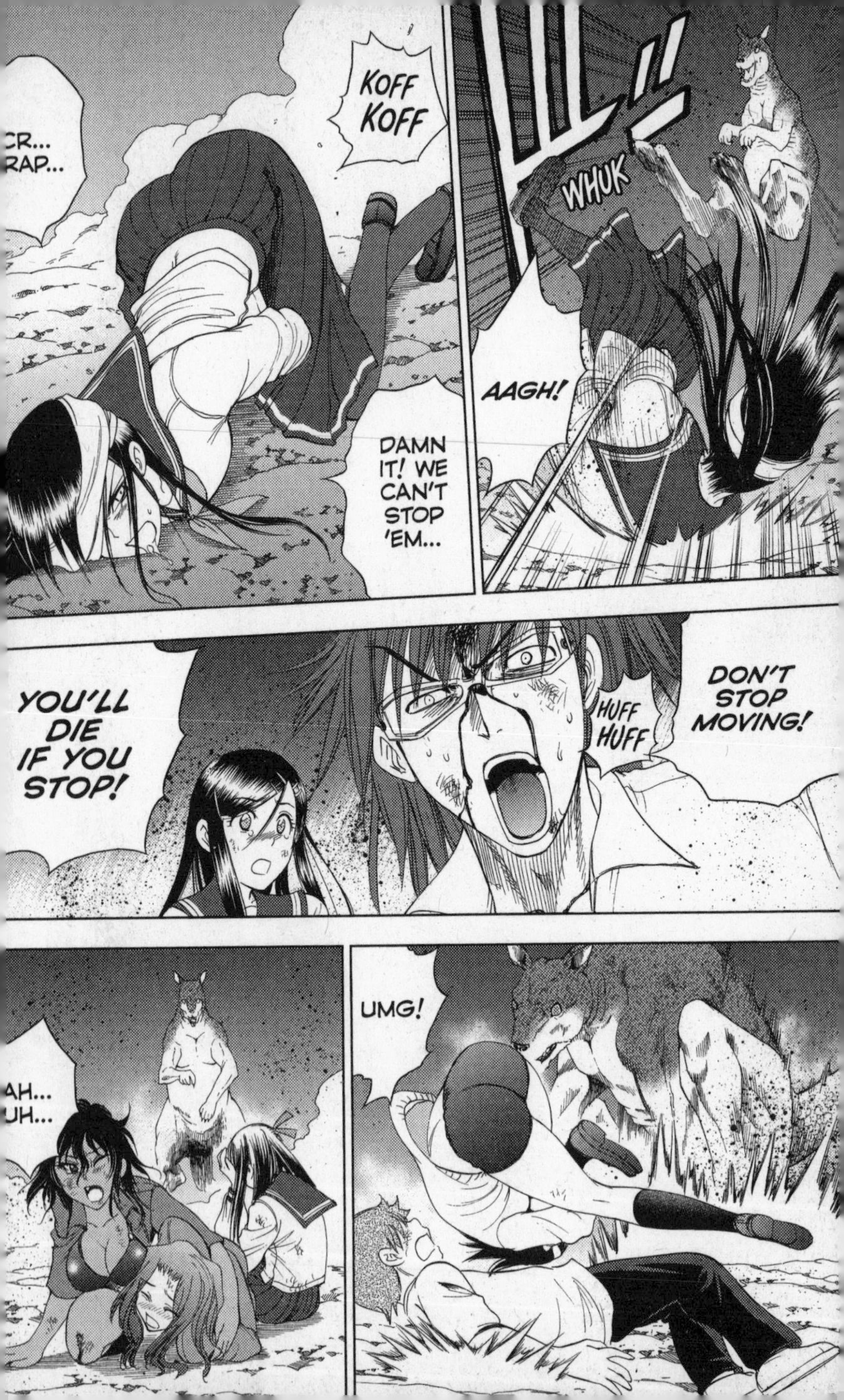
WHUK
AAGH!
DAMN IT! WE CAN'T STOP 'EM...
KOFF KOFF
CR... RAP...
DON'T STOP MOVING!
HUFF HUFF
YOU'LL DIE IF YOU STOP!
UMG!
AH... UH...

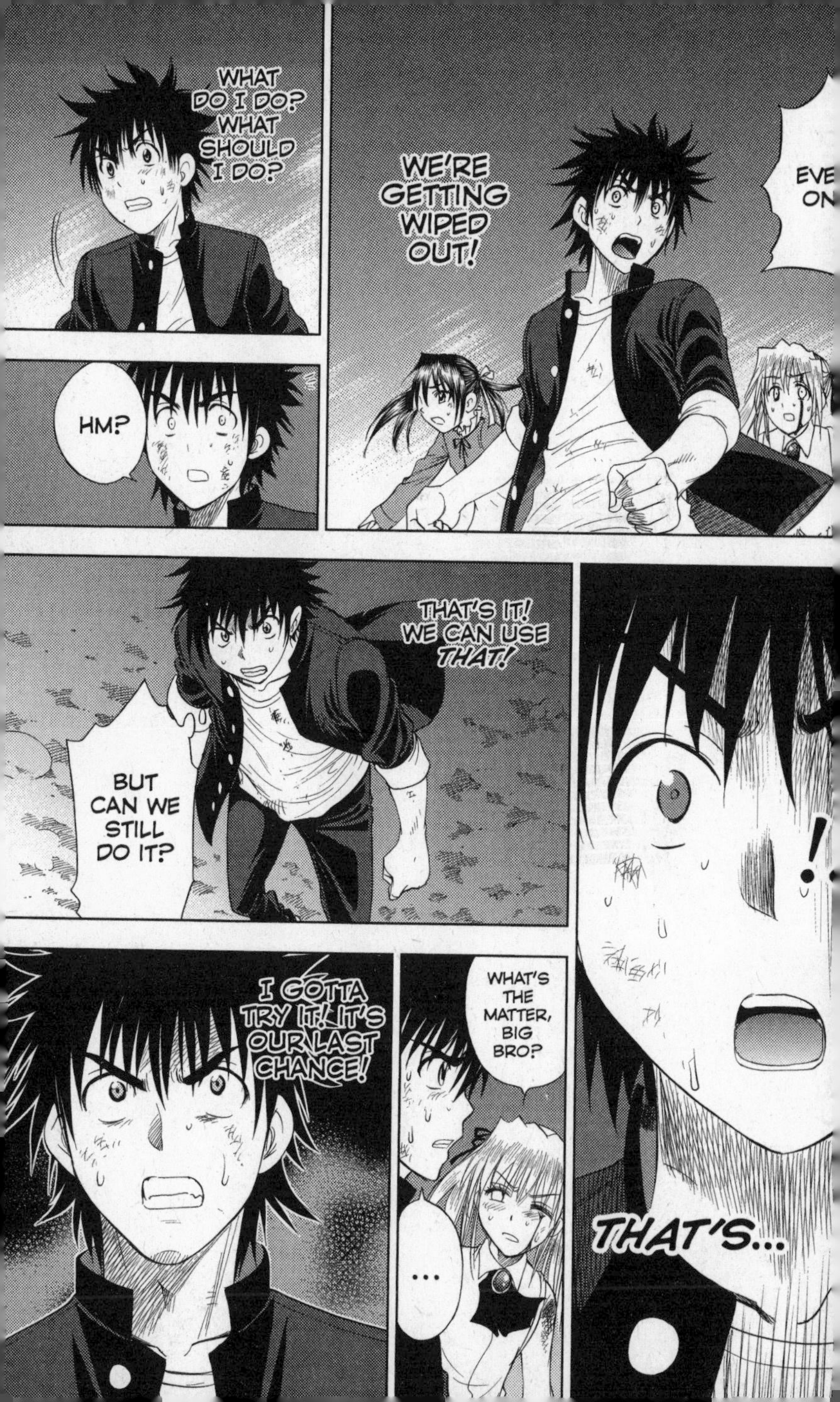

EVE ON
WE'RE GETTING WIPED OUT!
WHAT DO I DO? WHAT SHOULD I DO?
HM?
!!
THAT'S...
THAT'S IT! WE CAN USE *THAT!*
BUT CAN WE STILL DO IT?
WHAT'S THE MATTER, BIG BRO?
...
I GOTTA TRY IT! IT'S OUR LAST CHANCE!

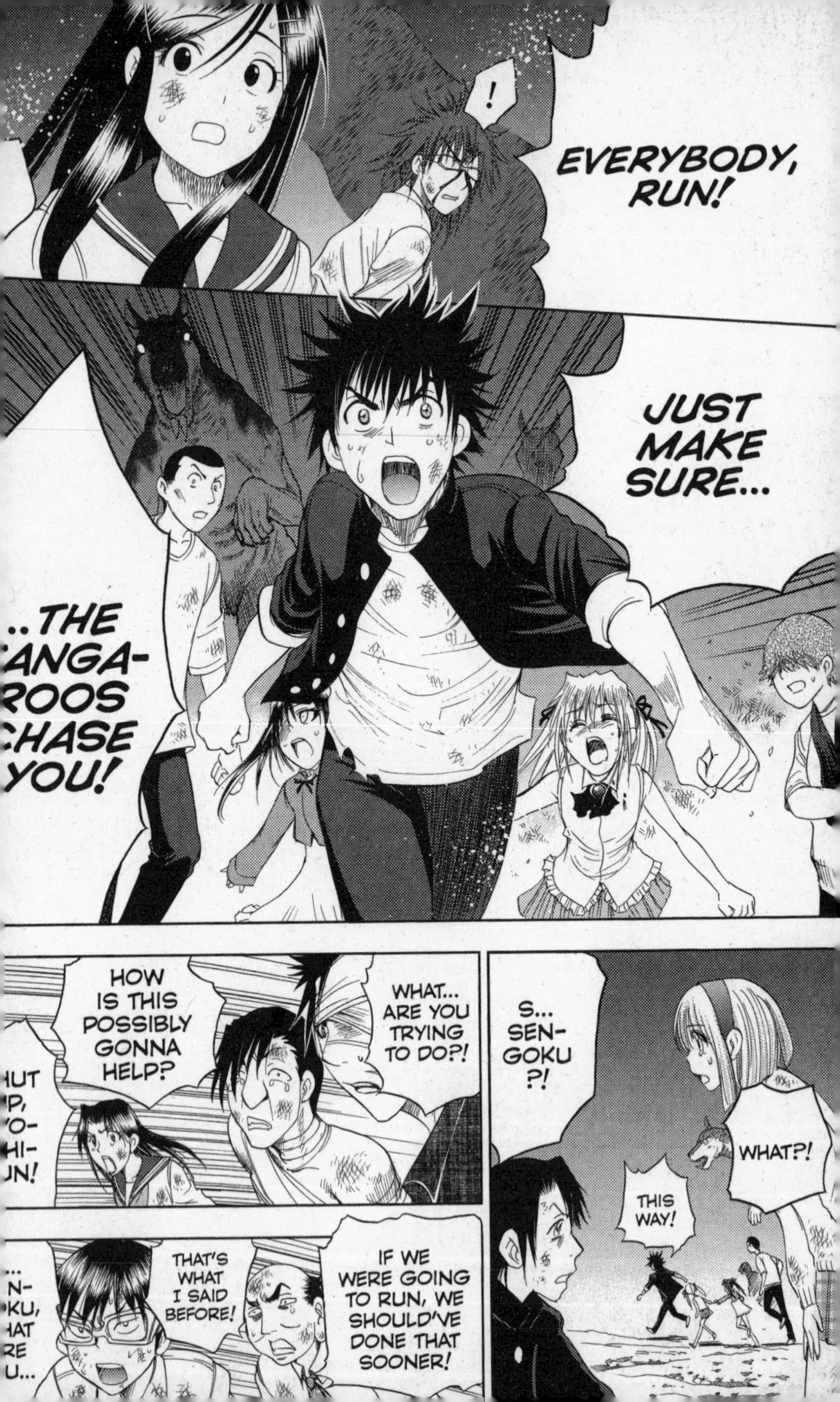
!
EVERYBODY, RUN!
JUST MAKE SURE...
..THE ANGA- ROOS HASE YOU!
S... SEN- GOKU ?!
WHAT?!
THIS WAY!
WHAT... ARE YOU TRYING TO DO?!
HOW IS THIS POSSIBLY GONNA HELP?
HUT P, O- HI- JN!
IF WE WERE GOING TO RUN, WE SHOULD'VE DONE THAT SOONER!
THAT'S WHAT I SAID BEFORE!
... N- KU, HAT RE U...

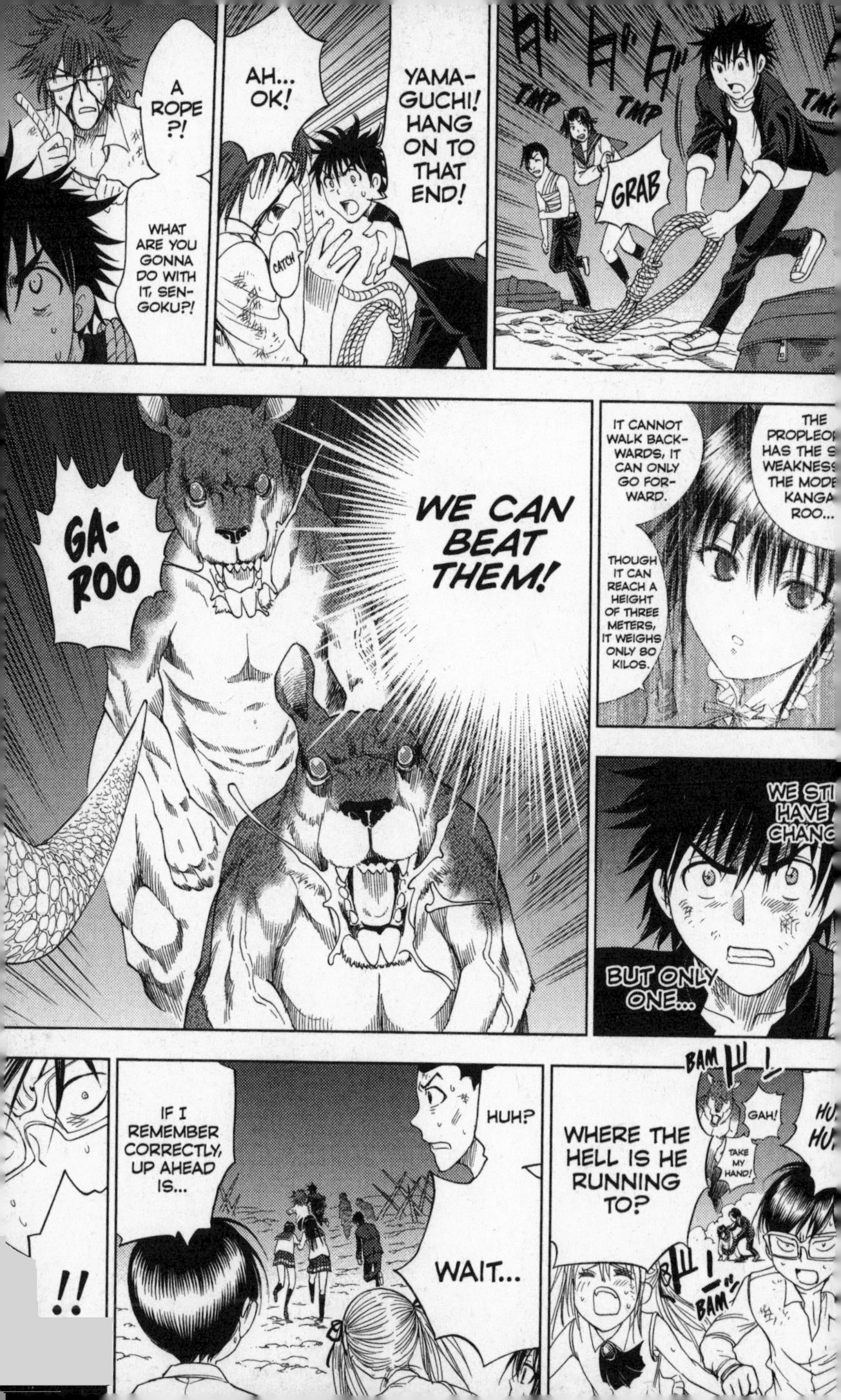

TMP
TMP
TMP
GRAB
YAMA-GUCHI! HANG ON TO THAT END!
AH... OK!
CATCH
A ROPE?!
WHAT ARE YOU GONNA DO WITH IT, SEN-GOKU?!
THE PROPLEOP HAS THE S WEAKNESS THE MODE KANGA ROO...
IT CANNOT WALK BACK-WARDS, IT CAN ONLY GO FOR-WARD.
THOUGH IT CAN REACH A HEIGHT OF THREE METERS, IT WEIGHS ONLY 80 KILOS.
WE STI HAVE CHANC
BUT ONLY ONE...
WE CAN BEAT THEM!
GA-ROO
BAM
GAH!
HU HU
TAKE MY HAND!
WHERE THE HELL IS HE RUNNING TO?
BAM
BAM
HUH?
IF I REMEMBER CORRECTLY, UP AHEAD IS...
WAIT...
!!

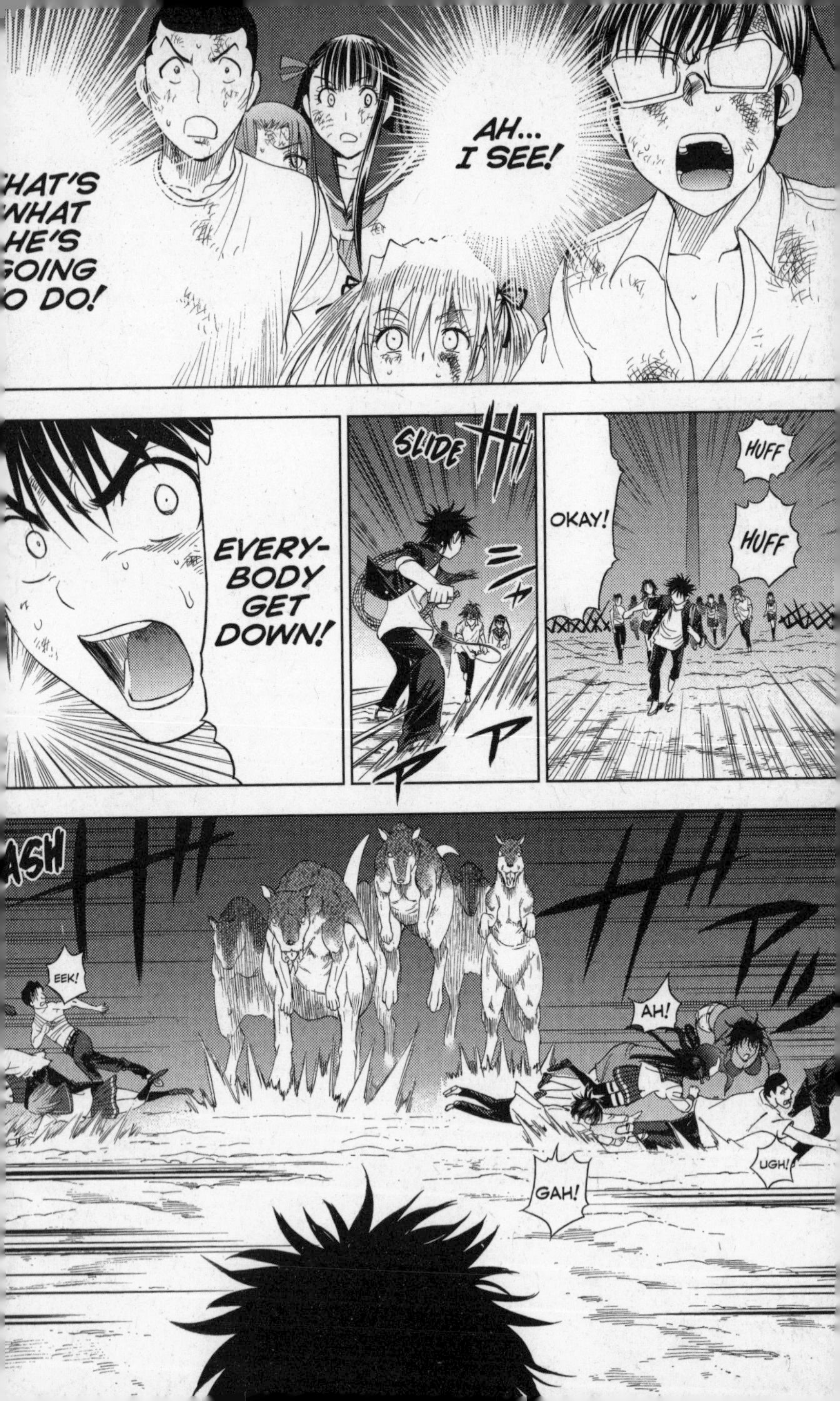
AH... I SEE!
HAT'S WHAT HE'S GOING O DO!
HUFF
HUFF
OKAY!
SLIDE
EVERY-BODY GET DOWN!
AH!
UGH!
GAH!
EEK!
ASH

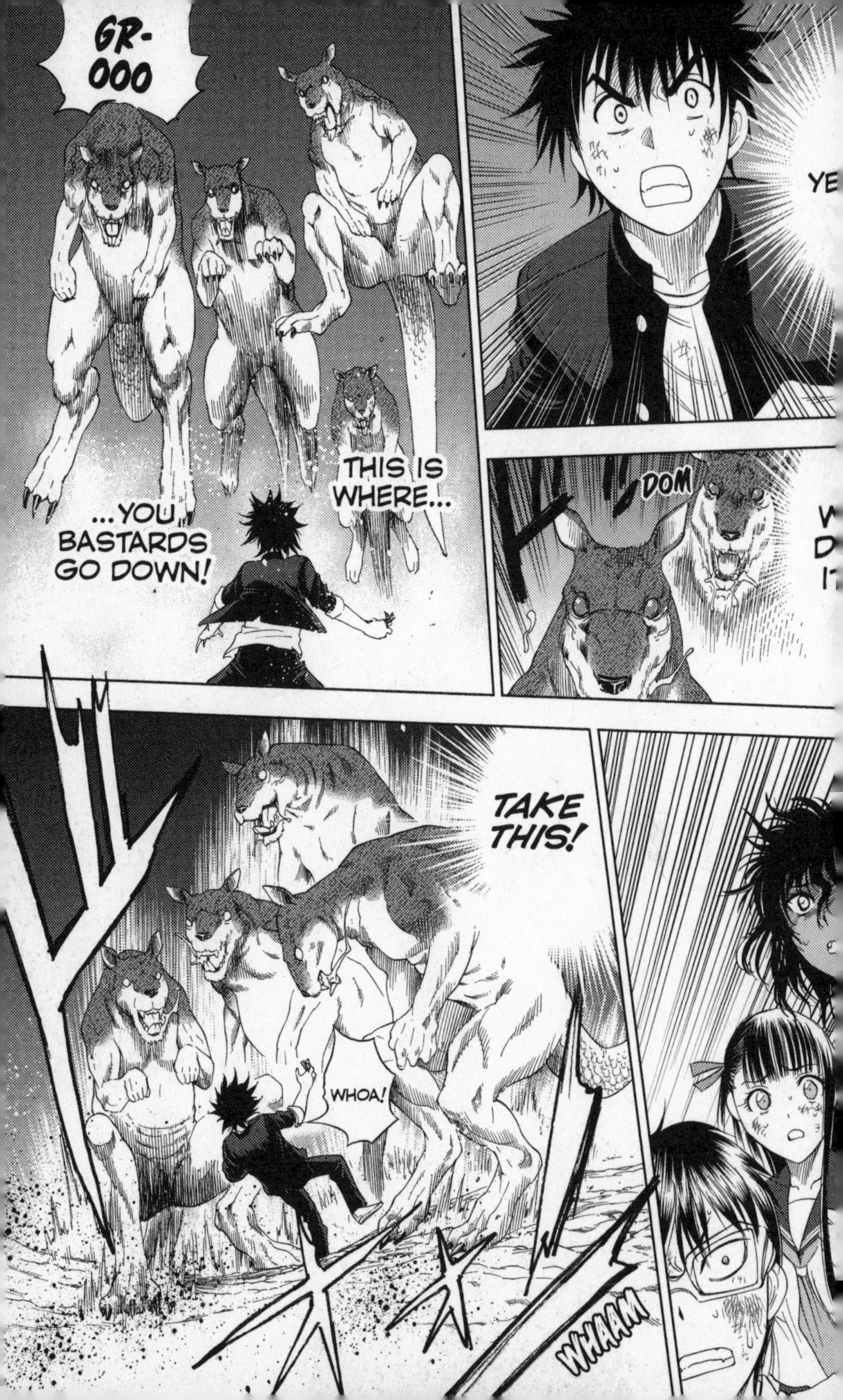
DOM
GR-OOO
THIS IS WHERE...
...YOU BASTARDS GO DOWN!
WHAAM
TAKE THIS!
WHOA!

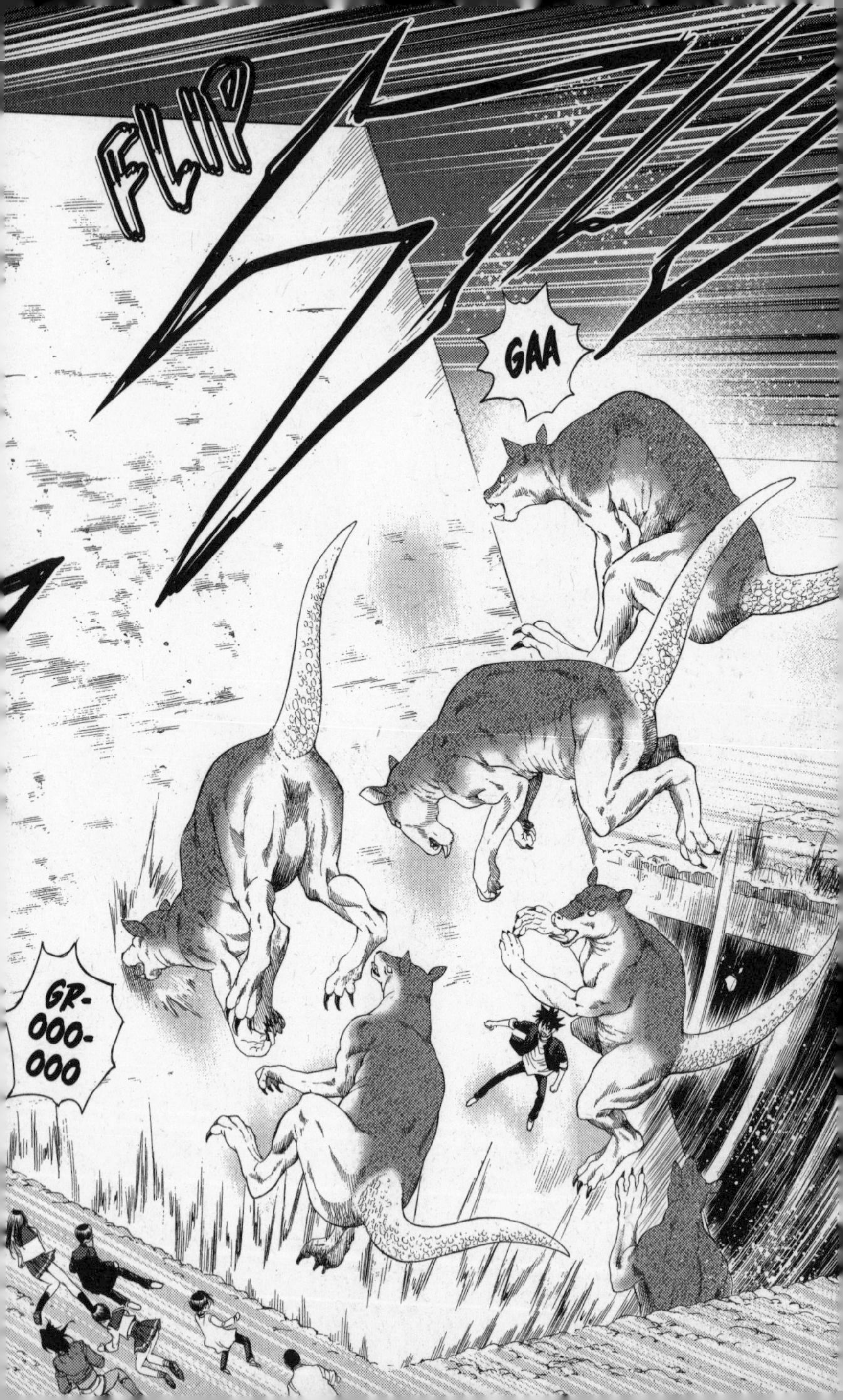
FLIP
GAA
GR-OOO-OOO

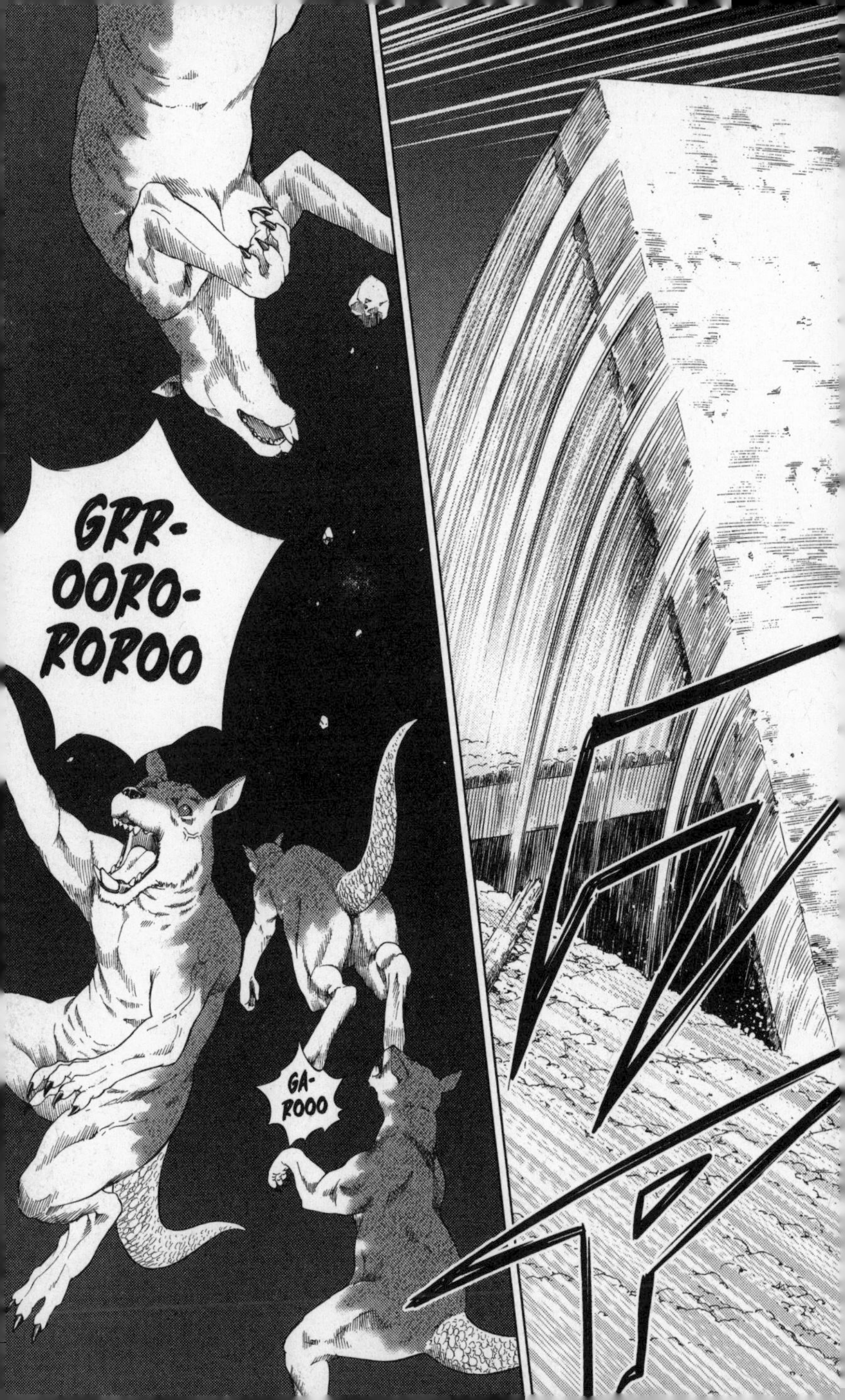
GRR-
OORO-
ROROO
GA-
ROOO

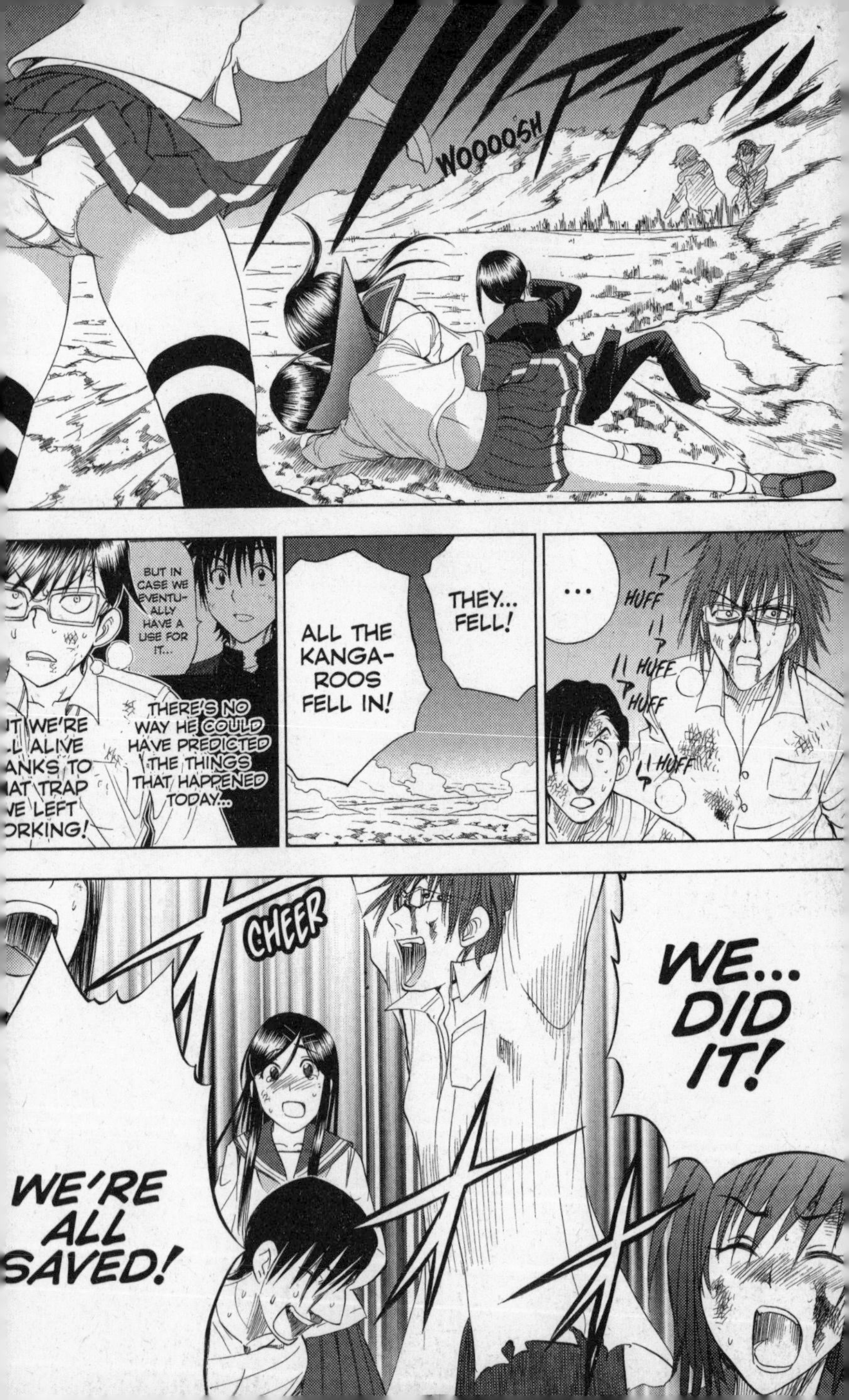
WOOOOSH
...
HUFF
HUFF
HUFF
HUFF
THEY... FELL!
ALL THE KANGAROOS FELL IN!
BUT IN CASE WE EVENTUALLY HAVE A USE FOR IT...
THERE'S NO WAY HE COULD HAVE PREDICTED THE THINGS THAT HAPPENED TODAY...
UT WE'RE L ALIVE ANKS TO AT TRAP VE LEFT ORKING!
CHEER
WE... DID IT!
WE'RE ALL SAVED!

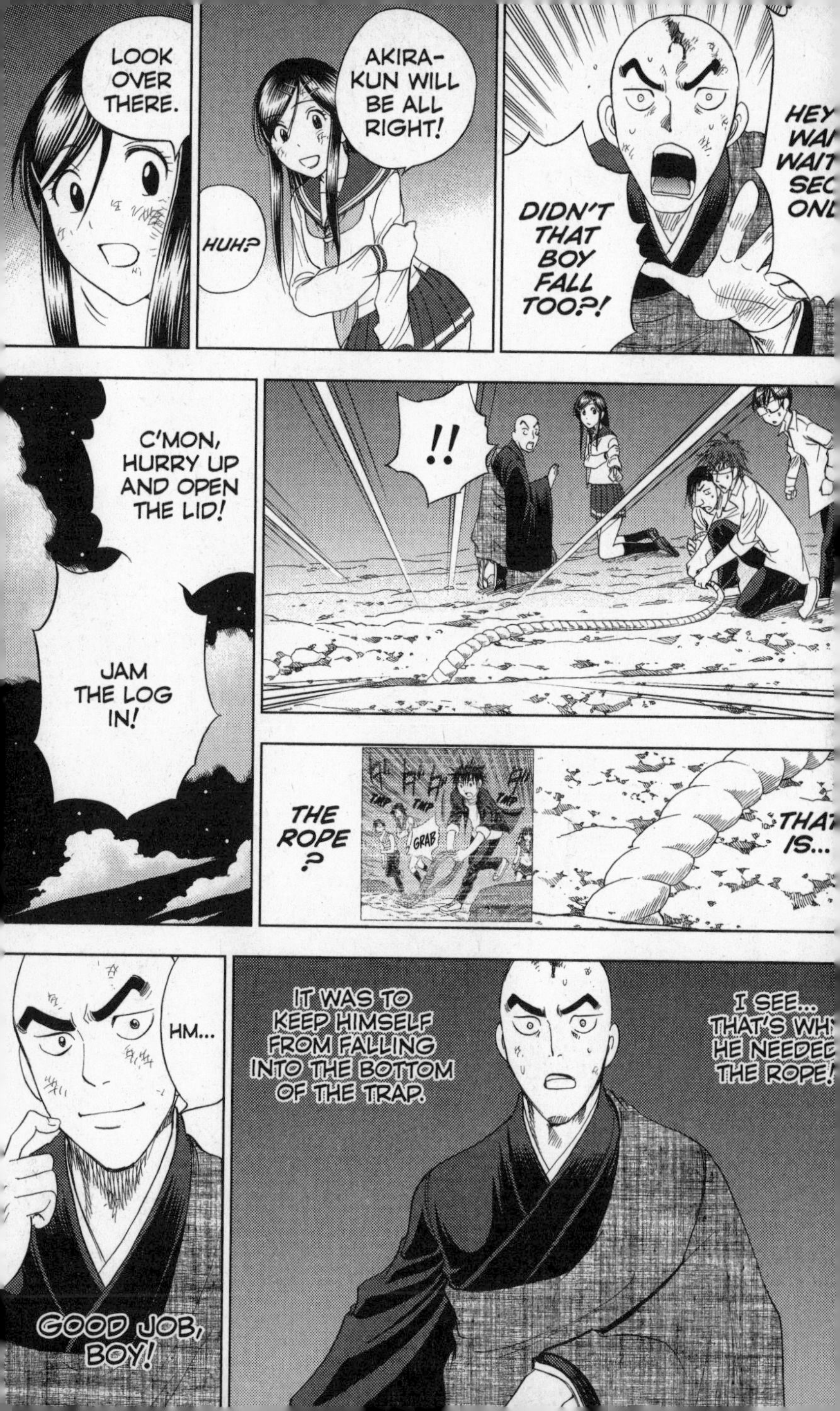
HEY WAI WAIT SEC ONL
DIDN'T THAT BOY FALL TOO?!
AKIRA-KUN WILL BE ALL RIGHT!
HUH?
LOOK OVER THERE.
!!
THAT IS...
THE ROPE?
GRAB
C'MON, HURRY UP AND OPEN THE LID!
JAM THE LOG IN!
I SEE... THAT'S WH HE NEEDED THE ROPE!
IT WAS TO KEEP HIMSELF FROM FALLING INTO THE BOTTOM OF THE TRAP.
HM...
GOOD JOB, BOY!

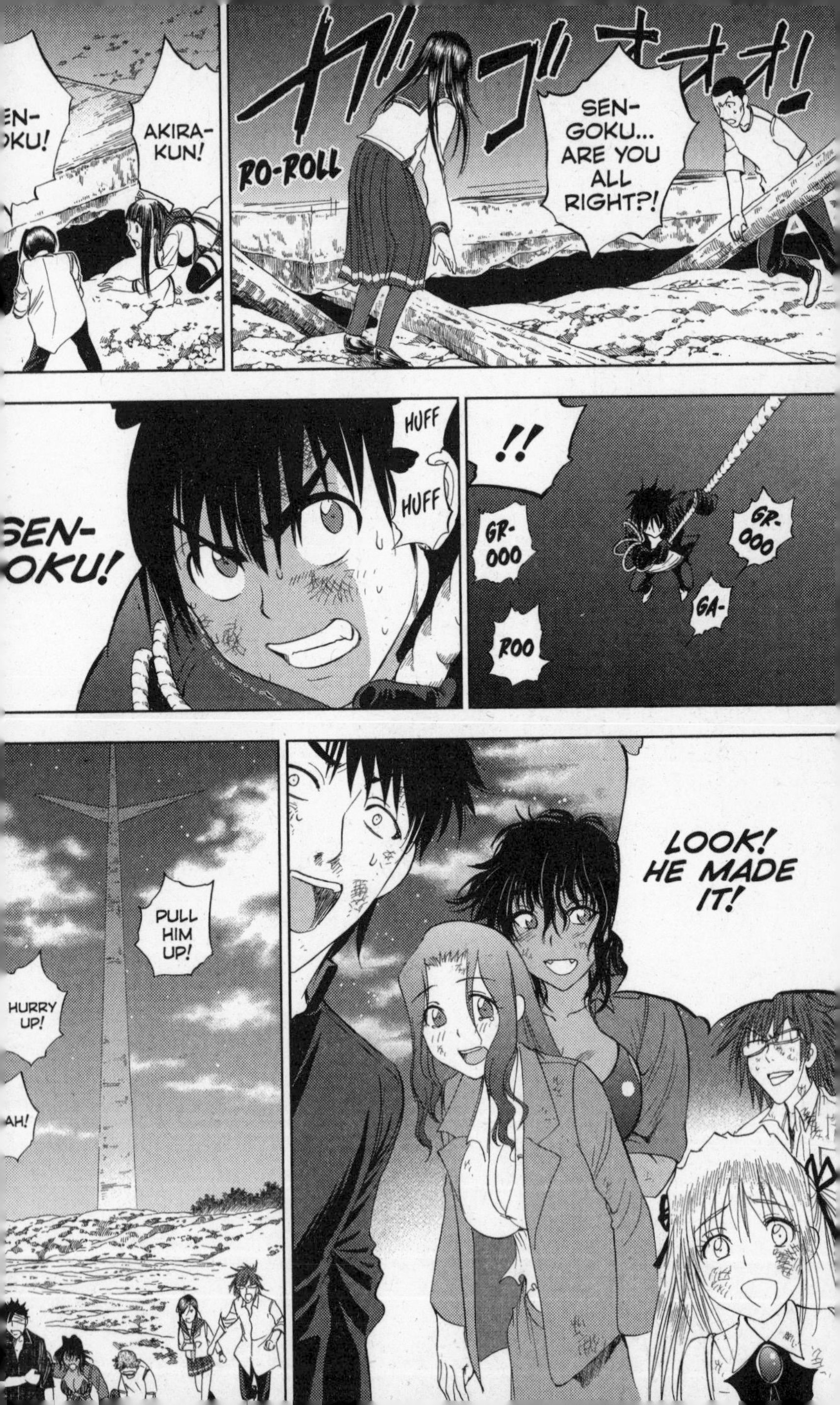
SEN-GOKU... ARE YOU ALL RIGHT?!
RO-ROLL
AKIRA-KUN!
EN-OKU!
!!
GR-OOO
GR-OOO
GA-
ROO
HUFF
HUFF
SEN-OKU!
LOOK! HE MADE IT!
PULL HIM UP!
HURRY UP!
AH!

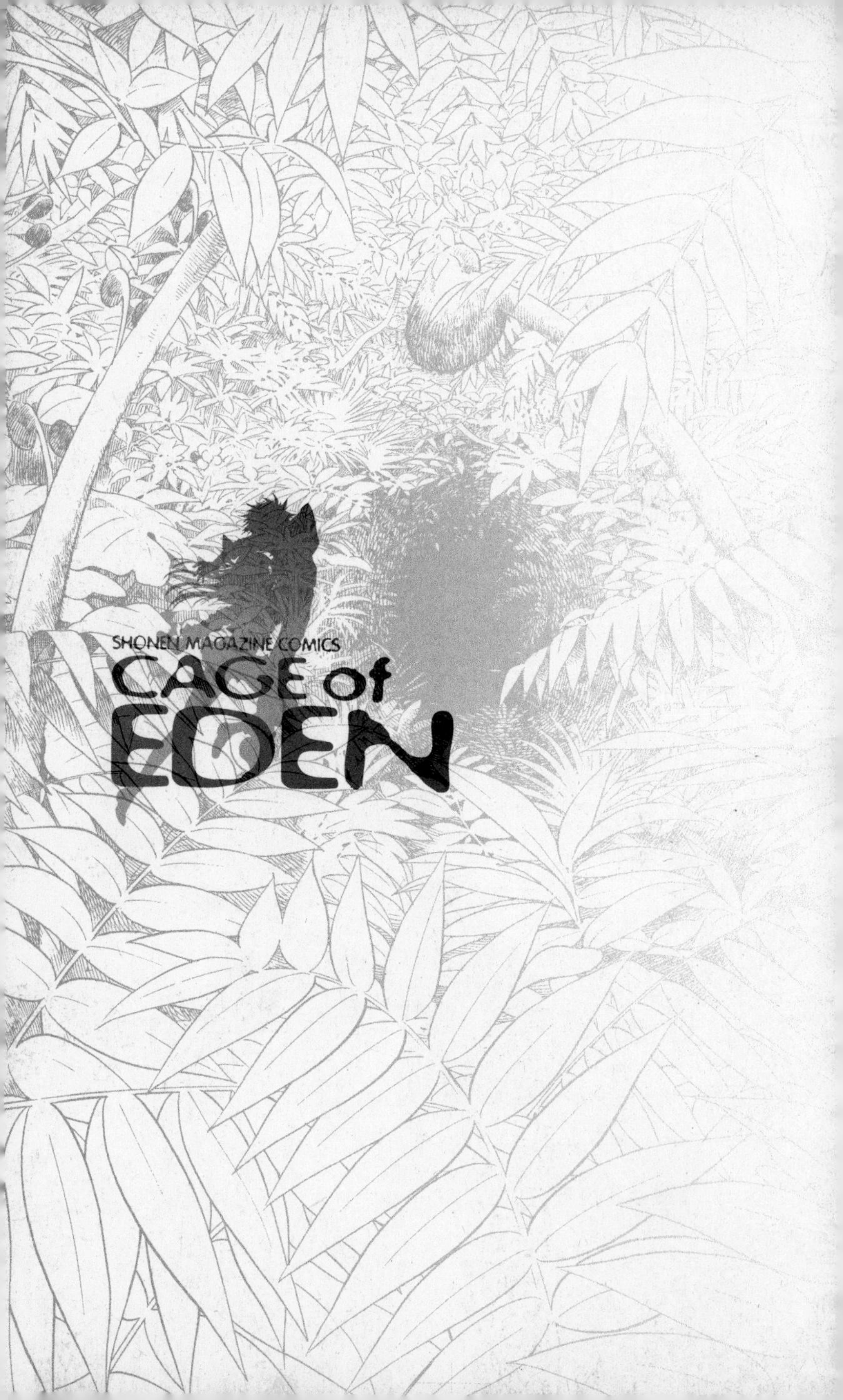
SHONEN MAGAZINE COMICS
CAGE of EDEN

Chapter 100: Excavation

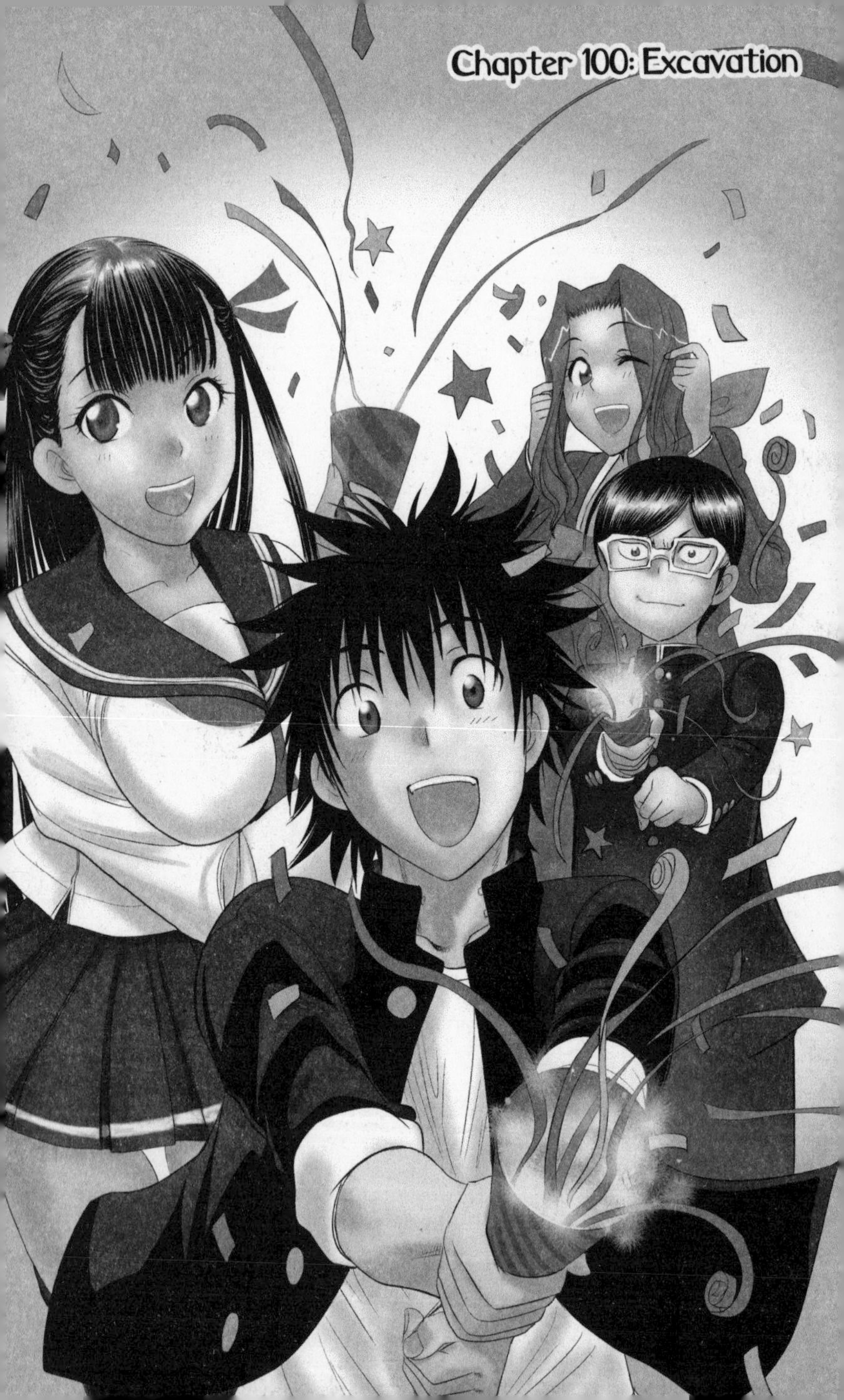

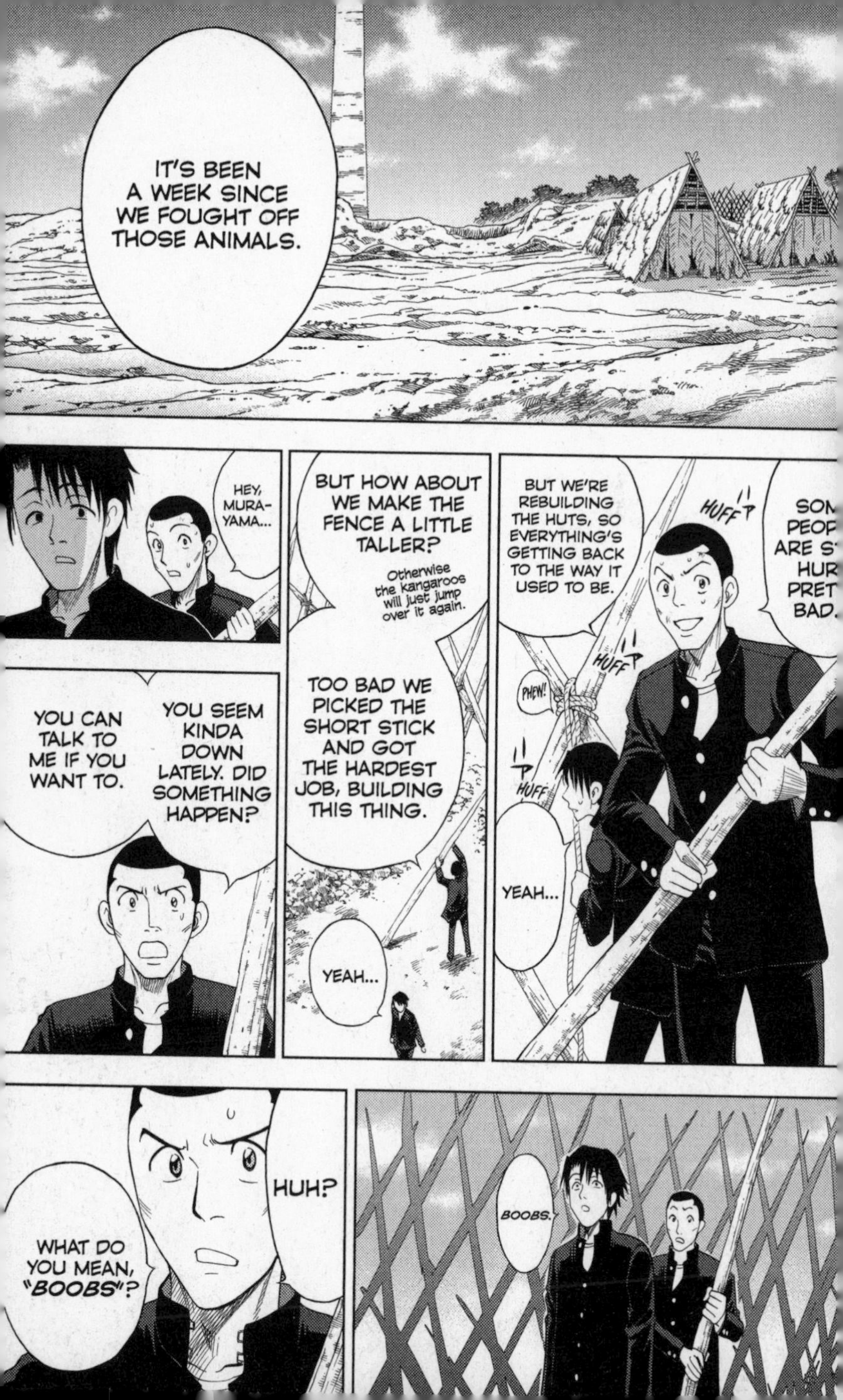
IT'S BEEN A WEEK SINCE WE FOUGHT OFF THOSE ANIMALS.
SOM PEOP ARE S HUR PRET BAD.
BUT WE'RE REBUILDING THE HUTS, SO EVERYTHING'S GETTING BACK TO THE WAY IT USED TO BE.
HUFF
HUFF
PHEW!
HUFF
YEAH...
BUT HOW ABOUT WE MAKE THE FENCE A LITTLE TALLER?
Otherwise the kangaroos will just jump over it again.
TOO BAD WE PICKED THE SHORT STICK AND GOT THE HARDEST JOB, BUILDING THIS THING.
YEAH...
HEY, MURA-YAMA...
YOU SEEM KINDA DOWN LATELY. DID SOMETHING HAPPEN?
YOU CAN TALK TO ME IF YOU WANT TO.
BOOBS.
HUH?
WHAT DO YOU MEAN, "BOOBS"?

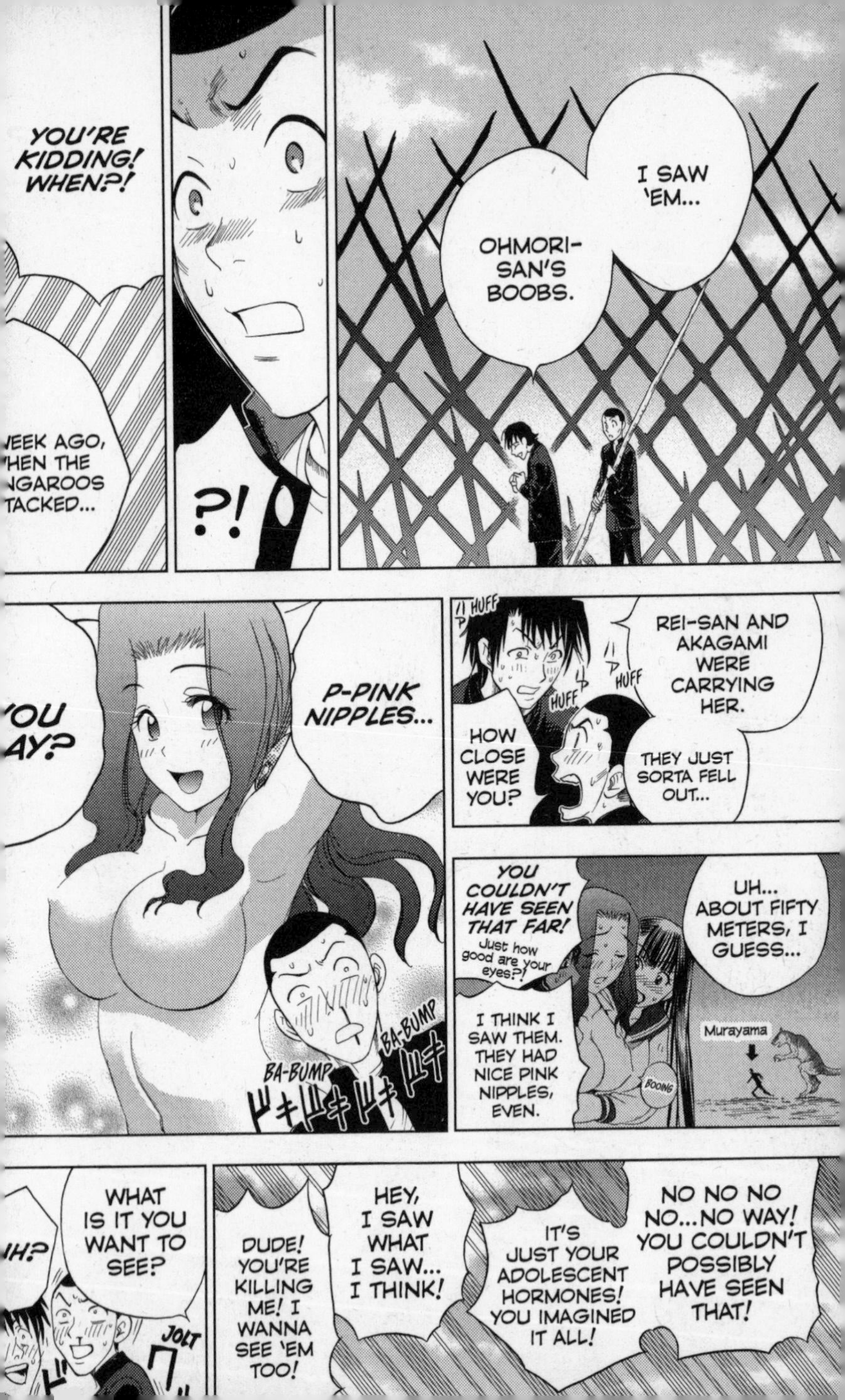
I SAW 'EM...
OHMORI-SAN'S BOOBS.
?!
YOU'RE KIDDING! WHEN?!
EEK AGO, HEN THE NGAROOS TACKED...
REI-SAN AND AKAGAMI WERE CARRYING HER.
HUFF
HUFF
HUFF
THEY JUST SORTA FELL OUT...
HOW CLOSE WERE YOU?
UH... ABOUT FIFTY METERS, I GUESS...
YOU COULDN'T HAVE SEEN THAT FAR!
Just how good are your eyes?!
I THINK I SAW THEM. THEY HAD NICE PINK NIPPLES, EVEN.
Murayama
BOOING
P-PINK NIPPLES...
BA-BUMP
BA-BUMP
OU AY?
NO NO NO NO...NO WAY! YOU COULDN'T POSSIBLY HAVE SEEN THAT!
IT'S JUST YOUR ADOLESCENT HORMONES! YOU IMAGINED IT ALL!
HEY, I SAW WHAT I SAW... I THINK!
DUDE! YOU'RE KILLING ME! I WANNA SEE 'EM TOO!
WHAT IS IT YOU WANT TO SEE?
JOLT
IH?

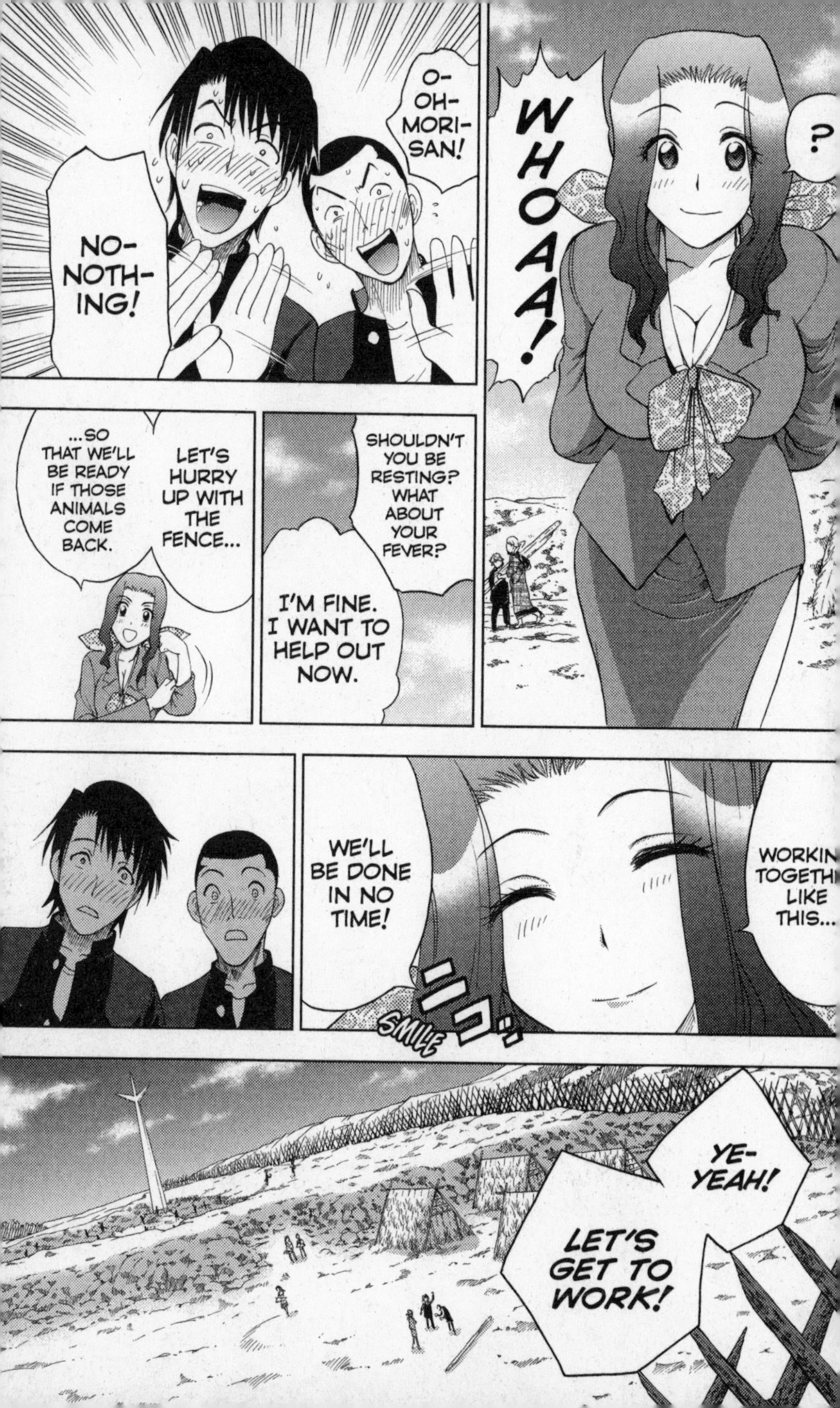
?
WHOAAA!
O-OH-MORI-SAN!
NO-NOTHING!
SHOULDN'T YOU BE RESTING? WHAT ABOUT YOUR FEVER?
I'M FINE. I WANT TO HELP OUT NOW.
LET'S HURRY UP WITH THE FENCE...
...SO THAT WE'LL BE READY IF THOSE ANIMALS COME BACK.
WORKIN TOGETH LIKE THIS...
WE'LL BE DONE IN NO TIME!
SMILE
YE-YEAH!
LET'S GET TO WORK!

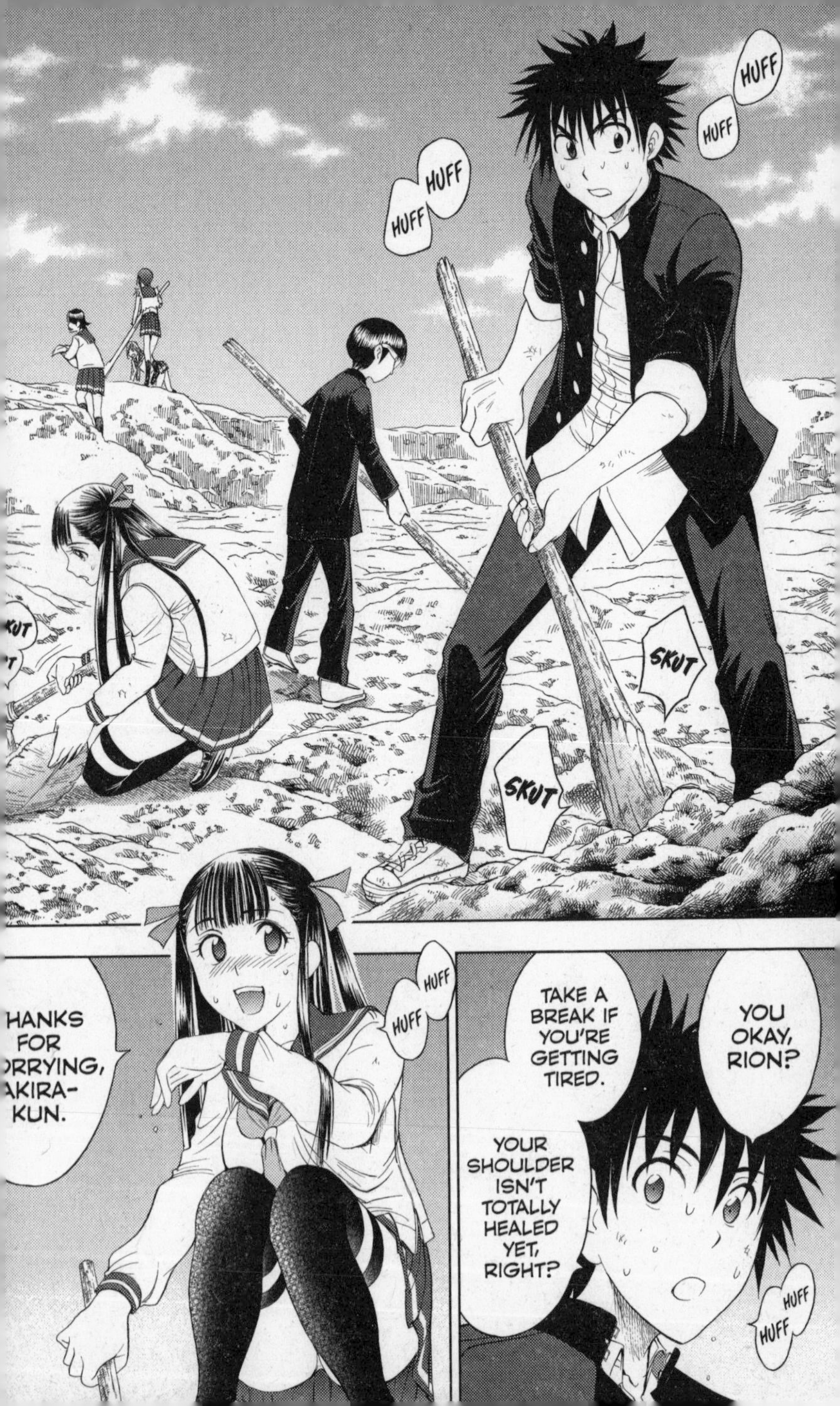

HUFF
HUFF
HUFF
HUFF
SKUT
SKUT
YOU OKAY, RION?
TAKE A BREAK IF YOU'RE GETTING TIRED.
YOUR SHOULDER ISN'T TOTALLY HEALED YET, RIGHT?
HUFF
HUFF
HUFF
HUFF
HANKS FOR ORRYING, AKIRA-KUN.

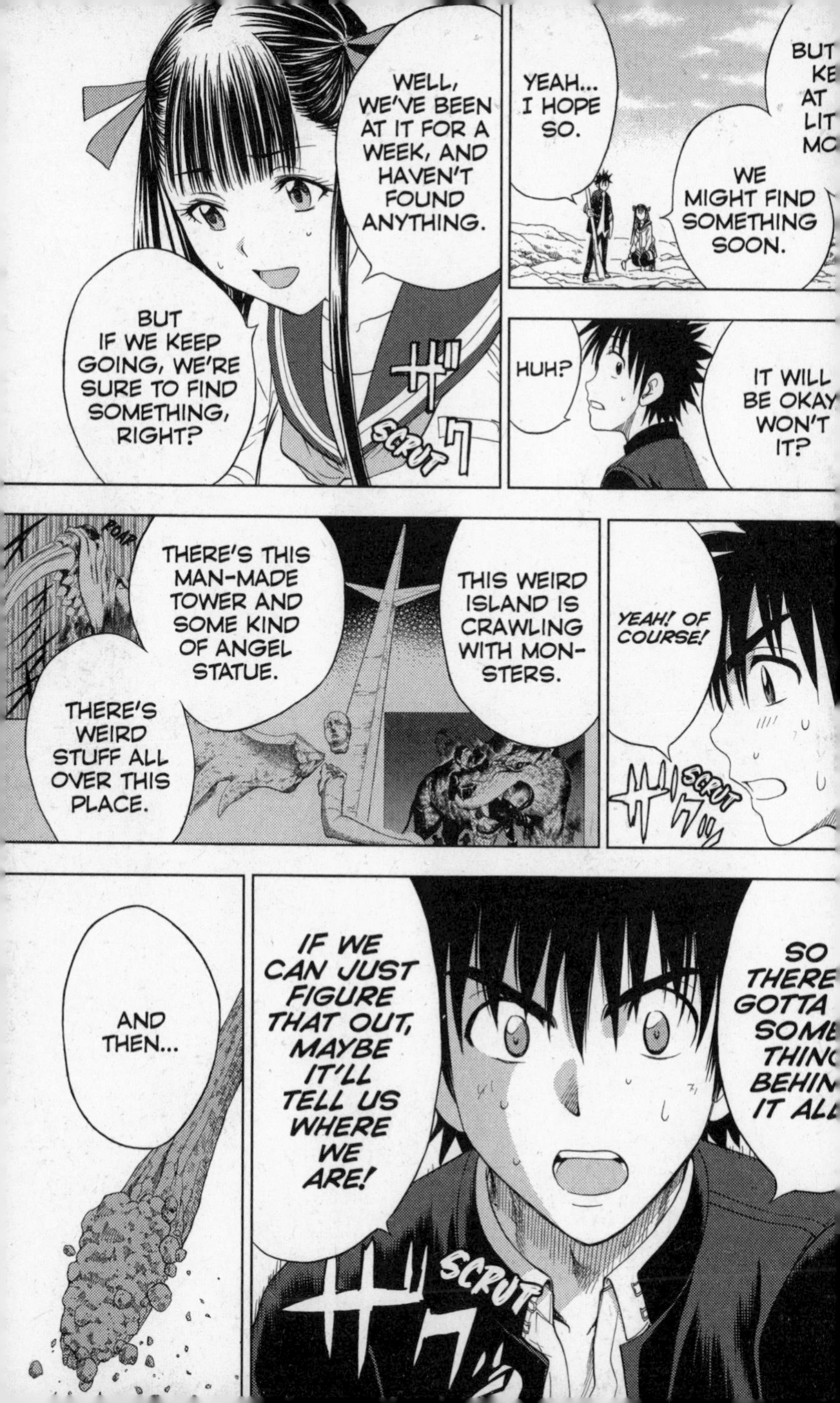
BUT KE AT LIT MO
WE MIGHT FIND SOMETHING SOON.
YEAH... I HOPE SO.
IT WILL BE OKAY WON'T IT?
HUH?
WELL, WE'VE BEEN AT IT FOR A WEEK, AND HAVEN'T FOUND ANYTHING.
BUT IF WE KEEP GOING, WE'RE SURE TO FIND SOMETHING, RIGHT?
SCRUT
YEAH! OF COURSE!
SCRUT
THIS WEIRD ISLAND IS CRAWLING WITH MON-STERS.
ROAR
THERE'S THIS MAN-MADE TOWER AND SOME KIND OF ANGEL STATUE.
THERE'S WEIRD STUFF ALL OVER THIS PLACE.
SO THERE GOTTA SOME THIN BEHIN IT AL
IF WE CAN JUST FIGURE THAT OUT, MAYBE IT'LL TELL US WHERE WE ARE!
SCRUT
AND THEN...

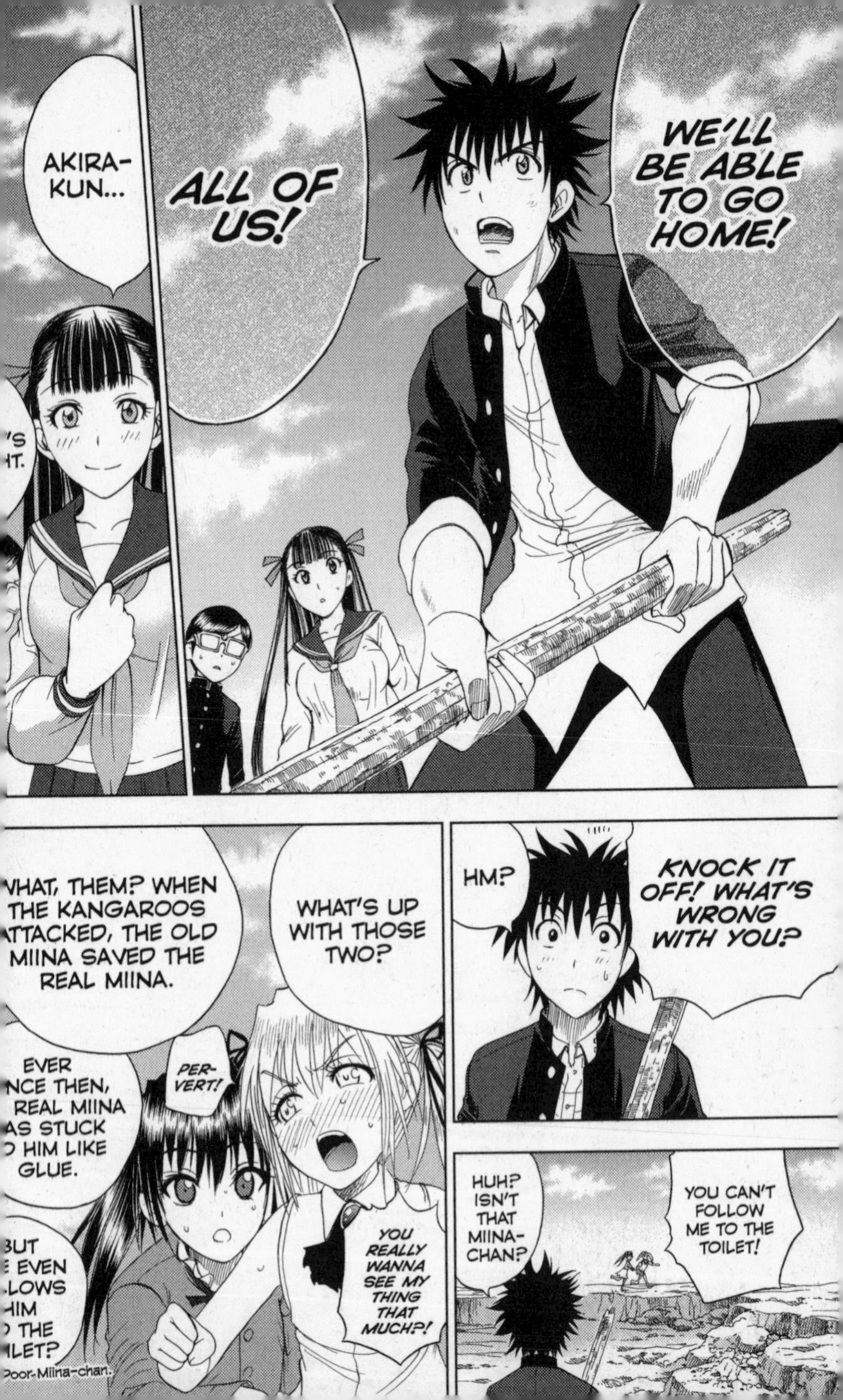
WE'LL BE ABLE TO GO HOME!
ALL OF US!
AKIRA-KUN...
'S
HT.
KNOCK IT OFF! WHAT'S WRONG WITH YOU?
HM?
YOU CAN'T FOLLOW ME TO THE TOILET!
HUH? ISN'T THAT MIINA-CHAN?
WHAT'S UP WITH THOSE TWO?
VHAT, THEM? WHEN THE KANGAROOS TTACKED, THE OLD MIINA SAVED THE REAL MIINA.
EVER NCE THEN, REAL MIINA AS STUCK O HIM LIKE GLUE.
YOU REALLY WANNA SEE MY THING THAT MUCH?!
PER-VERT!
BUT E EVEN LOWS HIM O THE ILET?
Poor-Miina-chan.

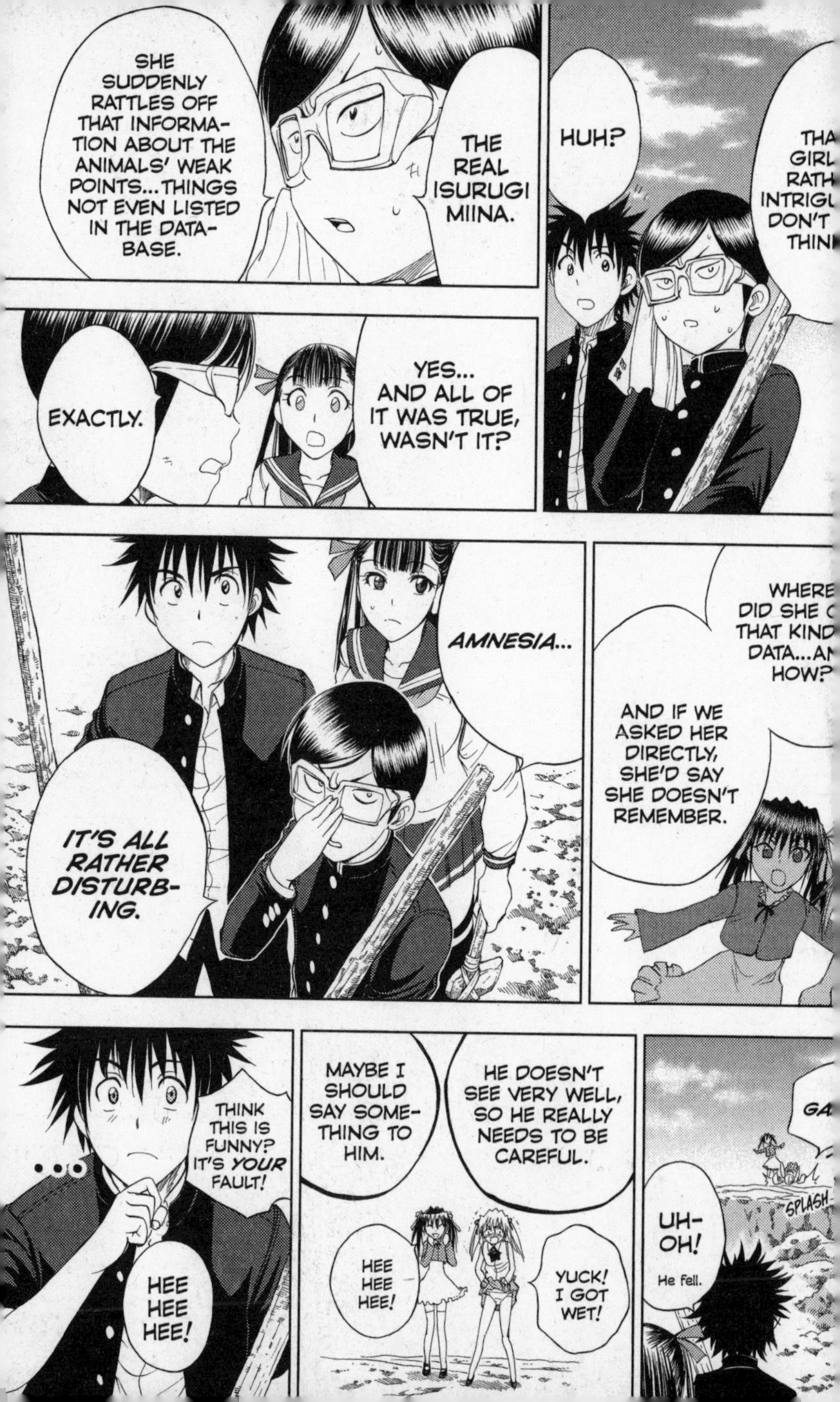
THA
GIRL
RATH
INTRIGU
DON'T
THIN
HUH?
THE REAL ISURUGI MIINA.
SHE SUDDENLY RATTLES OFF THAT INFORMATION ABOUT THE ANIMALS' WEAK POINTS...THINGS NOT EVEN LISTED IN THE DATABASE.
YES... AND ALL OF IT WAS TRUE, WASN'T IT?
EXACTLY.
WHERE DID SHE C THAT KIND DATA...AN HOW?
AND IF WE ASKED HER DIRECTLY, SHE'D SAY SHE DOESN'T REMEMBER.
AMNESIA...
IT'S ALL RATHER DISTURBING.
GA
SPLASH
UH-OH!
He fell.
HE DOESN'T SEE VERY WELL, SO HE REALLY NEEDS TO BE CAREFUL.
MAYBE I SHOULD SAY SOMETHING TO HIM.
YUCK! I GOT WET!
HEE HEE HEE!
THINK THIS IS FUNNY? IT'S YOUR FAULT!
...
HEE HEE HEE!

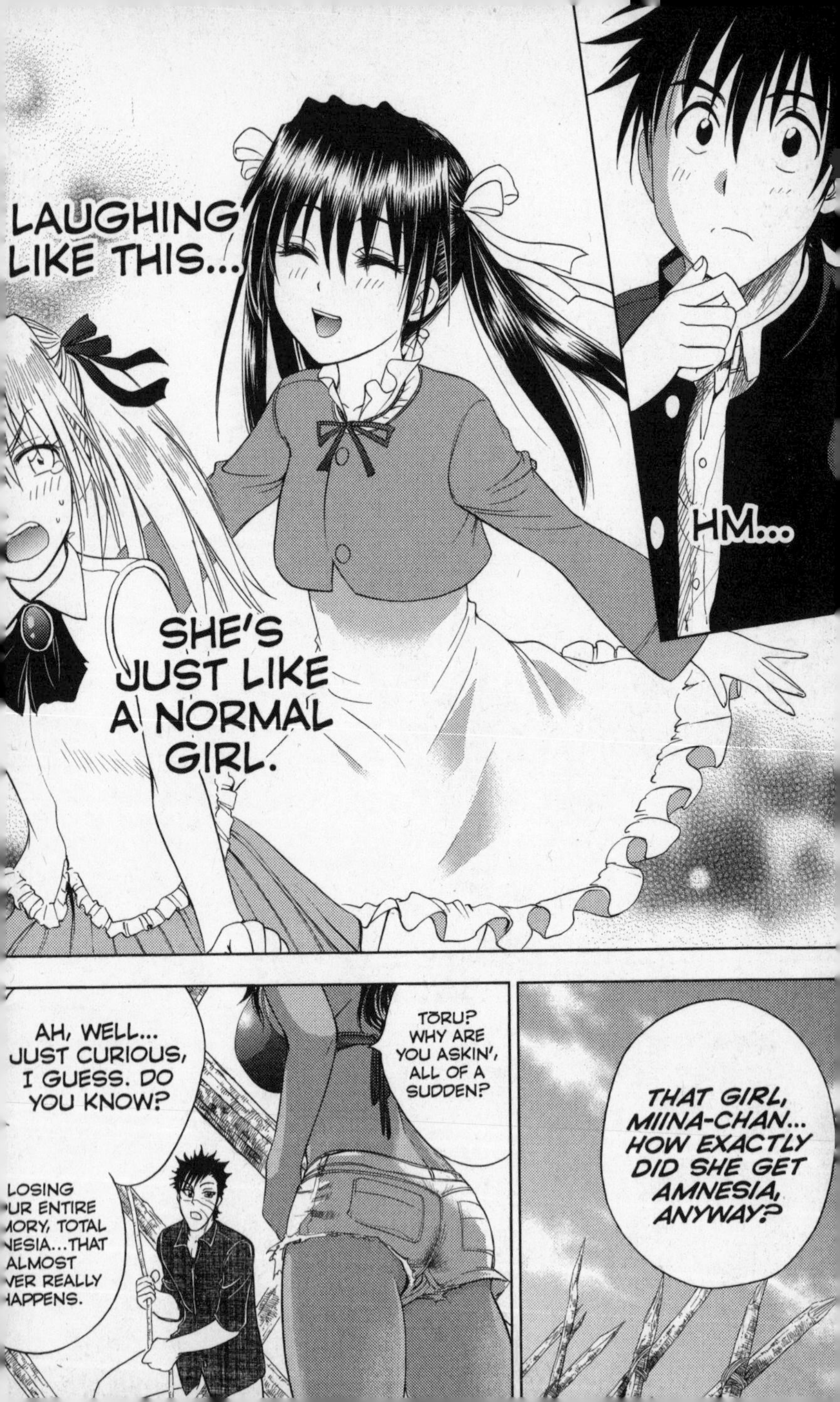
HM...
LAUGHING LIKE THIS...
SHE'S JUST LIKE A NORMAL GIRL.
THAT GIRL, MIINA-CHAN... HOW EXACTLY DID SHE GET AMNESIA, ANYWAY?
TŌRU? WHY ARE YOU ASKIN', ALL OF A SUDDEN?
AH, WELL... JUST CURIOUS, I GUESS. DO YOU KNOW?
LOSING UR ENTIRE ORY, TOTAL NESIA...THAT ALMOST VER REALLY APPENS.

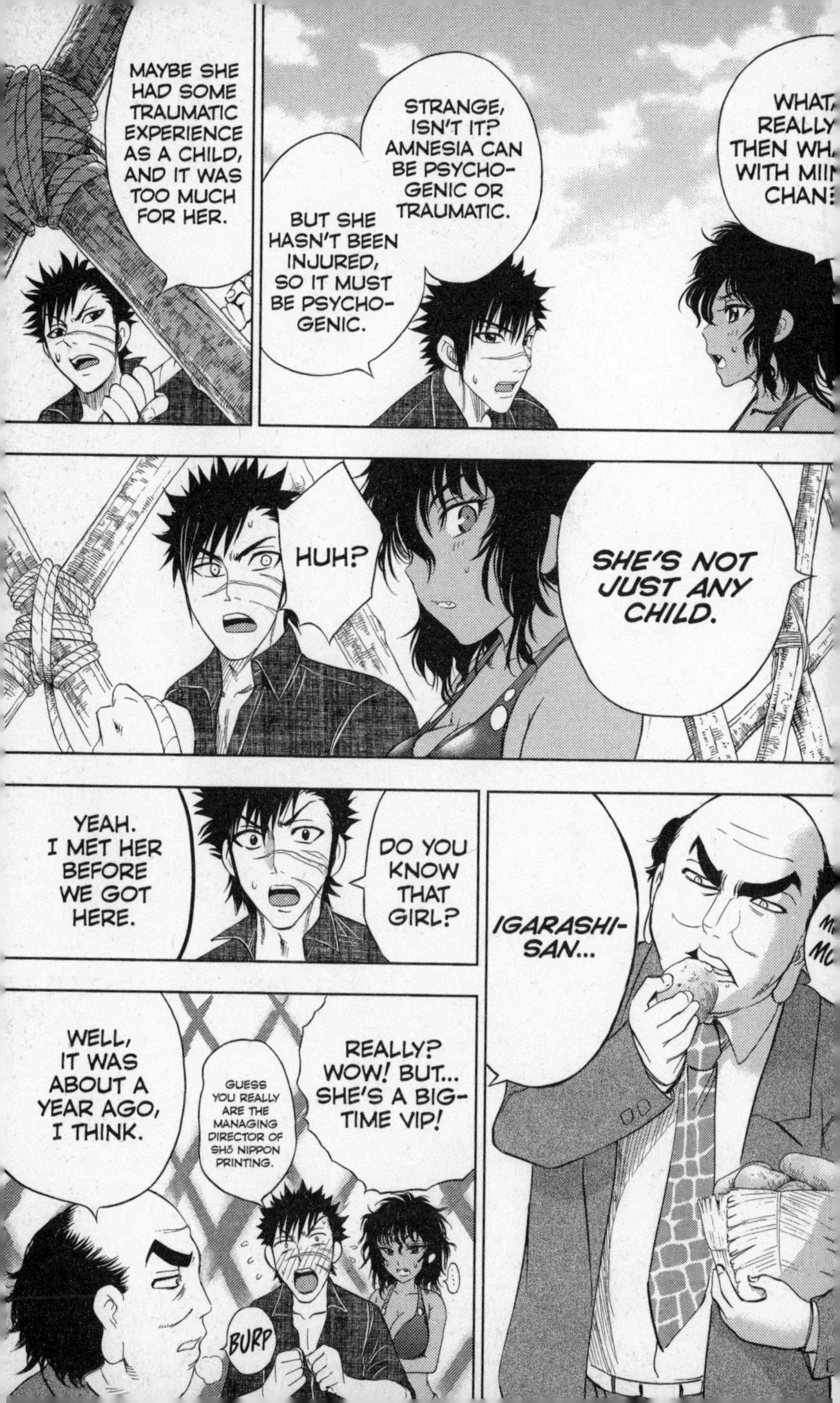
WHAT, REALLY THEN WH WITH MII CHAN
STRANGE, ISN'T IT? AMNESIA CAN BE PSYCHOGENIC OR TRAUMATIC.
BUT SHE HASN'T BEEN INJURED, SO IT MUST BE PSYCHOGENIC.
MAYBE SHE HAD SOME TRAUMATIC EXPERIENCE AS A CHILD, AND IT WAS TOO MUCH FOR HER.
SHE'S NOT JUST ANY CHILD.
HUH?
IGARASHI-SAN...
DO YOU KNOW THAT GIRL?
YEAH. I MET HER BEFORE WE GOT HERE.
REALLY? WOW! BUT... SHE'S A BIG-TIME VIP!
GUESS YOU REALLY ARE THE MANAGING DIRECTOR OF SHŌ NIPPON PRINTING.
WELL, IT WAS ABOUT A YEAR AGO, I THINK.
BURP

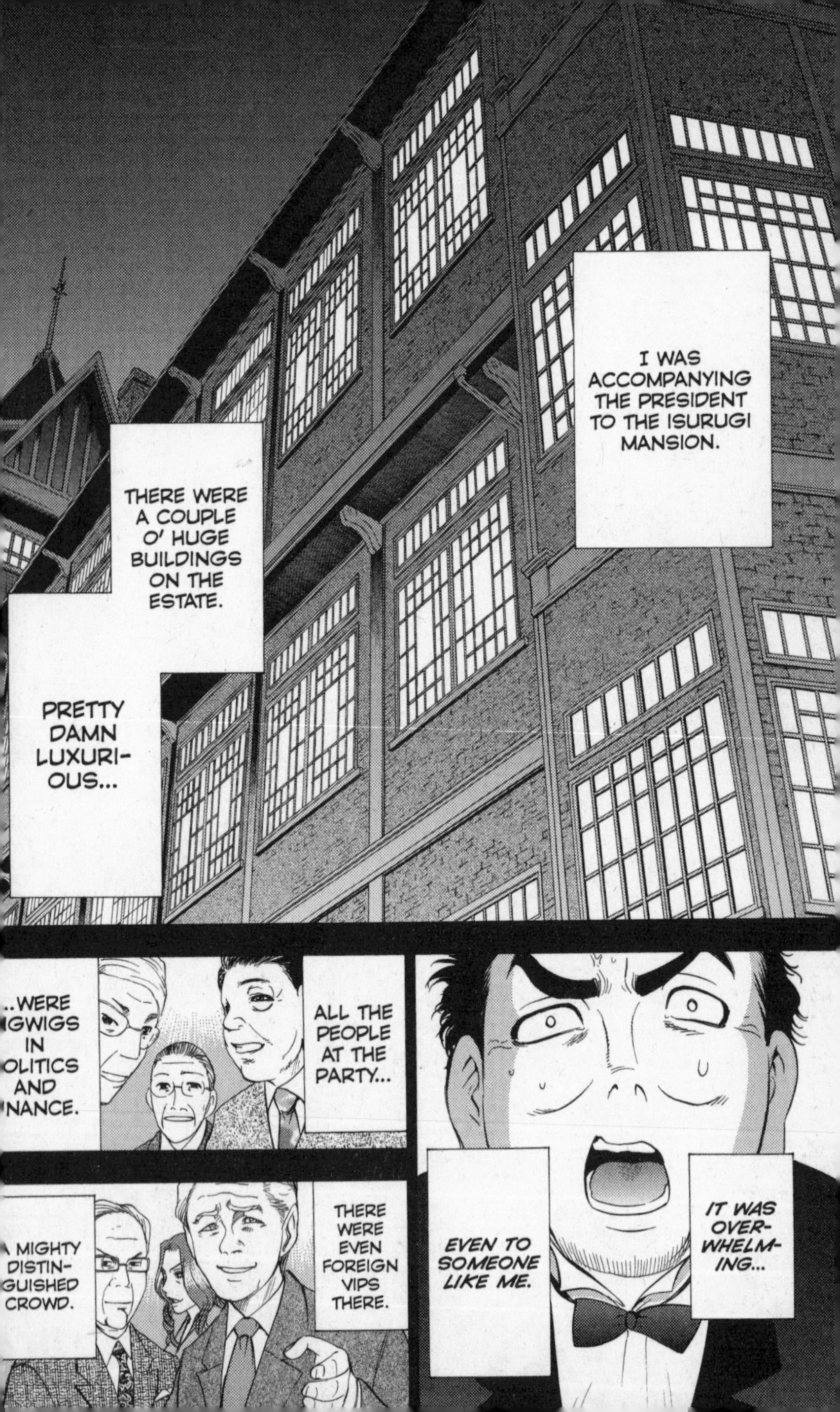

I WAS ACCOMPANYING THE PRESIDENT TO THE ISURUGI MANSION.
THERE WERE A COUPLE O' HUGE BUILDINGS ON THE ESTATE.
PRETTY DAMN LUXURI-OUS...
IT WAS OVER-WHELM-ING...
EVEN TO SOMEONE LIKE ME.
ALL THE PEOPLE AT THE PARTY...
..WERE IGWIGS IN OLITICS AND NANCE.
THERE WERE EVEN FOREIGN VIPS THERE.
MIGHTY DISTIN-GUISHED CROWD.

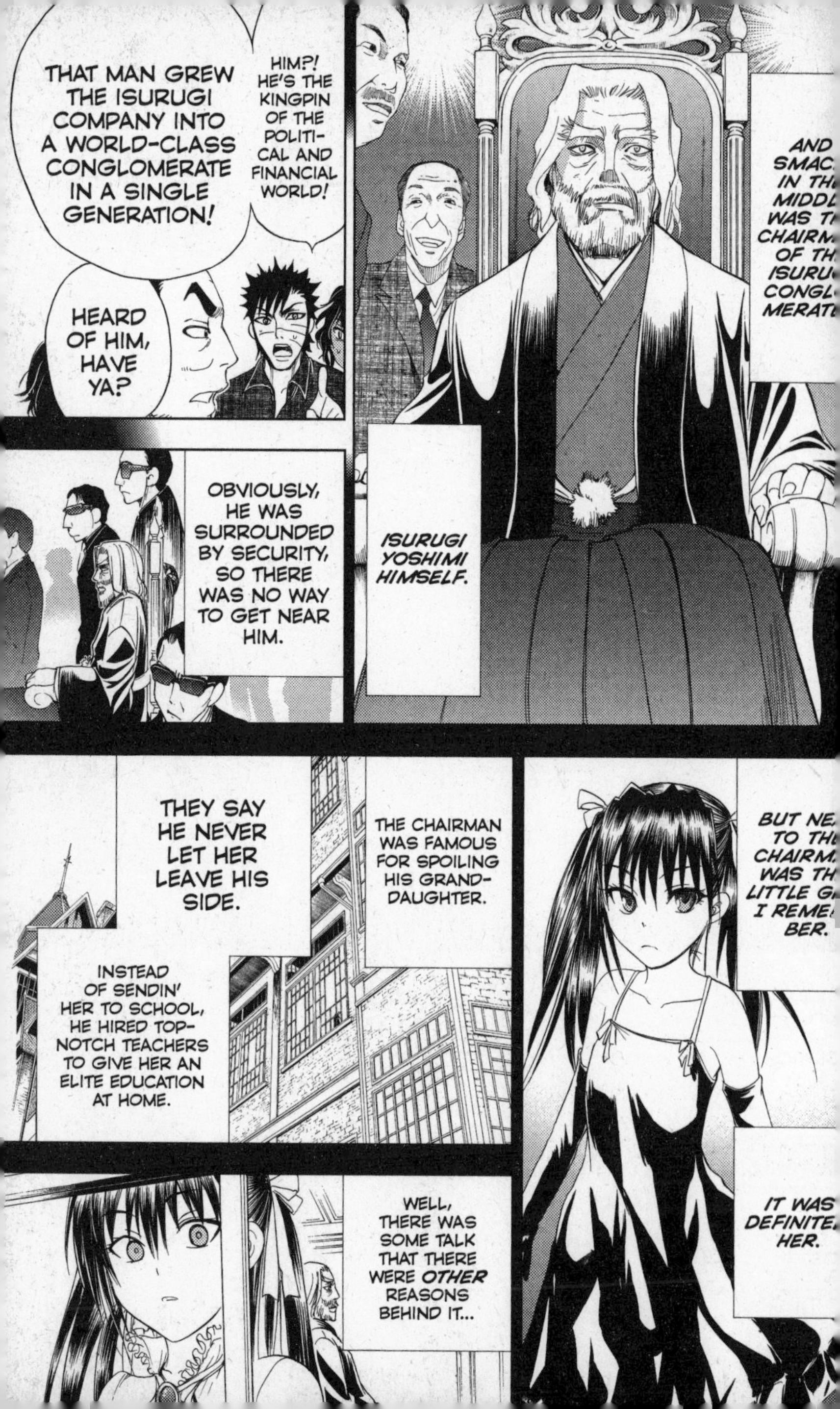

AND SMAC IN TH MIDDL WAS T CHAIRM OF TH ISURU CONGL MERAT
ISURUGI YOSHIMI HIMSELF.
HIM?! HE'S THE KINGPIN OF THE POLITI-CAL AND FINANCIAL WORLD!
THAT MAN GREW THE ISURUGI COMPANY INTO A WORLD-CLASS CONGLOMERATE IN A SINGLE GENERATION!
HEARD OF HIM, HAVE YA?
OBVIOUSLY, HE WAS SURROUNDED BY SECURITY, SO THERE WAS NO WAY TO GET NEAR HIM.
BUT NE TO TH CHAIRM WAS TH LITTLE G I REME BER.
IT WAS DEFINITE HER.
THE CHAIRMAN WAS FAMOUS FOR SPOILING HIS GRAND-DAUGHTER.
THEY SAY HE NEVER LET HER LEAVE HIS SIDE.
INSTEAD OF SENDIN' HER TO SCHOOL, HE HIRED TOP-NOTCH TEACHERS TO GIVE HER AN ELITE EDUCATION AT HOME.
WELL, THERE WAS SOME TALK THAT THERE WERE OTHER REASONS BEHIND IT...

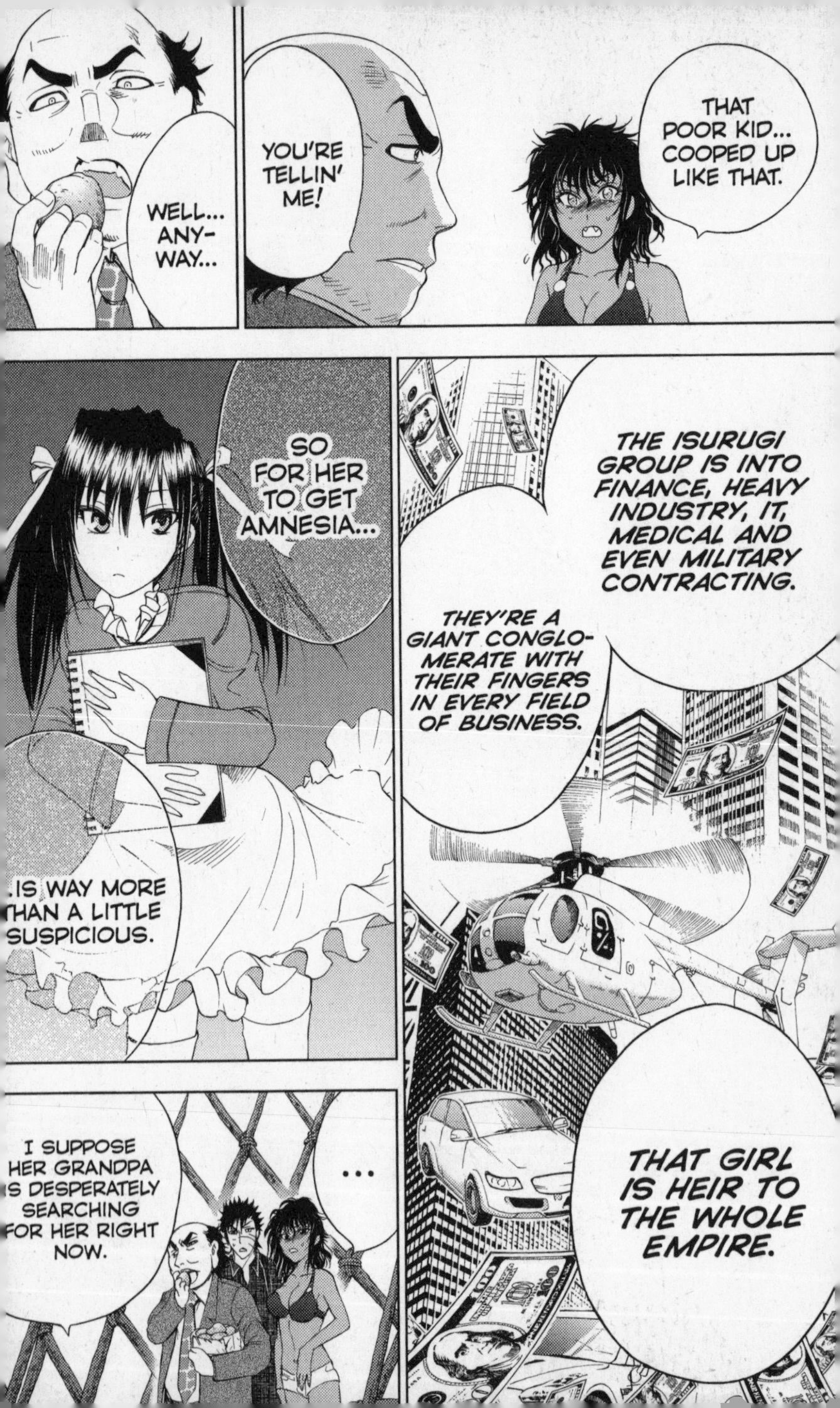
THAT POOR KID... COOPED UP LIKE THAT.
YOU'RE TELLIN' ME!
WELL... ANY-WAY...
THE ISURUGI GROUP IS INTO FINANCE, HEAVY INDUSTRY, IT, MEDICAL AND EVEN MILITARY CONTRACTING.
THEY'RE A GIANT CONGLO-MERATE WITH THEIR FINGERS IN EVERY FIELD OF BUSINESS.
THAT GIRL IS HEIR TO THE WHOLE EMPIRE.
SO FOR HER TO GET AMNESIA...
.IS WAY MORE THAN A LITTLE SUSPICIOUS.
...
I SUPPOSE HER GRANDPA IS DESPERATELY SEARCHING FOR HER RIGHT NOW.

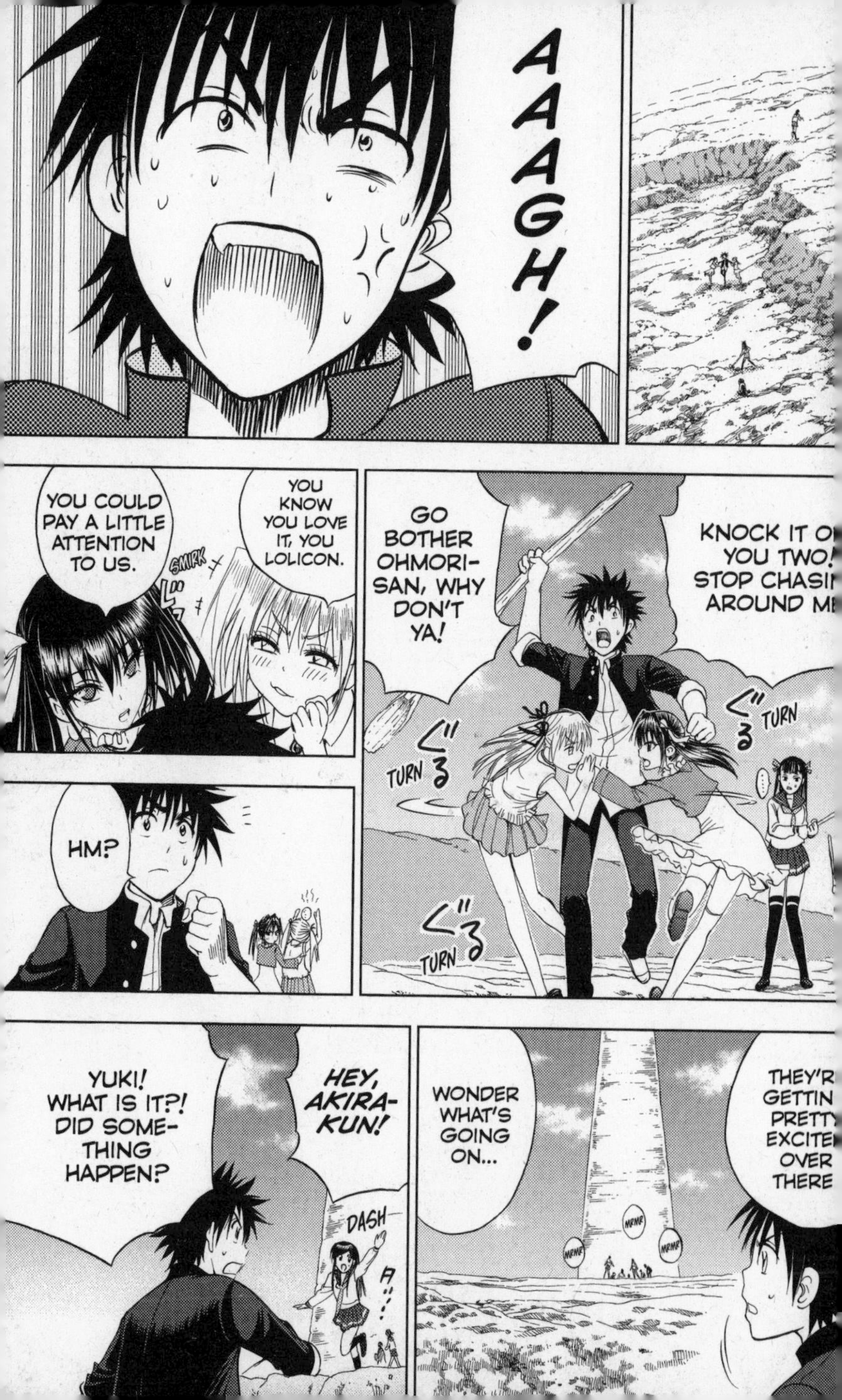
AAAGH!
KNOCK IT O YOU TWO! STOP CHASI AROUND M
GO BOTHER OHMORI-SAN, WHY DON'T YA!
TURN
TURN
TURN
YOU KNOW YOU LOVE IT, YOU LOLICON.
YOU COULD PAY A LITTLE ATTENTION TO US.
SMIRK
HM?
THEY'R GETTIN PRETT EXCITE OVER THERE
WONDER WHAT'S GOING ON...
MRMF
MRMF
MRMF
HEY, AKIRA-KUN!
YUKI! WHAT IS IT?! DID SOME-THING HAPPEN?
DASH

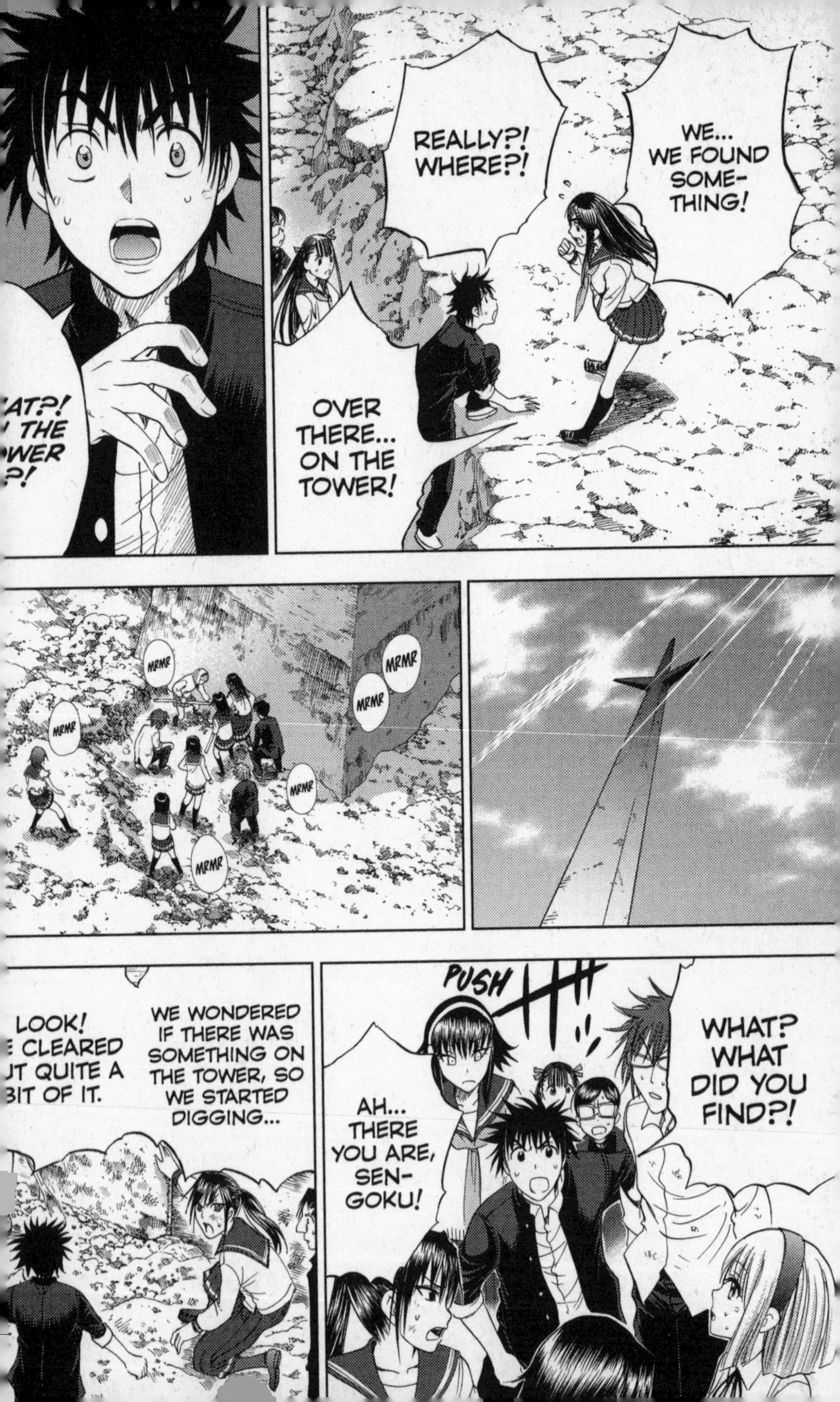
WE... WE FOUND SOME-THING!
REALLY?! WHERE?!
OVER THERE... ON THE TOWER!
AT?! N THE WER ?!
MRMR
MRMR
MRMR
MRMR
MRMR
PUSH
WHAT? WHAT DID YOU FIND?!
AH... THERE YOU ARE, SEN-GOKU!
WE WONDERED IF THERE WAS SOMETHING ON THE TOWER, SO WE STARTED DIGGING...
LOOK! E CLEARED UT QUITE A BIT OF IT.

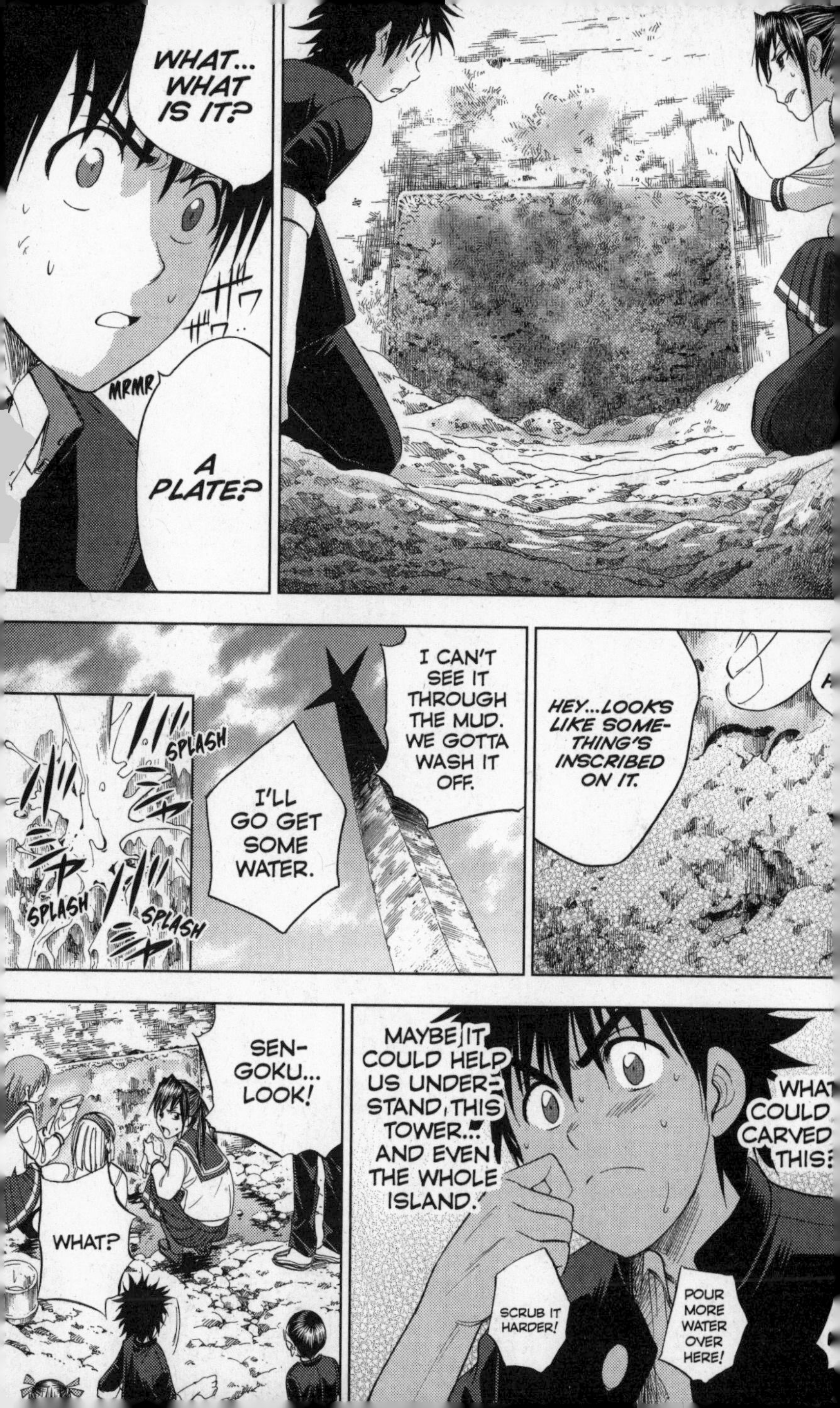

WHAT... WHAT IS IT?
ザワ ザワ…
MRMR
A PLATE?
HEY...LOOKS LIKE SOME-THING'S INSCRIBED ON IT.
I CAN'T SEE IT THROUGH THE MUD. WE GOTTA WASH IT OFF.
I'LL GO GET SOME WATER.
SPLASH
SPLASH
SPLASH
WHAT COULD CARVED THIS?
MAYBE IT COULD HELP US UNDER-STAND THIS TOWER... AND EVEN THE WHOLE ISLAND.
POUR MORE WATER OVER HERE!
SCRUB IT HARDER!
SEN-GOKU... LOOK!
WHAT?

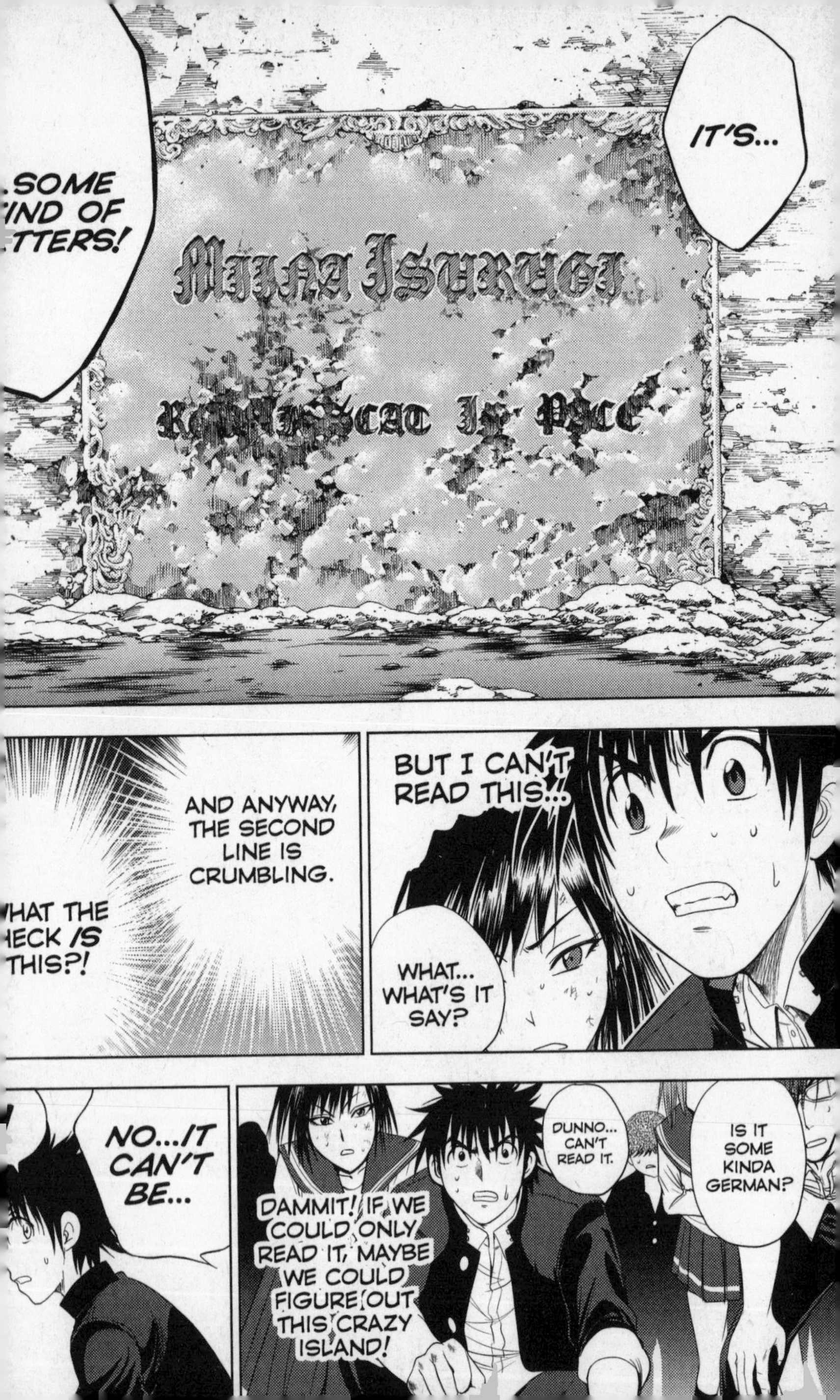

IT'S...
.SOME IND OF TTERS!
BUT I CAN'T READ THIS...
WHAT... WHAT'S IT SAY?
AND ANYWAY, THE SECOND LINE IS CRUMBLING.
HAT THE ECK *IS* THIS?!
IS IT SOME KINDA GERMAN?
DUNNO... CAN'T READ IT.
DAMMIT! IF WE COULD ONLY READ IT, MAYBE WE COULD FIGURE OUT THIS CRAZY ISLAND!
NO...IT CAN'T BE...

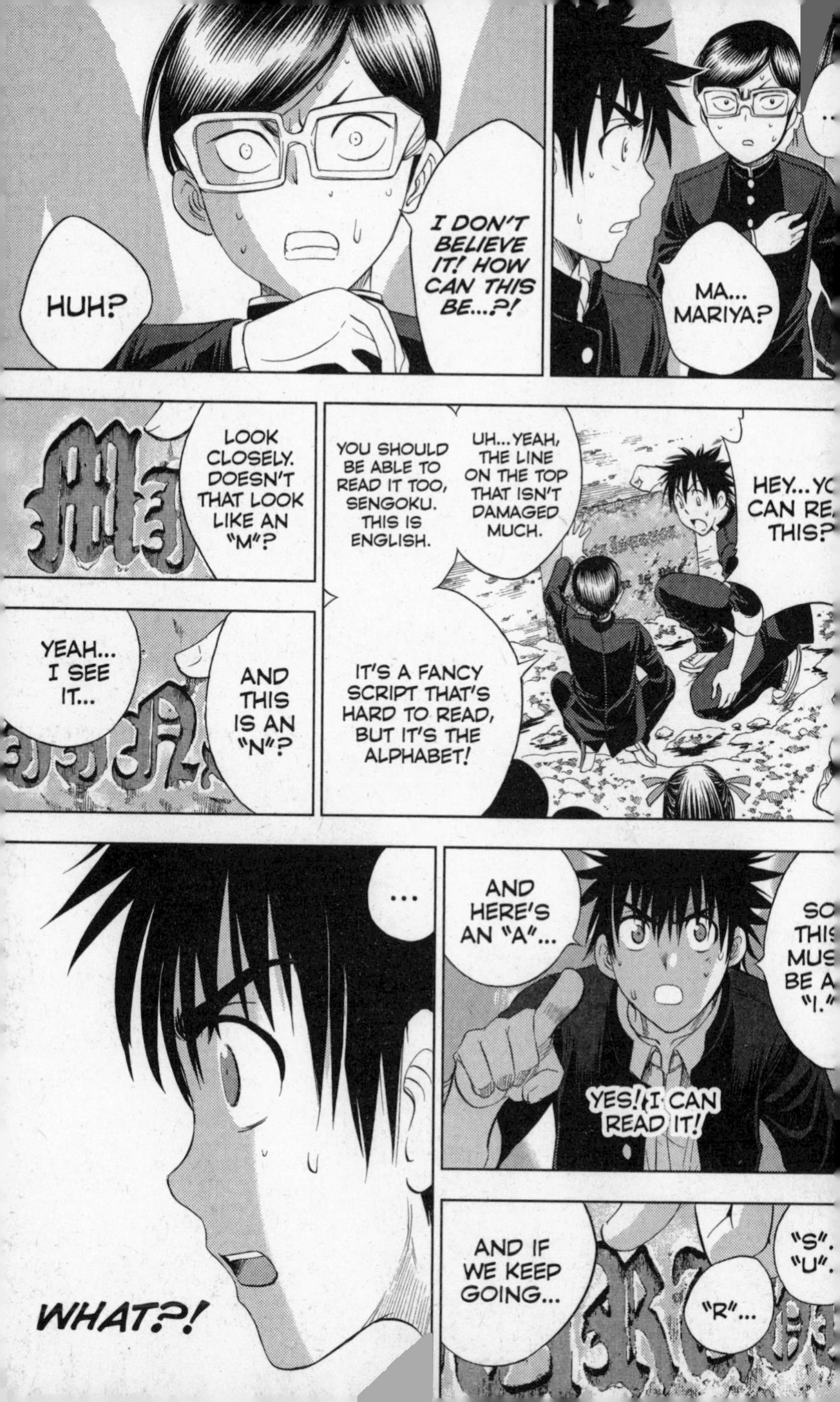
...
MA... MARIYA?
I DON'T BELIEVE IT! HOW CAN THIS BE...?!
HUH?
HEY...YC CAN RE THIS?
UH...YEAH, THE LINE ON THE TOP THAT ISN'T DAMAGED MUCH.
YOU SHOULD BE ABLE TO READ IT TOO, SENGOKU. THIS IS ENGLISH.
IT'S A FANCY SCRIPT THAT'S HARD TO READ, BUT IT'S THE ALPHABET!
LOOK CLOSELY. DOESN'T THAT LOOK LIKE AN "M"?
AND THIS IS AN "N"?
YEAH... I SEE IT...
SO THIS MUS BE A "I."
AND HERE'S AN "A"...
YES! I CAN READ IT!
"S"... "U"...
"R"...
AND IF WE KEEP GOING...
...
WHAT?!

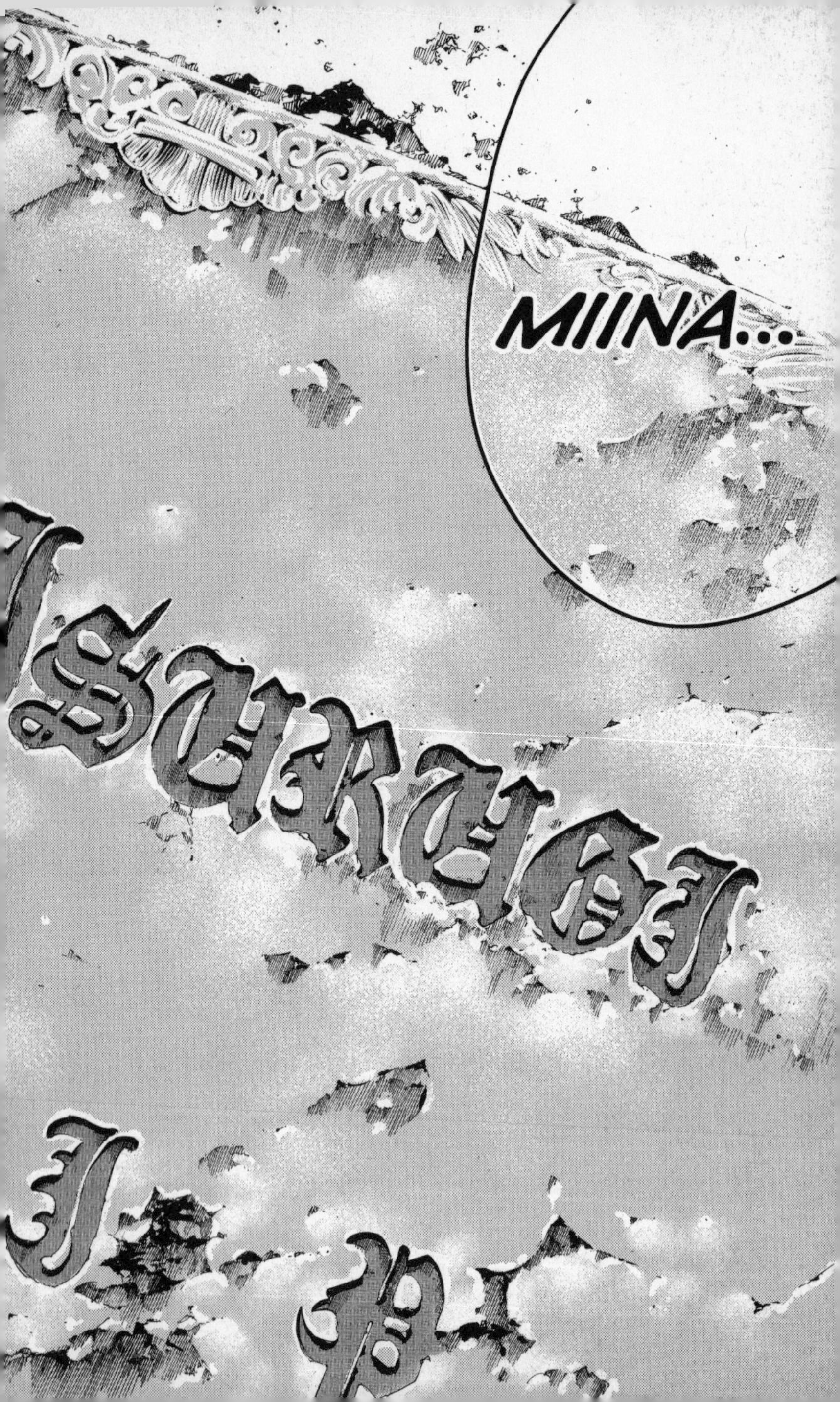
MIINA...

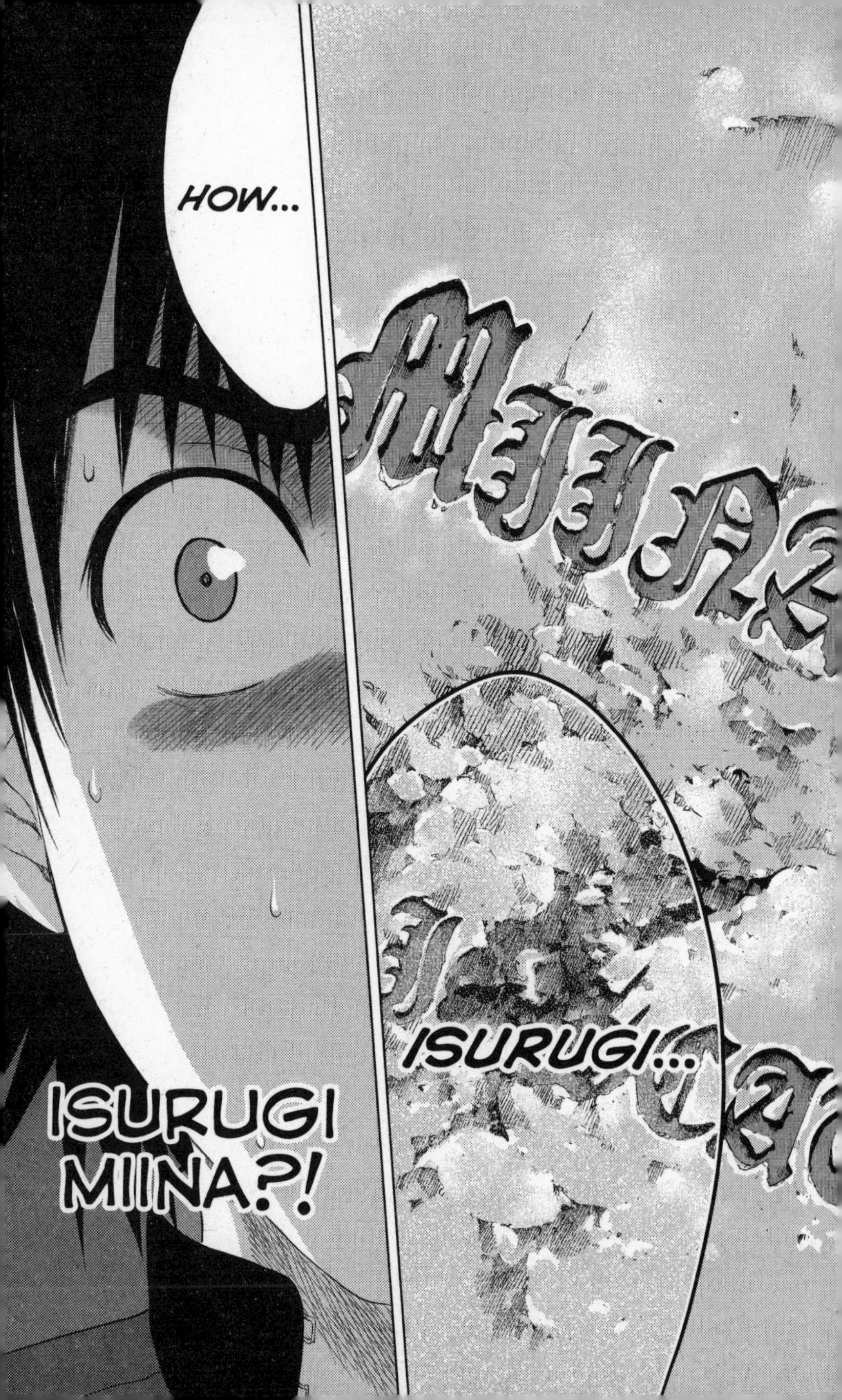
ISURUGI...
HOW...
ISURUGI MIINA?!

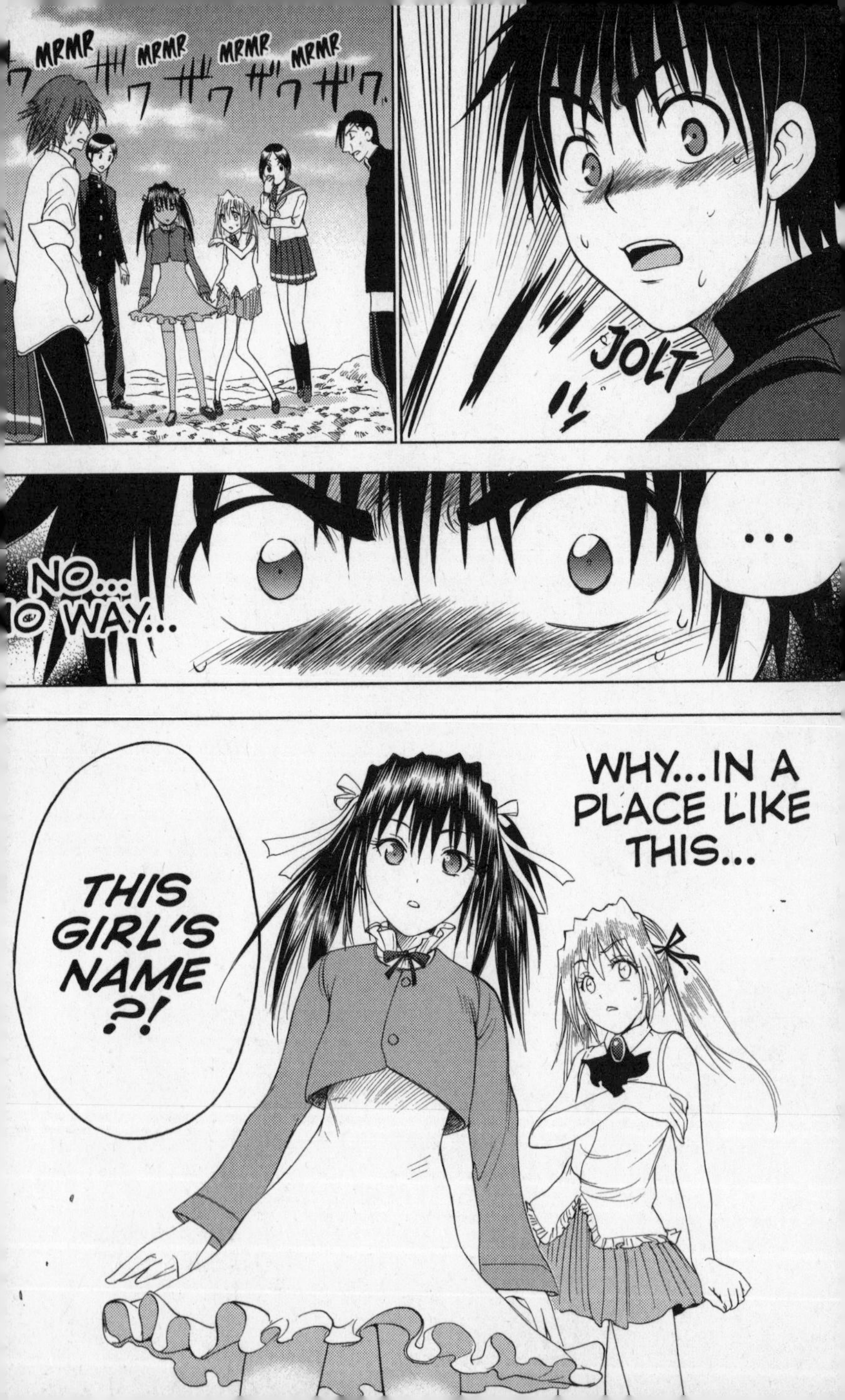
JOLT
!!
MRMR
MRMR
MRMR
MRMR
...
NO... NO WAY...
WHY...IN A PLACE LIKE THIS...
THIS GIRL'S NAME?!

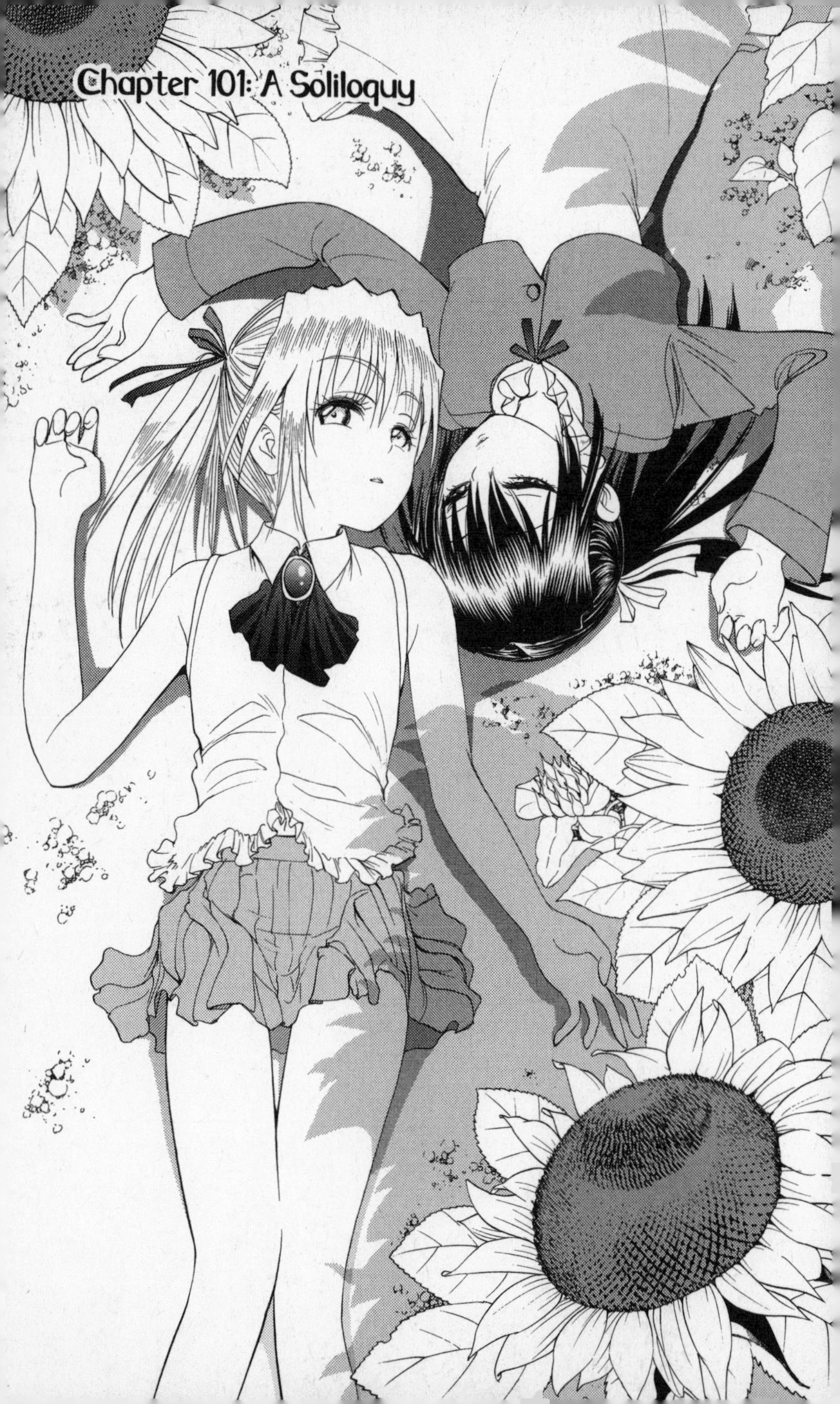
Chapter 101: A Soliloquy

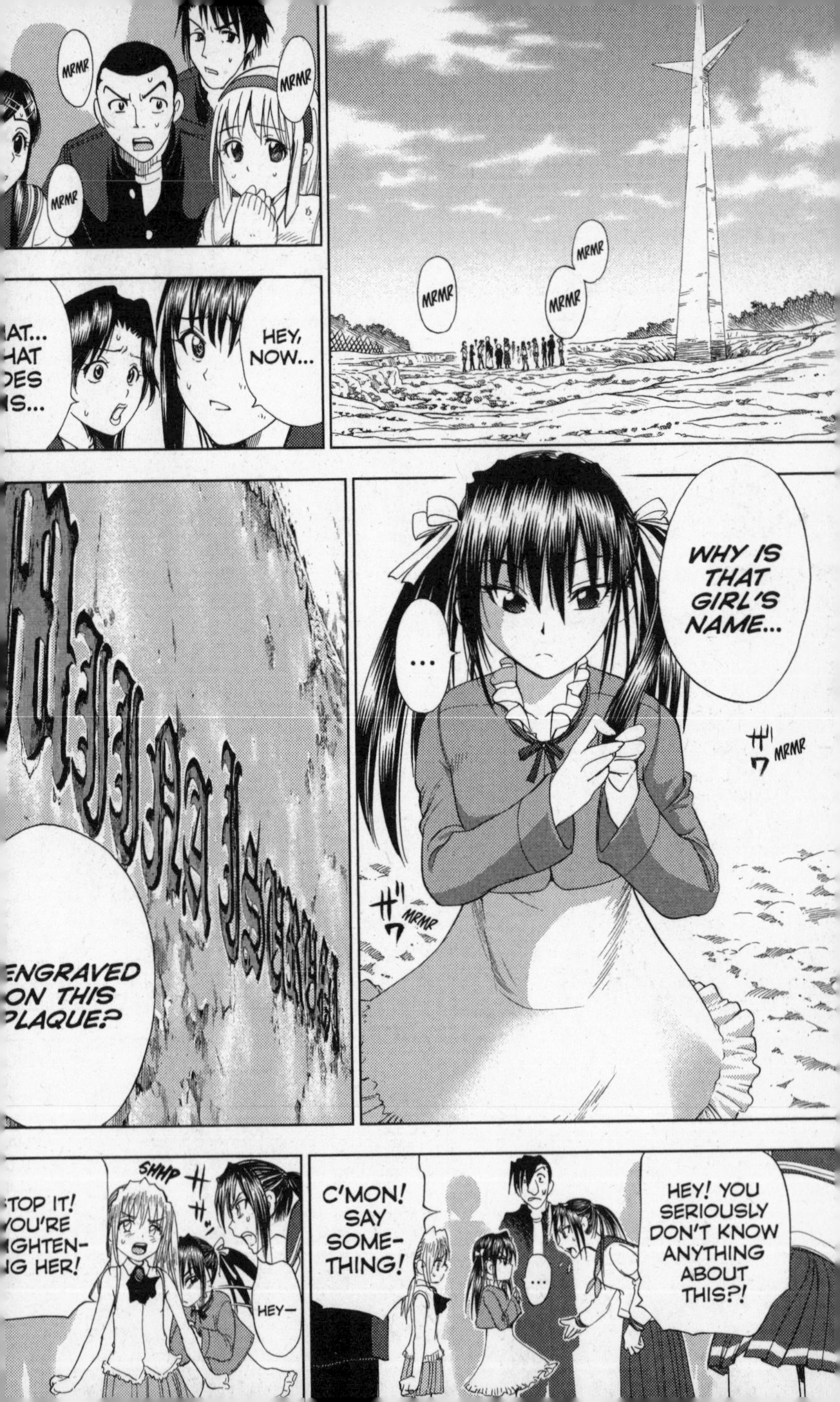
MRMR
MRMR
MRMR
MRMR
MRMR
MRMR
HEY, NOW...
AT... HAT DES S...
WHY IS THAT GIRL'S NAME...
...
ザワ MRMR
ザワ MRMR
ENGRAVED ON THIS PLAQUE?
HEY! YOU SERIOUSLY DON'T KNOW ANYTHING ABOUT THIS?!
C'MON! SAY SOME-THING!
...
SHHP
HEY—
TOP IT! YOU'RE IGHTEN-IG HER!

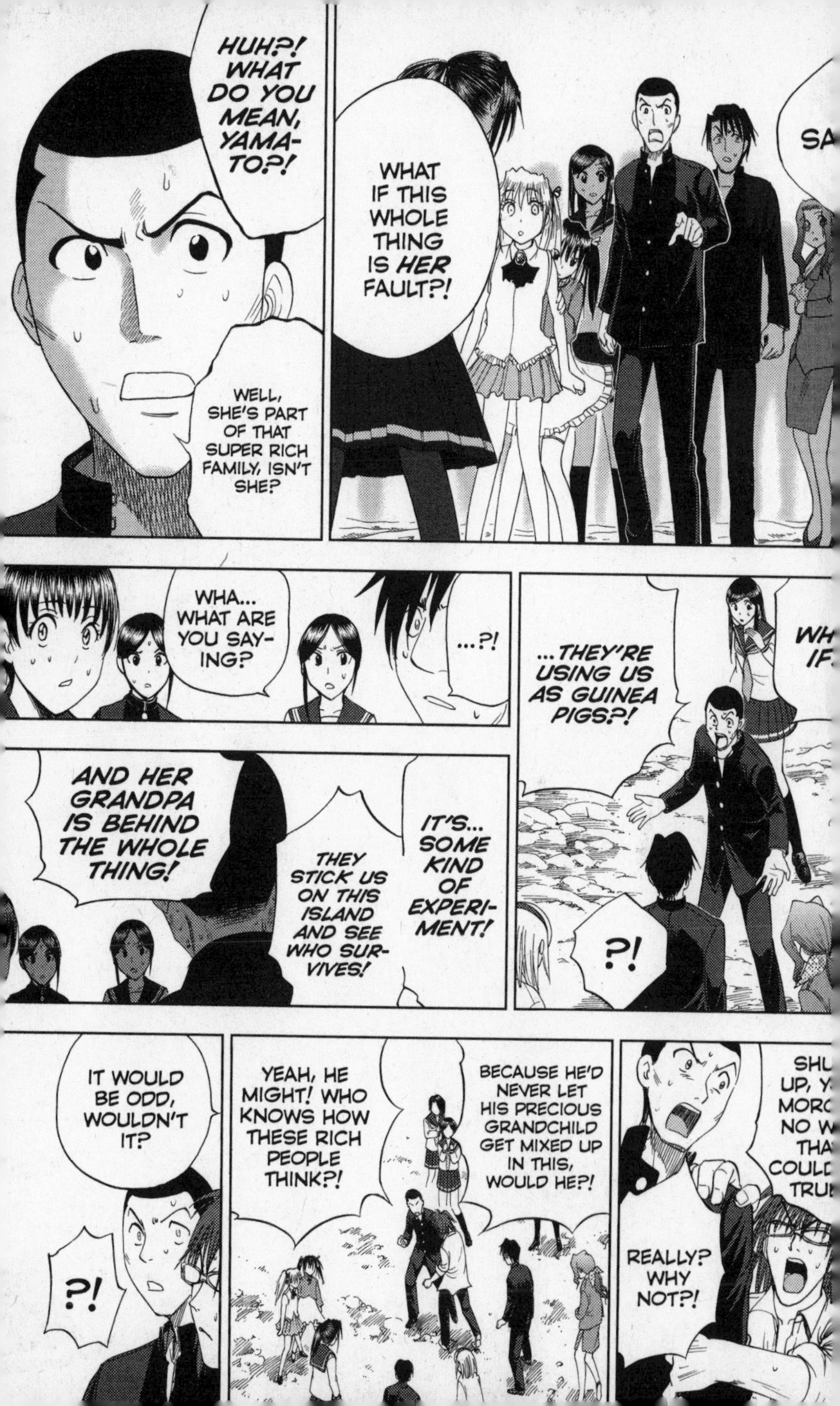

SA
WHAT IF THIS WHOLE THING IS HER FAULT?!
HUH?! WHAT DO YOU MEAN, YAMATO?!
WELL, SHE'S PART OF THAT SUPER RICH FAMILY, ISN'T SHE?
WH IF.
...THEY'RE USING US AS GUINEA PIGS?!
?!
...?!
WHA... WHAT ARE YOU SAYING?
IT'S... SOME KIND OF EXPERIMENT!
THEY STICK US ON THIS ISLAND AND SEE WHO SURVIVES!
AND HER GRANDPA IS BEHIND THE WHOLE THING!
SHU UP, Y MORO NO W THA COULD TRU
REALLY? WHY NOT?!
BECAUSE HE'D NEVER LET HIS PRECIOUS GRANDCHILD GET MIXED UP IN THIS, WOULD HE?!
YEAH, HE MIGHT! WHO KNOWS HOW THESE RICH PEOPLE THINK?!
IT WOULD BE ODD, WOULDN'T IT?
?!

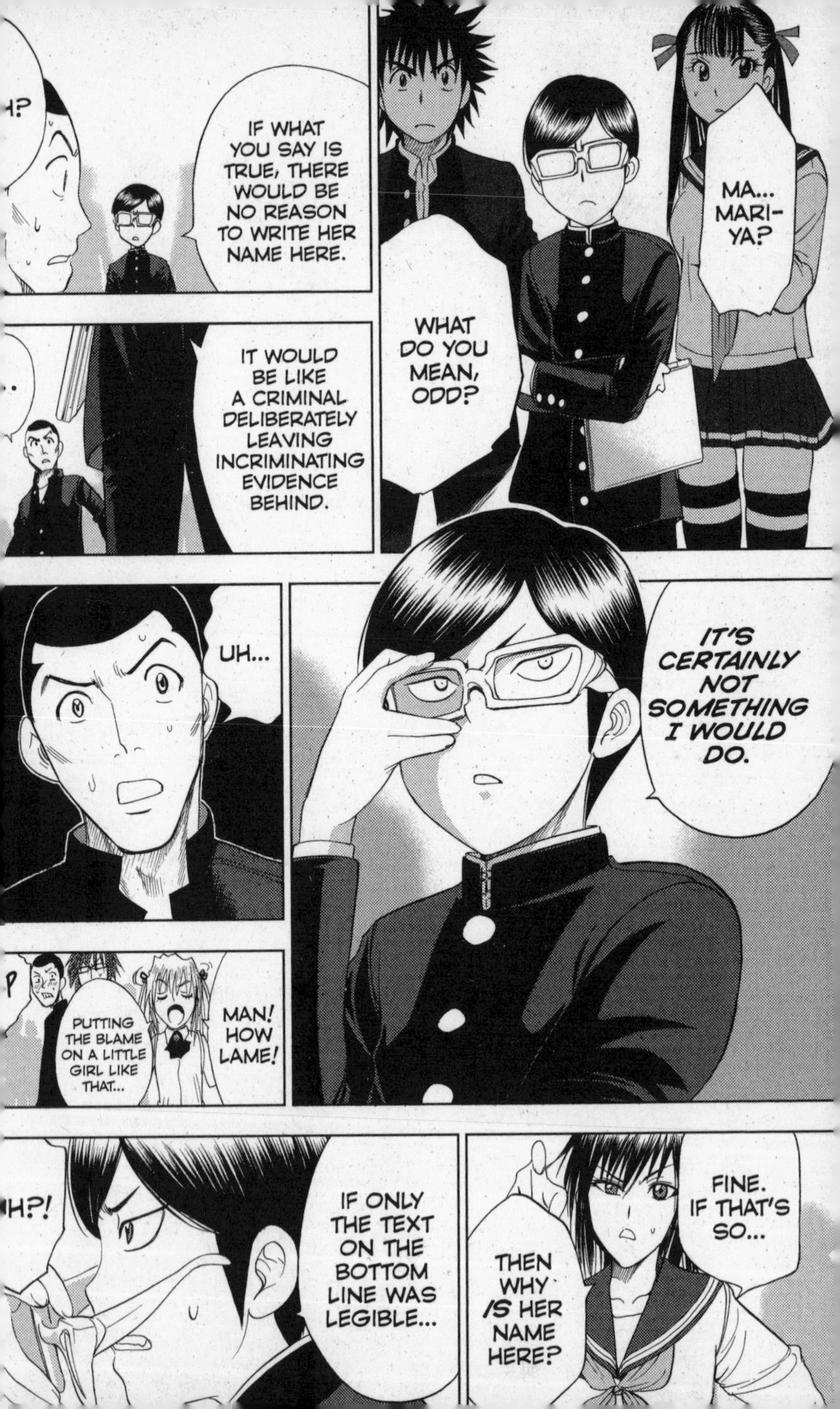
MA... MARI-YA?
WHAT DO YOU MEAN, ODD?
IF WHAT YOU SAY IS TRUE, THERE WOULD BE NO REASON TO WRITE HER NAME HERE.
IT WOULD BE LIKE A CRIMINAL DELIBERATELY LEAVING INCRIMINATING EVIDENCE BEHIND.
IT'S CERTAINLY NOT SOMETHING I WOULD DO.
UH...
MAN! HOW LAME!
PUTTING THE BLAME ON A LITTLE GIRL LIKE THAT...
FINE. IF THAT'S SO...
THEN WHY IS HER NAME HERE?
IF ONLY THE TEXT ON THE BOTTOM LINE WAS LEGIBLE...

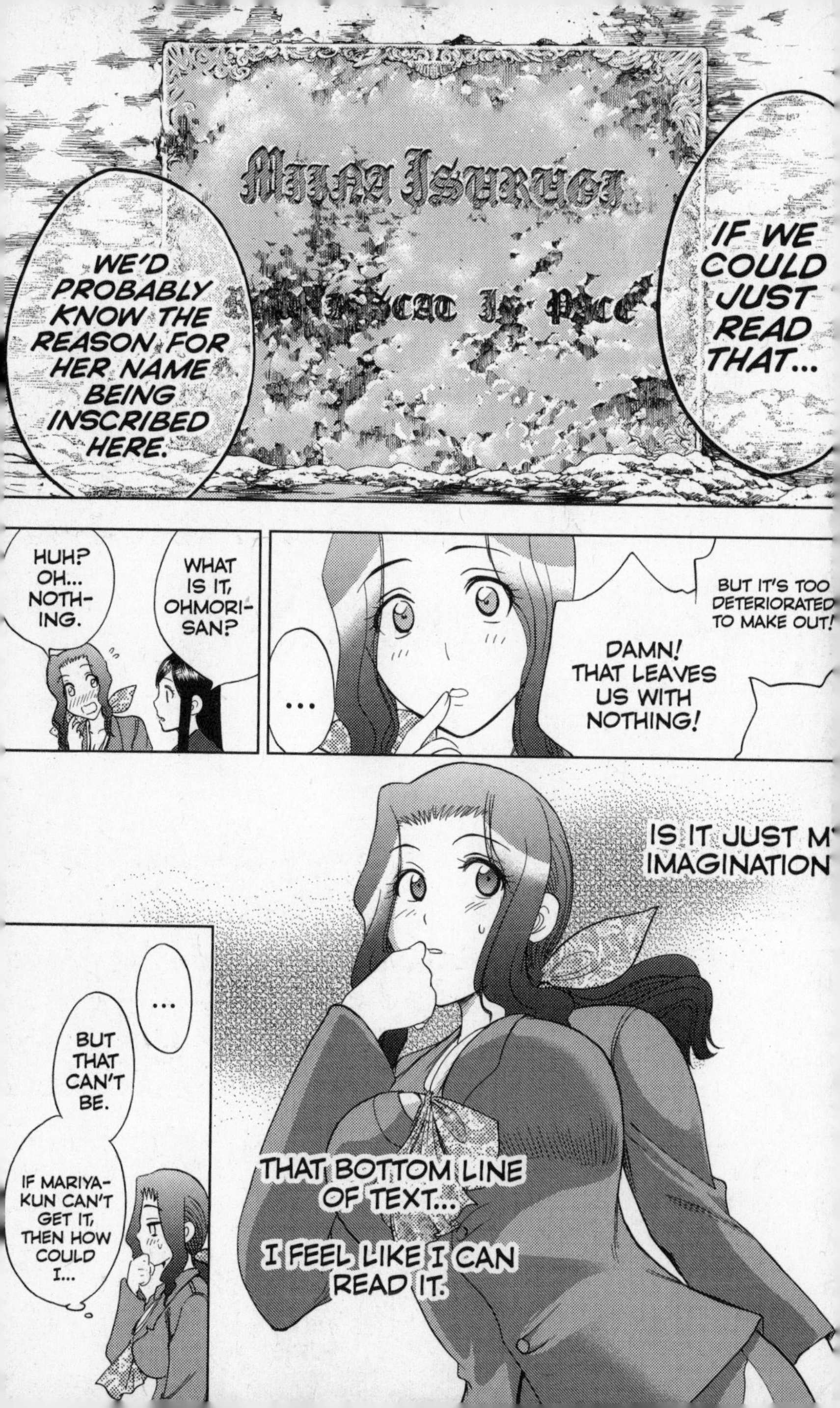
IF WE COULD JUST READ THAT...
WE'D PROBABLY KNOW THE REASON FOR HER NAME BEING INSCRIBED HERE.
BUT IT'S TOO DETERIORATED TO MAKE OUT!
DAMN! THAT LEAVES US WITH NOTHING!
...
WHAT IS IT, OHMORI-SAN?
HUH? OH... NOTH-ING.
IS IT JUST MY IMAGINATION
THAT BOTTOM LINE OF TEXT...
I FEEL LIKE I CAN READ IT.
...
BUT THAT CAN'T BE.
IF MARIYA-KUN CAN'T GET IT, THEN HOW COULD I...

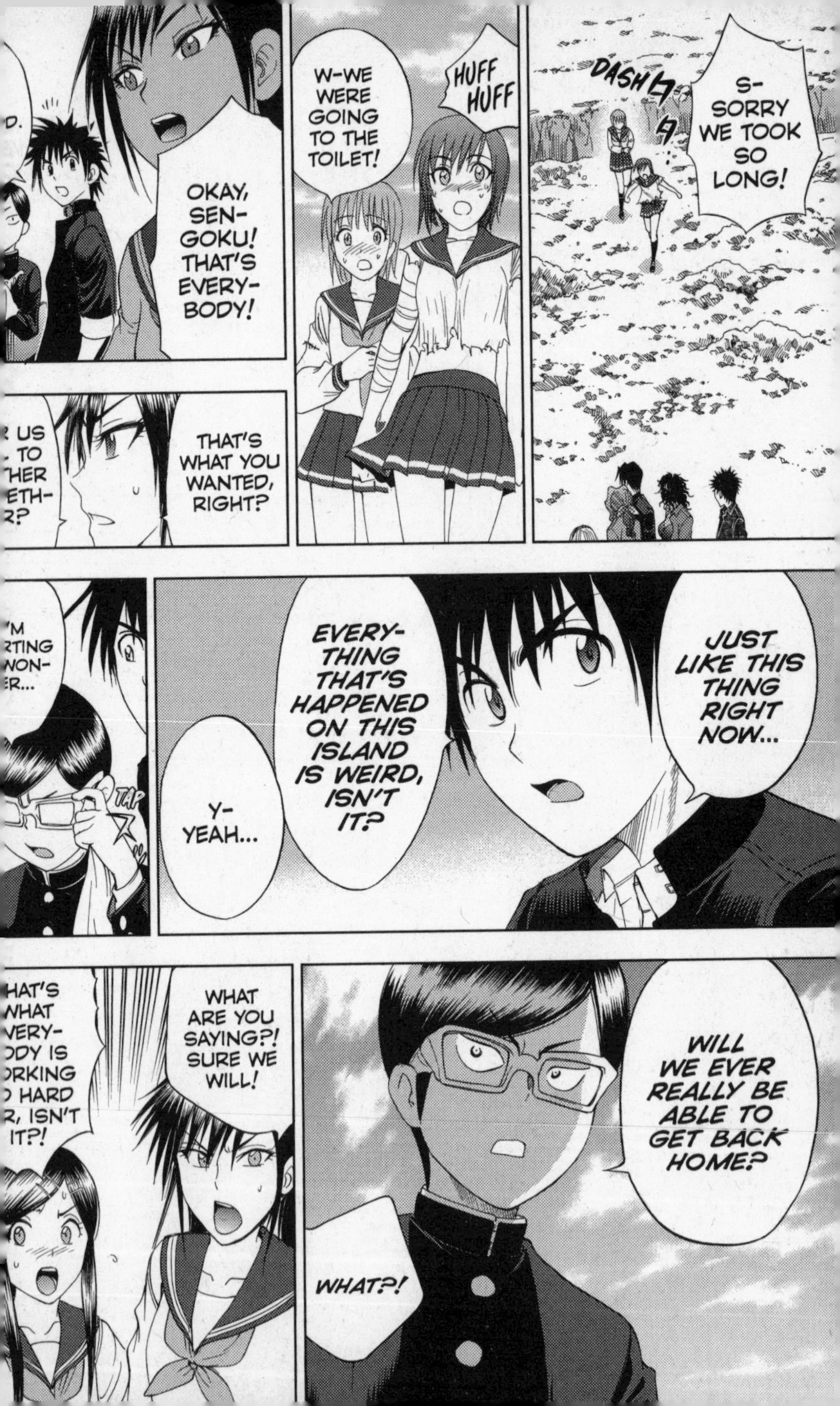
DASH
S-SORRY WE TOOK SO LONG!
HUFF HUFF
W-WE WERE GOING TO THE TOILET!
OKAY, SEN-GOKU! THAT'S EVERY-BODY!
THAT'S WHAT YOU WANTED, RIGHT?
JUST LIKE THIS THING RIGHT NOW...
EVERY-THING THAT'S HAPPENED ON THIS ISLAND IS WEIRD, ISN'T IT?
Y-YEAH...
TAP
WILL WE EVER REALLY BE ABLE TO GET BACK HOME?
WHAT?!
WHAT ARE YOU SAYING?! SURE WE WILL!

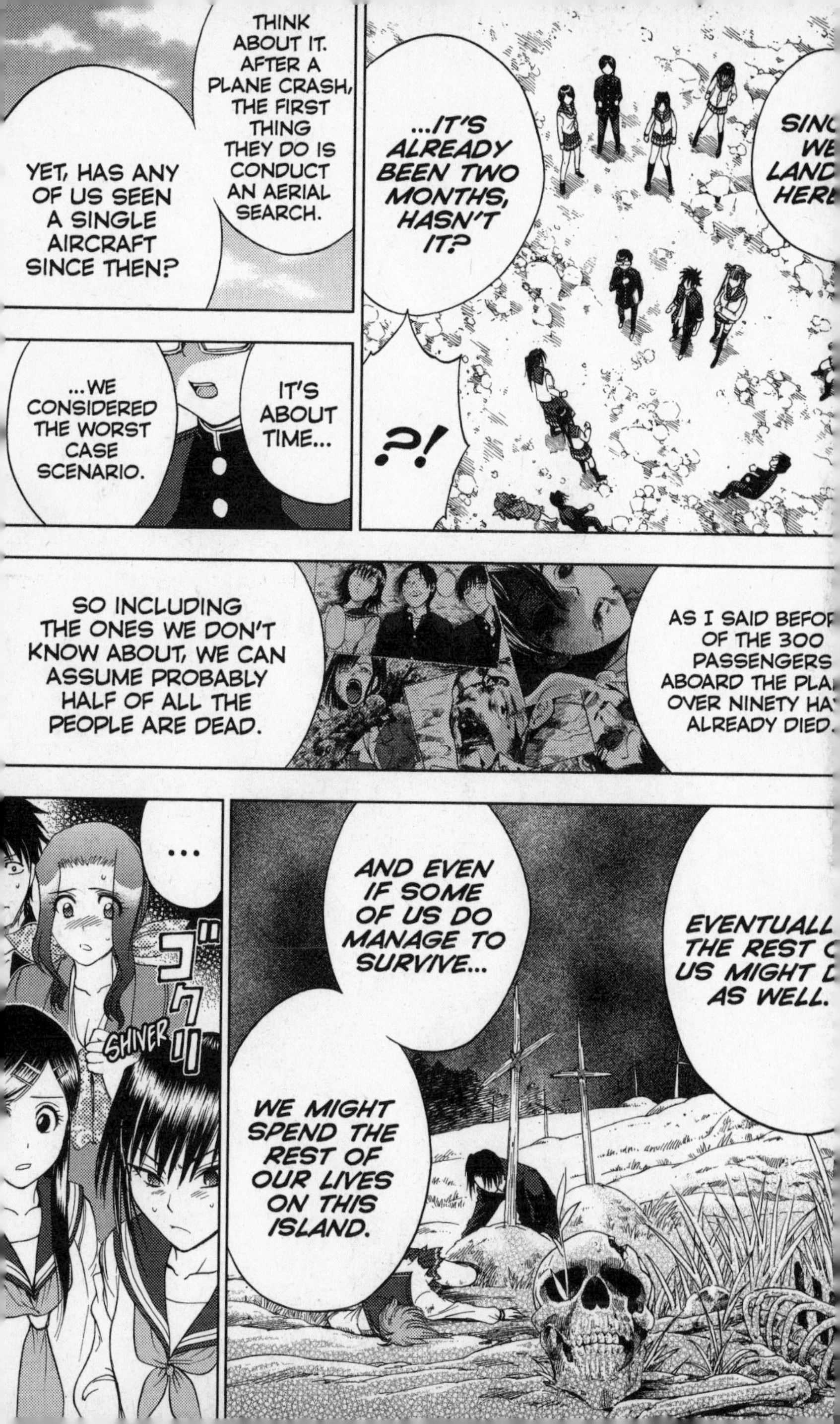
SINC WE LAND HERE
...IT'S ALREADY BEEN TWO MONTHS, HASN'T IT?
?!
THINK ABOUT IT. AFTER A PLANE CRASH, THE FIRST THING THEY DO IS CONDUCT AN AERIAL SEARCH.
YET, HAS ANY OF US SEEN A SINGLE AIRCRAFT SINCE THEN?
IT'S ABOUT TIME...
...WE CONSIDERED THE WORST CASE SCENARIO.
AS I SAID BEFOR OF THE 300 PASSENGERS ABOARD THE PLA OVER NINETY HA ALREADY DIED.
SO INCLUDING THE ONES WE DON'T KNOW ABOUT, WE CAN ASSUME PROBABLY HALF OF ALL THE PEOPLE ARE DEAD.
EVENTUALL THE REST O US MIGHT D AS WELL.
AND EVEN IF SOME OF US DO MANAGE TO SURVIVE...
WE MIGHT SPEND THE REST OF OUR LIVES ON THIS ISLAND.
...
SHIVER

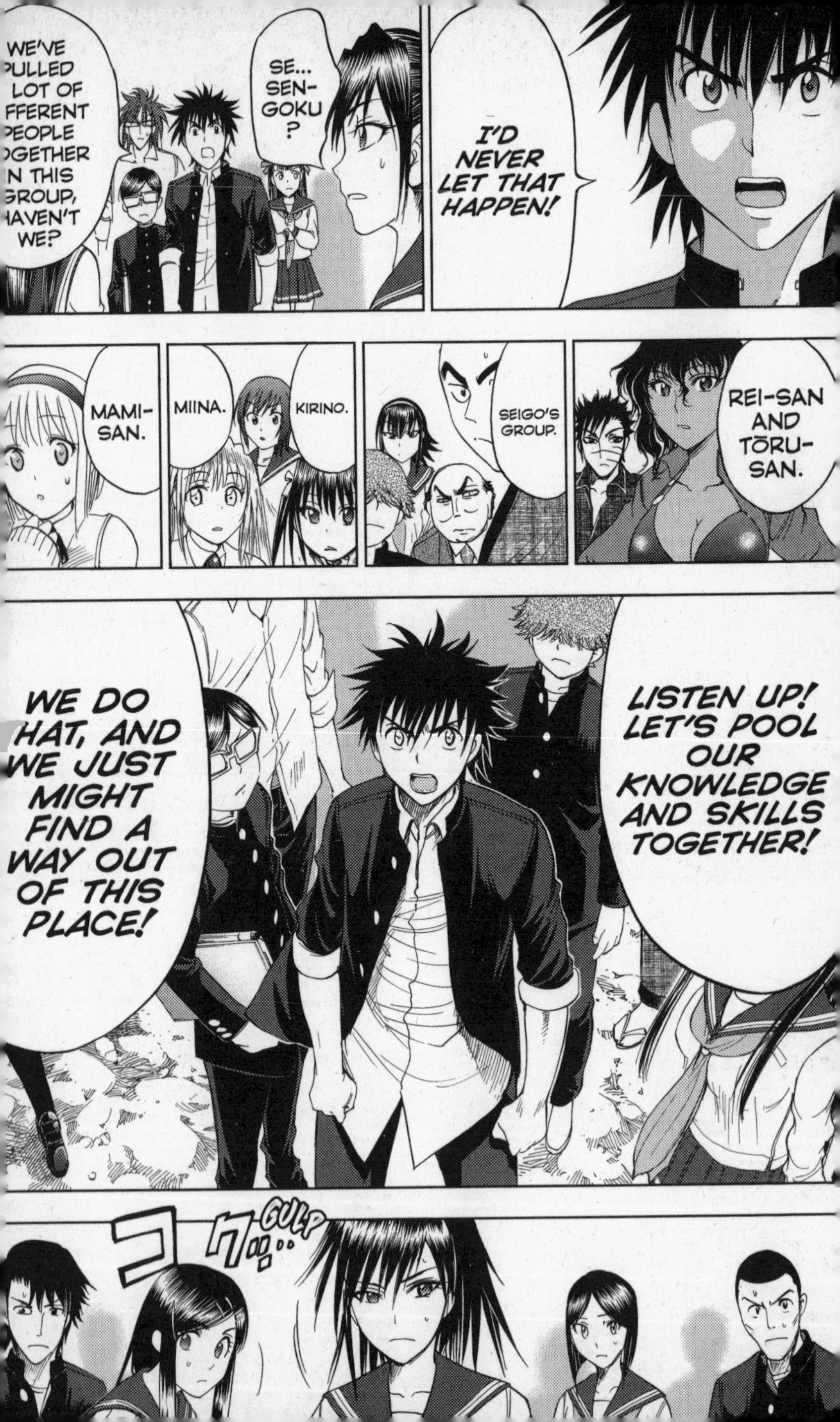
I'D NEVER LET THAT HAPPEN!
SE... SEN-GOKU?
WE'VE PULLED LOT OF FFERENT PEOPLE OGETHER N THIS GROUP, HAVEN'T WE?
REI-SAN AND TŌRU-SAN.
SEIGO'S GROUP.
KIRINO.
MIINA.
MAMI-SAN.
LISTEN UP! LET'S POOL OUR KNOWLEDGE AND SKILLS TOGETHER!
WE DO HAT, AND WE JUST MIGHT FIND A WAY OUT OF THIS PLACE!
コク
GULP

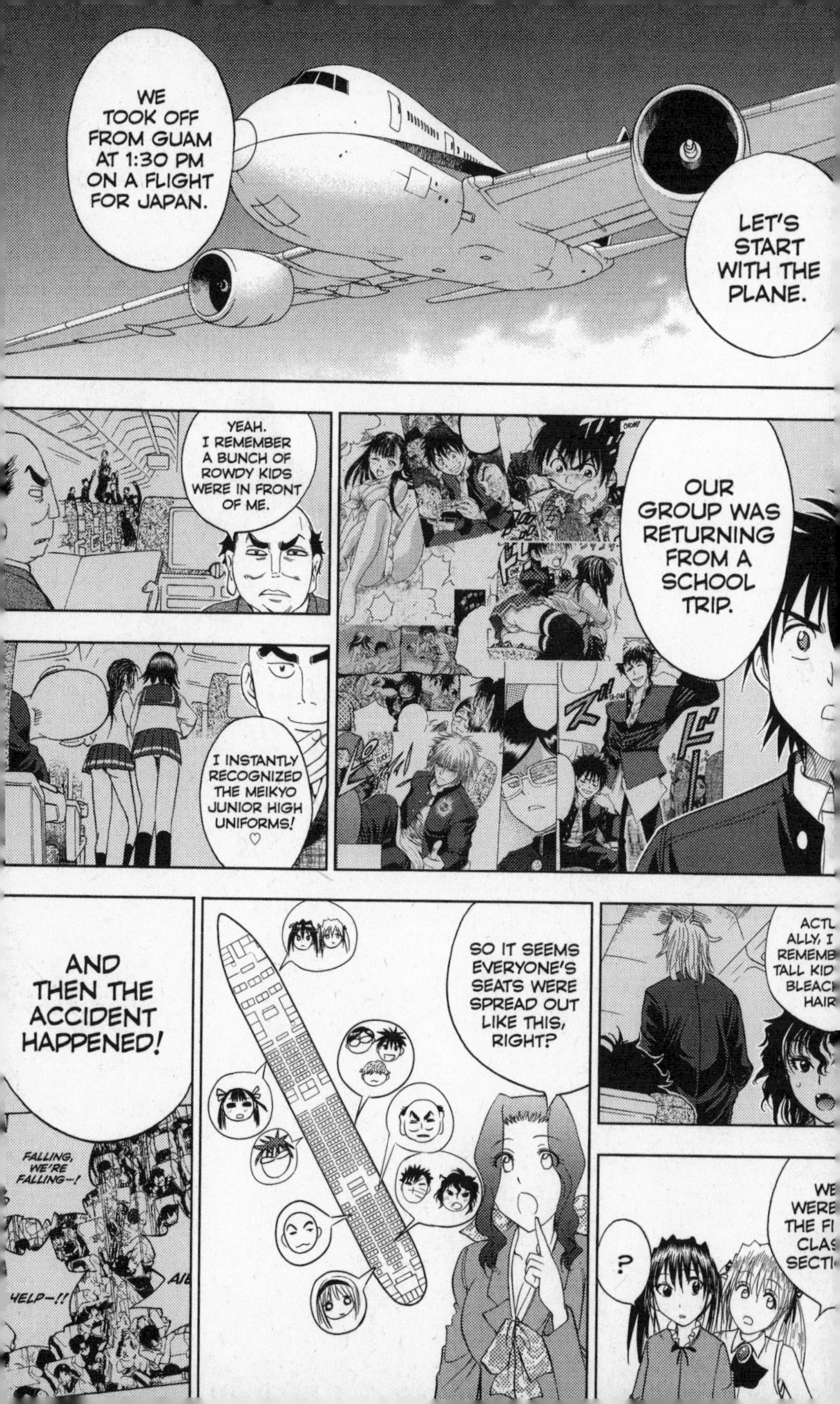
LET'S START WITH THE PLANE.
WE TOOK OFF FROM GUAM AT 1:30 PM ON A FLIGHT FOR JAPAN.
OUR GROUP WAS RETURNING FROM A SCHOOL TRIP.
YEAH. I REMEMBER A BUNCH OF ROWDY KIDS WERE IN FRONT OF ME.
I INSTANTLY RECOGNIZED THE MEIKYO JUNIOR HIGH UNIFORMS! ♡
ACTU ALLY, I REMEMB TALL KID BLEAC HAIR
WE WERE THE FI CLAS SECTI
?
SO IT SEEMS EVERYONE'S SEATS WERE SPREAD OUT LIKE THIS, RIGHT?
AND THEN THE ACCIDENT HAPPENED!
FALLING, WE'RE FALLING--!
AI
HELP--!!

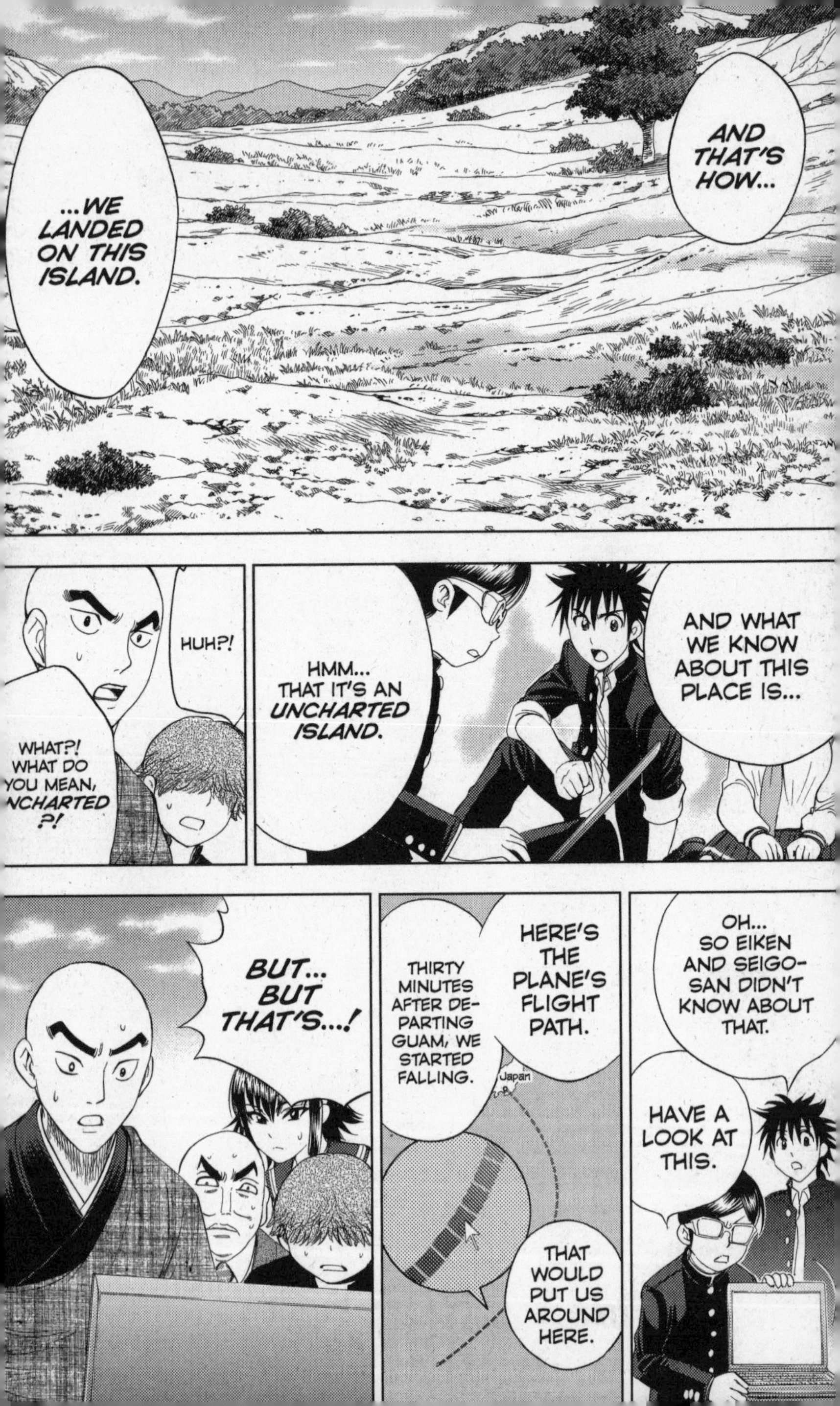
AND THAT'S HOW...
...WE LANDED ON THIS ISLAND.
AND WHAT WE KNOW ABOUT THIS PLACE IS...
HMM... THAT IT'S AN UNCHARTED ISLAND.
HUH?!
WHAT?! WHAT DO YOU MEAN, NCHARTED?!
OH... SO EIKEN AND SEIGO-SAN DIDN'T KNOW ABOUT THAT.
HAVE A LOOK AT THIS.
HERE'S THE PLANE'S FLIGHT PATH.
THIRTY MINUTES AFTER DE-PARTING GUAM, WE STARTED FALLING.
Japan
THAT WOULD PUT US AROUND HERE.
BUT... BUT THAT'S...!

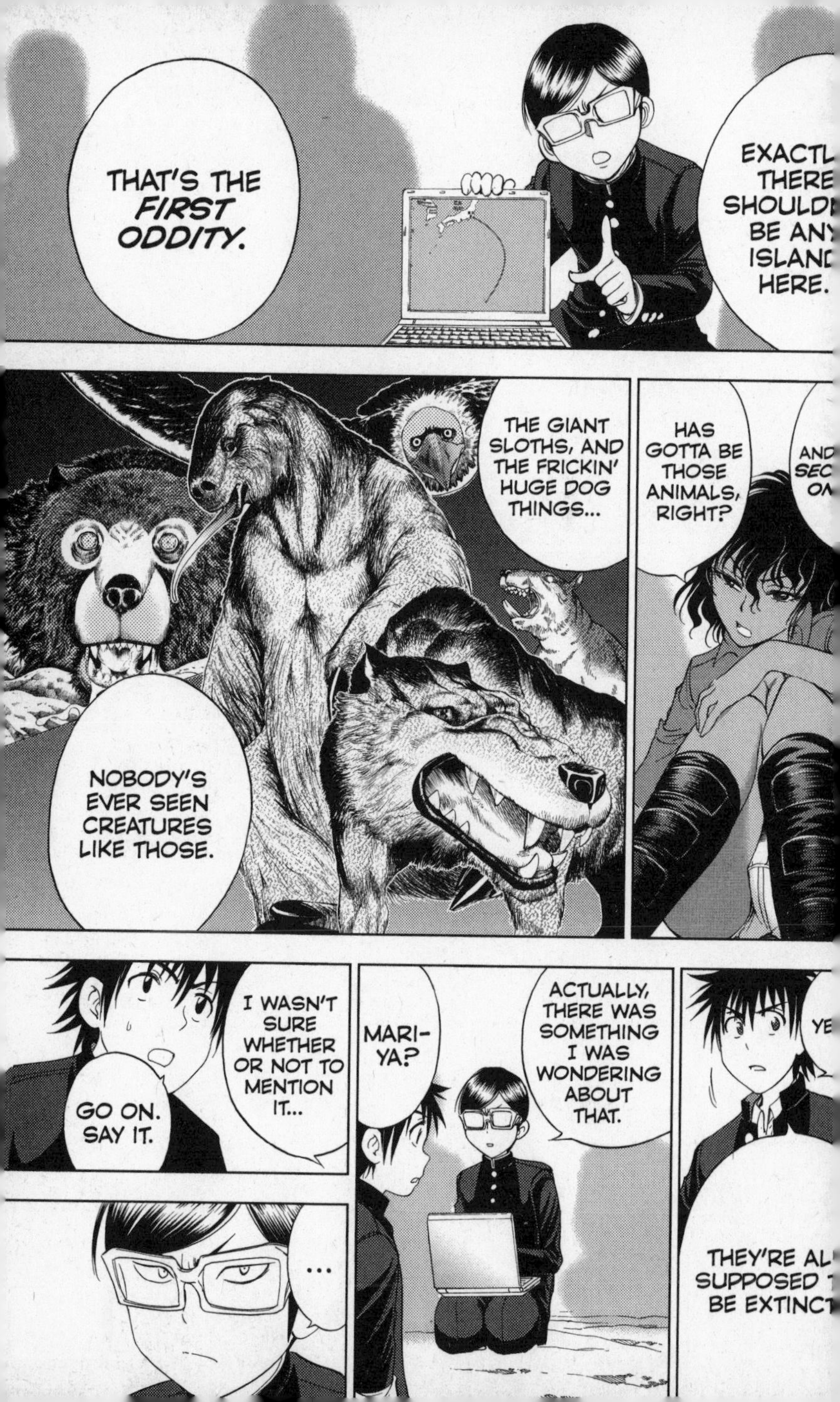

EXACTL THERE SHOULD BE AN ISLAN HERE.
THAT'S THE *FIRST ODDITY.*
AND SEC ON
HAS GOTTA BE THOSE ANIMALS, RIGHT?
THE GIANT SLOTHS, AND THE FRICKIN' HUGE DOG THINGS...
NOBODY'S EVER SEEN CREATURES LIKE THOSE.
YE
THEY'RE AL SUPPOSED T BE EXTINCT
ACTUALLY, THERE WAS SOMETHING I WAS WONDERING ABOUT THAT.
MARI-YA?
I WASN'T SURE WHETHER OR NOT TO MENTION IT...
GO ON. SAY IT.
...

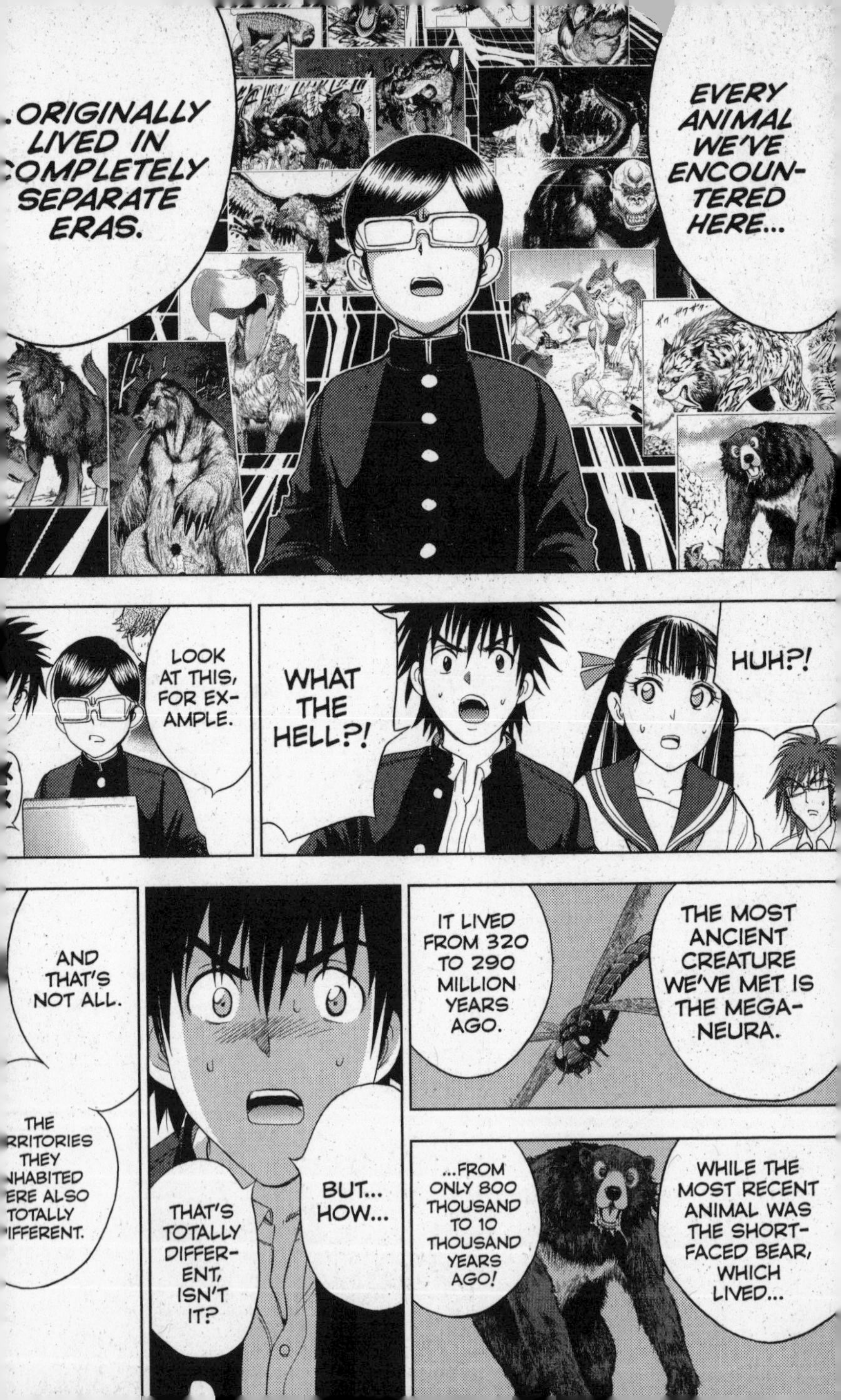
EVERY ANIMAL WE'VE ENCOUN-TERED HERE...
.ORIGINALLY LIVED IN COMPLETELY SEPARATE ERAS.
HUH?!
WHAT THE HELL?!
LOOK AT THIS, FOR EX-AMPLE.
THE MOST ANCIENT CREATURE WE'VE MET IS THE MEGA-NEURA.
IT LIVED FROM 320 TO 290 MILLION YEARS AGO.
WHILE THE MOST RECENT ANIMAL WAS THE SHORT-FACED BEAR, WHICH LIVED...
...FROM ONLY 800 THOUSAND TO 10 THOUSAND YEARS AGO!
BUT... HOW...
THAT'S TOTALLY DIFFER-ENT, ISN'T IT?
AND THAT'S NOT ALL.
RRITORIES THEY NHABITED ERE ALSO TOTALLY IFFERENT.

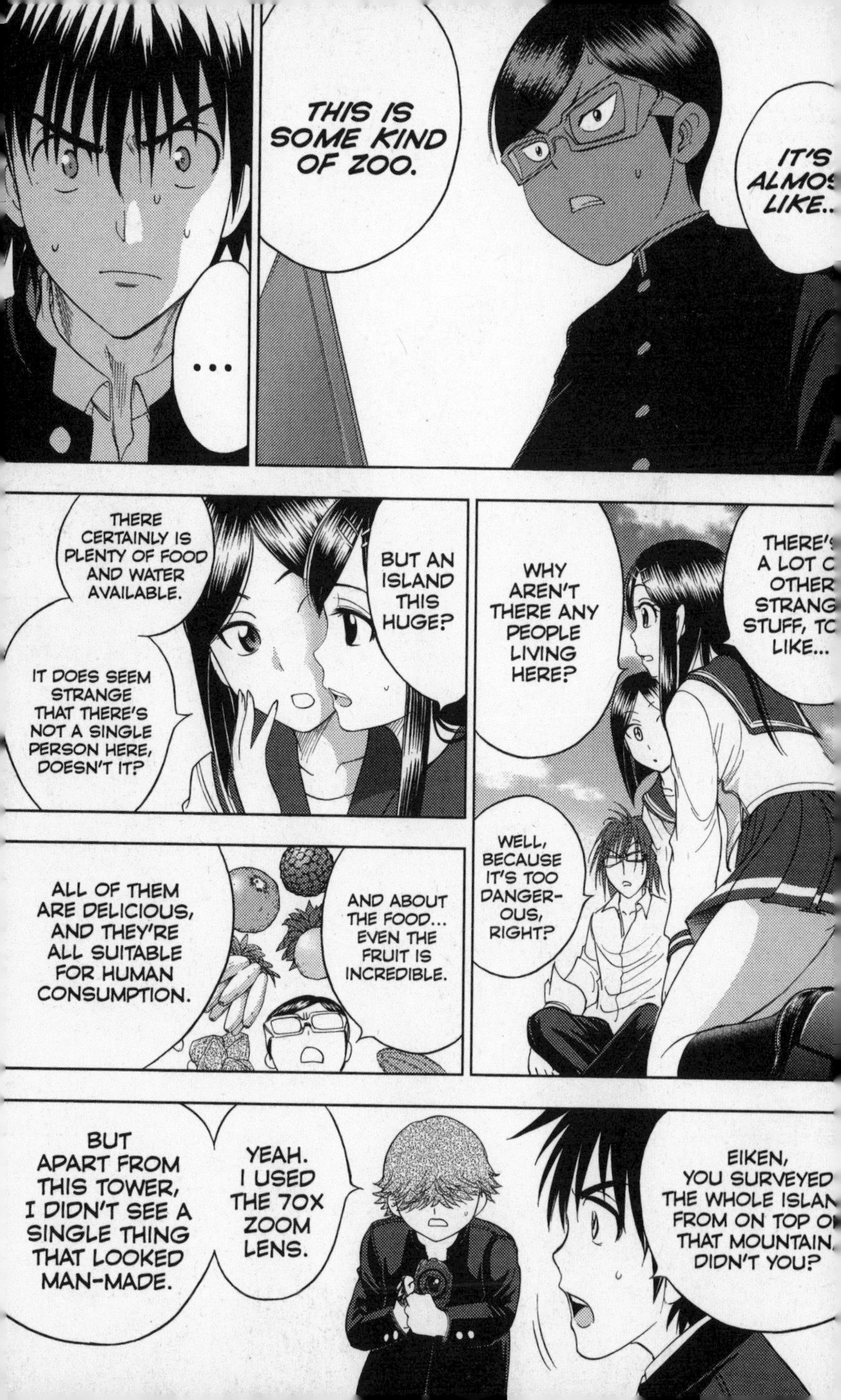

IT'S ALMOS LIKE..
THIS IS SOME KIND OF ZOO.
...
THERE'S A LOT C OTHER STRANG STUFF, TC LIKE...
WHY AREN'T THERE ANY PEOPLE LIVING HERE?
WELL, BECAUSE IT'S TOO DANGER-OUS, RIGHT?
BUT AN ISLAND THIS HUGE?
THERE CERTAINLY IS PLENTY OF FOOD AND WATER AVAILABLE.
IT DOES SEEM STRANGE THAT THERE'S NOT A SINGLE PERSON HERE, DOESN'T IT?
AND ABOUT THE FOOD... EVEN THE FRUIT IS INCREDIBLE.
ALL OF THEM ARE DELICIOUS, AND THEY'RE ALL SUITABLE FOR HUMAN CONSUMPTION.
EIKEN, YOU SURVEYED THE WHOLE ISLAN FROM ON TOP O THAT MOUNTAIN, DIDN'T YOU?
YEAH. I USED THE 70X ZOOM LENS.
BUT APART FROM THIS TOWER, I DIDN'T SEE A SINGLE THING THAT LOOKED MAN-MADE.

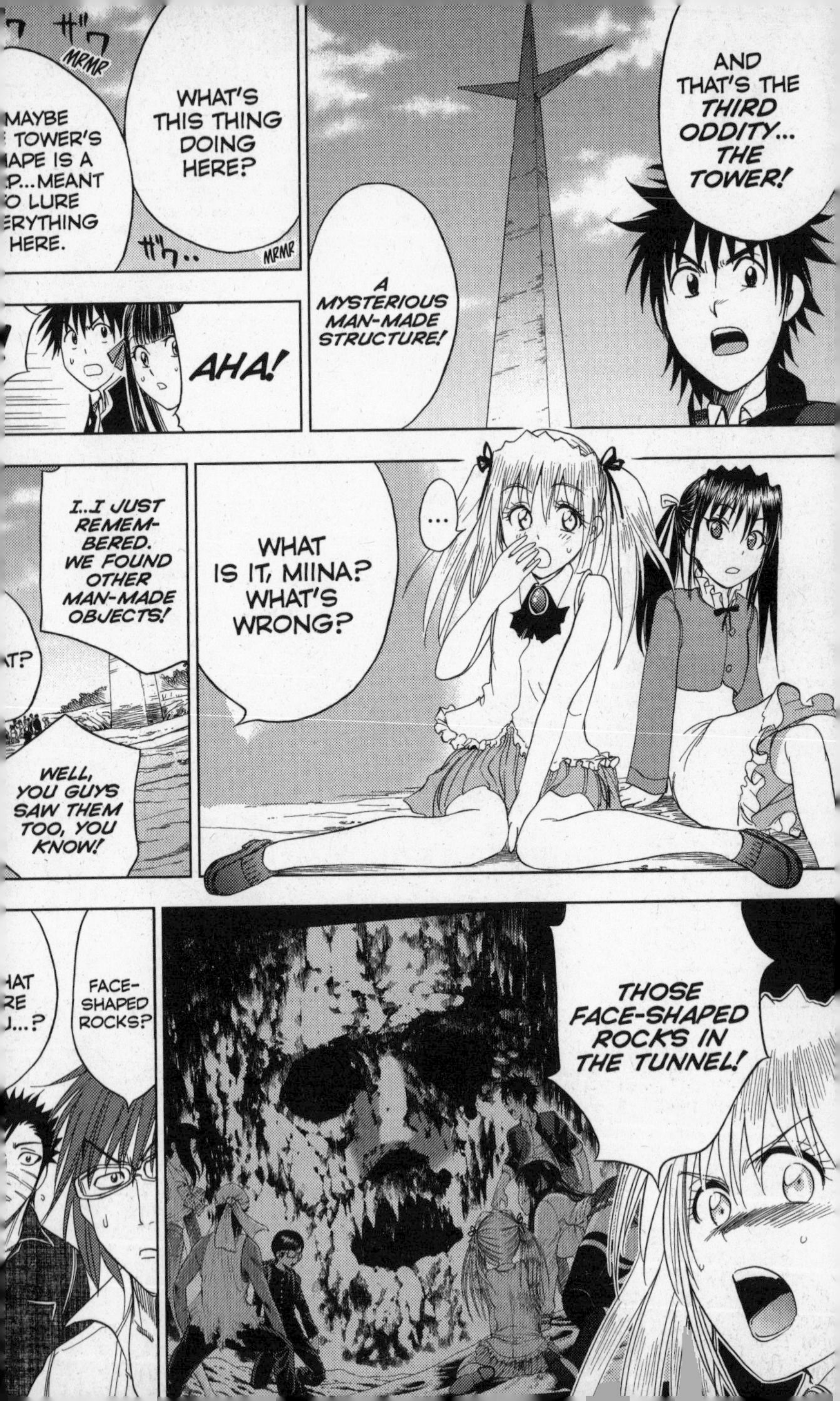
AND THAT'S THE THIRD ODDITY... THE TOWER!
A MYSTERIOUS MAN-MADE STRUCTURE!
WHAT'S THIS THING DOING HERE?
MRMR
MAYBE TOWER'S APE IS A P...MEANT O LURE ERYTHING HERE.
MRMR
AHA!
...
WHAT IS IT, MIINA? WHAT'S WRONG?
I..I JUST REMEMBERED. WE FOUND OTHER MAN-MADE OBJECTS!
AT?
WELL, YOU GUYS SAW THEM TOO, YOU KNOW!
THOSE FACE-SHAPED ROCKS IN THE TUNNEL!
FACE-SHAPED ROCKS?
HAT RE U...?

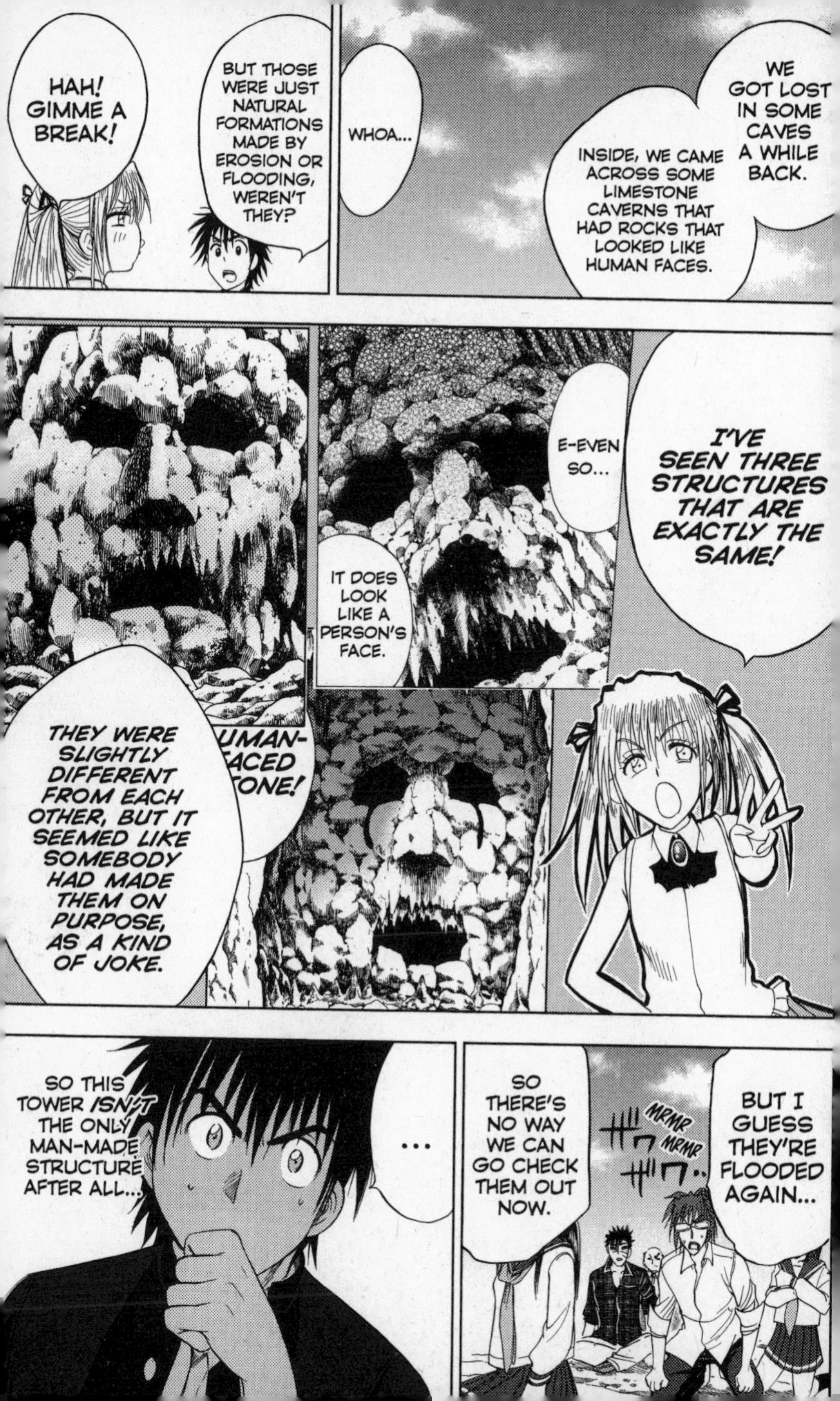
WE GOT LOST IN SOME CAVES A WHILE BACK.
INSIDE, WE CAME ACROSS SOME LIMESTONE CAVERNS THAT HAD ROCKS THAT LOOKED LIKE HUMAN FACES.
WHOA...
BUT THOSE WERE JUST NATURAL FORMATIONS MADE BY EROSION OR FLOODING, WEREN'T THEY?
HAH! GIMME A BREAK!
I'VE SEEN THREE STRUCTURES THAT ARE EXACTLY THE SAME!
E-EVEN SO...
IT DOES LOOK LIKE A PERSON'S FACE.
UMAN- ACED ONE!
THEY WERE SLIGHTLY DIFFERENT FROM EACH OTHER, BUT IT SEEMED LIKE SOMEBODY HAD MADE THEM ON PURPOSE, AS A KIND OF JOKE.
BUT I GUESS THEY'RE FLOODED AGAIN...
MRMR MRMR
SO THERE'S NO WAY WE CAN GO CHECK THEM OUT NOW.
...
SO THIS TOWER ISN'T THE ONLY MAN-MADE STRUCTURE AFTER ALL...

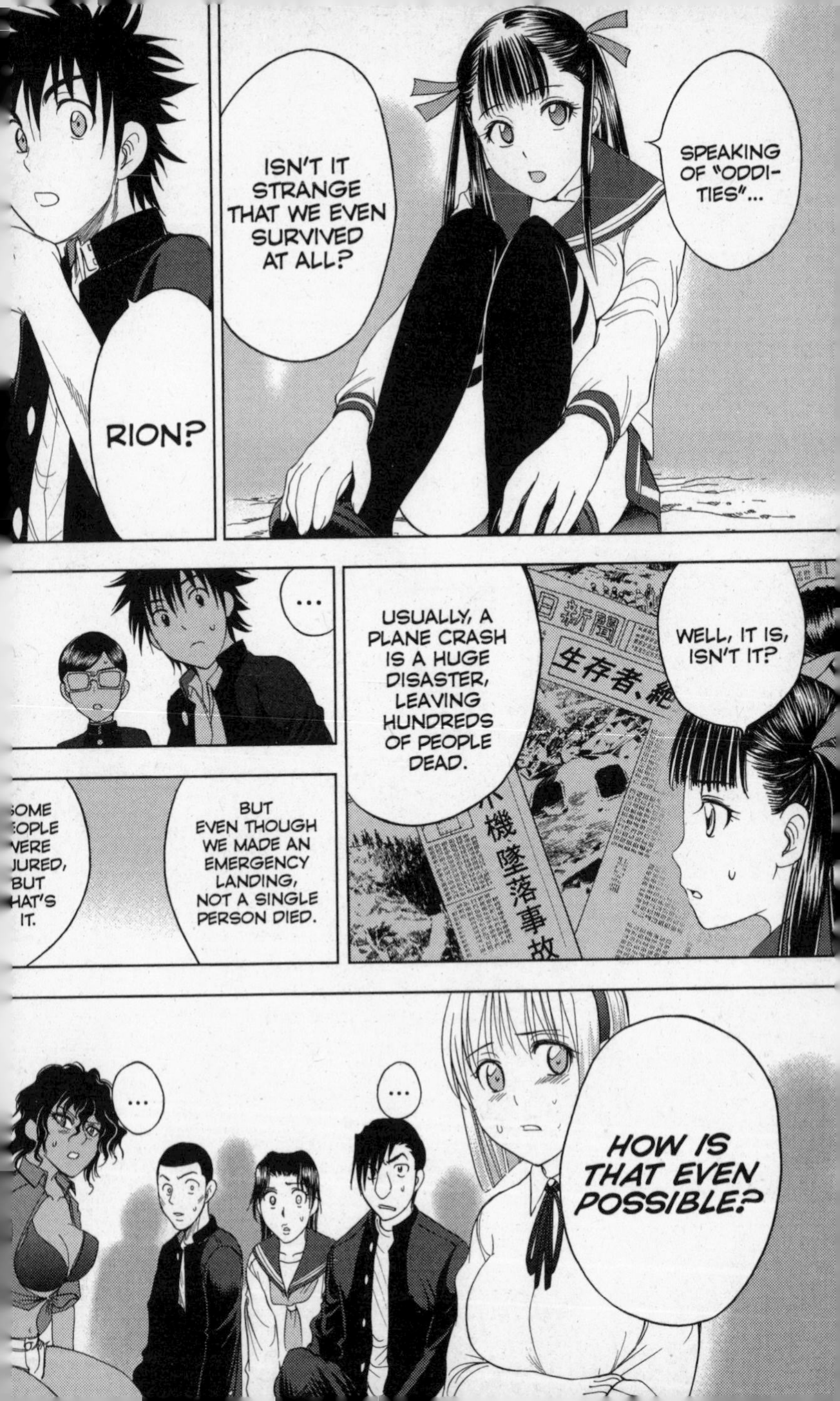
SPEAKING OF "ODDITIES"...
ISN'T IT STRANGE THAT WE EVEN SURVIVED AT ALL?
RION?
WELL, IT IS, ISN'T IT?
USUALLY, A PLANE CRASH IS A HUGE DISASTER, LEAVING HUNDREDS OF PEOPLE DEAD.
日新聞
生存者、絶
機墜落事故
...
BUT EVEN THOUGH WE MADE AN EMERGENCY LANDING, NOT A SINGLE PERSON DIED.
SOME EOPLE VERE JURED, BUT HAT'S IT.
HOW IS THAT EVEN POSSIBLE?
...
...

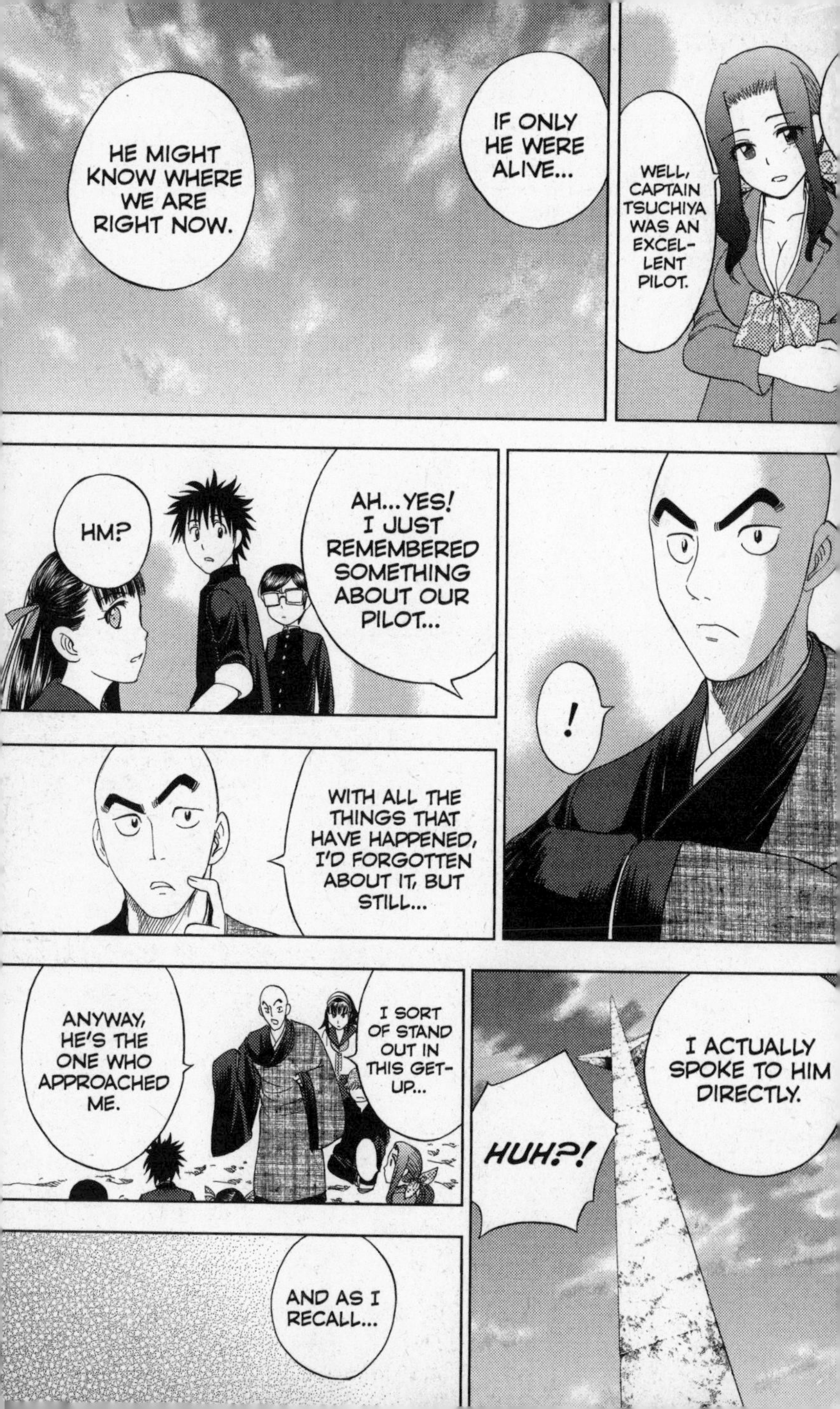
WELL, CAPTAIN TSUCHIYA WAS AN EXCEL-LENT PILOT.
IF ONLY HE WERE ALIVE...
HE MIGHT KNOW WHERE WE ARE RIGHT NOW.
!
AH...YES! I JUST REMEMBERED SOMETHING ABOUT OUR PILOT...
HM?
WITH ALL THE THINGS THAT HAVE HAPPENED, I'D FORGOTTEN ABOUT IT, BUT STILL...
I ACTUALLY SPOKE TO HIM DIRECTLY.
HUH?!
I SORT OF STAND OUT IN THIS GET-UP...
ANYWAY, HE'S THE ONE WHO APPROACHED ME.
AND AS I RECALL...

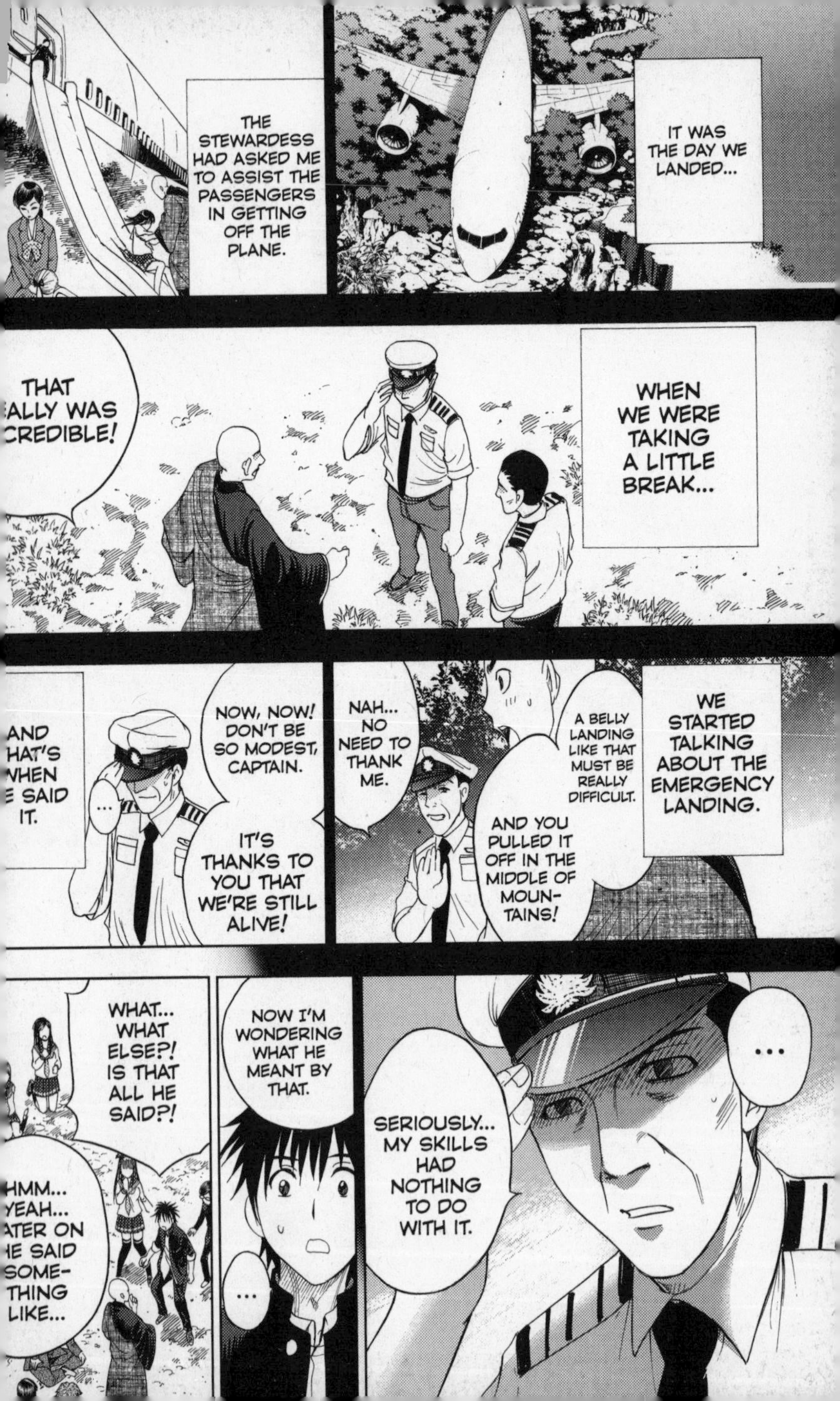
IT WAS THE DAY WE LANDED...
THE STEWARDESS HAD ASKED ME TO ASSIST THE PASSENGERS IN GETTING OFF THE PLANE.
WHEN WE WERE TAKING A LITTLE BREAK...
THAT ALLY WAS CREDIBLE!
WE STARTED TALKING ABOUT THE EMERGENCY LANDING.
A BELLY LANDING LIKE THAT MUST BE REALLY DIFFICULT.
AND YOU PULLED IT OFF IN THE MIDDLE OF MOUN-TAINS!
NAH... NO NEED TO THANK ME.
NOW, NOW! DON'T BE SO MODEST, CAPTAIN.
IT'S THANKS TO YOU THAT WE'RE STILL ALIVE!
...
AND HAT'S HEN SAID IT.
...
SERIOUSLY... MY SKILLS HAD NOTHING TO DO WITH IT.
NOW I'M WONDERING WHAT HE MEANT BY THAT.
...
WHAT... WHAT ELSE?! IS THAT ALL HE SAID?!
HMM... YEAH... ATER ON E SAID SOME-THING LIKE...

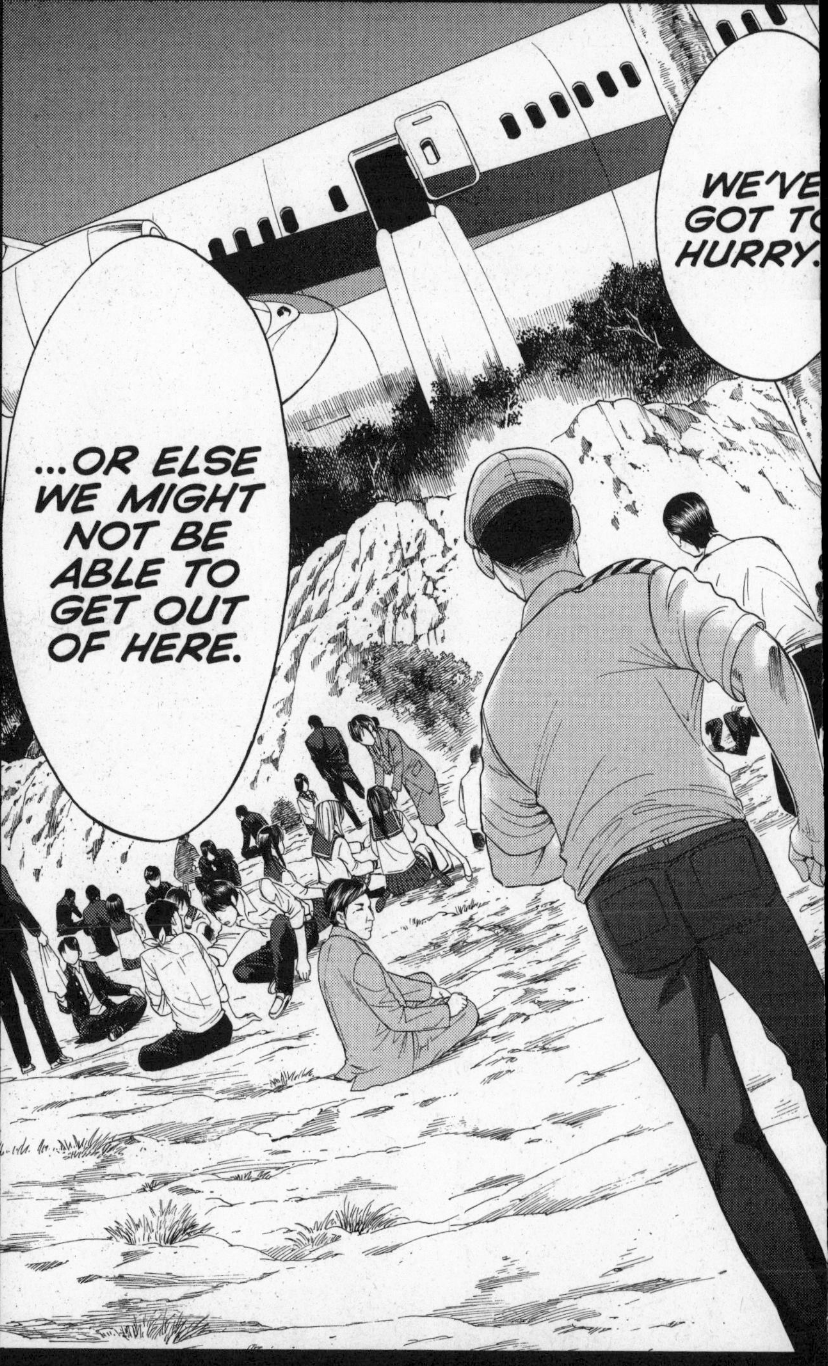
WE'VE GOT TO HURRY.
...OR ELSE WE MIGHT NOT BE ABLE TO GET OUT OF HERE.

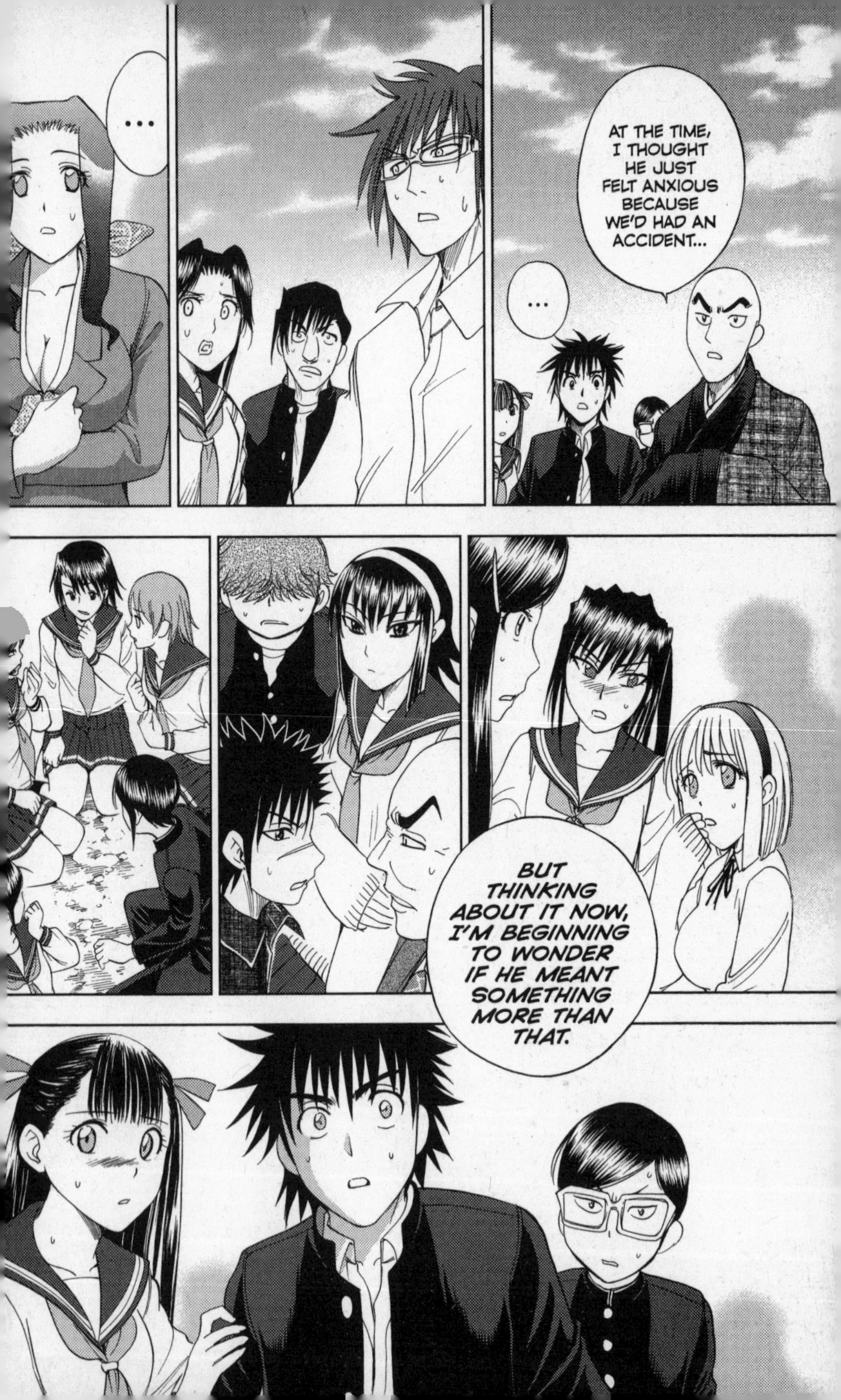
AT THE TIME, I THOUGHT HE JUST FELT ANXIOUS BECAUSE WE'D HAD AN ACCIDENT...
...
...
BUT THINKING ABOUT IT NOW, I'M BEGINNING TO WONDER IF HE MEANT SOMETHING MORE THAN THAT.

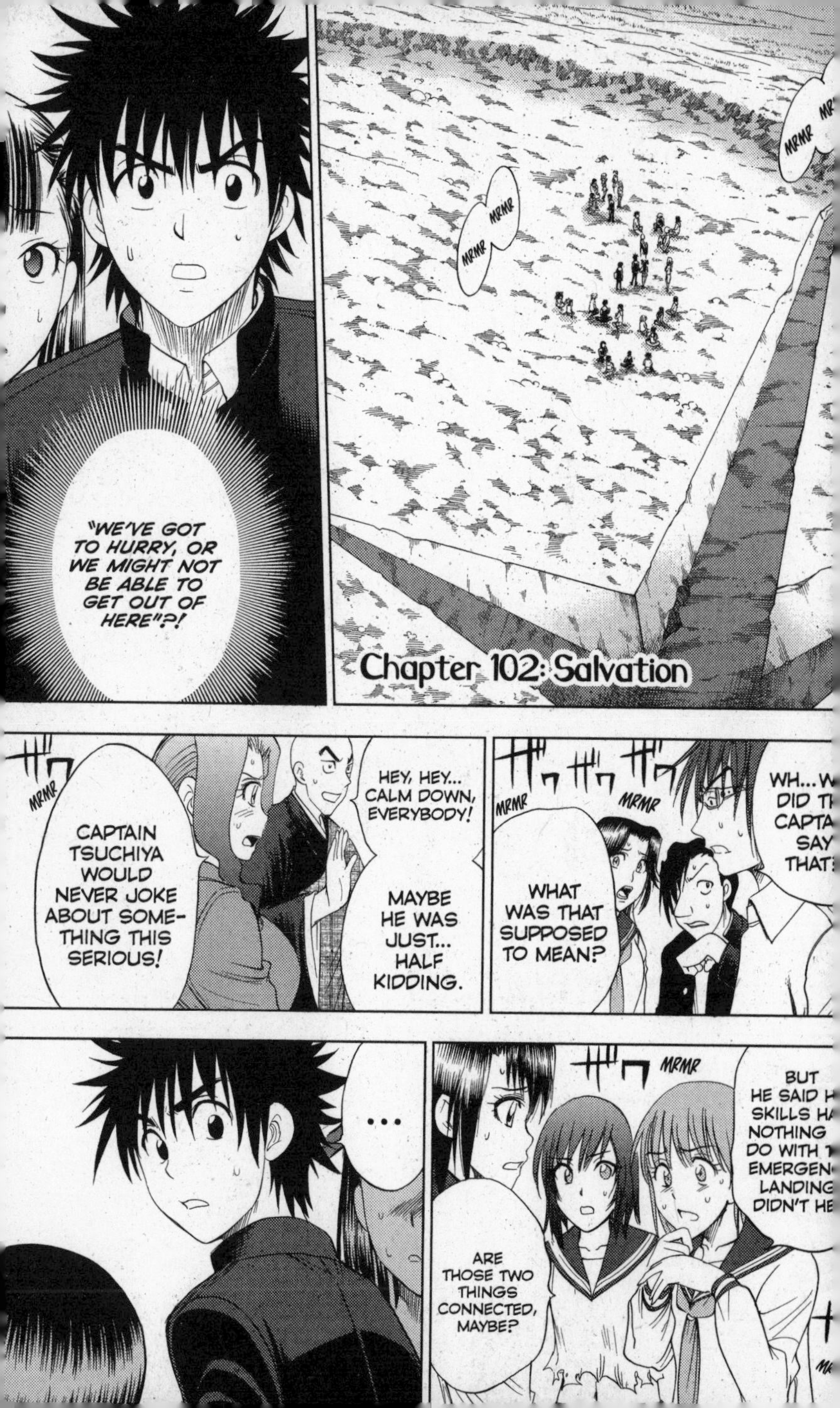
MRMR MRMR
MRMR MRMR
Chapter 102: Salvation
"WE'VE GOT TO HURRY, OR WE MIGHT NOT BE ABLE TO GET OUT OF HERE"?!
WH...W DID TH CAPTA SAY THAT
MRMR
MRMR
WHAT WAS THAT SUPPOSED TO MEAN?
HEY, HEY... CALM DOWN, EVERYBODY!
MAYBE HE WAS JUST... HALF KIDDING.
MRMR
CAPTAIN TSUCHIYA WOULD NEVER JOKE ABOUT SOME-THING THIS SERIOUS!
MRMR
BUT HE SAID H SKILLS HA NOTHING DO WITH T EMERGENC LANDING DIDN'T HE
ARE THOSE TWO THINGS CONNECTED, MAYBE?
...

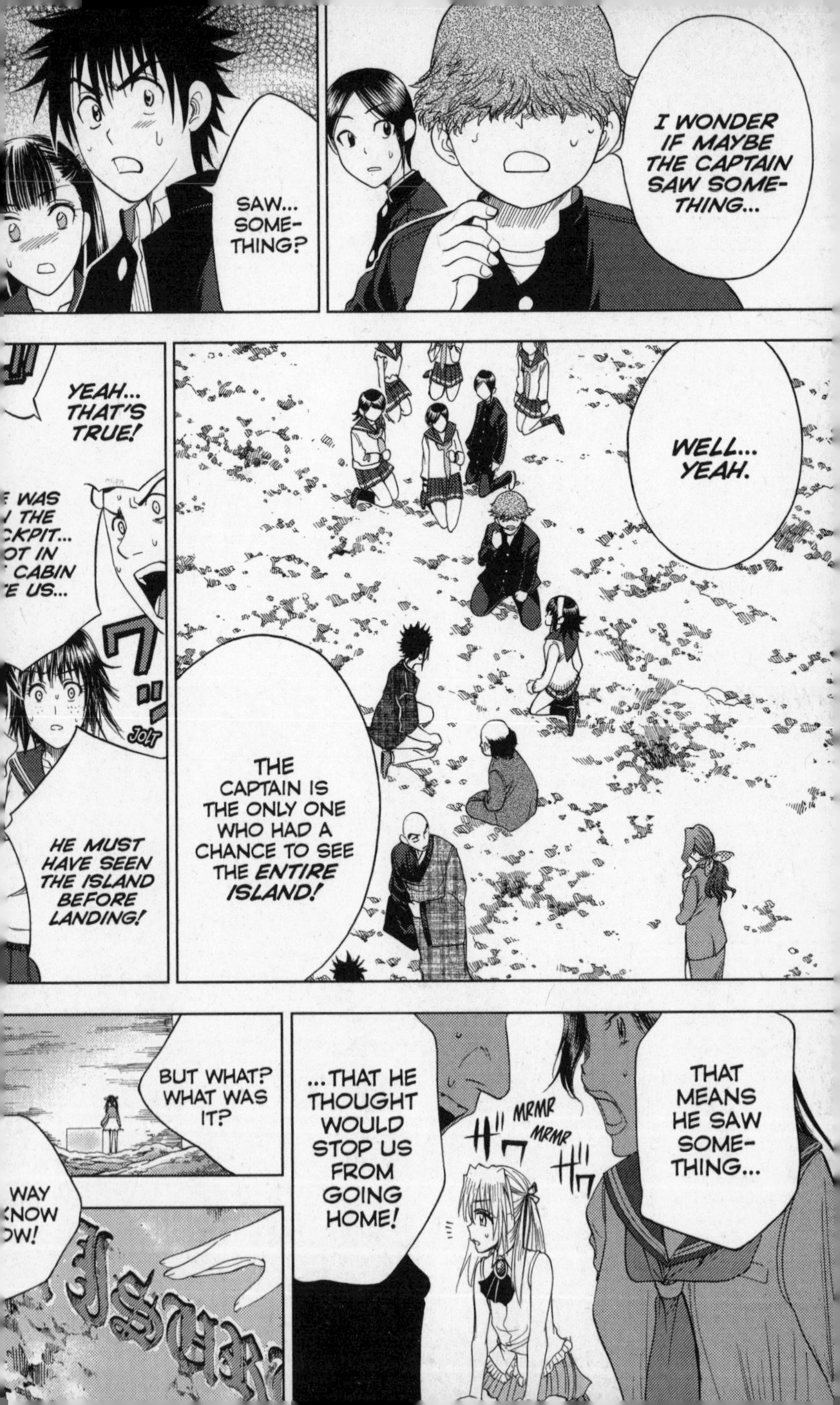
I WONDER IF MAYBE THE CAPTAIN SAW SOME-THING...
SAW... SOME-THING?
WELL... YEAH.
THE CAPTAIN IS THE ONLY ONE WHO HAD A CHANCE TO SEE THE *ENTIRE ISLAND!*
YEAH... THAT'S TRUE!
E WAS N THE CKPIT... OT IN CABIN E US...
JOLT
HE MUST HAVE SEEN THE ISLAND BEFORE LANDING!
THAT MEANS HE SAW SOME-THING...
MRMR
MRMR
...THAT HE THOUGHT WOULD STOP US FROM GOING HOME!
BUT WHAT? WHAT WAS IT?
WAY KNOW OW!

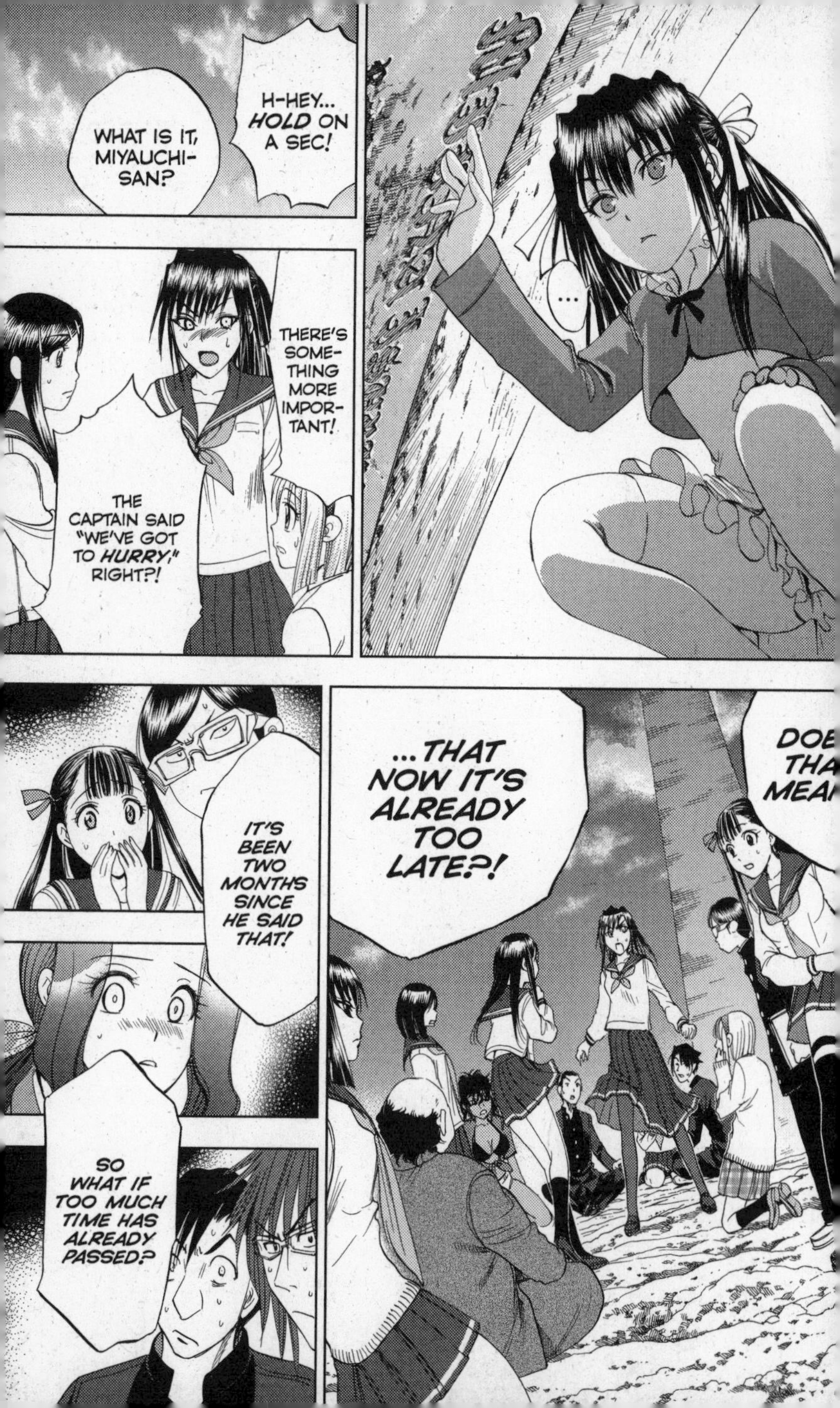
...
H-HEY... HOLD ON A SEC!
WHAT IS IT, MIYAUCHI-SAN?
THERE'S SOMETHING MORE IMPORTANT!
THE CAPTAIN SAID "WE'VE GOT TO HURRY," RIGHT?!
DOE THA MEA
...THAT NOW IT'S ALREADY TOO LATE?!
IT'S BEEN TWO MONTHS SINCE HE SAID THAT!
SO WHAT IF TOO MUCH TIME HAS ALREADY PASSED?

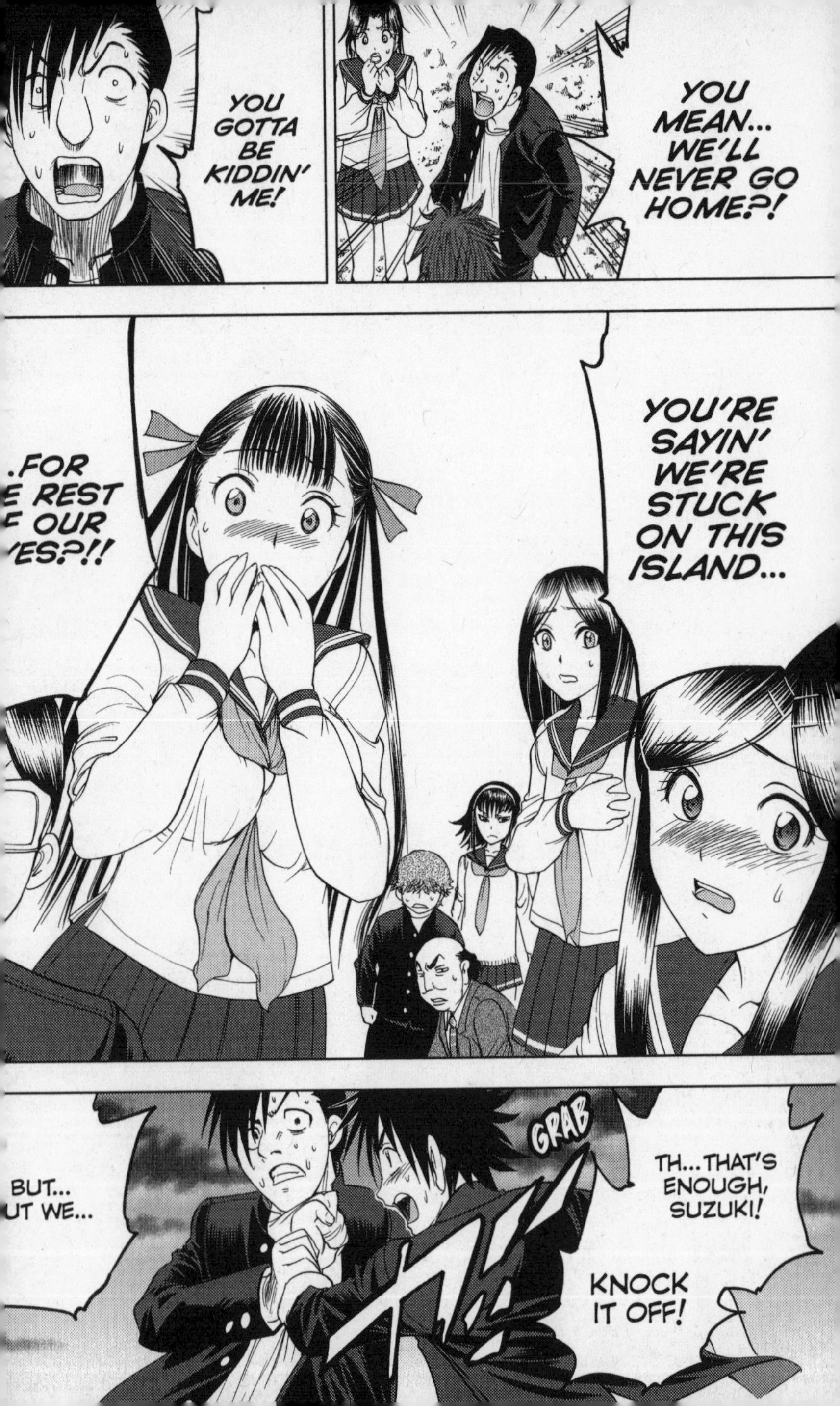
YOU MEAN... WE'LL NEVER GO HOME?!
YOU GOTTA BE KIDDIN' ME!
YOU'RE SAYIN' WE'RE STUCK ON THIS ISLAND...
.FOR E REST F OUR ES?!!
TH...THAT'S ENOUGH, SUZUKI!
GRAB
KNOCK IT OFF!
BUT... UT WE...

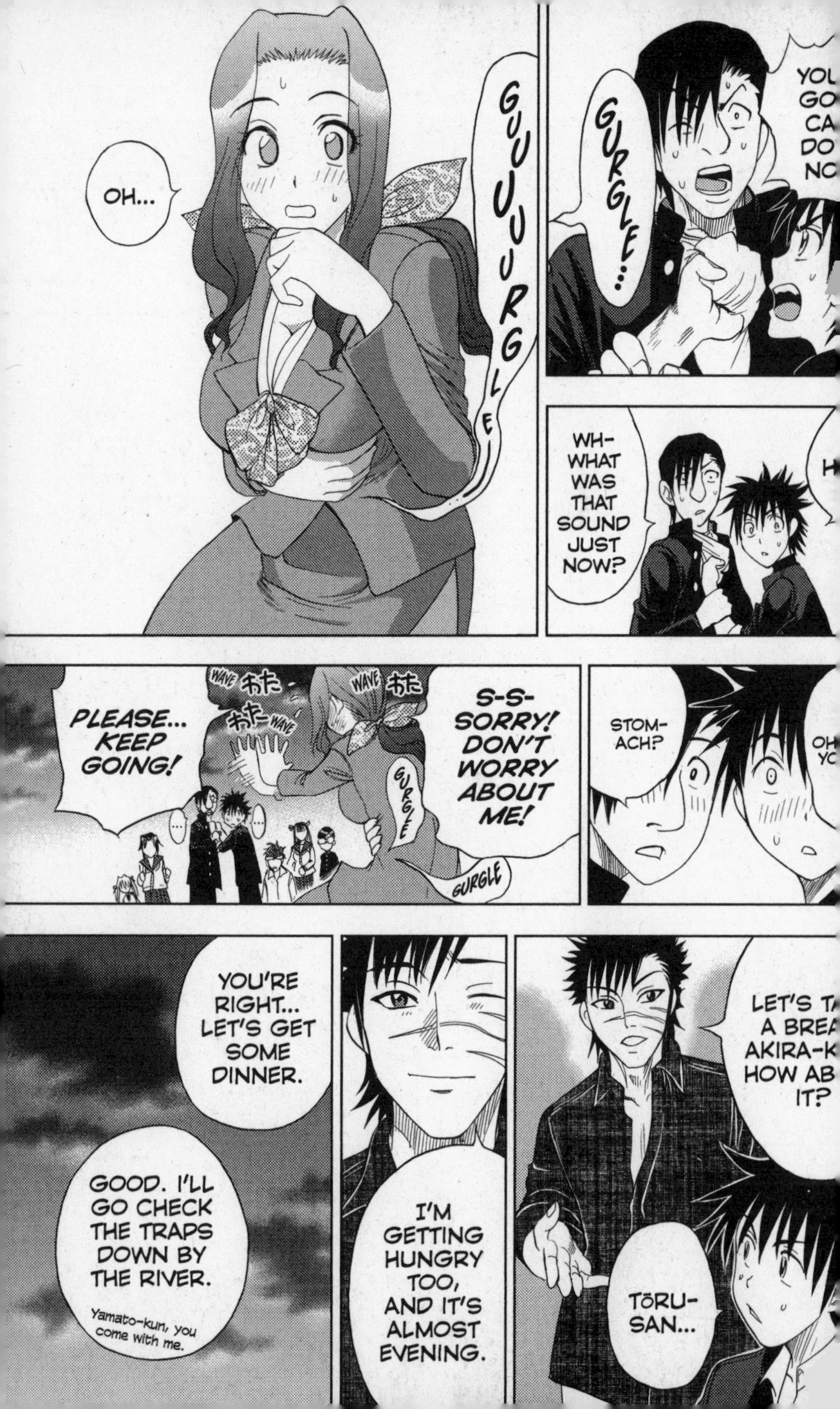

YOU GO CA DO NO
GURGLE...
WH- WHAT WAS THAT SOUND JUST NOW?
H
GUUUUURGLE
OH...
STOM- ACH?
OH YO
S-S-SORRY! DON'T WORRY ABOUT ME!
WAVE おた
おた WAVE
WAVE おた
PLEASE... KEEP GOING!
...
...
GURGLE
GURGLE
LET'S TA A BREA AKIRA-K HOW AB IT?
TŌRU- SAN...
YOU'RE RIGHT... LET'S GET SOME DINNER.
I'M GETTING HUNGRY TOO, AND IT'S ALMOST EVENING.
GOOD. I'LL GO CHECK THE TRAPS DOWN BY THE RIVER.
Yamato-kun, you come with me.

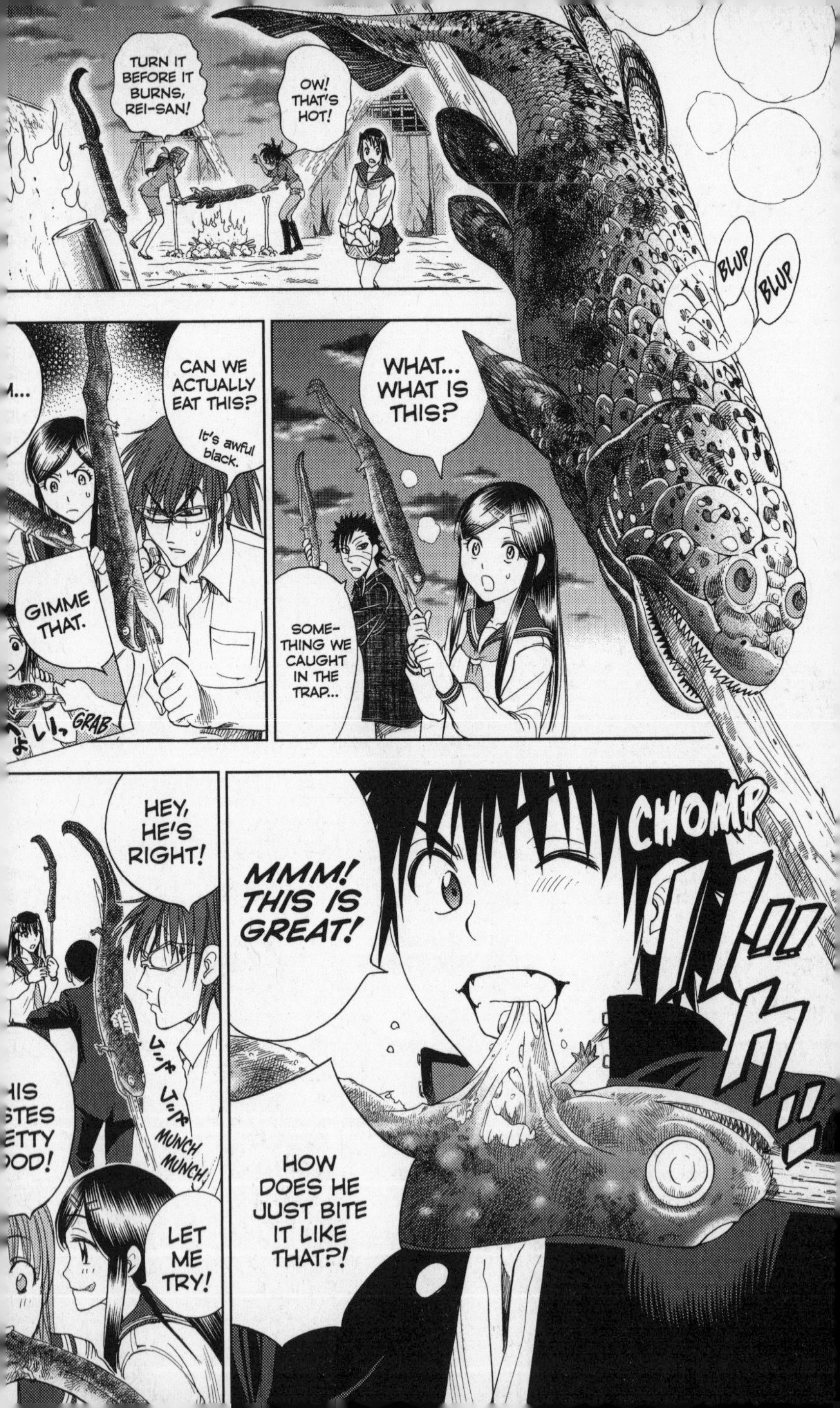
BLUP
BLUP
OW! THAT'S HOT!
TURN IT BEFORE IT BURNS, REI-SAN!
WHAT... WHAT IS THIS?
SOME-THING WE CAUGHT IN THE TRAP...
CAN WE ACTUALLY EAT THIS?
It's awful black.
GIMME THAT.
GRAB
CHOMP
MMM! THIS IS GREAT!
HOW DOES HE JUST BITE IT LIKE THAT?!
HEY, HE'S RIGHT!
MUNCH MUNCH
LET ME TRY!

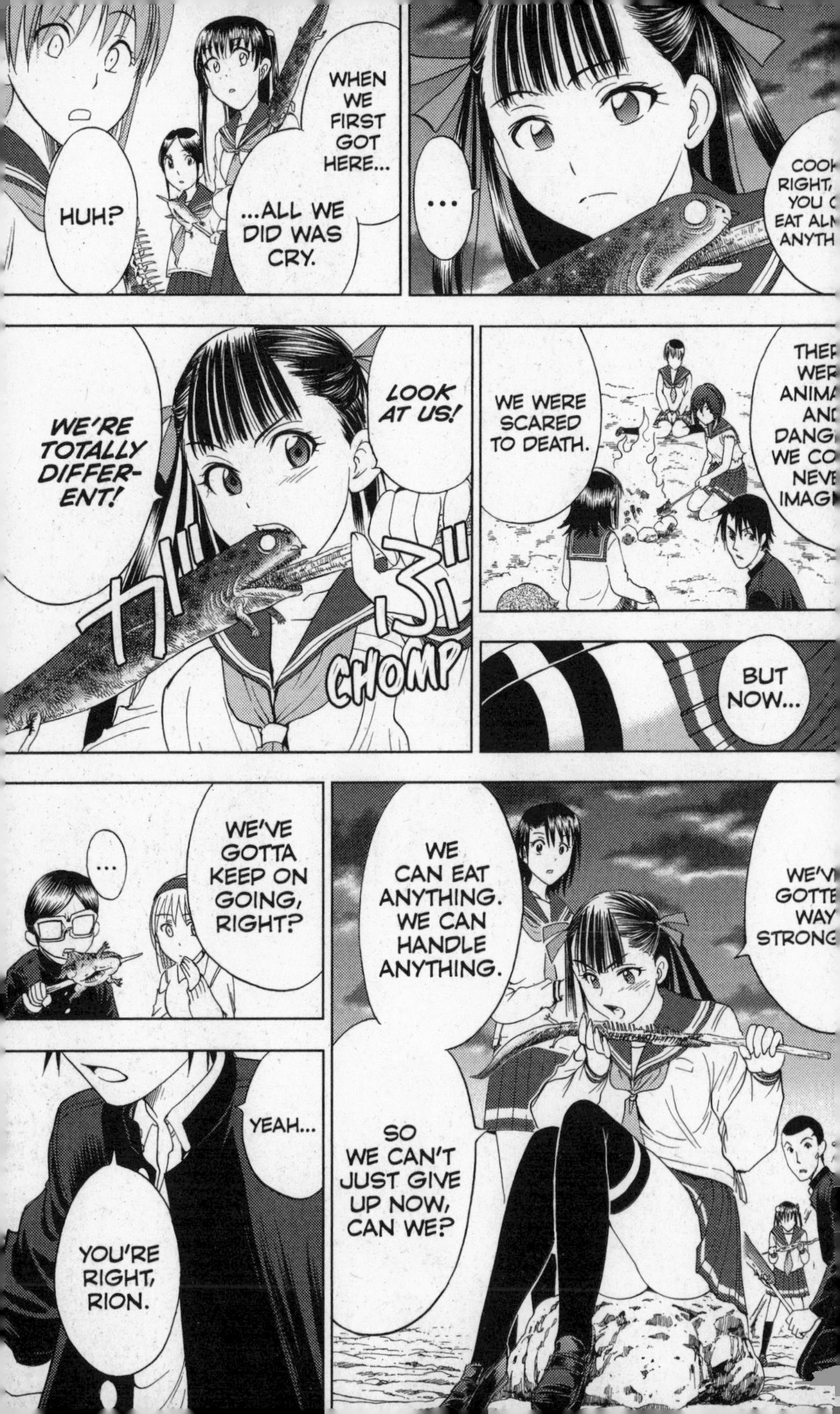
COOK RIGHT, YOU C EAT ALM ANYTH
...
WHEN WE FIRST GOT HERE...
...ALL WE DID WAS CRY.
HUH?
THEF WER ANIMA ANI DANG WE CO NEVE IMAG
WE WERE SCARED TO DEATH.
BUT NOW...
LOOK AT US!
WE'RE TOTALLY DIFFER-ENT!
CHOMP
WE'V GOTTE WAY STRONG
WE CAN EAT ANYTHING. WE CAN HANDLE ANYTHING.
SO WE CAN'T JUST GIVE UP NOW, CAN WE?
WE'VE GOTTA KEEP ON GOING, RIGHT?
...
YEAH...
YOU'RE RIGHT, RION.

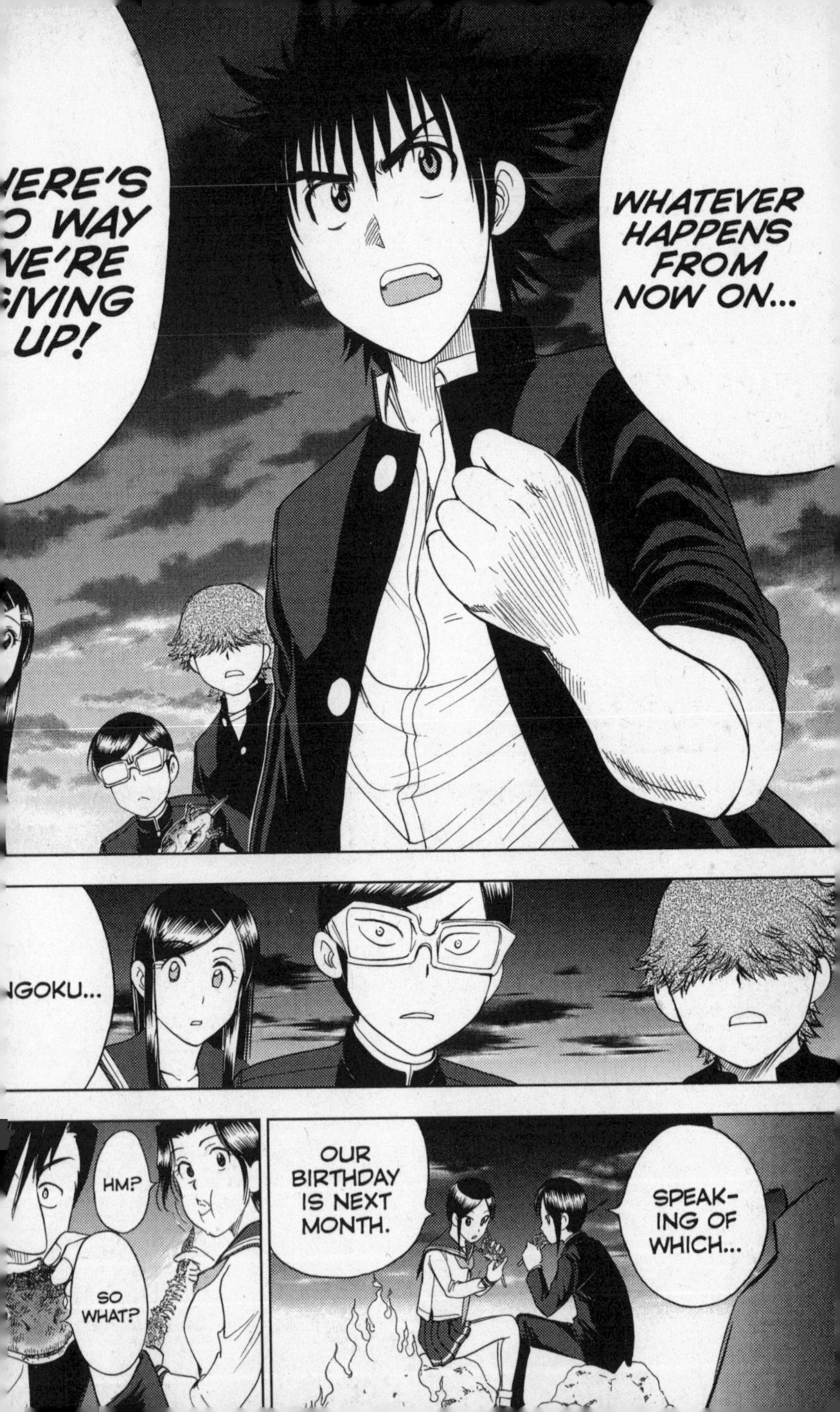

WHATEVER HAPPENS FROM NOW ON...
ERE'S WAY E'RE IVING UP!
NGOKU...
SPEAK-ING OF WHICH...
OUR BIRTHDAY IS NEXT MONTH.
HM?
SO WHAT?

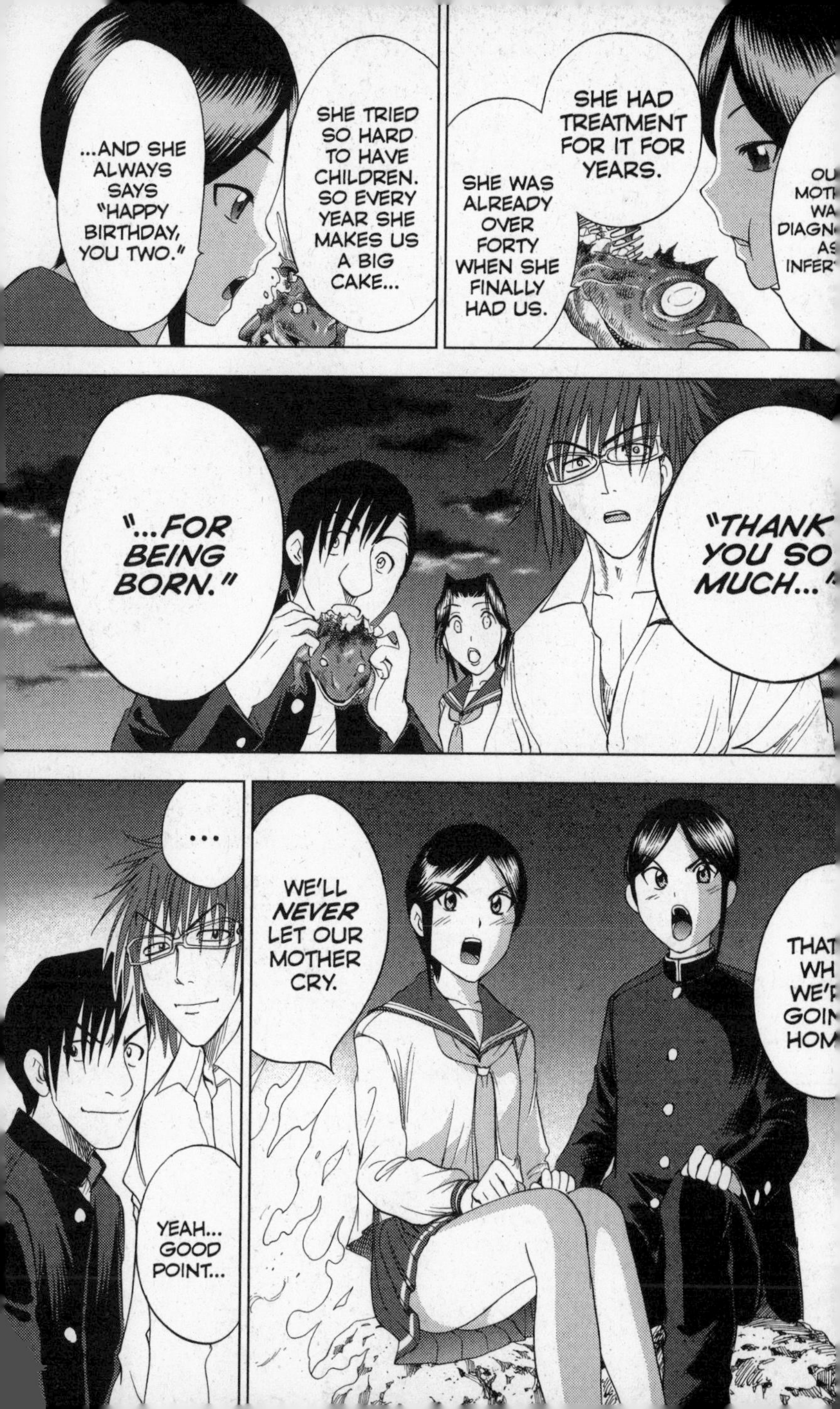
OU MOTH WA DIAGN AS INFER
SHE HAD TREATMENT FOR IT FOR YEARS.
SHE WAS ALREADY OVER FORTY WHEN SHE FINALLY HAD US.
SHE TRIED SO HARD TO HAVE CHILDREN. SO EVERY YEAR SHE MAKES US A BIG CAKE...
...AND SHE ALWAYS SAYS "HAPPY BIRTHDAY, YOU TWO."
"THANK YOU SO MUCH..."
"...FOR BEING BORN."
THAT WH WE'R GOIN HOM
WE'LL *NEVER* LET OUR MOTHER CRY.
...
YEAH... GOOD POINT...

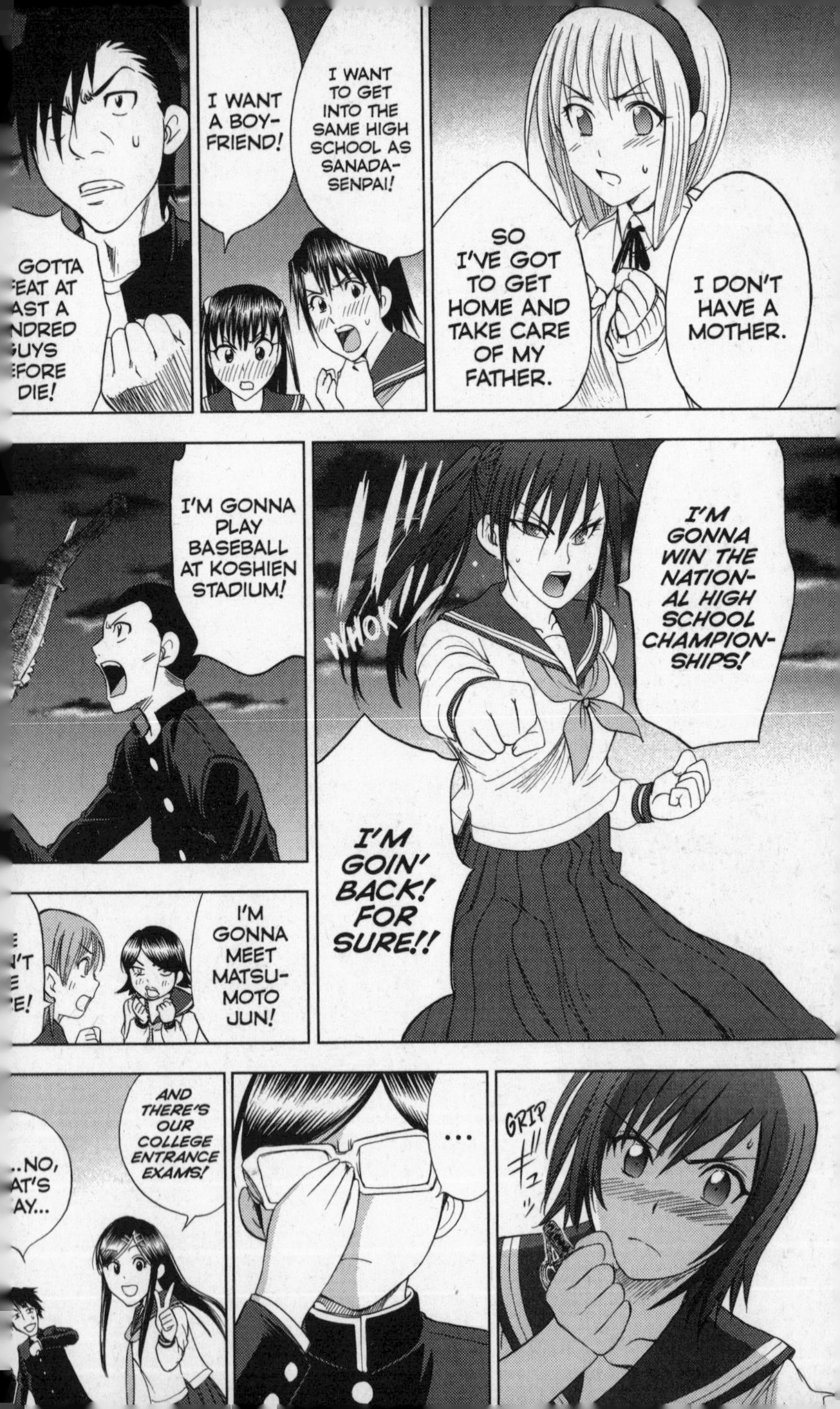
I DON'T HAVE A MOTHER.
SO I'VE GOT TO GET HOME AND TAKE CARE OF MY FATHER.
I WANT TO GET INTO THE SAME HIGH SCHOOL AS SANADA-SENPAI!
I WANT A BOY-FRIEND!
GOTTA FEAT AT AST A NDRED GUYS EFORE DIE!
I'M GONNA WIN THE NATION-AL HIGH SCHOOL CHAMPION-SHIPS!
WHOK
I'M GOIN' BACK! FOR SURE!!
I'M GONNA PLAY BASEBALL AT KOSHIEN STADIUM!
I'M GONNA MEET MATSU-MOTO JUN!
GRIP
...
AND THERE'S OUR COLLEGE ENTRANCE EXAMS!
...NO, AT'S AY...

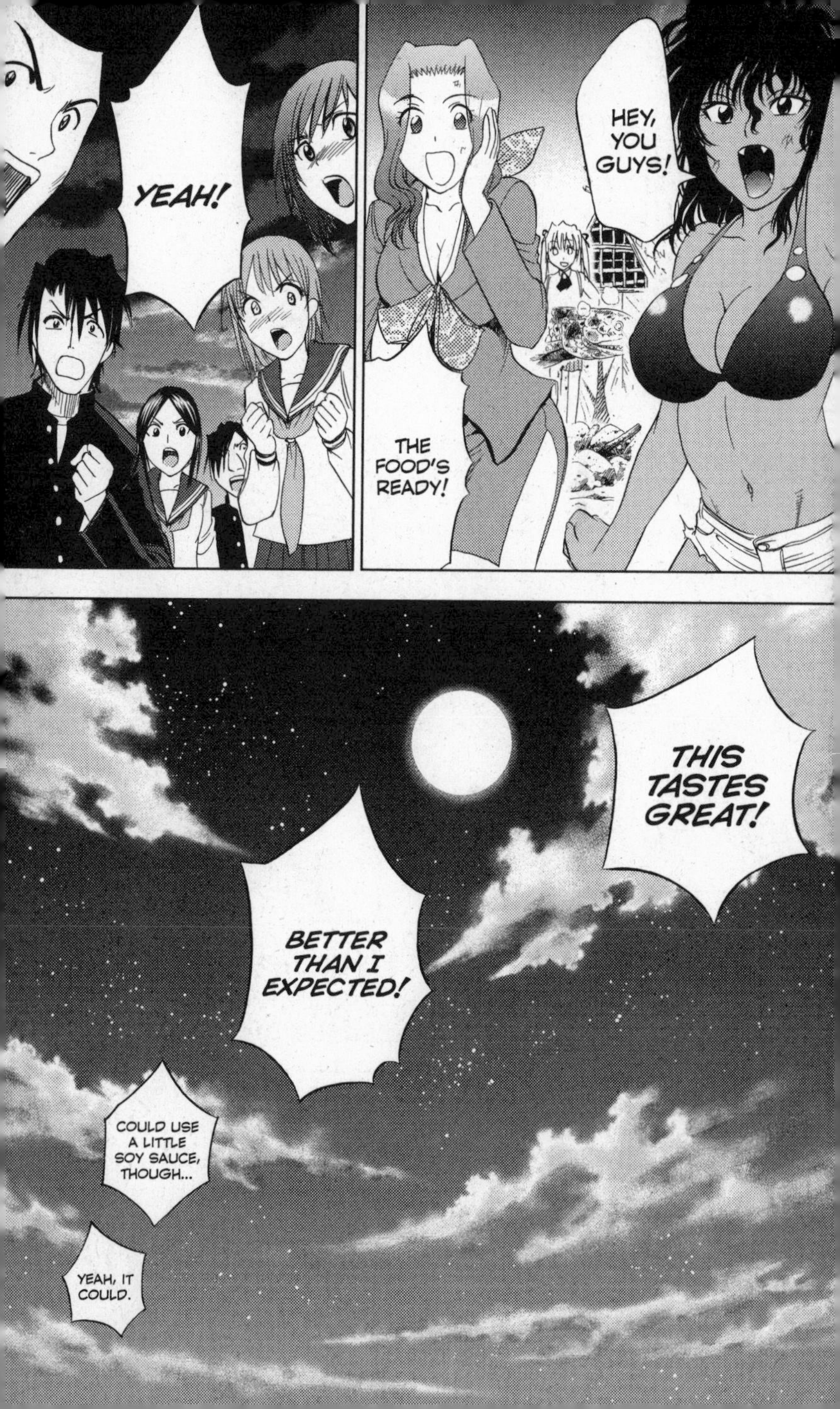
HEY, YOU GUYS!
THE FOOD'S READY!
YEAH!
THIS TASTES GREAT!
BETTER THAN I EXPECTED!
COULD USE A LITTLE SOY SAUCE, THOUGH...
YEAH, IT COULD.

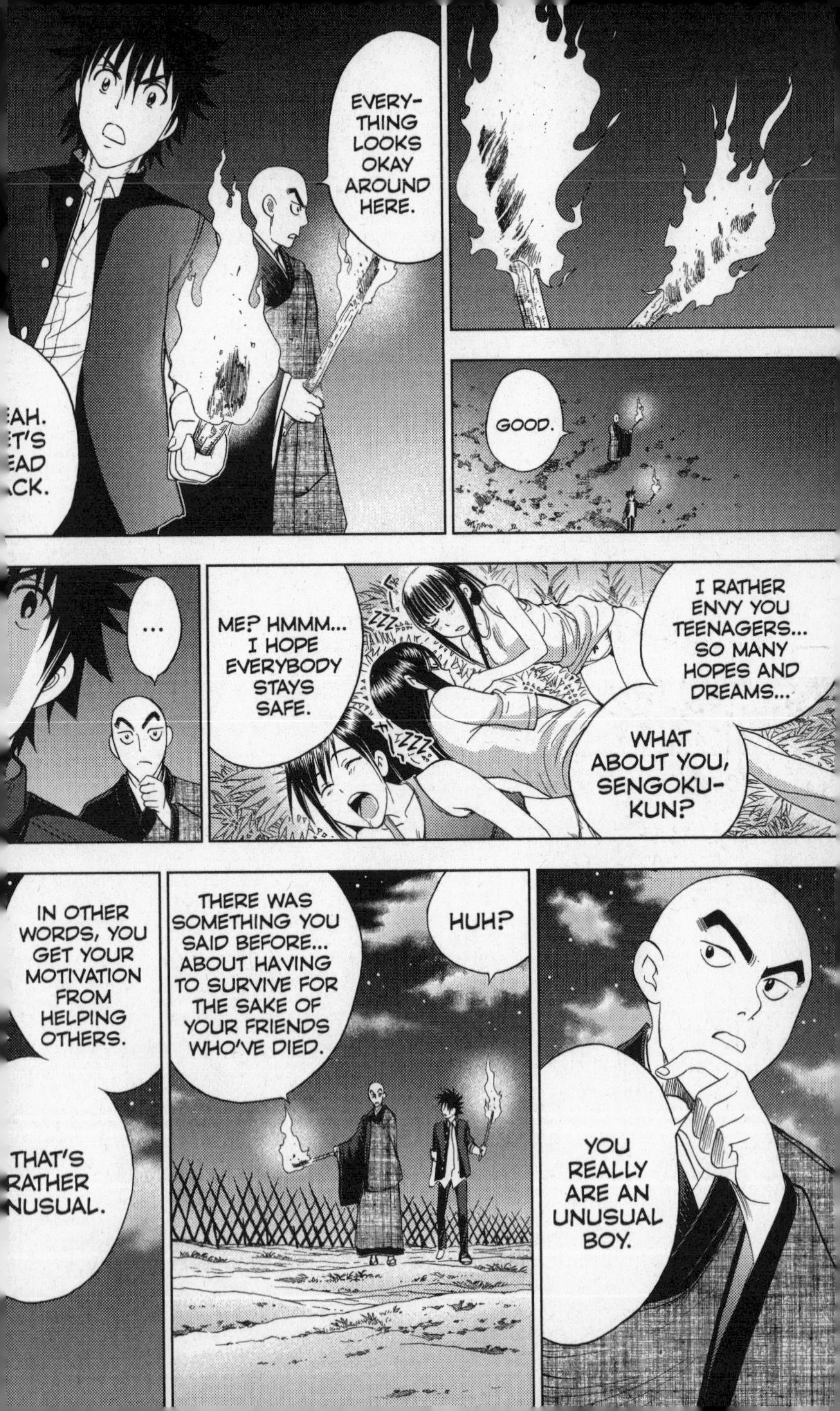
GOOD.
EVERY-THING LOOKS OKAY AROUND HERE.
EAH. ET'S EAD ACK.
I RATHER ENVY YOU TEENAGERS... SO MANY HOPES AND DREAMS...
WHAT ABOUT YOU, SENGOKU-KUN?
ME? HMMM... I HOPE EVERYBODY STAYS SAFE.
...
YOU REALLY ARE AN UNUSUAL BOY.
HUH?
THERE WAS SOMETHING YOU SAID BEFORE... ABOUT HAVING TO SURVIVE FOR THE SAKE OF YOUR FRIENDS WHO'VE DIED.
IN OTHER WORDS, YOU GET YOUR MOTIVATION FROM HELPING OTHERS.
THAT'S RATHER NUSUAL.

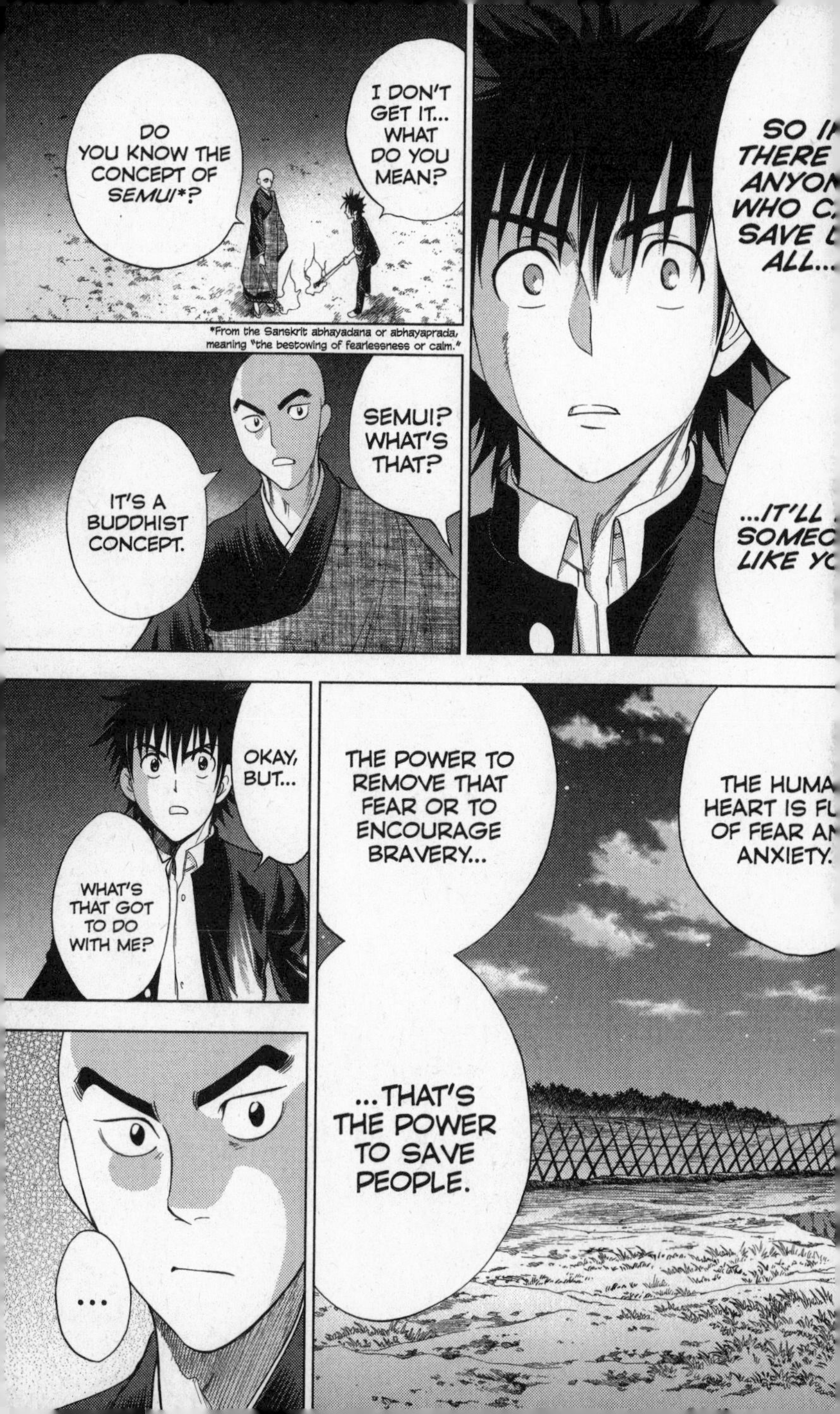
SO I THERE ANYON WHO C SAVE ALL...
...IT'LL SOMEC LIKE YO
I DON'T GET IT... WHAT DO YOU MEAN?
DO YOU KNOW THE CONCEPT OF SEMUI*?
SEMUI? WHAT'S THAT?
IT'S A BUDDHIST CONCEPT.
THE HUMA HEART IS FU OF FEAR AN ANXIETY.
THE POWER TO REMOVE THAT FEAR OR TO ENCOURAGE BRAVERY...
...THAT'S THE POWER TO SAVE PEOPLE.
OKAY, BUT...
WHAT'S THAT GOT TO DO WITH ME?
...

*From the Sanskrit abhayadana or abhayaprada, meaning "the bestowing of fearlessness or calm."

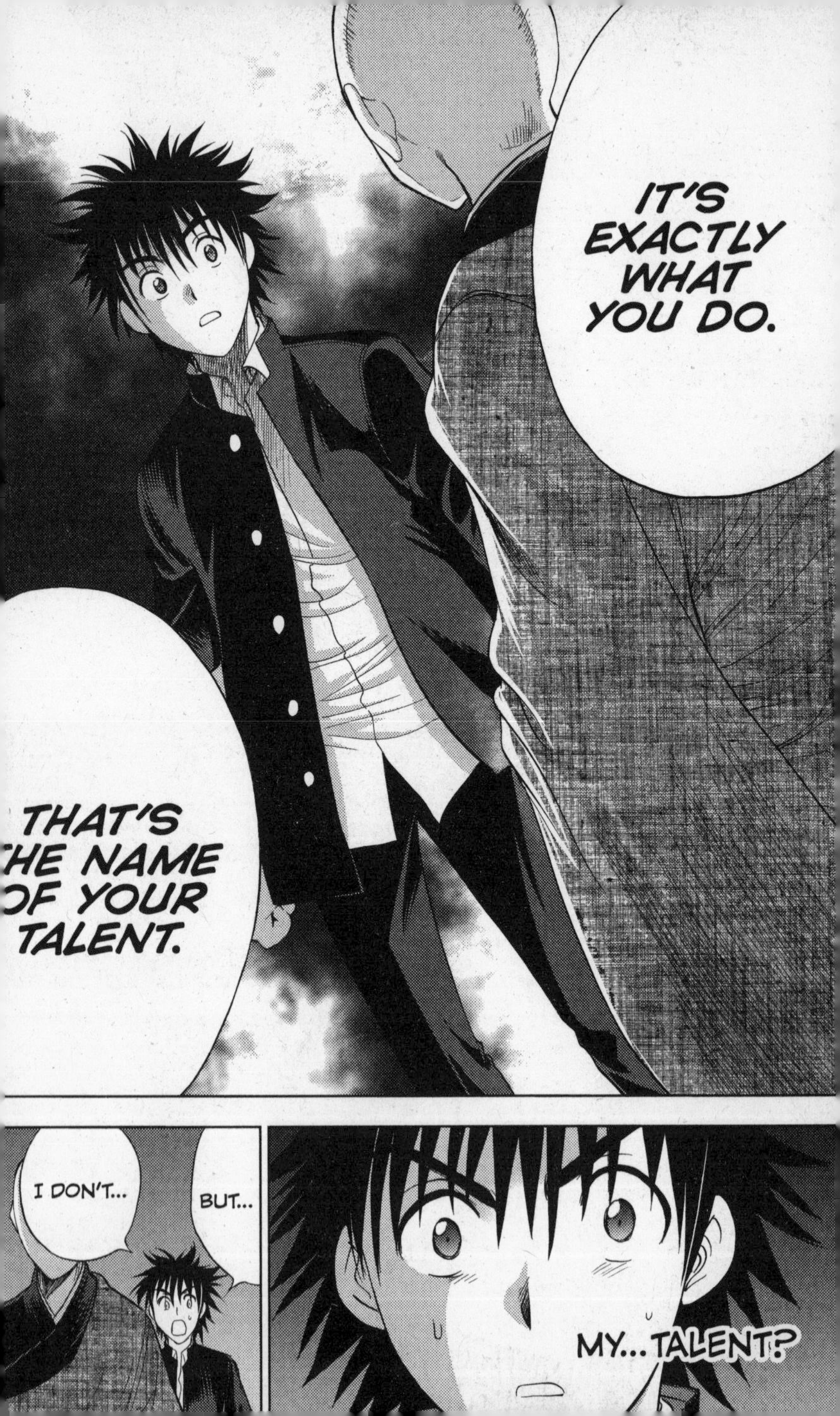
IT'S EXACTLY WHAT YOU DO.
THAT'S HE NAME OF YOUR TALENT.
MY... TALENT?
BUT...
I DON'T...

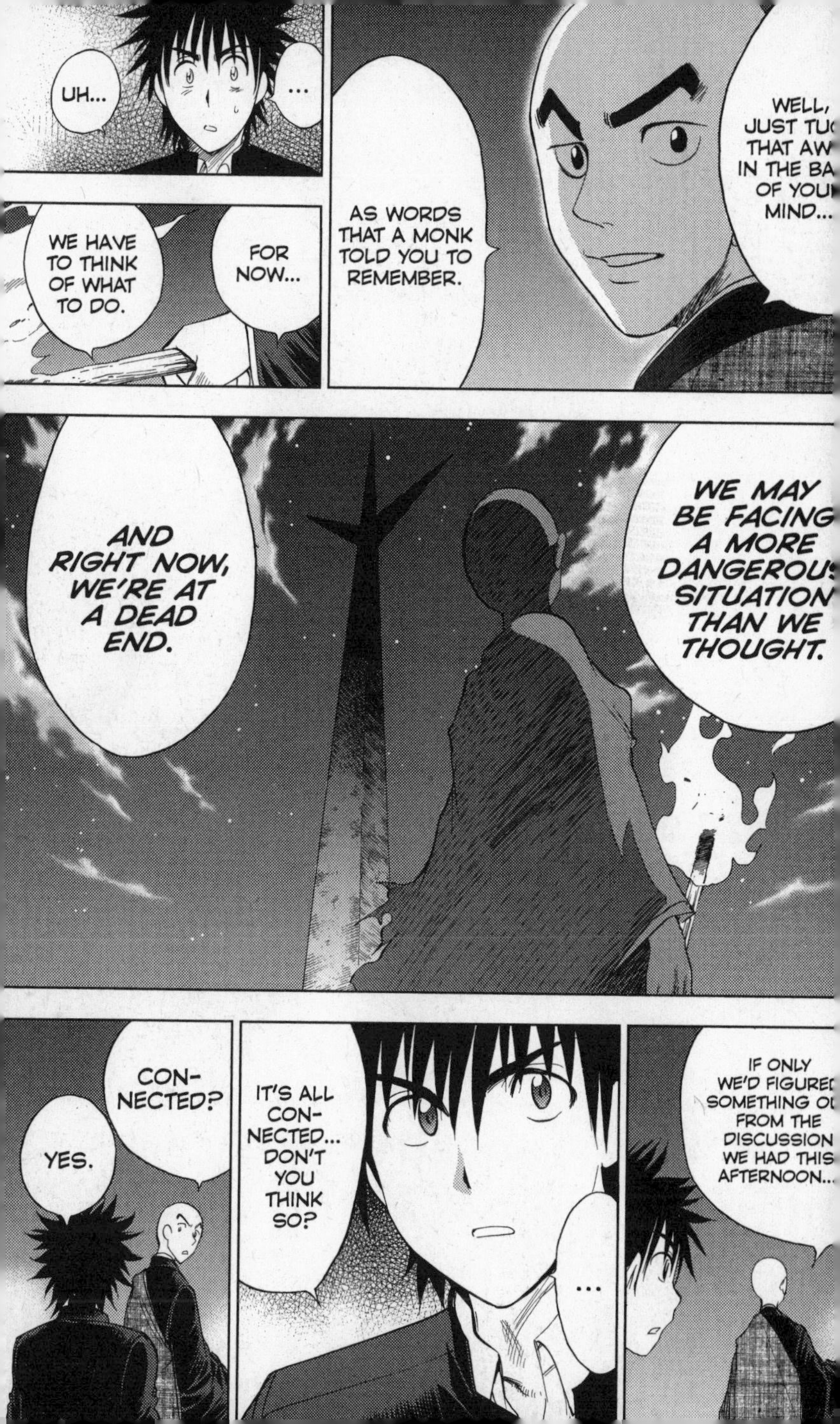
WELL, JUST TU THAT AW IN THE BA OF YOU MIND...
AS WORDS THAT A MONK TOLD YOU TO REMEMBER.
...
UH...
FOR NOW...
WE HAVE TO THINK OF WHAT TO DO.
WE MAY BE FACING A MORE DANGEROU SITUATION THAN WE THOUGHT.
AND RIGHT NOW, WE'RE AT A DEAD END.
IF ONLY WE'D FIGURE SOMETHING O FROM THE DISCUSSION WE HAD THIS AFTERNOON...
...
IT'S ALL CON-NECTED... DON'T YOU THINK SO?
CON-NECTED?
YES.

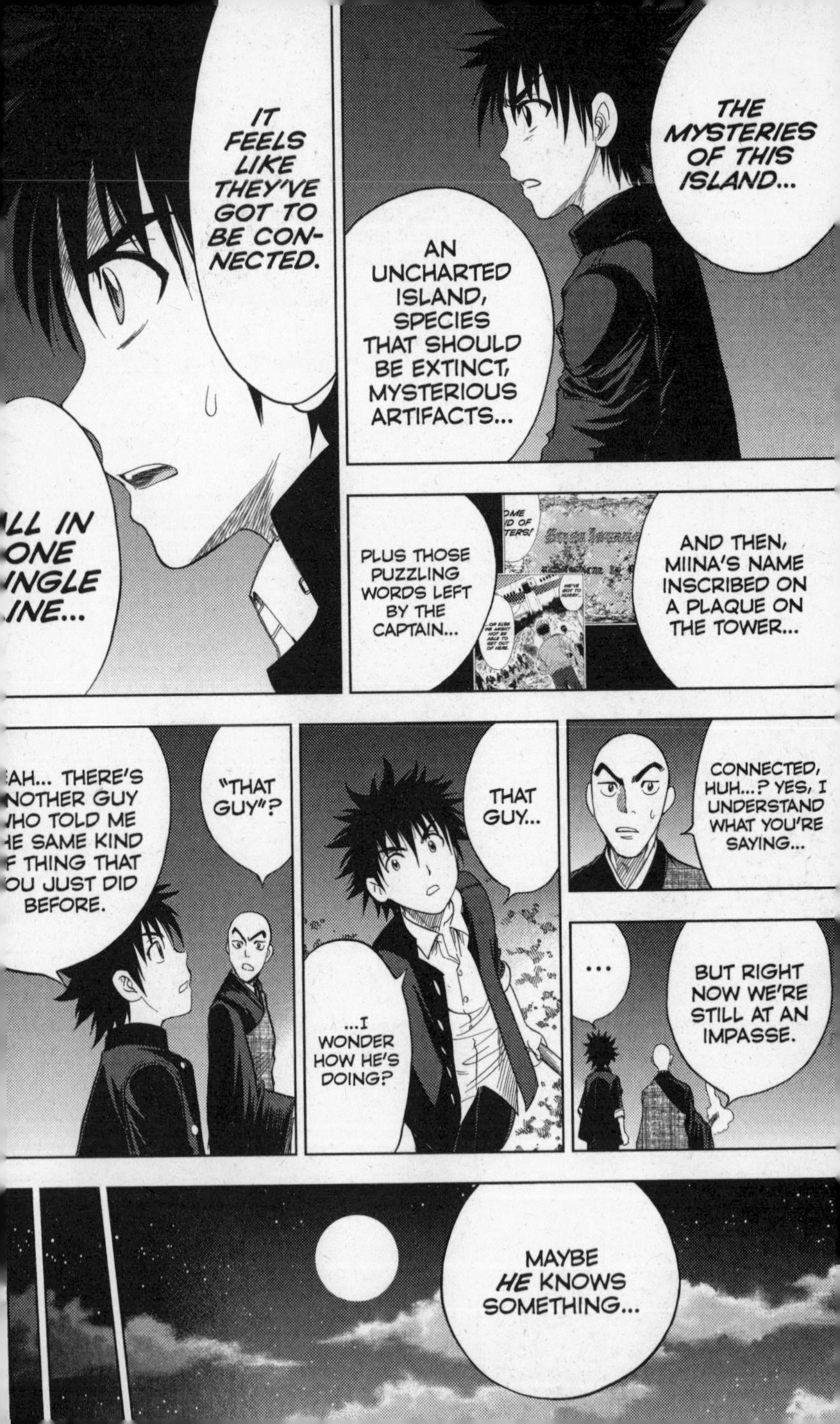
THE MYSTERIES OF THIS ISLAND...
AN UNCHARTED ISLAND, SPECIES THAT SHOULD BE EXTINCT, MYSTERIOUS ARTIFACTS...
AND THEN, MIINA'S NAME INSCRIBED ON A PLAQUE ON THE TOWER...
PLUS THOSE PUZZLING WORDS LEFT BY THE CAPTAIN...
IT FEELS LIKE THEY'VE GOT TO BE CONNECTED.
LL IN ONE INGLE INE...
CONNECTED, HUH...? YES, I UNDERSTAND WHAT YOU'RE SAYING...
BUT RIGHT NOW WE'RE STILL AT AN IMPASSE.
...
THAT GUY...
...I WONDER HOW HE'S DOING?
"THAT GUY"?
EAH... THERE'S NOTHER GUY HO TOLD ME HE SAME KIND F THING THAT OU JUST DID BEFORE.
MAYBE HE KNOWS SOMETHING...

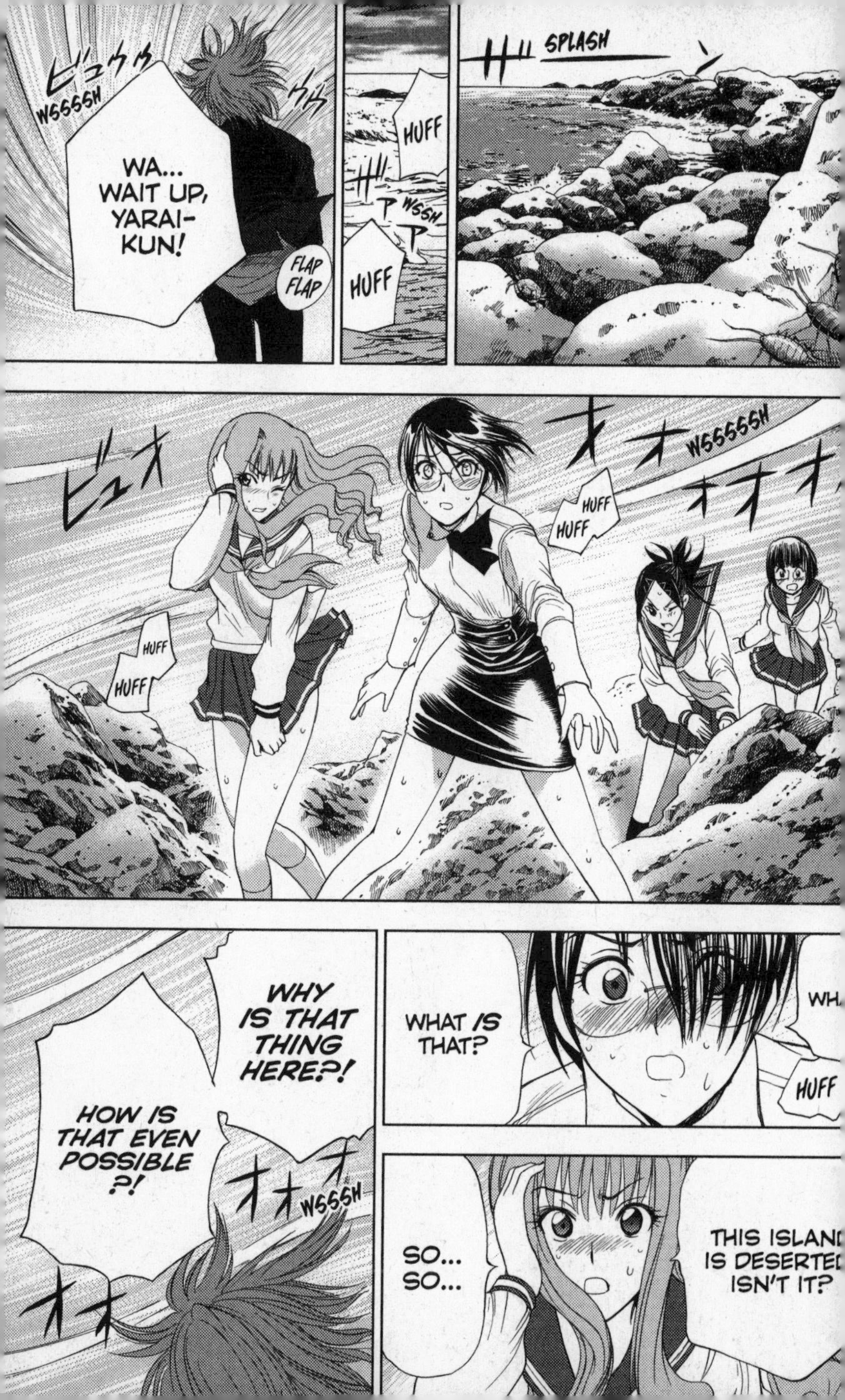
SPLASH
HUFF
WSSH
HUFF
WSSSSH
WA... WAIT UP, YARAI-KUN!
FLAP FLAP
WSSSSSH
HUFF HUFF
HUFF HUFF
WHA
HUFF
WHAT IS THAT?
THIS ISLAND IS DESERTED ISN'T IT?
SO... SO...
WHY IS THAT THING HERE?!
HOW IS THAT EVEN POSSIBLE?!
WSSSH

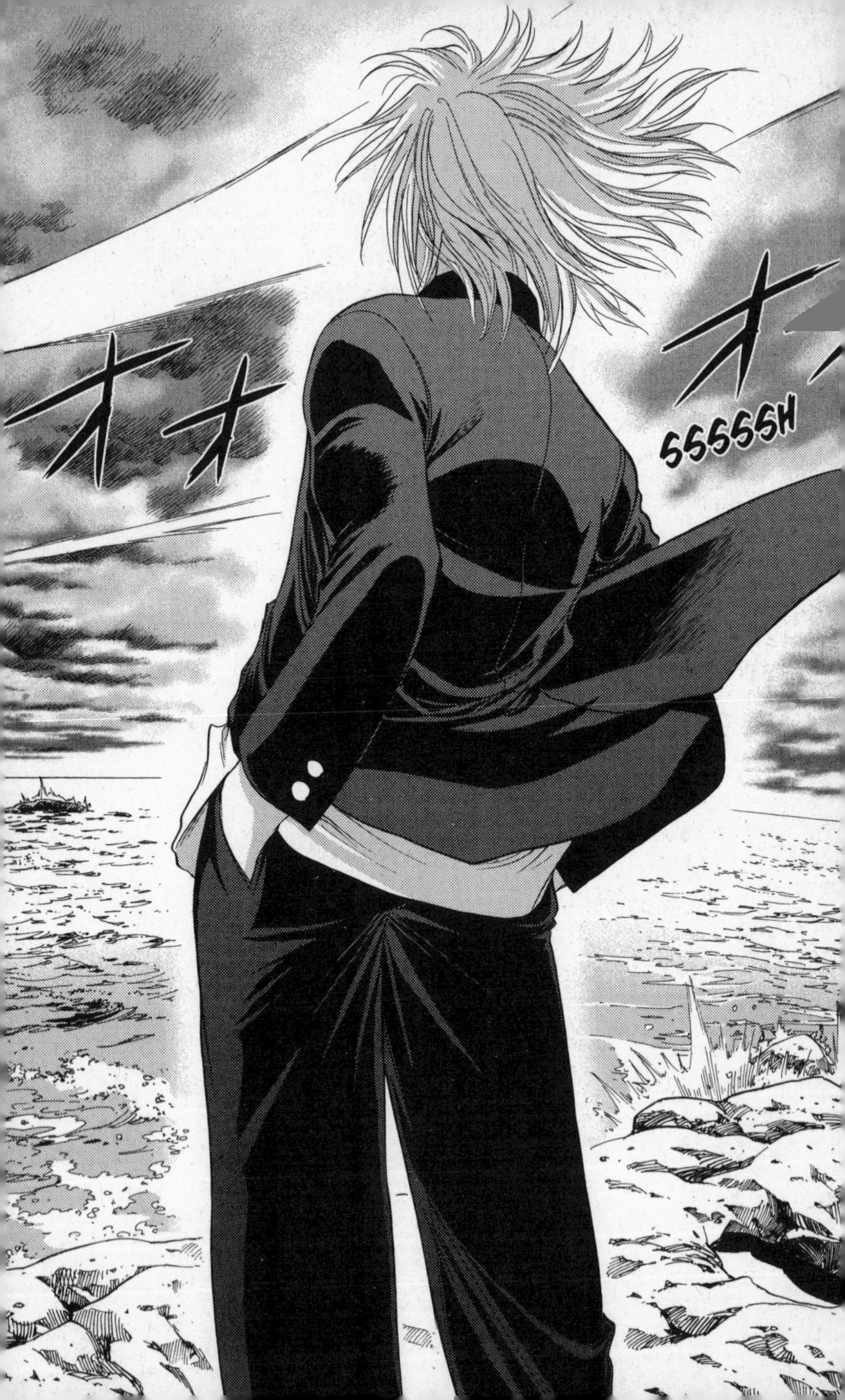
オォォ
SSSSSSH

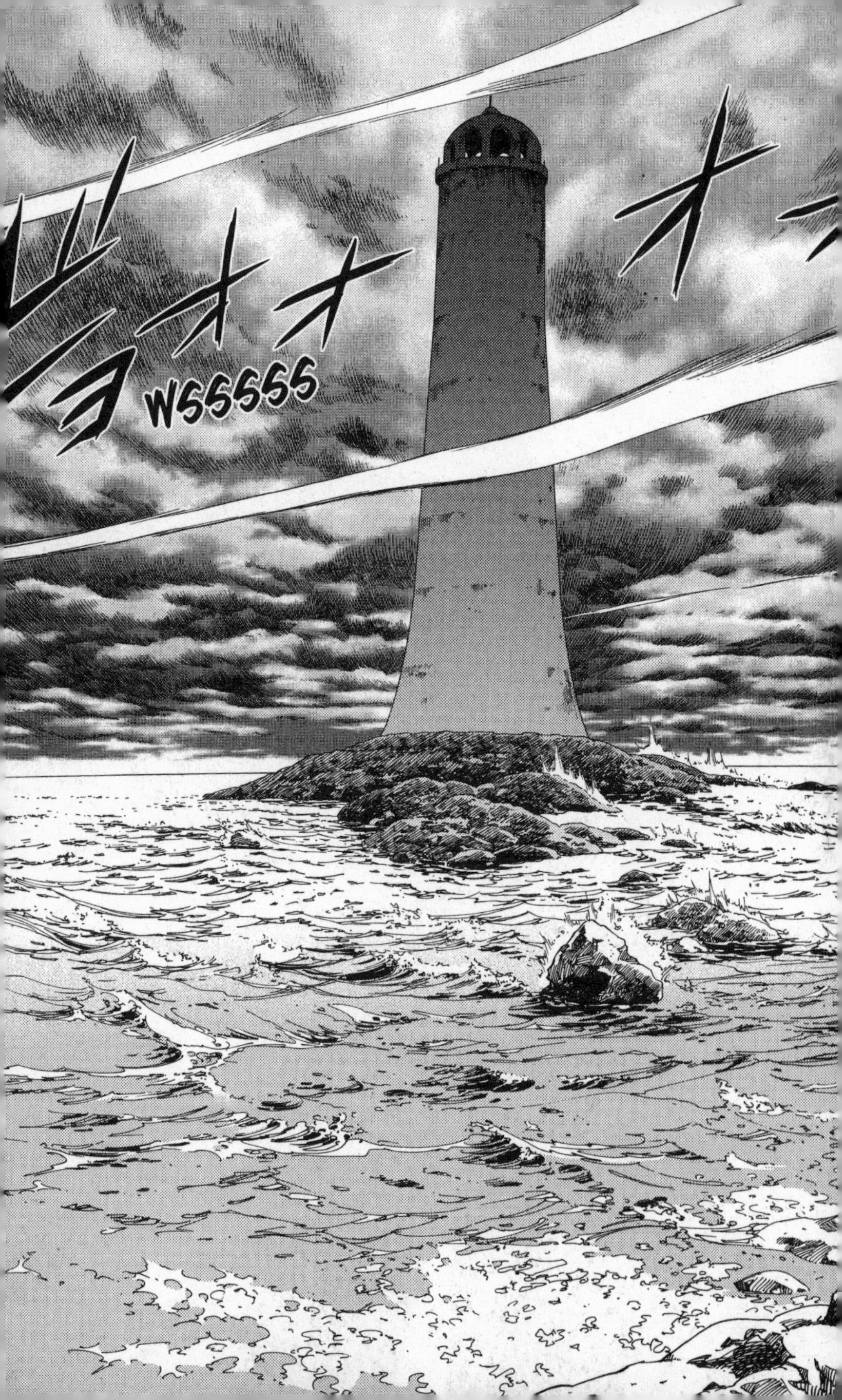
ヒュオオオオ
WSSSSS

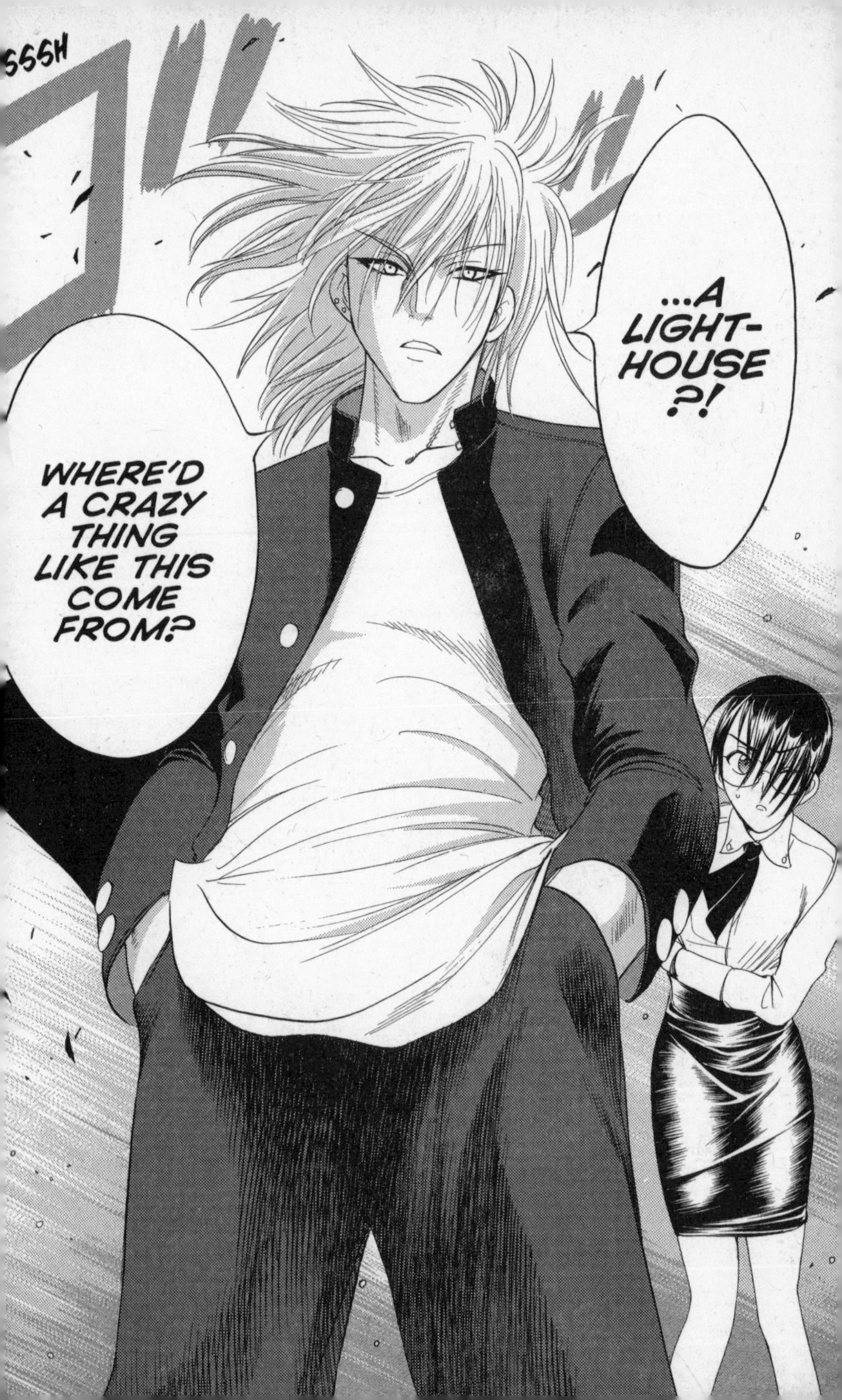
SSSH
...A LIGHT-HOUSE?!
WHERE'D A CRAZY THING LIKE THIS COME FROM?

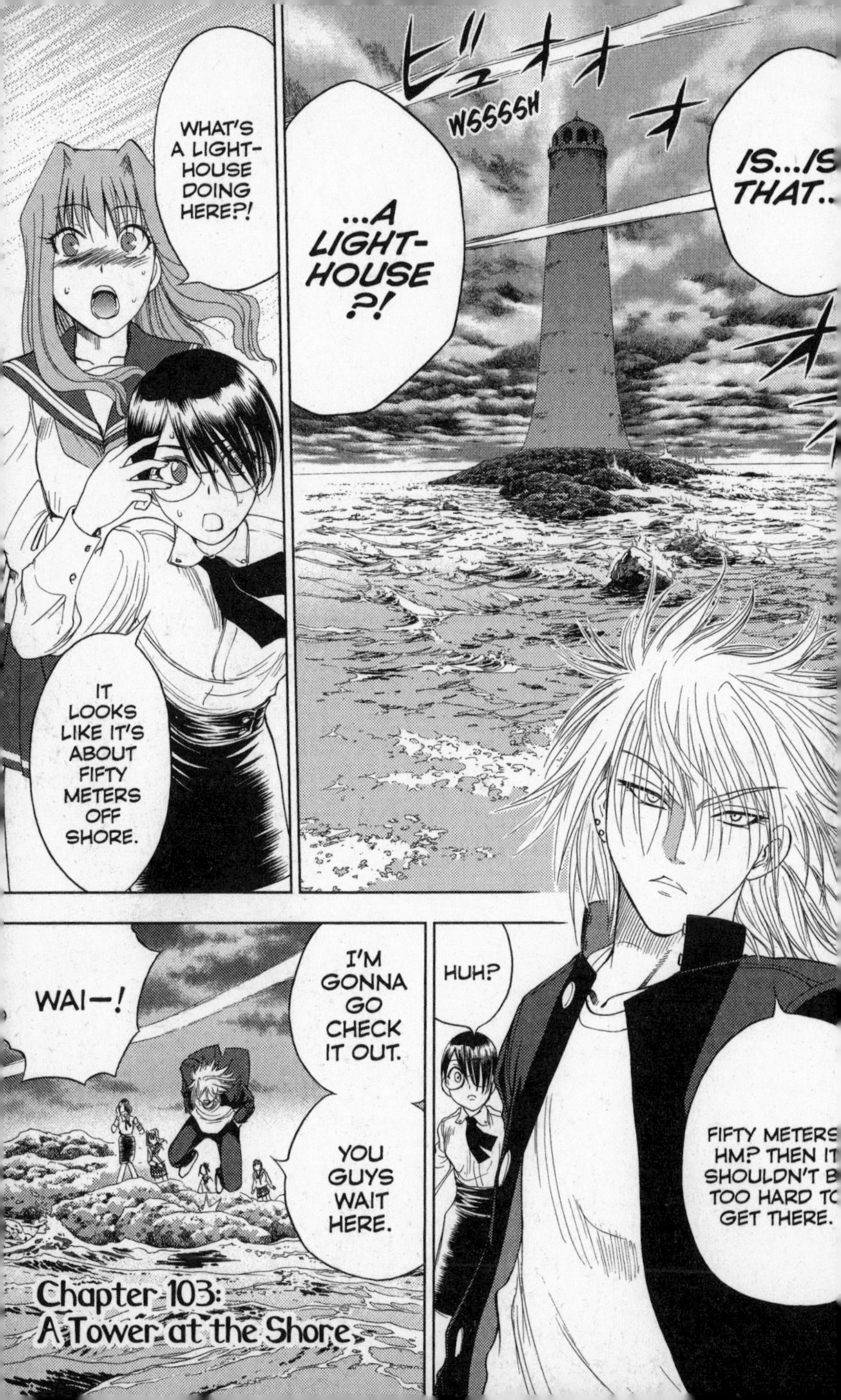
IS...IS THAT..
...A LIGHT-HOUSE?!
WSSSSH
WHAT'S A LIGHT-HOUSE DOING HERE?!
IT LOOKS LIKE IT'S ABOUT FIFTY METERS OFF SHORE.
FIFTY METERS HM? THEN IT SHOULDN'T B TOO HARD TO GET THERE.
HUH?
I'M GONNA GO CHECK IT OUT.
YOU GUYS WAIT HERE.
WAI—!
Chapter 103: A Tower at the Shore

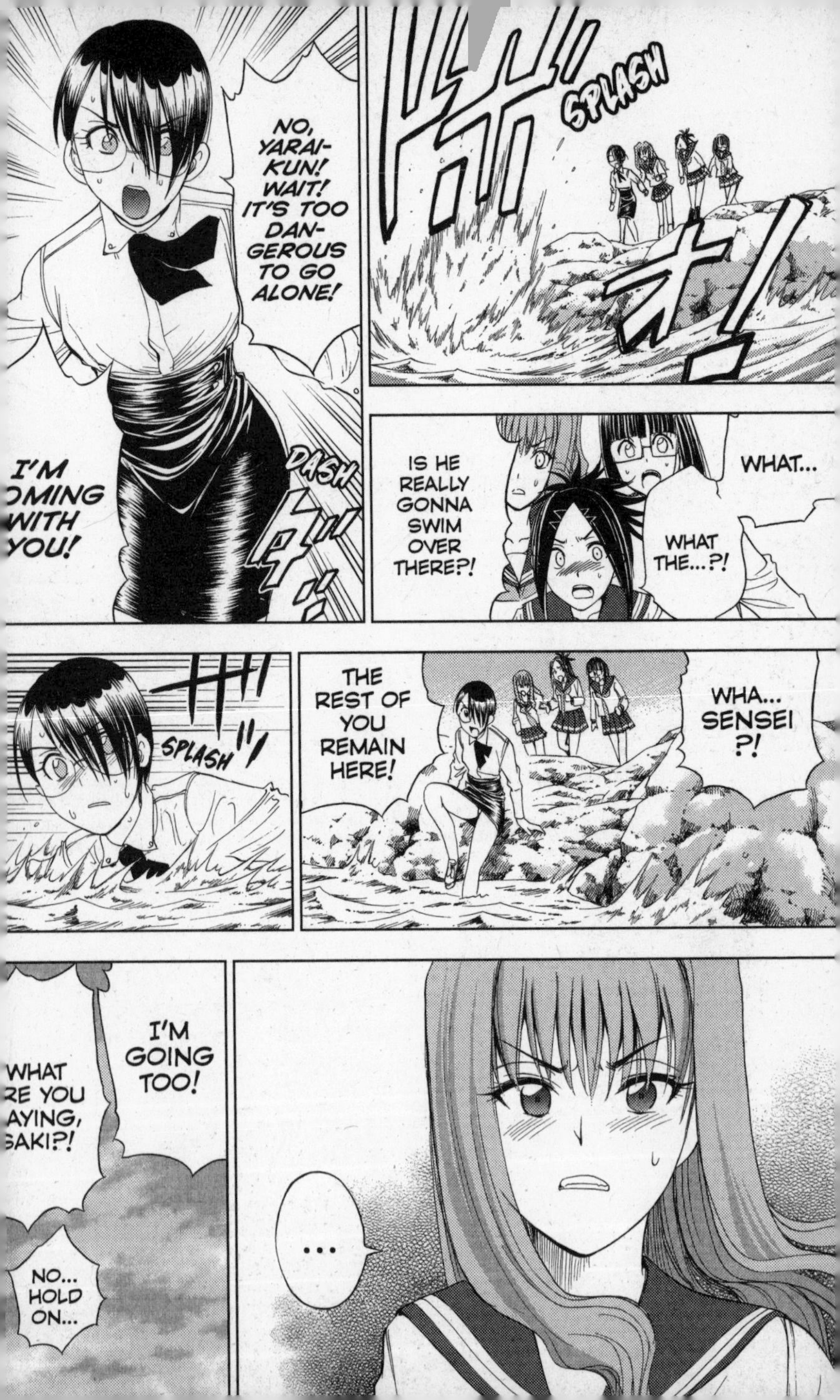
SPLASH
WHAT...
WHAT THE...?!
IS HE REALLY GONNA SWIM OVER THERE?!
NO, YARAI-KUN! WAIT! IT'S TOO DAN-GEROUS TO GO ALONE!
I'M OMING WITH YOU!
DASH
WHA... SENSEI?!
THE REST OF YOU REMAIN HERE!
SPLASH
...
I'M GOING TOO!
WHAT RE YOU AYING, SAKI?!
NO... HOLD ON...

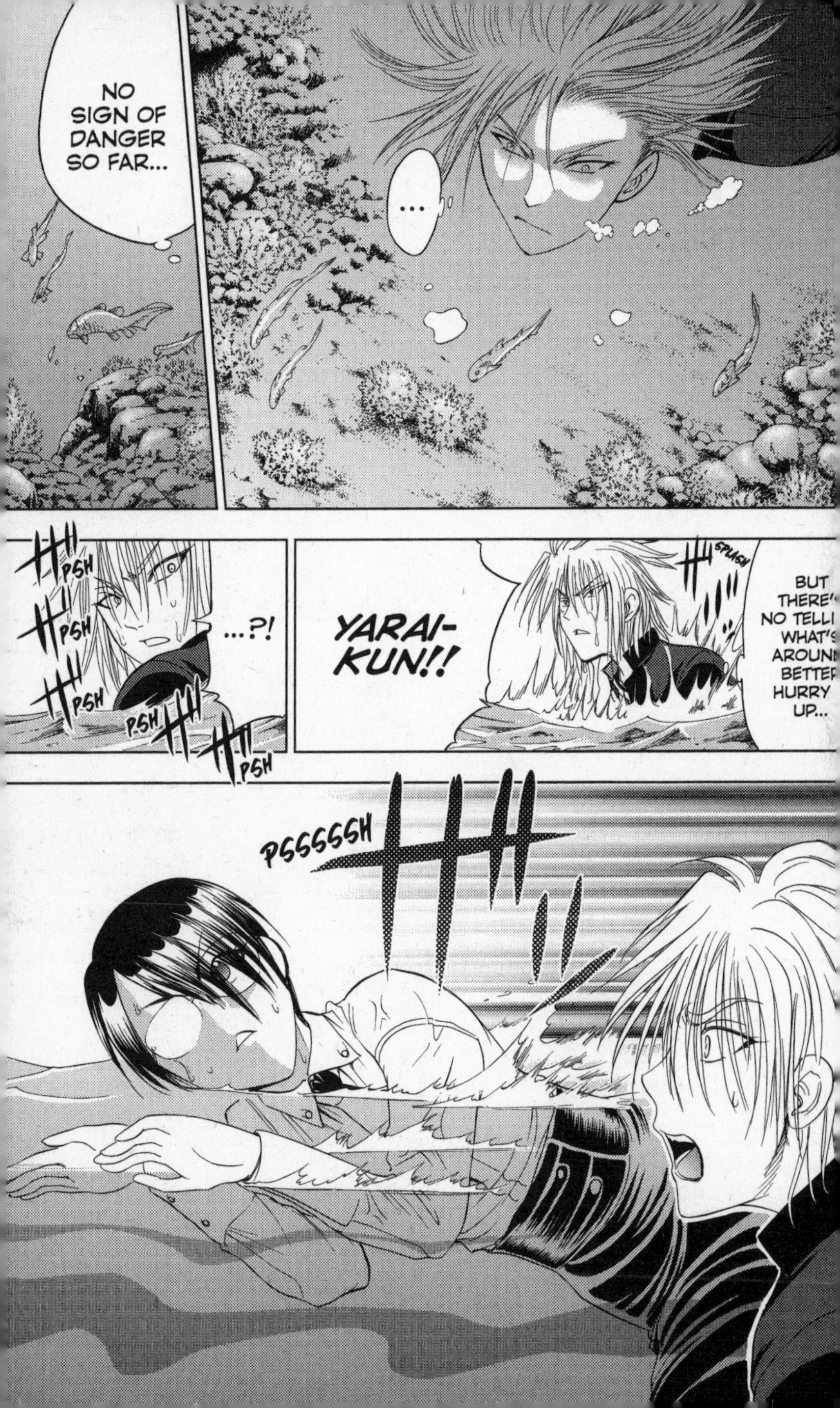
...
NO SIGN OF DANGER SO FAR...
BUT THERE' NO TELLI WHAT'S AROUN BETTER HURRY UP...
SPLASH
YARAI-KUN!!
PSH
PSH
PSH
...?!
PSH
PSH
PSSSSSH

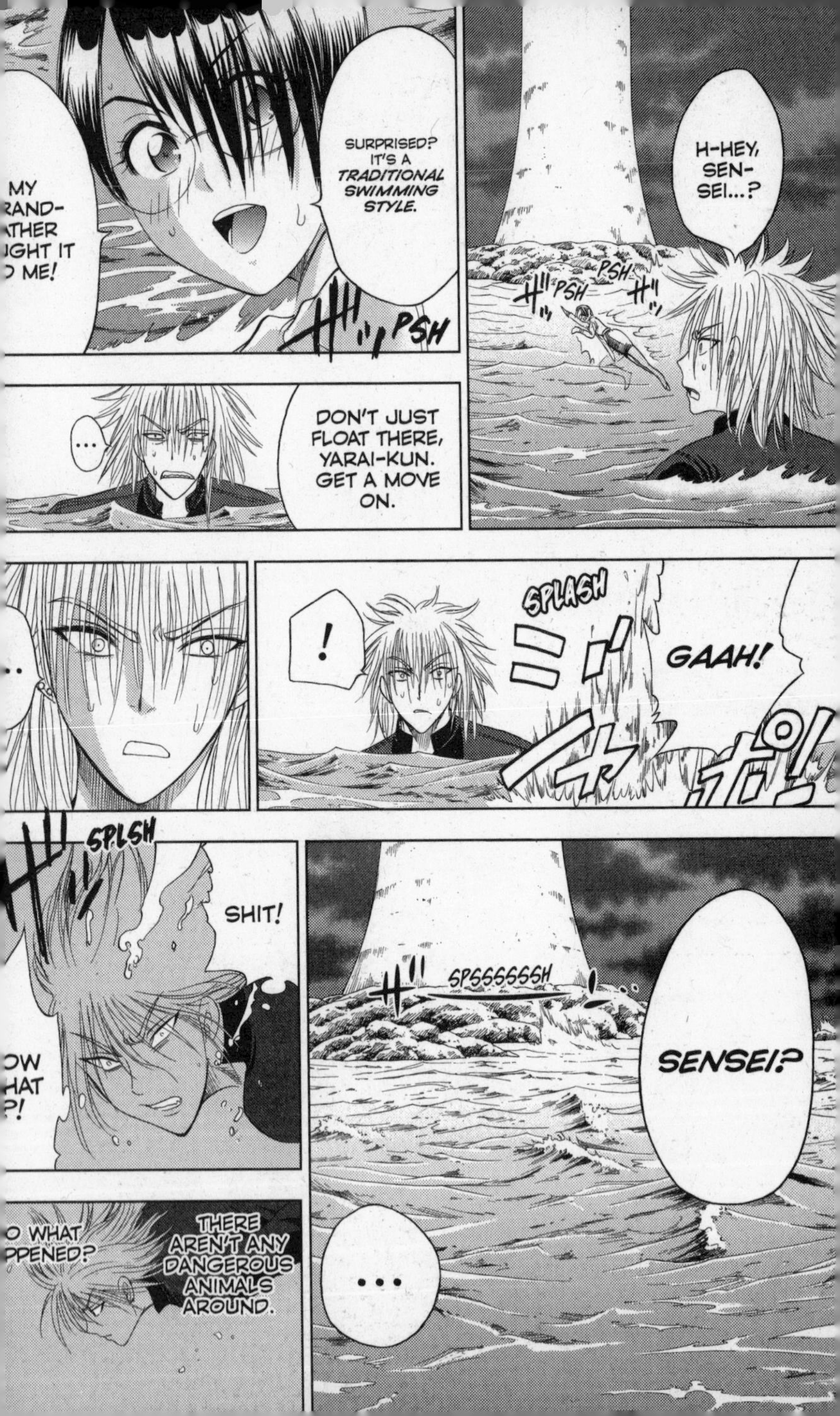
H-HEY, SEN-SEI...?
PSH
PSH
SURPRISED? IT'S A *TRADITIONAL* *SWIMMING* *STYLE.*
PSH
MY RAND- ATHER UGHT IT ME!
DON'T JUST FLOAT THERE, YARAI-KUN. GET A MOVE ON.
...
!
SPLASH
GAAH!
SPSSSSSSH
SENSEI?
...
SPLSH
SHIT!
OW HAT ?!
THERE AREN'T ANY DANGEROUS ANIMALS AROUND.
O WHAT PPENED?

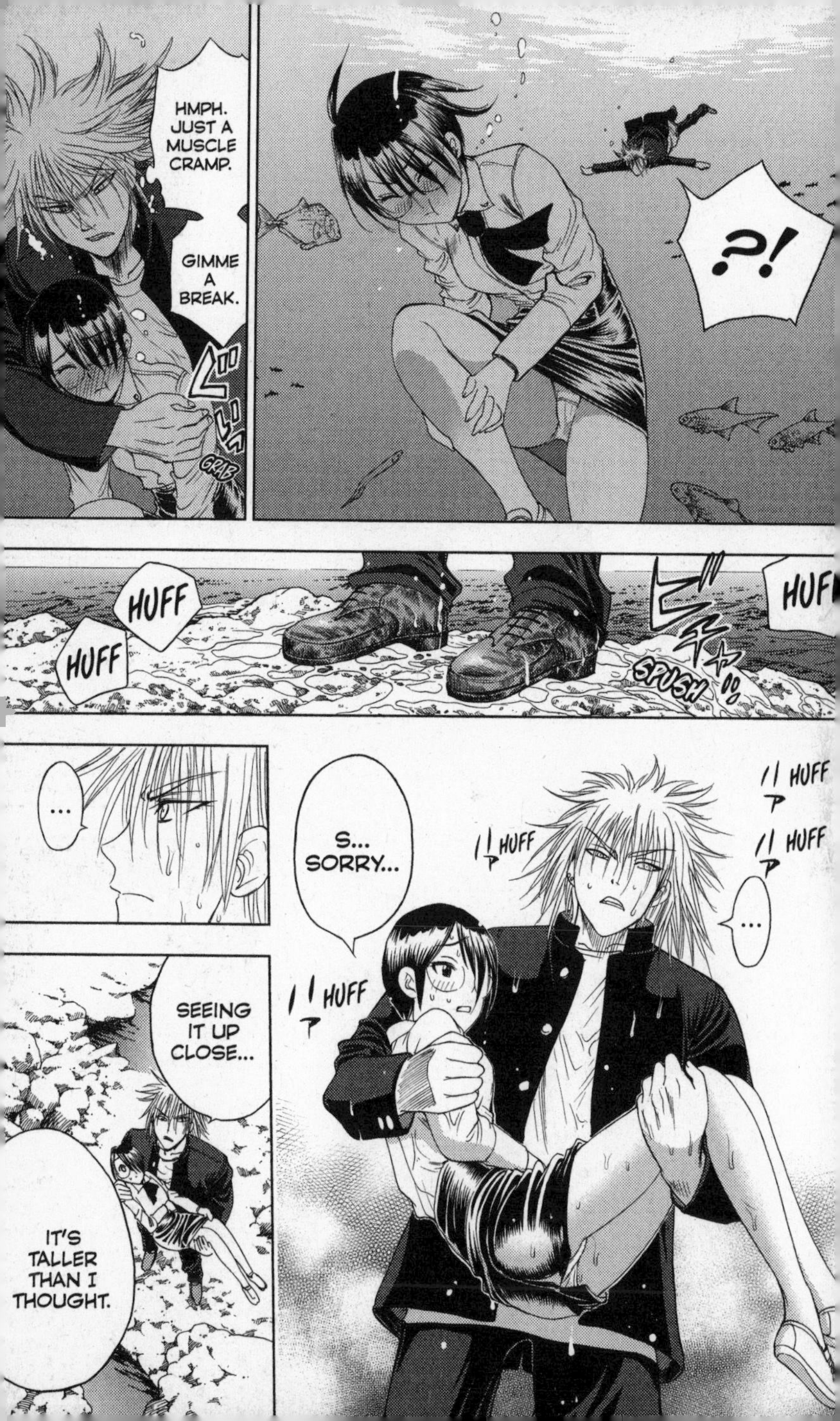
?!
HMPH. JUST A MUSCLE CRAMP.
GIMME A BREAK.
GRAB
HUF
SPUSH
HUFF
HUFF
HUFF
HUFF
...
HUFF
S... SORRY...
HUFF
...
SEEING IT UP CLOSE...
IT'S TALLER THAN I THOUGHT.

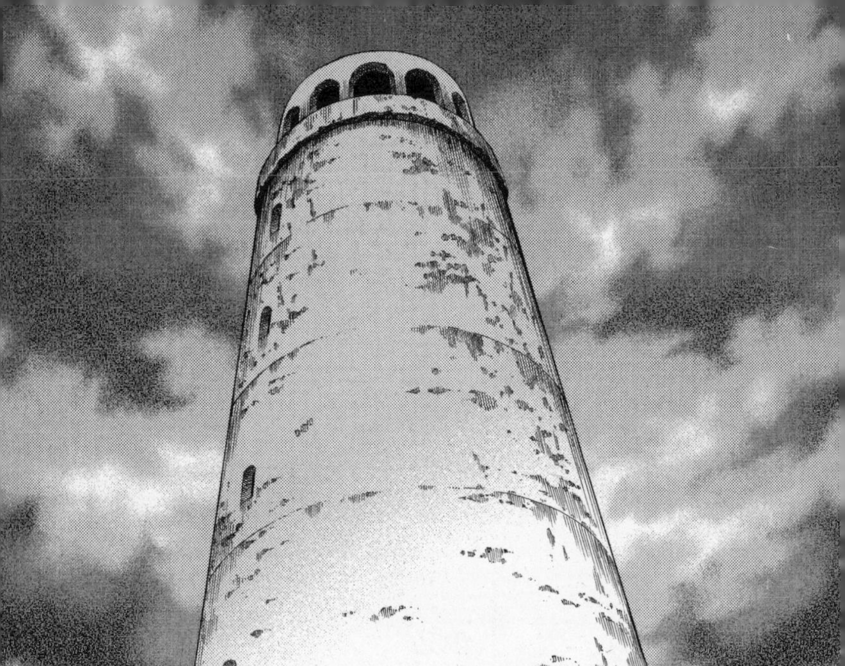

*About fifty feet.

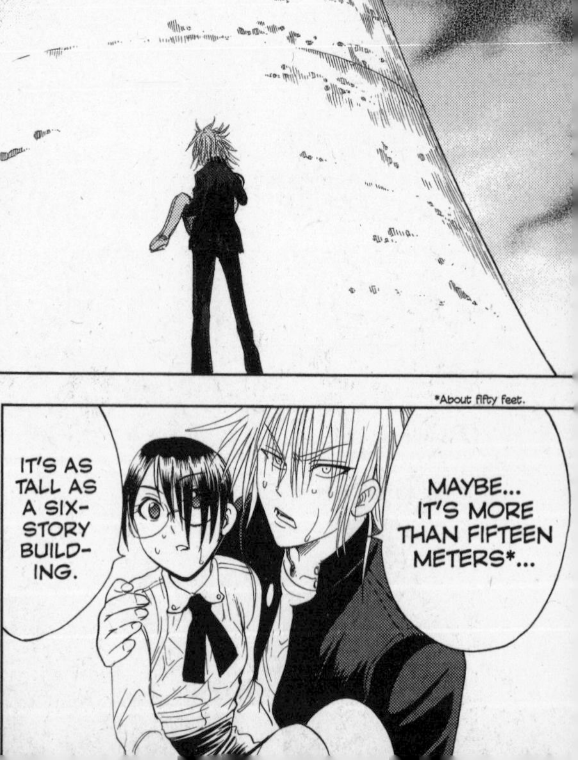
MAYBE... IT'S MORE THAN FIFTEEN METERS*...
IT'S AS TALL AS A SIX-STORY BUILD-ING.

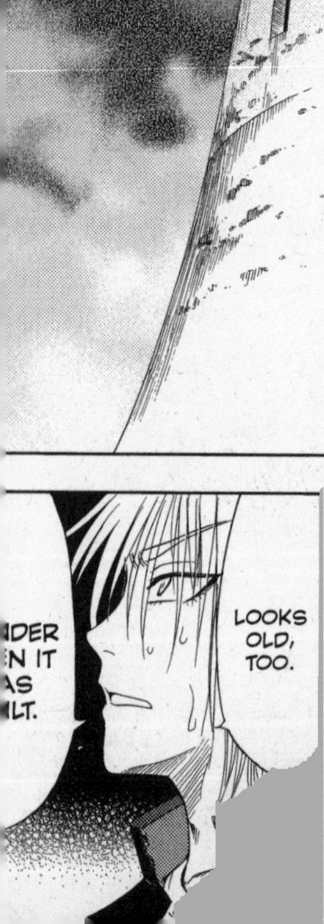
LOOKS OLD, TOO.
NDER EN IT AS ILT.

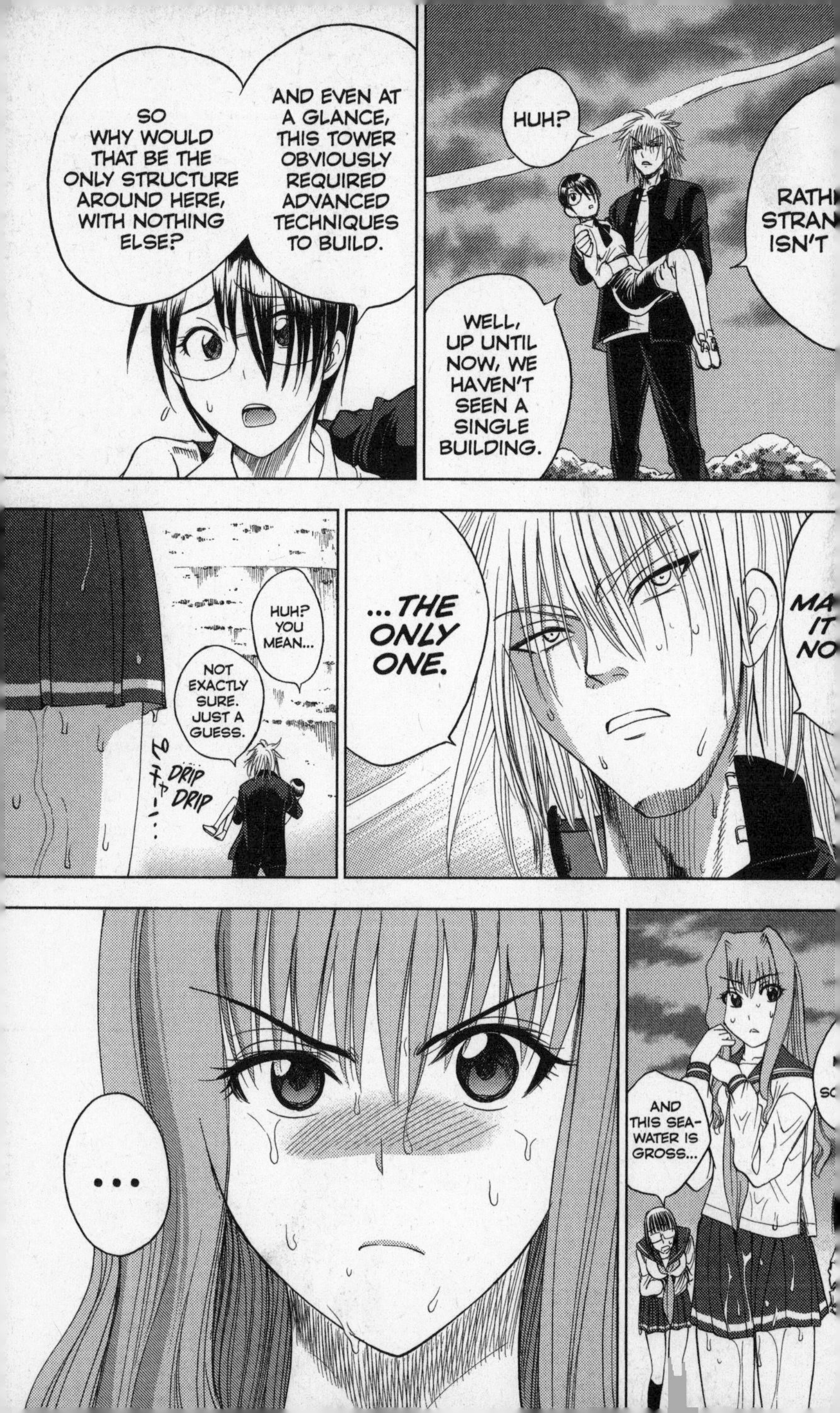

RATH STRAN ISN'T
HUH?
WELL, UP UNTIL NOW, WE HAVEN'T SEEN A SINGLE BUILDING.
AND EVEN AT A GLANCE, THIS TOWER OBVIOUSLY REQUIRED ADVANCED TECHNIQUES TO BUILD.
SO WHY WOULD THAT BE THE ONLY STRUCTURE AROUND HERE, WITH NOTHING ELSE?
MA IT NO
...THE ONLY ONE.
HUH? YOU MEAN...
NOT EXACTLY SURE. JUST A GUESS.
DRIP DRIP
SO
AND THIS SEA-WATER IS GROSS...
...

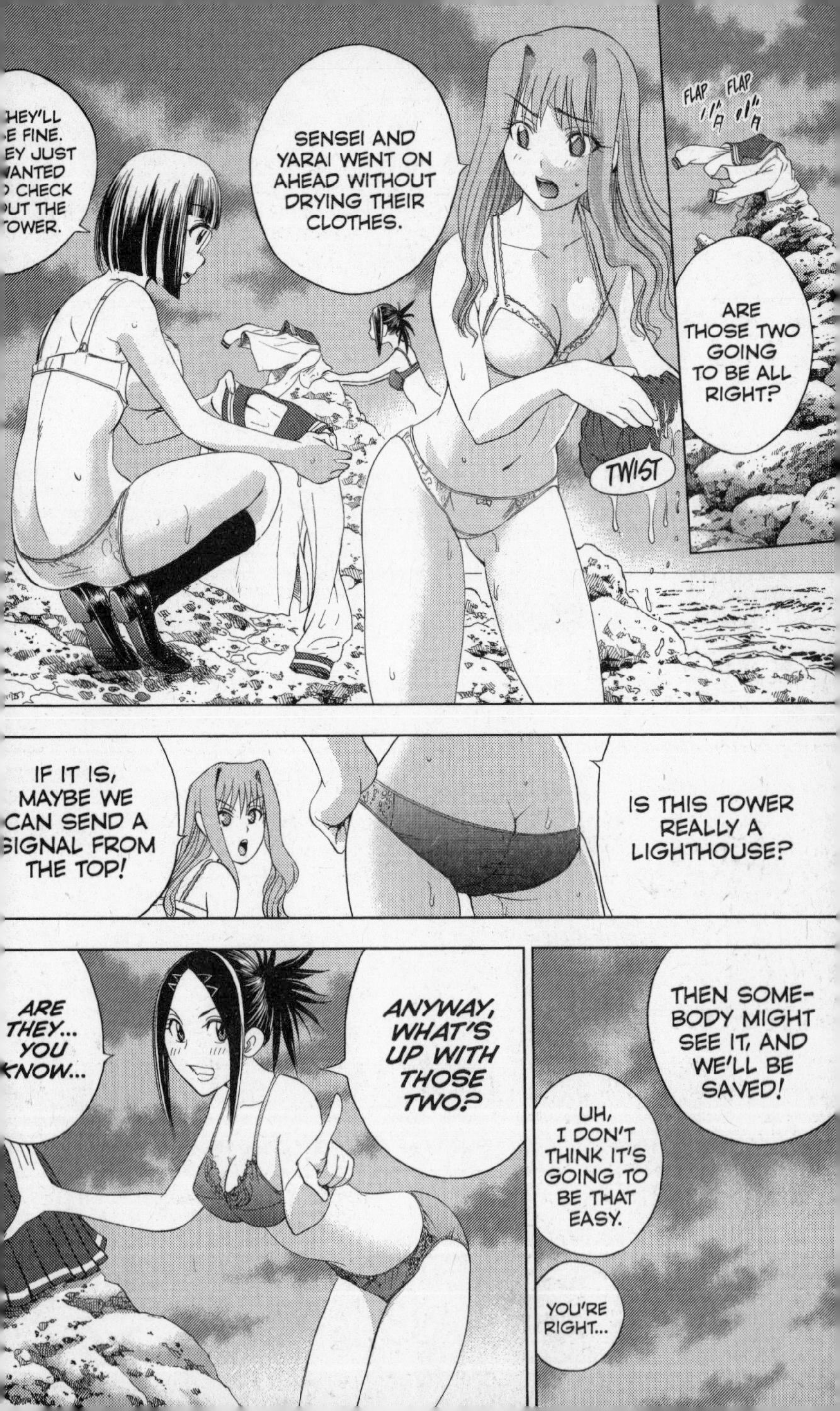
FLAP FLAP
ARE THOSE TWO GOING TO BE ALL RIGHT?
SENSEI AND YARAI WENT ON AHEAD WITHOUT DRYING THEIR CLOTHES.
TWIST
HEY'LL E FINE. EY JUST VANTED D CHECK UT THE TOWER.
IS THIS TOWER REALLY A LIGHTHOUSE?
IF IT IS, MAYBE WE CAN SEND A IGNAL FROM THE TOP!
THEN SOME-BODY MIGHT SEE IT, AND WE'LL BE SAVED!
UH, I DON'T THINK IT'S GOING TO BE THAT EASY.
YOU'RE RIGHT...
ANYWAY, WHAT'S UP WITH THOSE TWO?
ARE THEY... YOU NOW...

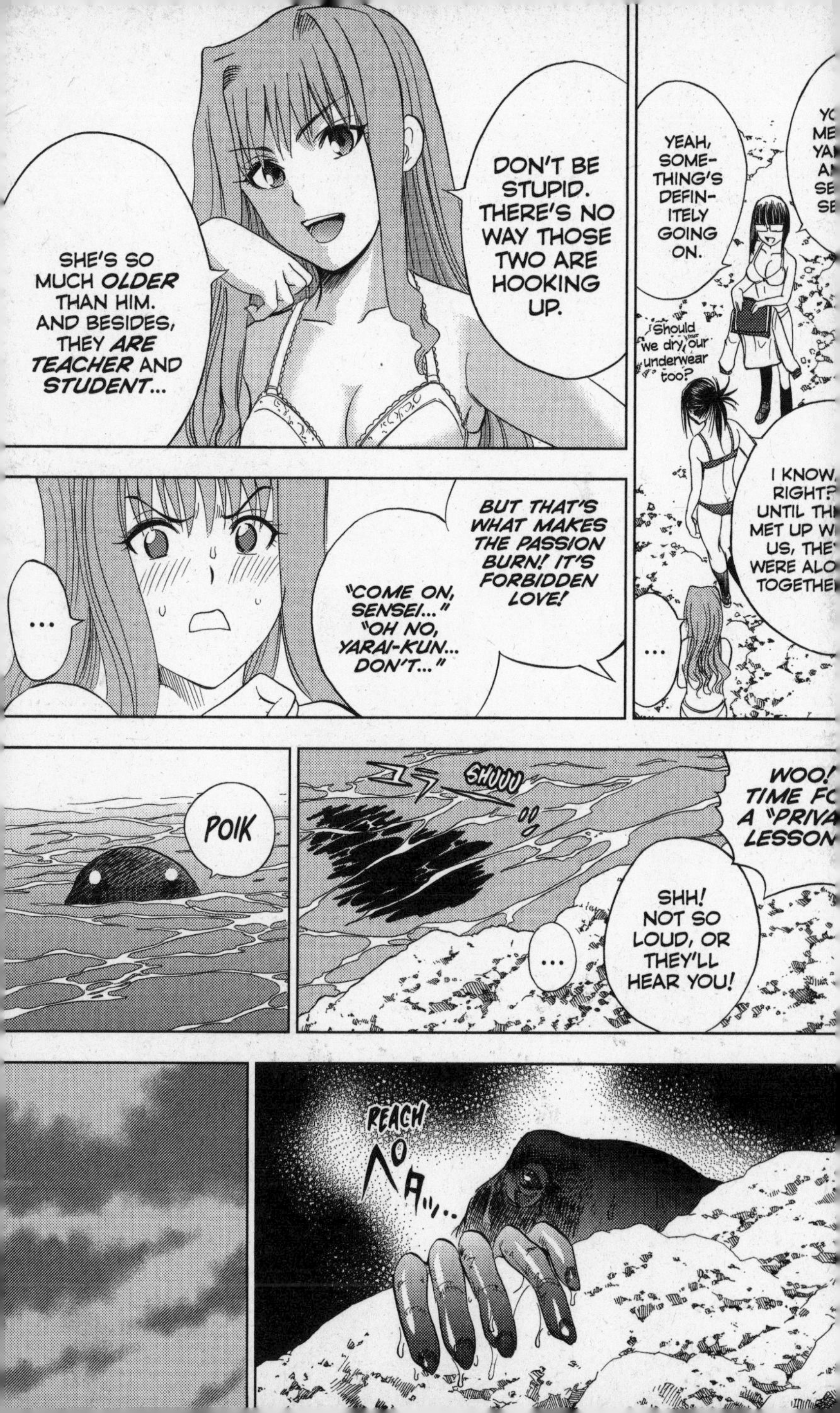
YO
ME
YA
AN
SE
SE
YEAH, SOMETHING'S DEFINITELY GOING ON.
Should we dry our underwear too?
I KNOW, RIGHT? UNTIL TH
MET UP W
US, THE
WERE ALO
TOGETHE
...
DON'T BE STUPID. THERE'S NO WAY THOSE TWO ARE HOOKING UP.
SHE'S SO MUCH *OLDER* THAN HIM. AND BESIDES, THEY *ARE TEACHER* AND *STUDENT*...
BUT THAT'S WHAT MAKES THE PASSION BURN! IT'S FORBIDDEN LOVE!
"COME ON, SENSEI..." "OH NO, YARAI-KUN... DON'T..."
...
WOO! TIME FO A "PRIVA LESSON
SHUUU
SHH! NOT SO LOUD, OR THEY'LL HEAR YOU!
...
POIK
REACH

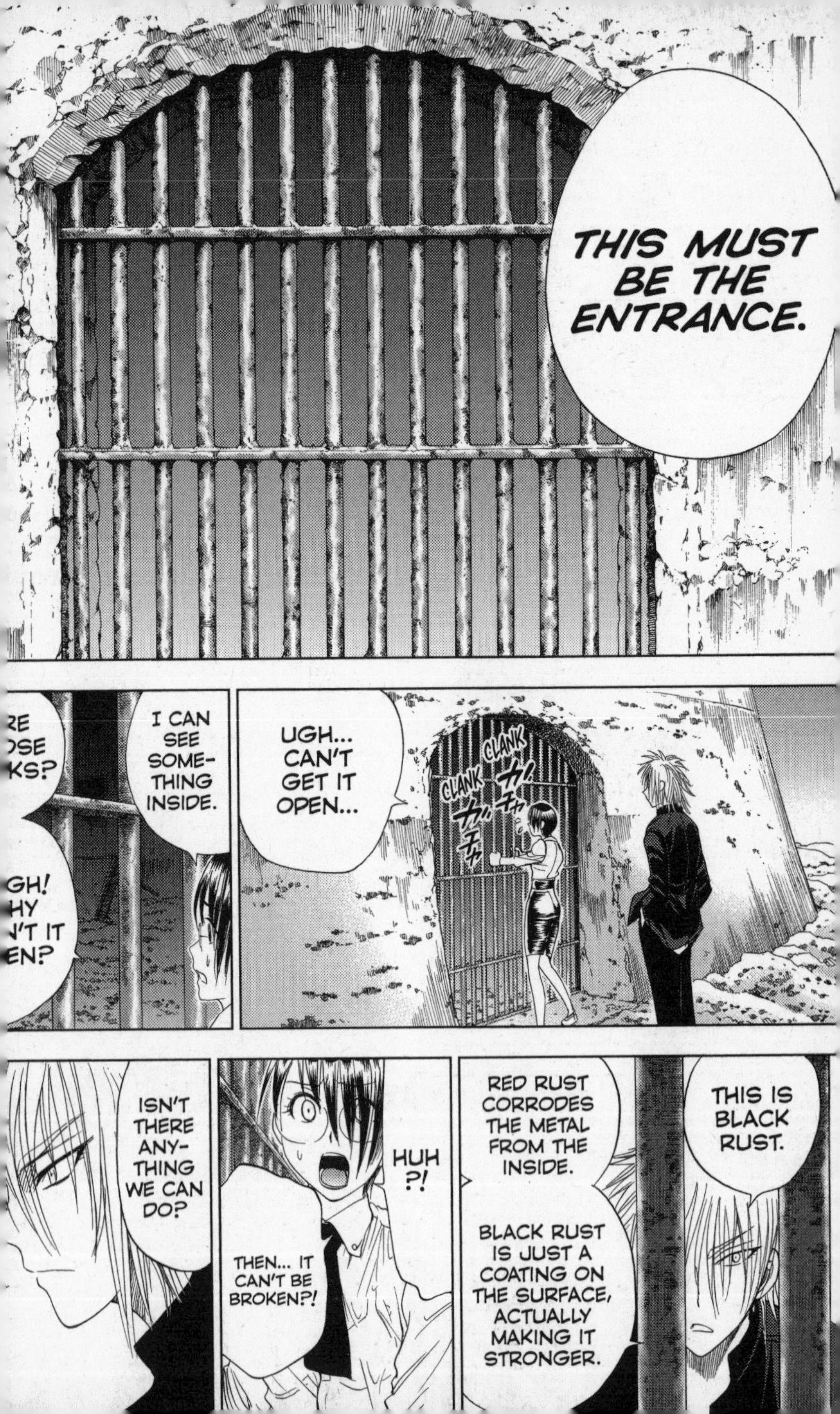
THIS MUST BE THE ENTRANCE.
UGH... CAN'T GET IT OPEN...
CLANK
CLANK
I CAN SEE SOME-THING INSIDE.
THIS IS BLACK RUST.
RED RUST CORRODES THE METAL FROM THE INSIDE.
BLACK RUST IS JUST A COATING ON THE SURFACE, ACTUALLY MAKING IT STRONGER.
HUH?!
THEN... IT CAN'T BE BROKEN?!
ISN'T THERE ANYTHING WE CAN DO?

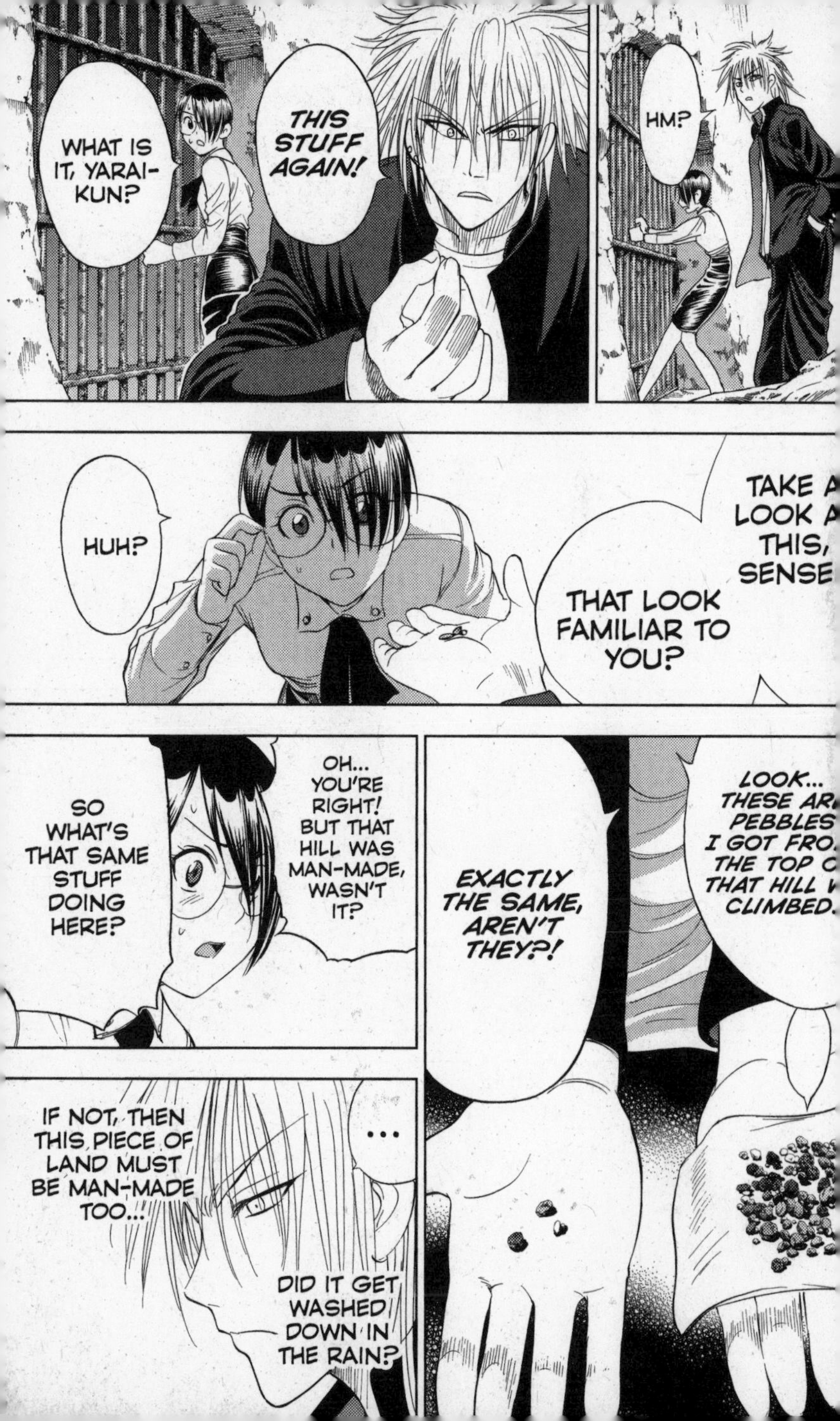

HM?
THIS STUFF AGAIN!
WHAT IS IT, YARAI-KUN?
TAKE A LOOK A THIS, SENSE
THAT LOOK FAMILIAR TO YOU?
HUH?
LOOK... THESE AR PEBBLES I GOT FRO THE TOP O THAT HILL W CLIMBED.
EXACTLY THE SAME, AREN'T THEY?!
OH... YOU'RE RIGHT! BUT THAT HILL WAS MAN-MADE, WASN'T IT?
SO WHAT'S THAT SAME STUFF DOING HERE?
...
DID IT GET WASHED DOWN IN THE RAIN?
IF NOT, THEN THIS PIECE OF LAND MUST BE MAN-MADE TOO...!

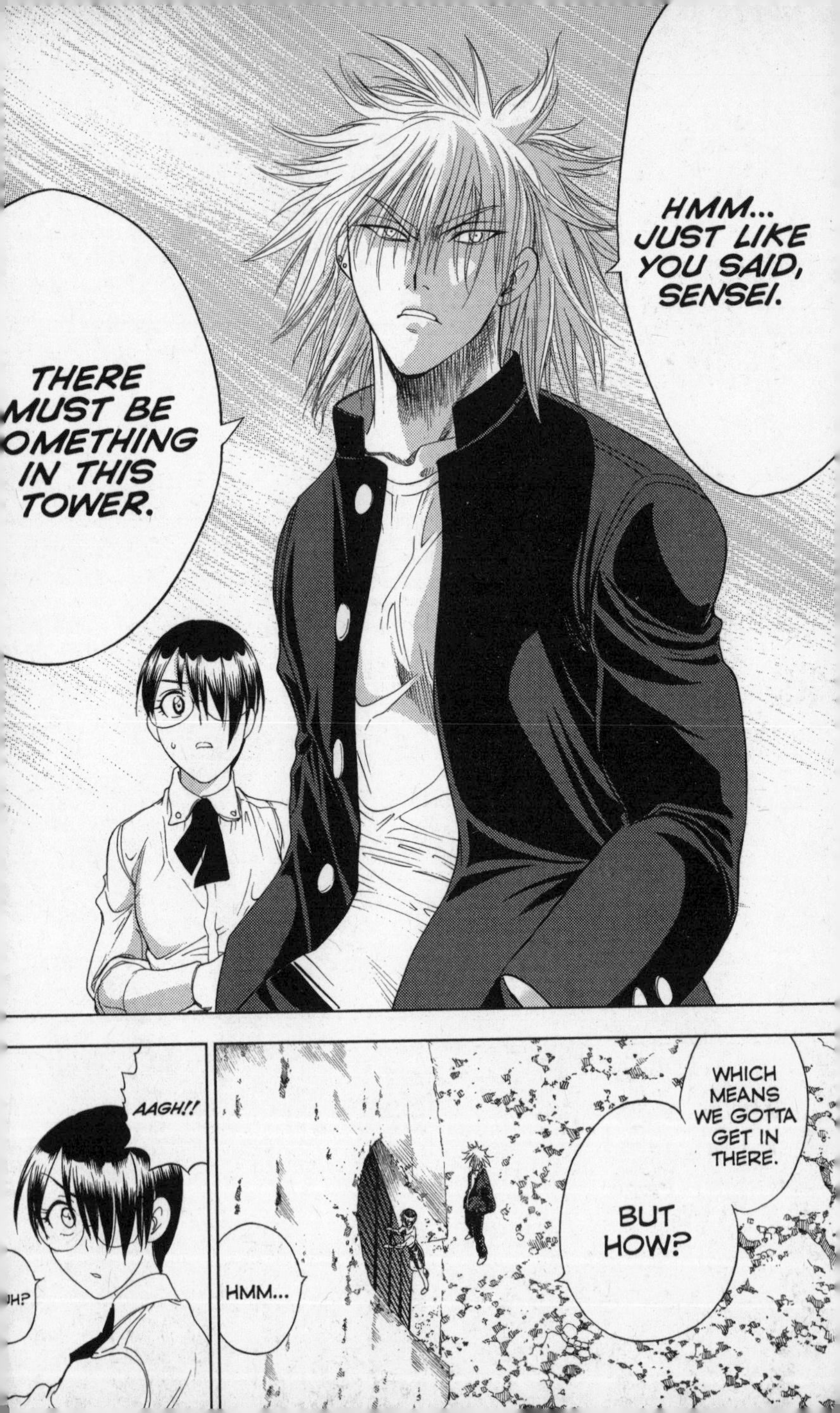
HMM... JUST LIKE YOU SAID, SENSEI.
THERE MUST BE OMETHING IN THIS TOWER.
WHICH MEANS WE GOTTA GET IN THERE.
BUT HOW?
HMM...
AAGH!!

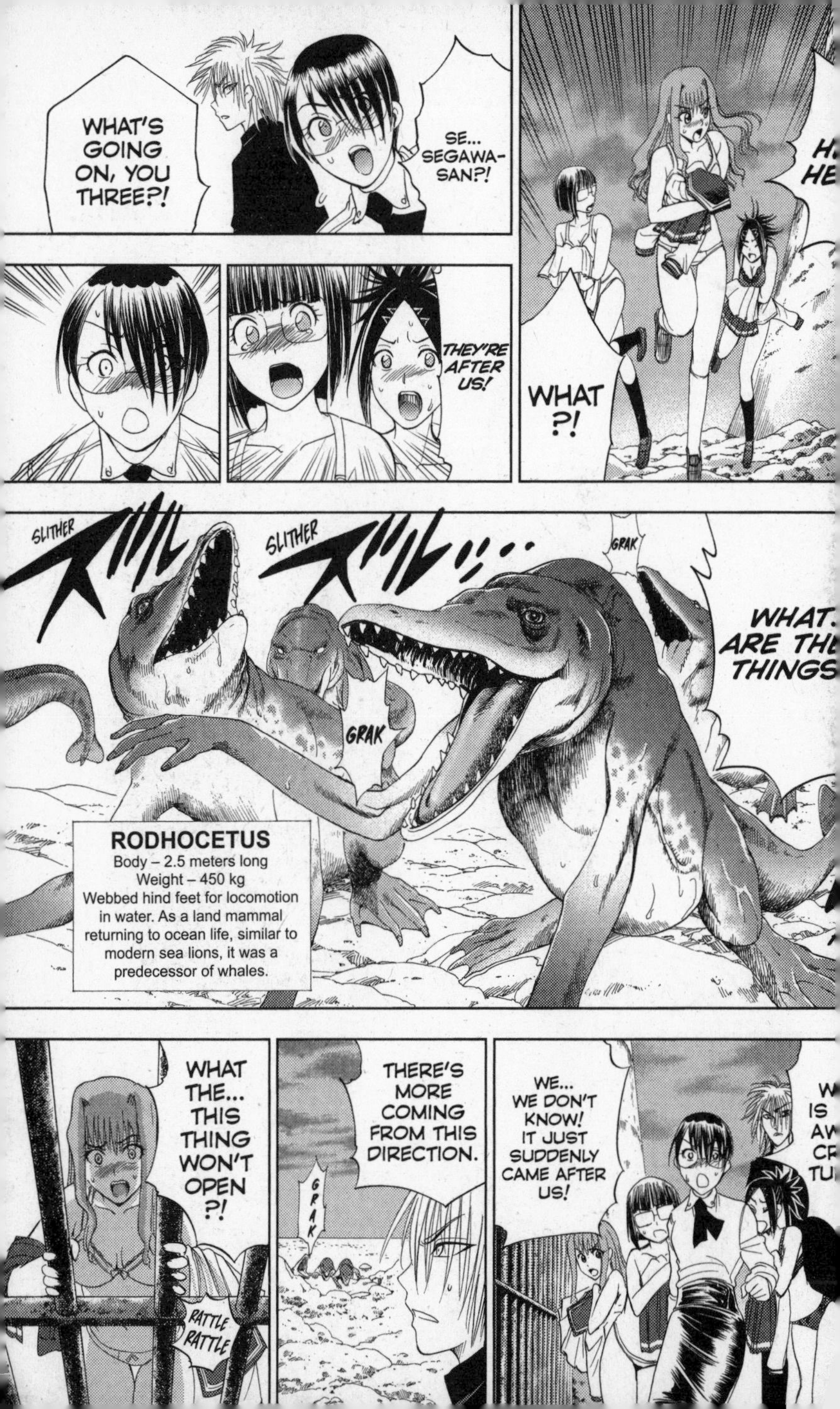
WHAT ?!
SE... SEGAWA-SAN?!
WHAT'S GOING ON, YOU THREE?!
THEY'RE AFTER US!
GRAK
WHAT. ARE THE THINGS
SLITHER
SLITHER
GRAK
RODHOCETUS
Body – 2.5 meters long
Weight – 450 kg
Webbed hind feet for locomotion in water. As a land mammal returning to ocean life, similar to modern sea lions, it was a predecessor of whales.
WE... WE DON'T KNOW! IT JUST SUDDENLY CAME AFTER US!
THERE'S MORE COMING FROM THIS DIRECTION.
GRAK
WHAT THE... THIS THING WON'T OPEN ?!
RATTLE RATTLE

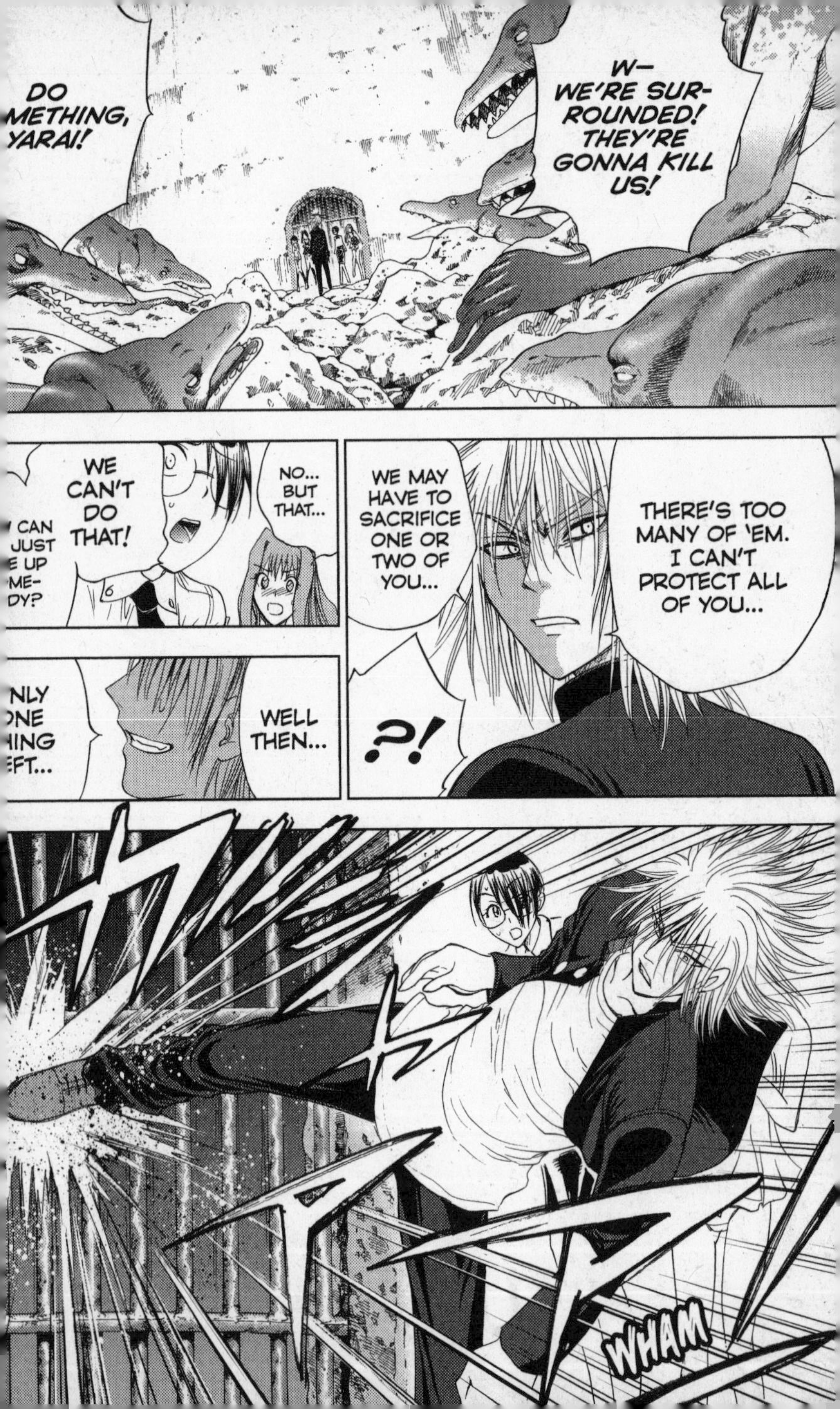
W— WE'RE SUR-ROUNDED! THEY'RE GONNA KILL US!
DO METHING, YARAI!
THERE'S TOO MANY OF 'EM. I CAN'T PROTECT ALL OF YOU...
WE MAY HAVE TO SACRIFICE ONE OR TWO OF YOU...
?!
NO... BUT THAT...
WE CAN'T DO THAT!
CAN JUST E UP ME- DY?
WELL THEN...
NLY ONE HING EFT...
WHAM

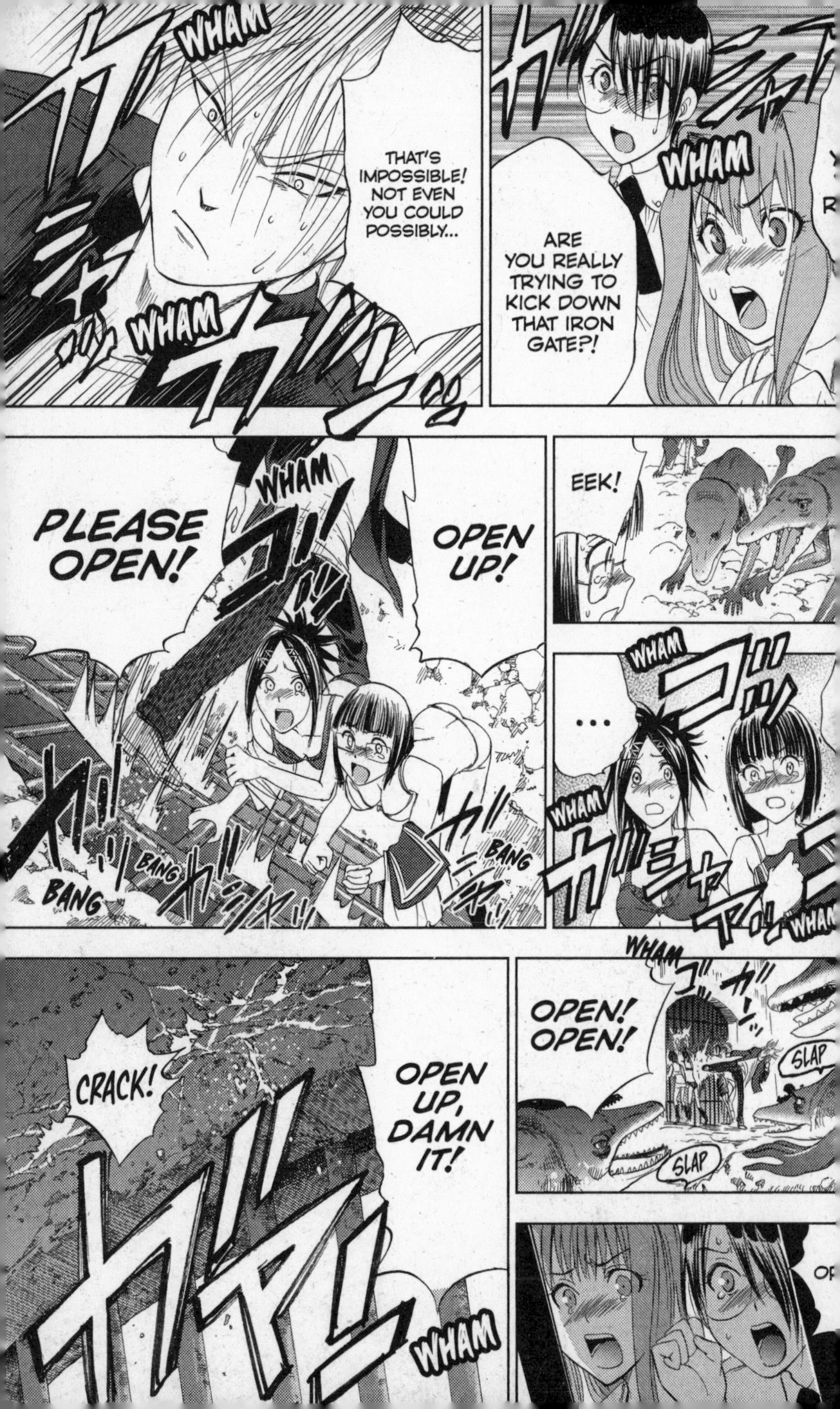
WHAM
ARE YOU REALLY TRYING TO KICK DOWN THAT IRON GATE?!
WHAM
THAT'S IMPOSSIBLE! NOT EVEN YOU COULD POSSIBLY...
WHAM
EEK!
WHAM
...
WHAM
WHAM
OPEN UP!
WHAM
PLEASE OPEN!
BANG
BANG
BANG
WHAM
OPEN! OPEN!
SLAP
SLAP
OPEN UP, DAMN IT!
CRACK!
WHAM

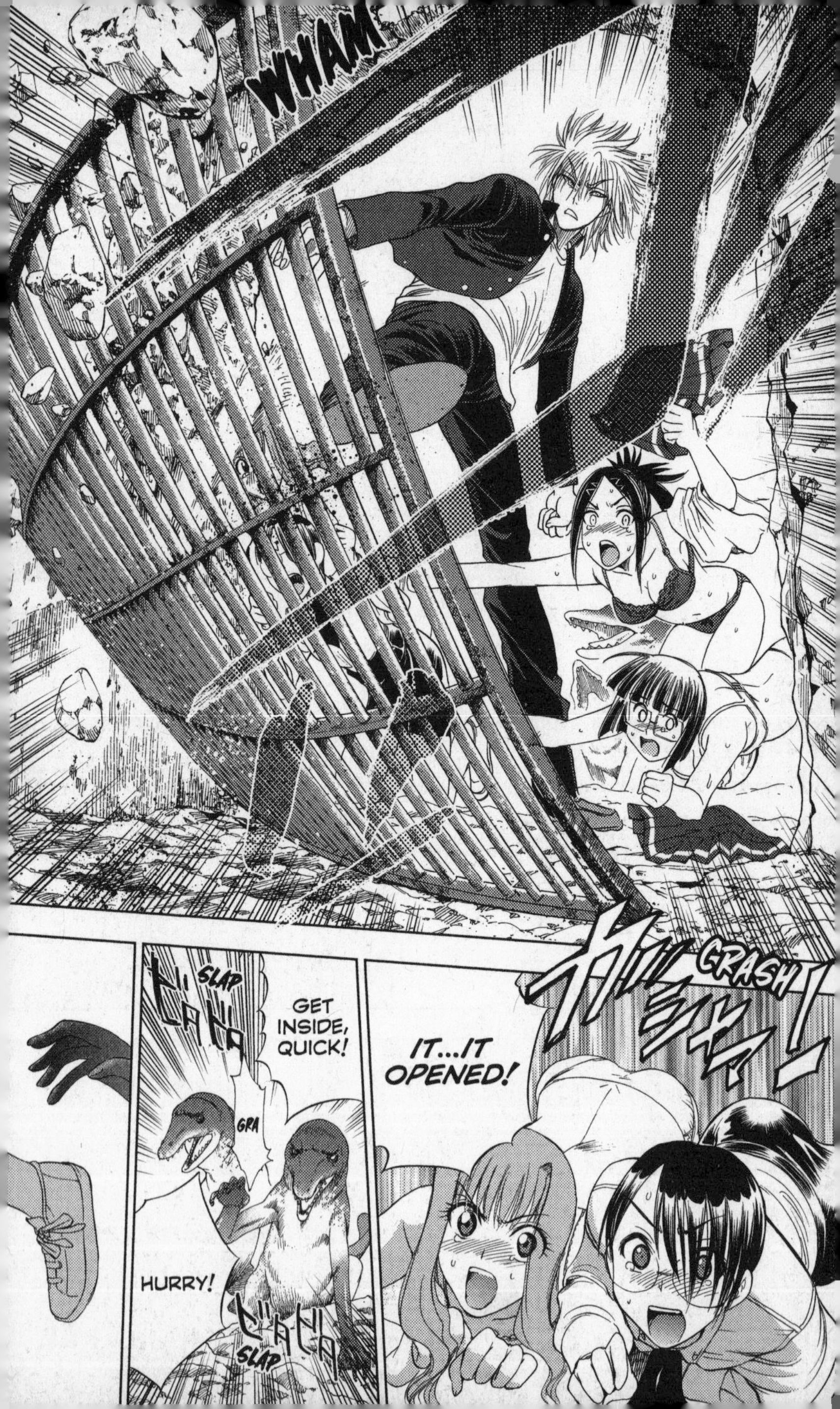
WHAM
CRASH
IT...IT OPENED!
GET INSIDE, QUICK!
SLAP
GRA
HURRY!
SLAP

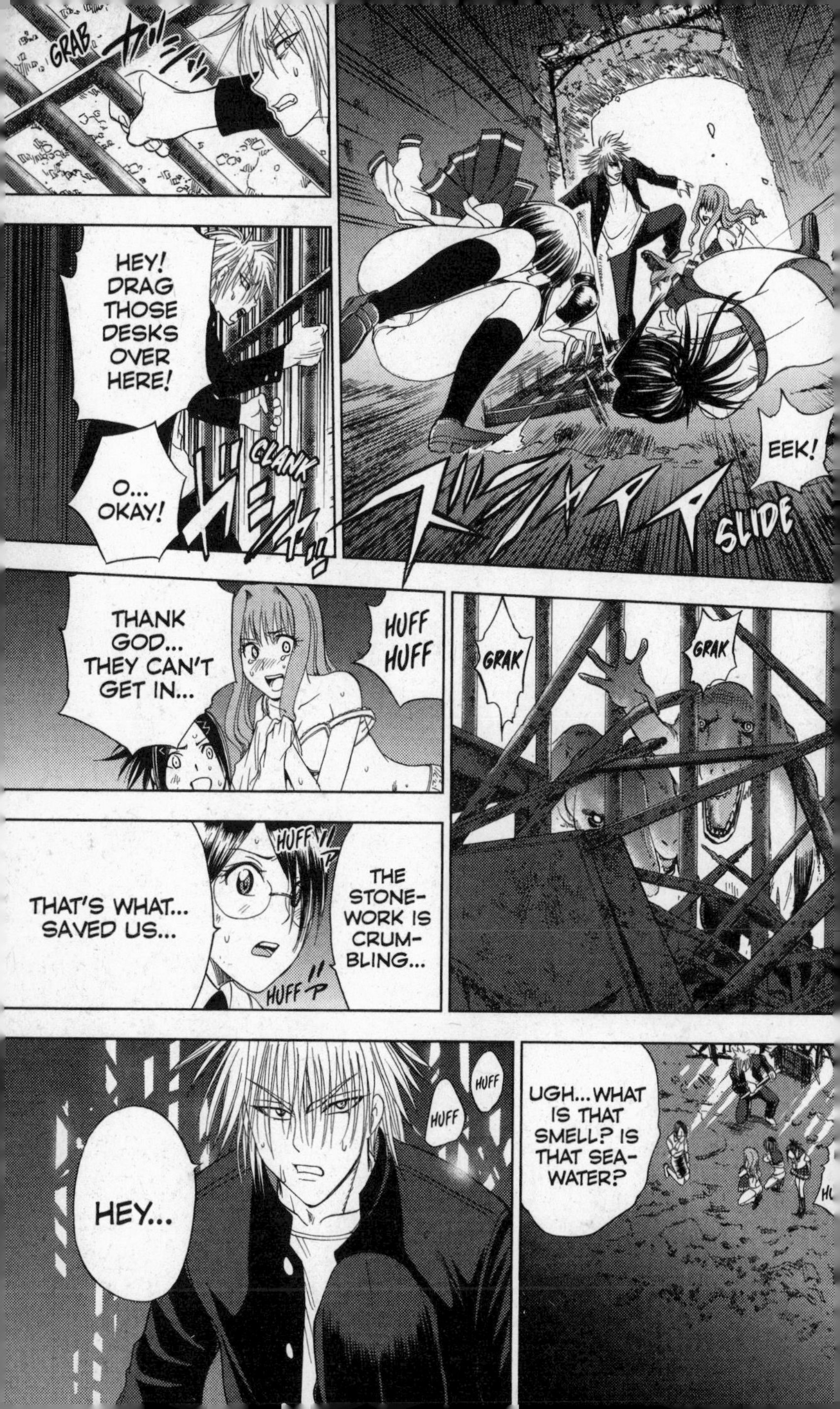
EEK!
SLIDE
GRAB
HEY! DRAG THOSE DESKS OVER HERE!
CLANK
O... OKAY!
GRAK
GRAK
HUFF HUFF
THANK GOD... THEY CAN'T GET IN...
THE STONE-WORK IS CRUM-BLING...
HUFF
HUFF
THAT'S WHAT... SAVED US...
UGH...WHAT IS THAT SMELL? IS THAT SEA-WATER?
HUFF
HUFF
HEY...

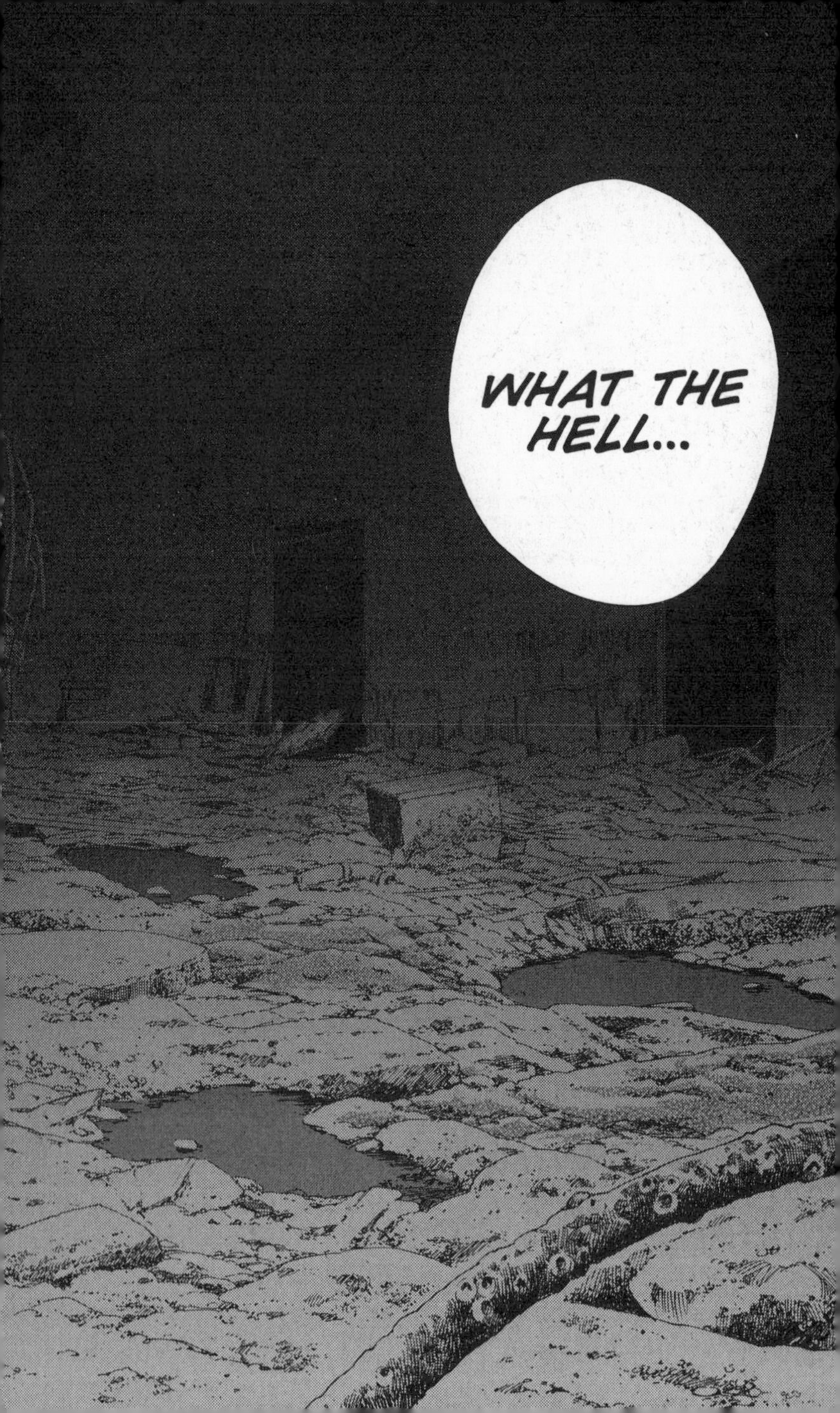
WHAT THE HELL...

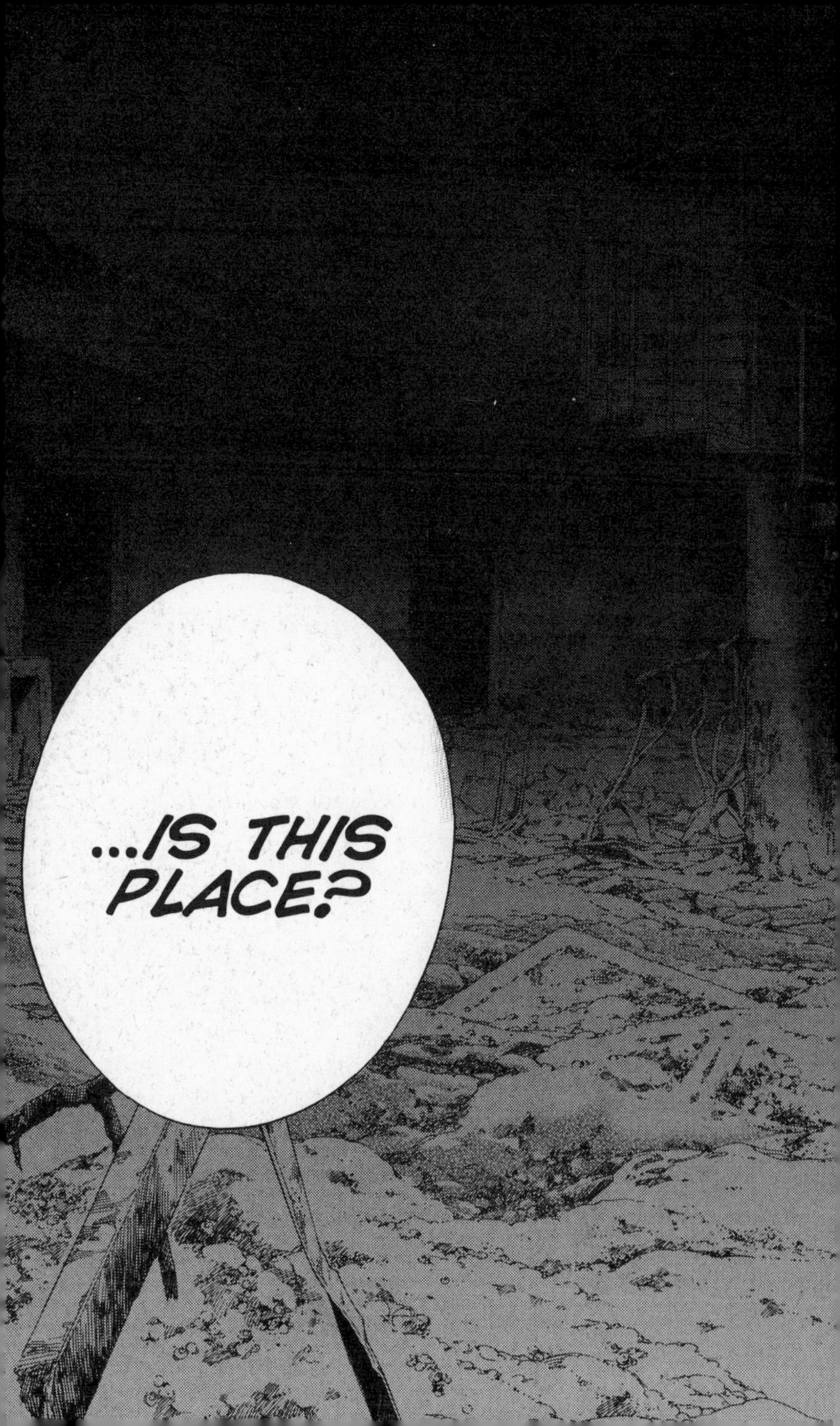
...IS THIS PLACE?

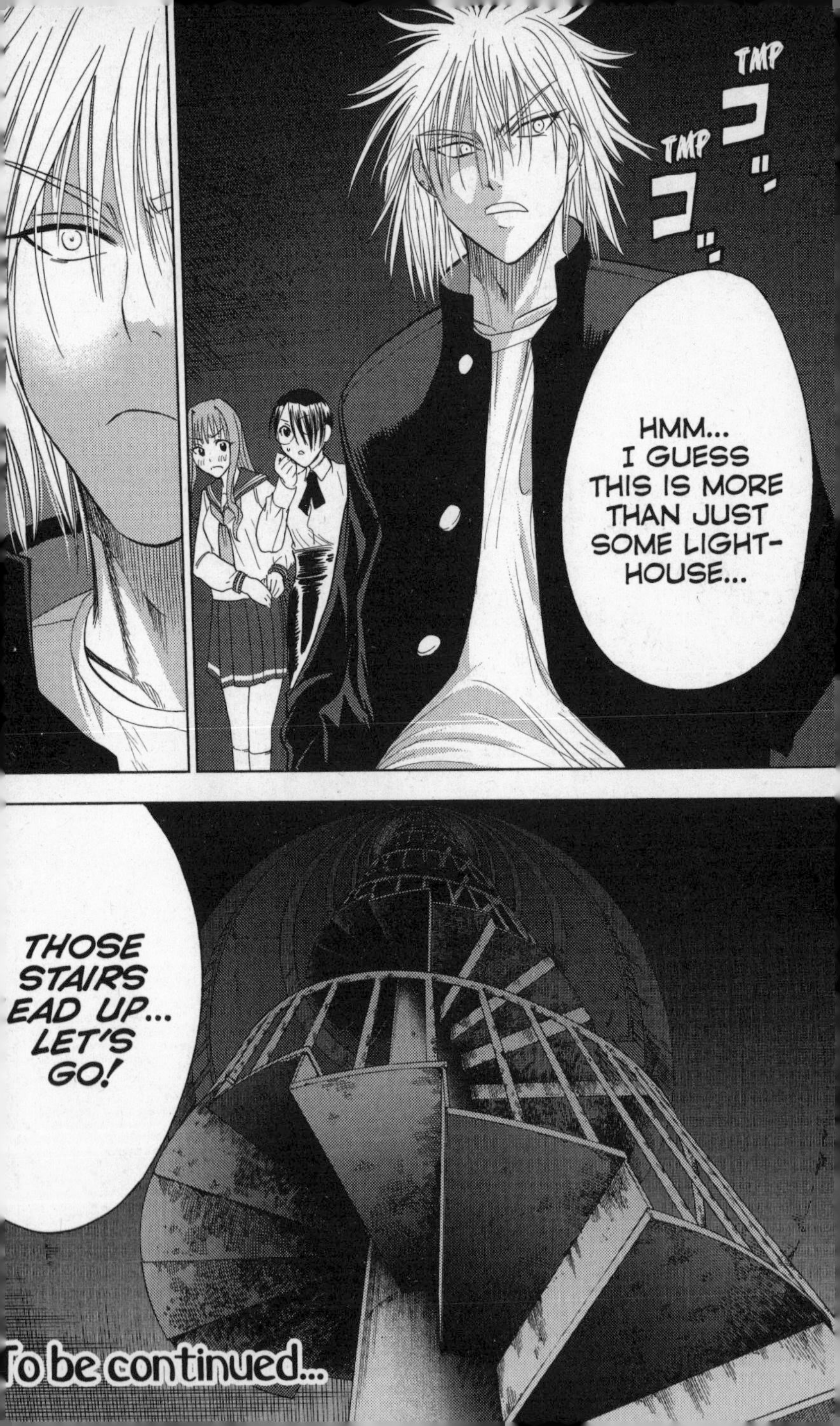
TMP
TMP
HMM... I GUESS THIS IS MORE THAN JUST SOME LIGHT-HOUSE...
THOSE STAIRS EAD UP... LET'S GO!
To be continued...

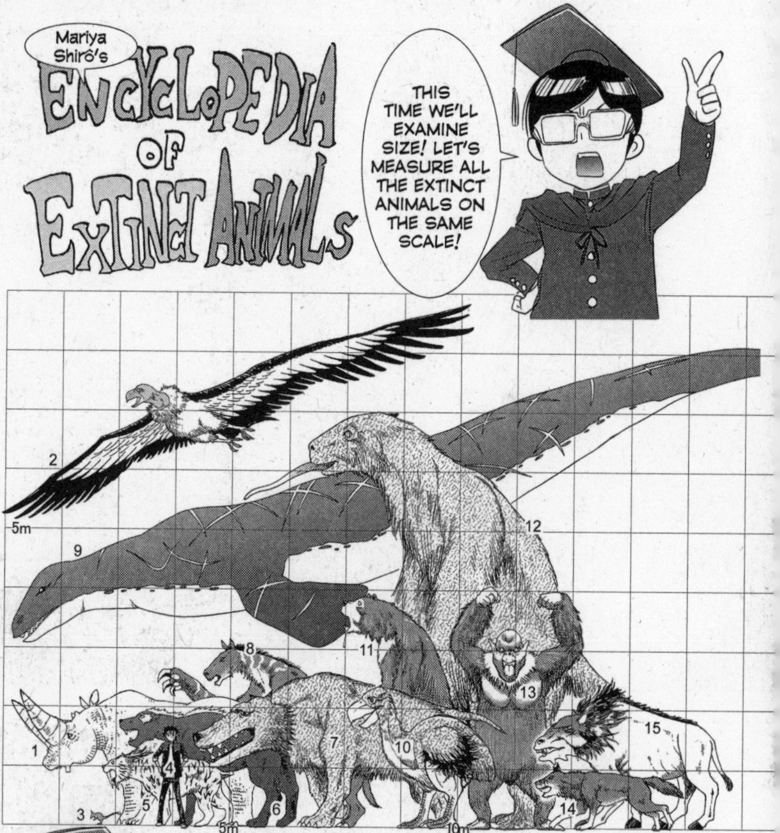
Mariya Shirô's
ENCYCLOPEDIA OF EXTINCT ANIMALS
THIS TIME WE'LL EXAMINE SIZE! LET'S MEASURE ALL THE EXTINCT ANIMALS ON THE SAME SCALE!
5m
5m
10m
1
2
3
4
5
6
7
8
9
10
11
12
13
14
15

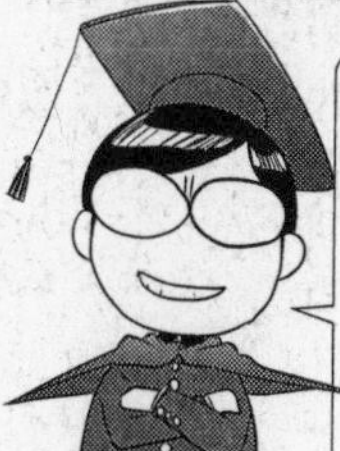

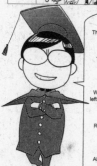

1. **ARSINOITHERIUM**
Appearance: Vol. 2-3
This proved the accuracy of my field guide.

2. **ARGENTAVIS**
Appearance: Vol. 6-7
The largest flying bird in natural history.
The first animal we ever defeated.

3. **PTILODUS**
Appearance: From Vol. 1
We haven't seen these recently, since we left the forest. It's a little lonely without them.

4. **SENGOKU AKIRA**
Appearance: From Vol. 1
Rather short for a human. However, able to survive because of his wits.

5. **SMILODON**
Appearance: Vol. 1, 5, 11-12
Also called saber-tooth tiger. The top star in the world of extinct animals.

6. **HYAENODON**
Appearance: Vol. 4
Even among the extinct animals, some speculate that this is the strongest species.

7. **ANDREWSARCHUS**
Appearance: Vol. 1-2
When this one attacked, we thought we were done for.

8. **CHALICOTHERIUM**
Appearance: Vol. 8
Caution: Although an herbivore, it's still highly dangerous!

9. **BASILOSAURUS**
Appearance: Vol. 2
I regret that I didn't have a chance to come in contact with this one. Really!

10. **DIATRYMA**
Appearance: Vol. 1
The first extinct species I ever came face-to-face with.

11. **SHORT-FACED BEAR**
Appearance: Vol. 6
A carnivore widespread during the Pleistocene age. An extremely fast runner.

12. **MEGATHERIUM**
Appearance: Vol. 2
An enormous body, but a quiet personality. Relative of the sloth.

13. **GIGANTOPITHECUS**
Appearance: Vol. 9-10
It's considered to be the origin of the stories of abominable snowman.

14. **DIRE WOLF**
Appearance: Vol. 6
Its cubs were born all right, but Akagami was rather worried about them.

15. **ENTELODONT**
Appearance: Vol. 3-4
A.K.A. the boar from hell. Will eat anything.

Cage of Eden Coloring Page

This design is from a set of three glasses made in honor of our second year of serialization. As only 100 sets were made, this design is provided for all readers who did not win. The three panels can connect into one long picture.

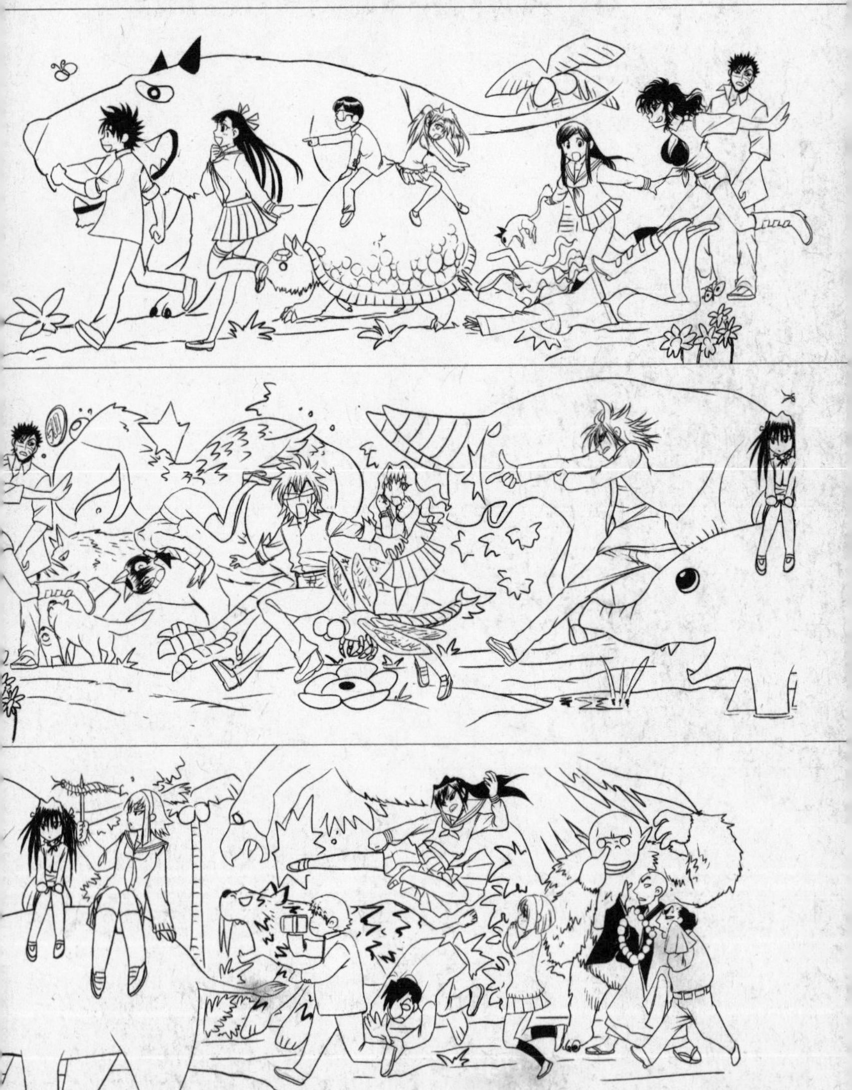